THE RETURN OF BIPOLARITY IN WORLD POLITICS

The Return of Bipolarity in World Politics

CHINA, THE UNITED STATES,
AND GEOSTRUCTURAL REALISM

Øystein Tunsjø

Columbia University Press

New York

Publishers Since 1893
New York   Chichester, West Sussex
cup.columbia.edu

Copyright © 2018 Columbia University Press

Library of Congress Cataloging-in-Publication Data
A complete CIP record is available from the Library of Congress
ISBN 978-0-231-17654-5 (cloth : alk. paper)
ISBN 978-0-231-54690-4 (e-book)

Columbia University Press books are printed on permanent
and durable acid-free paper.
Printed in the United States of America

Cover design: Chang Jae Lee

CONTENTS

Acknowledgments   vii

1. Introduction: A New Bipolar System   1

PART I: PAST AND PRESENT POLARITY

2. Explaining and Understanding Polarity   23

3. Contemporary U.S.-China Bipolarity   50

4. Distinguishing Top-Ranking States and Comparing Bipolarity   76

PART II: SYSTEMIC EFFECTS: PATTERNS OF BEHAVIOR AND STABILITY

5. Strong Balancing Postponed   99

6. U.S.-China Relations and the Risk of War   126

7. The Return of Bipolarity: Global and Regional Effects   150

8. Conclusion: Geostructural Realism   178

Notes   189

Bibliography   241

Index   261

ACKNOWLEDGMENTS

Among the debts that I am happy to acknowledge, the greatest is to the Norwegian Institute for Defence Studies and the Norwegian Defence University College. These institutions have entirely sponsored this research, and I would like to add that the Norwegian Research Council has several times declined to support my research. Every time the Research Council has rejected my applications, I have been fortunate to have the support of the Institute for Defence Studies and the Defence University College. I am also very grateful that Columbia University Press was willing to support this contrarian and original book project. A special thanks to my editor, Stephen Wesley, and my former editor, Anne Routon, who shepherded this manuscript through a long and thorough peer-review process.

My students, mostly officers, were introduced to the bipolarity thesis at an early stage in my research. Many were skeptical, and some were even frustrated that they had to rely on my assessments and assumptions, since there existed no other publications on the topic. They have provided valuable criticism and ideas that pushed my research forward. It is with great satisfaction that I now can point to this publication, and I sincerely hope that my former and current students will appreciate this book.

In 2013, a leading journal in the field of international relations rejected an article I wrote based on the first part of this book. The decision was a "borderline revise and resubmit" and based on three comprehensive peer reviews. This was a turning point. While all the reviewers criticized my examination of the distribution of capabilities and the bipolarity thesis, the most important takeaway from this review process was the "so what" question posed by one of the reviewers. I understood that I needed to develop what now is the second part of the book: Why does a return to bipolarity matter, and what are the effects and outcome of such a polarity shift? This pushed me to develop chapters 5, 6, and 7 and focus on balancing, stability, and global effects, and I thank the three anonymous reviewers for their comprehensive comments.

The manuscript also benefited enormously from two rounds of comments by two peer reviewers at Columbia University Press. I sharpened my definition of a superpower and emphasized that, from a structural-realist perspective, the definition of a superpower relies on the distribution of capabilities in the international system rather than the power attributes of states. I further had to develop and nuance my empirical assessment of the contemporary distribution of capabilities. I am extremely grateful to the two reviewers that twice read and commented on my entire manuscript.

I have presented various drafts of this book at numerous conferences and workshops where I have received comments from many. Stephen Walt visited the Norwegian Institute for Defence Studies in 2013 and summed up his criticism of my bipolarity thesis by pointing out that it was "too early." I hope this book might push him to reconsider. I am grateful to Ian Bowers, Daniel W. Drezner, Bjørn Grønning, Taylor Fravel, Chung-in Moon, James Reilly, Robert S. Ross, and Wang Dong, who participated in two workshops in Beijing, November 2013, and in Oslo, May 2014, and especially to Randall L. Schweller for his comments as a discussant on my paper. Again, the comments were not that favorable at the time, but Schweller now recognizes that the argument for the return of bipolarity is more convincing. I thank the participants in the international politics group for their comments on a chapter draft I presented at the annual Norwegian Political Science meeting in 2014.

I have presented my bipolarity thesis to several institutions and researchers in China. Wu Zhengyu has welcomed me several times at Renmin University. Zhou Qi hosted a meeting at Tsinghua University. Wang Yizhou, Yu Tiejun, Zhang Qingming, and Wang Dong at Peking University's School of International Studies have always been forthcoming and have commented and shared their knowledge. Discussions and collaboration with Zhang Tuosheng were most helpful. In the United States, I owe a special thanks to Peter Dutton, Andrew S. Erickson, Lyle Goldstein, and Bernard D. Cole.

My biggest intellectual debt is to Robert S. Ross. I have benefited immensely from working with Bob on numerous research projects and coedited volumes for a decade. With his realist approach and emphasis on geography, Bob has been truly inspirational. He is not too fond of structural realism or entirely convinced by my bipolarity thesis, but our friendship has always overcome such differences. Johannes Rø has been another intellectual inspiration, and his comments and criticism have always been invaluable.

I have benefited greatly from working at the Centre for Asian Security Studies at my institute. Jo Inge Bekkevold has headed this Asian Centre and provided all possible support, which has made this book project doable. His organizational and management skills were crucial in allowing me to concentrate on my research, and he was always available and willing to discuss scholarly issues. I thank those that have participated in seminars organized by the Asian Centre, where various chapters of the book were presented. I would also like to thank others at my institute: director Kjell Inge Bjerga, former director Sven Holtsmark, former director Rolf Tamnes, head of research Helge Danielsen, and former head of research Torunn Haaland have all been supportive and allowed my research to develop and flourish.

My family, and especially my wife, Hege, have learned more about bipolarity than anyone can imagine. Hege's unwavering support through the ups and downs has been remarkable. This book is dedicated to her and my two sons, Axel and Felix.

THE RETURN OF BIPOLARITY IN WORLD POLITICS

Chapter 1

INTRODUCTION: A NEW BIPOLAR SYSTEM

Whether the post–Cold War unipolar international system is sustainable or will morph into multipolarity is currently under debate. In that context, this book sees the United States as a state in relative decline but contends against conventional wisdom and the mainstream view that the international system has returned to bipolarity, not multipolarity, nonpolarity, or sustained unipolarity. An era of unprecedented unipolarity has come to an end as China's rise has changed the underlying distribution of power in the international system. While China is not equal to the United Sates in power aggregate, it has narrowed the power gap significantly and vaulted into top ranking. Equally important, no other state is strong enough to serve as a competitor to these two. Since the top two states are now much more powerful than any third state, the structure of the international system has changed from unipolarity to bipolarity.

The shift in the contemporary distribution of capabilities in the international system is important because a system of two top-ranking powers (bipolarity) shapes and shoves international politics differently than a system of one (unipolarity) or a system of three or more (multipolarity). Kenneth N. Waltz argued that a bipolar system is more stable than a multipolar system. He further maintained that the international system tends toward balancing and that states' balancing behavior is different in bipolar and multipolar systems.[1] However, no studies have compared states' balancing behavior or examined the relative stability between two bipolar systems. This book refines Waltz's structural-realist theory and develops a new geostructural-realist theory. Geostructural realism contends that although it is important whether the international system is bipolar or has some other structure, stability and balancing are heavily affected by geopolitics and by how geography affects the two superpowers and their relationship. These core arguments, that the distribution of capabilities in the international system is now bipolar and that such a polarity shift matters to a few important issues in international politics, namely, balancing and stability, are developed in two steps in the pages that follow.

The first part of the book draws on structural-realist work to define power and uses three criteria to establish that the distribution of capabilities in the international system is indeed bipolar. First, I examine the power gap between the number-one power (the United States) and the number-two power (China) and demonstrate that it has narrowed considerably. While China has not obtained power parity with the United States, the relative increase in China's combined capabilities places it in the top ranking with the United States, even if only "barely."[2]

Second, I scrutinize the power gap between the two top-ranking powers and the third and lower powers and find both that no other states are within reach of the United States and China and that within the foreseeable future no third state will be capable of developing a combined capability comparable to either.[3] The power gap between China and the nation next in rank has become so large as to warrant the notion of a new bipolar system.

Third, I compare the distribution of capabilities in the current bipolar system with the distribution at the start of the previous bipolar system. I find that the distribution is roughly similar, which strongly suggests that the contemporary international system is bipolar. Accordingly, the combined effect of the narrowing power gap between China and the United States, the widening power gap between China and the third-ranking power, and the roughly similar bipolar distribution of capabilities between the current international system and the bipolar system in the twentieth century all indicate the return of bipolarity.

The second part of the book builds on structural realism and Waltz's assumptions that the international system tends toward balance, that top-ranking states' balancing is different in bipolar and multipolar systems, and that a bipolar system is more stable than a multipolar system. However, this only provides a starting point for analysis. I refine Waltz's theory by pointing out that contemporary balancing in a new bipolar system is not as strong as structural-realist theory expects. Moreover, neorealist theory says nothing about whether one bipolar system is relatively more stable than another.

I show that the new bipolar system is different in three fundamental ways from the previous bipolar period and the Cold War. First, geopolitics and the importance of the "stopping power of water"[4] postpone contemporary strong balancing[5] in the new bipolar system concentrated on maritime East Asia. The United States and China are unlikely in the near future to pursue an arms race and the strong balancing characteristic of the U.S.-Soviet pattern of behavior during the early Cold War.

Second, in some respects there will likely be more instability at the new power center in East Asia than there was in Europe during the previous bipolar era.[6] While the risk of superpower conflict in the new bipolar era remains low, there is a higher risk of a limited war between the superpowers in the twenty-first century than there was in the twentieth century. Water barriers may prevent a third world war, but the rivalry between the United States and China is mainly at sea, which makes a limited naval war between the superpowers in the first half of this century more likely. Geopolitical factors make superpower rivalry in a bipolar system concentrated on maritime East Asia more prone to conflict than in a bipolar system concentrated on continental Europe, despite contemporary strong economic interdependence, the existence of an international institutional order, limited ideological confrontation, and nuclear second-strike capability.

Third, I argue that China and the United States will be preoccupied with instability, rivalries, and conflict in maritime East Asia, all of which will help subdue global-security confrontations and involvement in proxy wars by the superpowers in other regions. This is different from the relative stability that emerged in Europe and the global rivalry and conflict that developed between the superpowers during the previous bipolar period.

In sum, the new bipolar system in the twenty-first century is unlikely to evolve into another cold war. This book develops a new geostructural-realist theory in order for the first time to compare states' patterns of behavior in two bipolar systems. I contend that "geography trumps structure."[7] Although polarity is important, the way in which the new bipolar system shapes international politics is heavily affected by geopolitical factors.

THE BIPOLARITY THESIS AND ITS CRITICS

Most books and current polarity debates in IR journals do not address the issue of bipolarity. There is a debate between "unipolarists" and "multipolarists," but the polarity debate is relatively limited to academic conferences and the existing literature.[8] No other studies in the fields of IR and security have examined in detail U.S.-China relations, the most important bilateral relationship of our time, on the basis of a bipolarity perspective.[9] This book argues against the scholarly community.

Critics of arguments for bipolarity emphasize that China does not possess the attributes of a superpower. Much of the critique of the bipolarity thesis points out that China lacks enough power to compete on a quasi-equal basis with the United States. It lacks global power-projection capabilities, has few allies, and has not obtained regional hegemony. Others scholars question whether China even has a reliable nuclear second-strike capability and argue that China's innovative and technological skills remain inadequate for superpower status. In short, many observers still contend that the international system remains unipolar and that it is too early to tell if it will transition to bipolarity.

I deal with such criticism throughout the book, especially in chapter 2. It is sufficient to note here that a response to such counterarguments requires definitional clarification and a comparative historical perspective. Drawing on structural-realist theory, I define polarity—unipolarity (one superpower), bipolarity (two superpowers), or multipolarity (three or more great powers)—according to the distribution of capabilities in the international system. We can examine states' possession of various capabilities, whether nuclear weapons, aircraft-carrier battle groups, technological sophistication, soft power, economic strength, diplomatic skills, and so on, when considering states' aggregated power. These are the attributes of states in the international system. However, the distribution of capabilities across states is not an attribute of states. The distribution of capabilities is rather "a system-wide concept."[10]

From a structural-realist theoretical perspective it is not the characteristics of the states that define a superpower or determine the polarity of the international system. What matters in determining whether a state is a pole (a superpower) in a bipolar international structure is its relative standing compared to other states and how power is distributed in the international system. Whether a state is a regional hegemon, has global power-projection capabilities, possesses nuclear second-strike capability, or has formed a number of alliances does not define or determine superpower status or polarity. That is, international political structure is defined by counting the number of top-ranking states, not by examining the qualities and the nature of the interaction among states.[11]

The concept of superpower has been and continues to be a controversial issue. William T. R. Fox coined the term, but his usage is different from that of Hans J. Morgenthau.[12] This book draws on Morgenthau in order to distinguish superpowers in a bipolar system from great powers in a multipolar system. The Soviet Union and the United States were much more powerful relative to any other state in the international system in the post–World War II period and much more powerful relative to the great powers of the past. Thus, Morgenthau labeled these two great powers as superpowers. Similarly, the United States and China are superpowers today because they are much more powerful relative to any other states in the international system and relatively much more powerful than the great powers of past multipolar systems. They are not more powerful than the great powers of the past because they have more advanced weapons but because they are the only two top-ranking powers according to the contemporary distribution of capabilities.

A bipolar system, as Waltz pointed out, is "a system in which no third power is able to challenge the top two."[13] As Barry R. Posen writes, the "Soviet Union was only barely in the US league for most of the Cold War in terms of economic capacity but we think of the era as a bipolar order, in part because the gap between the Soviet Union and the third ranking power in the immediate aftermath of World War Two and for much of the Cold War was so great."[14] Since no other countries are able to match China's aggregate power, two states, the United States and China, are now much more powerful than the rest. The contemporary power distribution in the international system has become bipolar.

Simultaneously, China is not as powerful as the United States, and it is far from dominating or ruling the world. But China does not need to overtake the United States before the international system can be considered bipolar. The Soviet Union was never as powerful as the United States during the previous bipolar period, but it was still regarded as a superpower and a pole in a new bipolar system. The United States was a regional hegemon in the Western Hemisphere; the Soviet Union never dominated Europe in a similar way. The United States possessed global power-projection capability throughout the previous bipolar era; the Soviet Union had not acquired global power-projection capability at the start of the previous bipolar era—for example, it deployed its first aircraft carrier only in the late 1970s. The Soviet Union lacked nuclear capability at the origins of the previous bipolar system; the United States had already acquired such capability. Despite the asymmetric power relation between the United States and the Soviet Union, most scholars and policy makers considered the Soviet Union a superpower and a pole in the previous bipolar system because the United States and the Soviet Union were much more powerful relative to all other states. The distribution of capabilities in the post–World War II period had become bipolar. Similarly, despite the fact that China has not obtained power parity with the United States, the contemporary distribution of capabilities in the international system has now returned to bipolarity.

I now proceed with a more thorough exposition of how this book challenges conventional views on polarity and U.S.-China rivalry in the twenty-first century, how it refines Waltz's structural-realist theory, and how it develops a new geostructural-realist theory of international politics.

THE POLARITY DEBATE

There is broad consensus in the field of international relations that whether the international system is multipolar, bipolar, or unipolar, the international system affects state behavior and conditions the possibility of peace and stability. Determining polarity is important because it allows for predictions and enhances explanations and understanding. While most IR scholars acknowledge that polarity matters, there has been no consensus among academics or within policy-making circles about the polarity of the post–Cold War era.[15] Basing their assumptions on balance-of-power theory, some realists argued in the 1990s that "multipolarity is developing before our eyes."[16] Several scholars have sought to demonstrate the firmly unipolar state of the international system in the more than two decades since the end of the Cold War.[17] Nonetheless, since the 2007 financial crisis (the "Great Recession"), certain studies argued that U.S. unipolarity is on the wane.[18] Many academics and policy makers believe the current international system is becoming multipolar,[19] and others seek to develop empirical data in addition to theoretical assumptions to sustain the argument that the end of unipolarity is real and that the unipolar moment is over.[20] One observer even finds "the evidence that the international system is rapidly becoming multipolar" is now so clear that it is "impossible to deny."[21] However, "unipolarists" do not agree with the claim that unipolarity is ending.[22]

Nonetheless, "unipolarists" recognize a contemporary shift in the distribution of capabilities. Stephen G. Brooks and William C. Wohlforth have modified Barry Buzan's "1+X" terminology for describing the post–Cold War unipolar system. They now see the need for distinguishing between great powers that are not in a position to bid for superpower status and those that are by examining a "1+Y+X" system, "in which one or more Y powers have the potential to rise to superpower status or are moving in this direction and thus need to be differentiated from the other great powers." Their conclusion is that we have moved from a "1+X" to "1+1+X" system, "with the United States set to long remain the sole superpower, followed by China as the only emerging potential superpower."[23]

Strikingly, in 2011, Wohlforth, John G. Ikenberry, and Michael Mastanduno contended that the "bottom line" is that the "current international system is as *unambiguously* unipolar as past systems were multi- and bipolar."[24] This book contends that in explaining the current power shift it is unnecessary to refine Buzan's terminology for the unipolar system and stretch the definition of unipolarity. The new "1+1+X" terminology for describing the current distribution of capabilities in the international system is roughly similar to the asymmetric U.S.-Soviet relations and the distribution of capabilities during the previous bipolar system. The system has returned to bipolarity and moved from a "1+X" to a "2+X" system, not a "1+1+X" system.

Unipolarists and multipolarists correctly ask whether China has reached top ranking. However, this debate neglects or underemphasizes that the growing power gap between the second- and the third-ranking power is as important, if not more important, as that between the leading and the second-ranked power when it comes to determining the polarity of the international system. It was not the asymmetric power relationship between the United States and the Soviet Union at the start of the previous bipolar system that preoccupied observers when defining the international system of the post–World War II period. Instead, scholars such as Morgenthau maintained that the international system had shifted from multipolarity to bipolarity in the aftermath of the Second World War because the United States and the Soviet Union, "in view of their enormous superiority over the power next in rank [Great Britain], deserved to be called superpowers."[25] Insofar as it was the growing power gap between the Soviet Union (#2) and Great Britain (#3) that had a greater effect on the restructuring of the international system from multipolarity to bipolarity between 1945 and 1950 than changes in the gap between the United States (#1) and the Soviet Union, it will be contended here that a similar power gap is developing today between China and the third-ranking power.

In addition, as highlighted in chapter 4, if we compare the distribution of capabilities at the origins of the previous bipolar system with today, we find that the distribution is roughly similar. This strongly suggests that the international system has returned to bipolarity.

CHALLENGING EXISTING SCHOLARSHIP

In the current debate about the characteristics of U.S.-China relations, scholars and policy makers are grappling with two overarching questions: Will China's rise be peaceful? What will U.S.-China relations in the twenty-first century look like? Henry A. Kissinger writes that the "presidents of the major twenty-first-century competitors—the United States and China—have vowed to avoid repeating Europe's tragedy through a 'new type of great power relations.' The concept awaits joint elaboration."[26] As a start, we need to establish whether China and the United States will be peer competitors within a bipolar or a multipolar system. This will affect the risk of war, stability, their pattern of behavior, and how a new world order will be constructed.

Basing their assumptions on a contemporary transition to multipolarity, some scholars contend that U.S.-China relations are ripe for conflict and tragedy.[27] Analogies to rivalry and the likelihood of war are drawn from former multipolar systems.[28] However, with the return of bipolarity we might expect another period of the "long peace" that characterized the previous bipolar system.[29] From a structural-realist account,[30] U.S.-China relations are likely to be more stable with the return of bipolarity than if the international system had returned to multipolarity.[31]

While leading scholars do approach the U.S.-China rivalry from a multipolar perspective, it provides a misleading starting point for an examination of this vital bilateral relationship. Kissinger, for example, sees Germany's emergence as posing a challenge to the system in twentieth-century Europe, and the "emergence of China poses a comparable structural challenge in the twenty-first century," he argues.[32] However, Germany rose within a multipolar system that allowed for instability and a balancing behavior that contributed to war: the dynamics of chain-ganging prior to World War I and buck-passing prior to World War II.[33] Chain-ganging and buck-passing behavior are much less likely within a bipolar system.

Joseph S. Nye Jr. and Graham Allison pose the analogy of the Thucydides trap, the rivalry between the rising power of Athens and the established power of Sparta, in ancient Greece.[34] Although Raymond Aron has pointed out that rivalry in ancient Greece is not directly comparable with the modern state system,[35] as the top-ranking powers at the time, Sparta and Athens's rivalry might resemble that of the United States and China under bipolarity. However, Allison compares this power struggle with Germany challenging Britain in the early twentieth century. Thirteen of Allison's sixteen cases reflect multipolar systems and "in 12 of 16 cases over the past 500 years, the result was war." So "based on the current trajectory," Allison concludes, "war between the United States and China in the decades ahead is not just possible, but much more likely than recognized at the moment," even if it is not inevitable.[36] Allison does not take into account the bipolar-stability thesis and does not address what type of great-power war is likely to erupt.

The U.S.-Soviet case during the previous bipolar system in Allison's dataset did not result in war. To follow Allison's argument we have to assume U.S.-China rivalry under multipolarity. But Allison provides no evidence that the current international system is multipolar or will remain multipolar in the decades ahead. Instead, both Allison and Nye's analysis emphasize the unprecedented rise of China and how only China can rival the United States. Their analysis implies it is more likely that the current system is already or is becoming bipolar even though China has not obtained power parity with the United States.[37] Allison argues that structural factors lay the foundations for the outbreak of war and conditions how crises are managed. The argument is exemplified by pointing to the outbreak of the First World War and the management of the Cuban missile crisis during the Cold War, but there is no discussion of how rivalry under multipolar and bipolar systems shaped the different outcomes of these two cases.[38] Neither does Allison examine whether the United States and China are destined for war or another "long peace" under a new bipolar system.

The United States and China are on a path to tragedy in the form of increased competition, confrontation, and conflict, which both states might seek to avoid. Nonetheless, the tragedy of great-power politics is significantly different under multipolar and bipolar systems. This is acknowledged by John J. Mearsheimer in his historical analysis of the causes of great-power war,[39] although he has neglected it in his contemporary assessment of U.S.-China rivalry. Britain and Germany's rivalry and balancing in a multipolar system led to two world wars, while the United States and Soviet Union's intense confrontation sustained a cold war. U.S.-China rivalry will be shaped by a new bipolar system with its own unique characteristics. While predicting and urging the avoidance of "a repetition of previous tragedies,"[40] participants in the current debate about U.S.-China relations need to address bipolarity.

According to Thomas J. Christensen, the United States can manage and shape the choices posed by a rising China through a balanced strategy of deterrence and reassurance and adjustments in its diplomacy. His comprehensive analysis draws a distinction between the current interdependent and globalized world and the great-power politics of the nineteenth and twentieth centuries. As with most other IR and U.S.-China-relations studies, analogies are based on the previous multipolar system, not the relative superpower stability that persisted through the previous bipolar era.[41] A similar argument to Christensen's analysis is found in James Steinberg and Michael O'Hanlon's emphasis on strategic reassurance and resolve, and Lyle Goldstein has emphasized how the United States and China can ease bilateral tension through compromise.[42] These studies provide some of the best guidelines for avoiding unnecessary U.S.-China competition; however, the effects of a return to bipolarity are not developments that can be remedied simply with improved policy making. We need to examine how a new bipolar system will shape U.S.-China relations and other states' strategic adjustments in new and unprecedented ways.

The reasons for the outbreak of war are multiple. The argument here is not that perceptions or misperceptions, perceived advantages of offense and defense, incentives for a preventive war, miscalculations, wishful thinking, complacency, greed, idiosyncrasies, ideology, domestic politics, nationalism, the quest for natural resources, technological progress, and other factors are insignificant. They undoubtedly all play a part in the outbreak of war. It is that polarity conditions the risk of war and shapes and molds how these unit-level and idiosyncratic factors influence policy making and the course of great-power politics.

By establishing that the international system has returned to bipolarity and by examining U.S.-China relations from a bipolar perspective, this book challenges the polarity debate between advocates of continued unipolarity and those predicting a transition to multipolarity, reconsiders current multipolar-tragedy analogies, and proposes using the bipolar-stability thesis and the analogy of the "long peace" as a new starting point for analyzing U.S.-China relations in the twenty-first century. No comprehensive studies have examined contemporary U.S.-China relations from a bipolar perspective or compared bipolar systems.

REFINING WALTZ'S STRUCTURAL-REALIST THEORY

The book tests neorealist propositions about the stability, balancing, and "sameness" of a bipolar system. Waltz's thesis that a bipolar system is more stable than a multipolar system provides an important starting point for my analysis. Nonetheless, Waltz's theory remains unfinished because he did not compare bipolar systems. Structural realism seeks to explain "changes across systems, not within them." It describes "the range of likely outcomes of actions and interactions of states within a given system and shows how the range of expectations varies as systems change."[43] However, neorealism cannot account for how and why actions and interactions change between roughly similar structures and systems. It cannot predict whether a new bipolar system in the twenty-first century will be more or less stable than the bipolar system of the twentieth, especially not when the two bipolar systems are concentrated on two different geographic regions. A geostructural-realist theory is needed to enable informed analysis of likely political trends based on comparative research that better explains current developments and better predicts future state behavior. Because the future is unknown, we must use theories to predict what is likely to transpire in international politics. The objective is not to try to foretell the future but to outline assumptions that are useful. Geostructural realism can supplement existing approaches and theories. It can identify a more plausible range of possible futures, thereby contributing to a more comprehensive understanding of contemporary and future U.S.-China relations.

The rise of China has validated Waltz's long-held assumption that the international system tends toward balance.[44] The international system is no longer as unbalanced as it was in the unipolar era.[45] As expected by neorealist theory, balances form recurrently.[46] In addition, the prediction "that states will engage in balancing behavior" captures the increased balancing in contemporary U.S.-China relations, which corresponds to a systemic shift from unipolarity to bipolarity.[47] At the same time, U.S. and China moderate balancing at the onset of a new bipolar system does not fit the strong balancing pursued by the United States and the Soviet Union at the beginning of the previous bipolar system, in the late 1940s and early 1950s. This questions neorealism's emphasis on the endurance of predictable patterns of balancing and international politics as long as the structure remains the same.[48]

Christensen and Jack Snyder have demonstrated how and why European powers chain-ganged as a response to the German threat before World War I but buck-passed when faced with a similar threat prior to World War II, despite the similar multipolar configuration of power.[49] Just as multipolar systems of the past encompassed various balancing behaviors by the great powers and have been both stable and war prone, patterns of behavior and structural effects are likely to display differences across bipolar systems.[50] Waltz stated that his theory does not aim to explain foreign policy, and he evinced no interest in predicting the type of state behavior that will appear in particular circumstances.[51] Nonetheless, neorealist theory predicts that states will tend toward "sameness" and balancing behavior.[52]

Superpowers and great powers seeking to survive in an anarchic and competitive self-help system are compelled to emulate the successes of others, which will manifest itself in a tendency of states to engage in balancing behavior. From the structure of the international system, "we can infer some things about the expected behavior and fate of the units: namely, how they will have to compete with and adjust to one another if they are to survive and flourish."[53] Since the two superpowers cannot rely on buck-passing in a bipolar system but have to compensate for external balancing by intensifying their internal efforts,[54] and since chain-ganging is not a likely outcome of systemic effects under bipolarity, the incentives for the two competitors to "imitate each other and become socialized to their system"[55] should be stronger in a bipolar than a multipolar system. Against Waltz's theoretical assumptions emphasizing continuity within systems and differences between systems, it is argued that structural effects on balancing and stability are different, mainly as a result of distinct geopolitics, despite a roughly similar distribution of power between the bipolar systems of the twentieth and twenty-first centuries.

COMBINING GEOPOLITICS AND NEOREALIST THEORY

A reexamination and modification of Waltz's unfinished neorealist theory and the development of a new geostructural-realist theory allow us to give a better explanation and predict a few "big and important things."[56] The book does not examine domestic politics or seek to penetrate the black box of states' policy making to explain states' foreign policy. Following Waltz, its main objective is to deal "with the forces that are in play at the international level, and not at the national level,"[57] and to add geopolitics to the parsimonious structural realism he developed. Neorealism gives us an important first look at the relative stability of a bipolar system, at balancing behavior, and at the role of alliances under different polarities. However, this theory doesn't take us far enough.

The new U.S.-China bipolar system has unique features, ones unlike those of the previous bipolar system. These distinct features can be explained and understood by combining geopolitics and structural realism. Geopolitics operates to influence state behavior from forces outside the state.[58] Geopolitics or a geostrategic approach is distinct from geopolitik or a more organic approach.[59] This book draws on geopolitics. Another distinction is between classical geopolitics and critical geopolitics. I rely on the former tradition and follow Kelly in emphasizing that "classical geopolitics focuses upon the structural, international, or strategic level, and within this broader aspect it involves the study of the impacts of certain geographical features, such as states' and regions' positions and locations, resources, distances, topography, shapes and sizes, and the like, upon states' foreign policies and behaviors as an aid to statecraft and as a sources for theory."[60]

During the previous bipolar system centered on Europe, the United States preserved the balance of power in Europe through its military presence on the European continent. In the contemporary bipolar system centered on East Asia, the United States relies on its naval power and dominance in the maritime theater to maintain the balance of power in East Asia and to resist Chinese regional hegemony. During the Cold War, the sea was secondary for strategic competition when compared with the U.S.-Soviet divide that dominated continental Europe. Today, maritime East Asia is the primary area of the superpowers' strategic competition and interaction. The relative importance of land and sea power in the two bipolar systems and the differences between rivalry and balancing on land and at sea illustrate how geopolitics shapes the effects of bipolarity.

In the confrontation on the land mass of Western Europe, the strategic space was physically close to the Soviet Union, geographically impossible to defend from Soviet attack because of a lack of natural barriers, and susceptible to occupation and control by ground forces. The contemporary confrontation in maritime East Asia is, by contrast, in a wide expanse of water, so that neither power can occupy the contested space; the arena of strategic competition is the nonmainland areas of Northeast and Southeast Asia, where the stopping power of water makes it difficult for China to attack American allies and for the United States to invade China; the rivalry at sea is largely in an ungoverned space and a global common used by all;[61] and the wide sea expanse exacts a cost on U.S. power because it has to project power all the way across the Pacific Ocean before it can begin to contain Chinese power.[62]

The geopolitical factors informing the following analysis include (1) comparing the relatively flat, barrier-free geography of the European continent with the desert, mountains, jungles, and permafrost of the East Asian mainland; (2) contrasting superpower rivalry on land in Europe with rivalry at sea in East Asia and distinguishing between continental powers and sea powers in general;[63] (3) comparing a fragile status quo and contested spheres of influence in maritime East Asia with recognized spheres of influences, status quo–oriented superpowers, and clearly marked red lines or "trip wires"[64] between the East and the West in the European continent during the previous bipolar era; (4) contrasting between distinct power vacuums and examining their role in shaping patterns of behavior between bipolar systems; (5) comparing the importance of the stopping power of water and contrasting the vastness of the Pacific Ocean[65] and the limited geographical space available to the United States for a forward military presence in East Asia, in contrast to the shorter route across the Atlantic and abundance of space for forward U.S. military bases and facilities in Western Europe (in contrast to Europe, there are few places on the East Asian mainland where the United States can establish a military foothold to counterbalance China); and (6) pointing out that China is geographically as large as the European continent and that there are fewer states on the East Asian mainland than in Europe. As the distribution of capabilities between the two bipolar systems is roughly similar, these geopolitical factors are combined with neorealism and highlighted in order to account for similar and different patterns of stability and behavior.

Waltz only noted anarchy and the distribution of capabilities as systemic factors, but geopolitics has important regional and systemic effects. Geopolitics is a longstanding school of thought, and many realists and historians have drawn extensively on insights derived from geography and geographical conditions.[66] Since Waltz's theory disregarded the importance of geopolitics, the explanatory power of his theory proved too limited. Moreover, since Waltz could not compare and contrast bipolar systems, his neorealist theory was too Eurocentric. Insofar as the role of geopolitics was undertheorized in Waltz's neorealist theory, this book seeks to incorporate geopolitics into a structural-realist analysis and works toward a refinement of neorealism by developing a new geostructural-realist theory. It builds on the emphasis on geography in the work of other structural realists[67] and draws on the scholarship of other realists on the importance of geography in understanding U.S.-China relations and balance-of-power politics.[68]

This does not mean that neorealism is rejected. While I build on the work of scholars such as Christopher Layne, Jack S. Levy, and Robert S. Ross, who contend that great-power politics takes place predominantly at a regional level and stress the importance of "specifying the geographical scope of the system,"[69] Waltz's emphasis on the systemic distribution of capabilities is my starting point.[70] I seek to demonstrate that shifts in the systemic distribution of capabilities, such as a narrowing power gap between the United States and China and a widening power gap between

China and any third-ranking power, have important regional effects. Indeed, the return of bipolarity is the most important factor explaining increased balancing, assertiveness, and strategic adjustments in East Asia. If the distribution of capabilities had remained unipolar or shifted to multipolarity, then balancing and stability in East Asia would have looked very different. It is not just China's rise and its growing capabilities that have allowed China to assert its interest and challenge the United States in its sphere of influence in maritime East Asia since 2009. Equally important is the shifting distribution of capabilities and the fact that China has become relatively so much more powerful than all other states.

China and Russia had about the same nominal GDP in 1993. In 2016, China's GDP was more than ten times larger than Russia's. If Russia, for example, had been able to maintain a GDP half the size of China's in the post–Cold War era, it would have had the world's third-largest GDP today. Furthermore, with such a hypothetical GDP, and if Russia's defense spending as a share of GDP had been the same as it is today (5.4 percent in 2015), then its defense expenditure would have rivaled the United States and been two to three times larger than China's. But the distribution of capabilities is not multipolar; it is bipolar. The dramatic and enduring relative decline of Russia over the last two decades suggests that Russia will not be able to challenge Chinese security on the East Asian mainland. Instead, it allows China to challenge the United States in maritime East Asia. As a result of shifts in the systemic distribution of capabilities, China now enjoys both the necessary economic strength and geopolitical conditions to dominate the Asian mainland and to focus its efforts in the near and medium term on developing naval capabilities to challenge the United States in East Asian waters in a bid for regional hegemony, potentially fulfilling this ambition in the long term. The ambitious Belt and Road initiative is also an effect of China's rising power and the shifting distributions of capabilities.

Russia's decline also compels the United States to prioritize between its flanking regions and adjust its presence in Europe. Since the enormous rise in China's relative power has shifted the distribution of capabilities to bipolarity, the United States is seeking to concentrate more and more of its forces in East Asia. Had the international system transitioned to multipolarity, there would have been strong systemic incentives for the United States to pull back its forces from its two flanking regions and let regional great powers sustain a power equilibrium. Instead, the United

States is most likely to balance China, its only peer competitor, and become more drawn into East Asia in a bipolar system.

Waltz's neorealism remains important when comparing the stability of bipolar and multipolar systems, but when we can compare and contrast bipolar systems, an endeavor Waltz could not undertake, we find variations from structural-realist theory, primarily because of the geopolitical differences between a bipolar system concentrated on East Asia rather than Europe and with superpower rivalry and balancing concentrated more on the maritime domain than on land. We therefore need to understand the new bipolar system, distinguish its stabilizing from its destabilizing characteristics, and examine its effects on behavior and outcomes. Geopolitics must be added to structural-realist theory not only to account for "the different expected effects of different international systems"[71] but to identify variation in the prospects for stability in roughly similar international systems, enhancing in the process structural realism's explanatory and predictive power.

PLAN OF THE BOOK

The book is divided into eight chapters. Following this introductory chapter, chapter 2 first discusses how states' power and rankings are measured before examining how polarity can be established according to the distribution of capabilities in the international system. Three criteria are suggested for determining whether polarity changes and for studying shifts in the distribution of capabilities among the top-ranking powers. The meaning of bipolarity is then explored by answering the question "what was bipolarity?"[72] The theoretical underpinnings of the book are emphasized by explaining why polarity matters in international politics.

Chapter 3 examines the current distribution of capabilities in the international system. Drawing on the discussion of method and theory in chapter 2, it is contended that China's current combined capabilities place it in the top echelon alongside the United States, despite their lack of symmetry and power parity.

No other great powers can compete with China's combined score, it is suggested in chapter 4. China is catching up with the United States faster than any other great power is catching up with China. The power gap between China and the third-ranking power is now so great that we can start thinking of the international system as bipolar. This argument is reinforced by an examination of the distribution of capabilities in the early stages of the previous bipolar system, which shows a roughly similar distribution to that of the current bipolar system. After challenging the conventional and mainstream polarity debate in the first part of the book and establishing the bipolar nature of the contemporary international system, three main arguments follow in the second part.

The first argument (chapter 5) is that strong balancing will be postponed at the start of the new bipolar system. Balancing on land in Europe was more intense during the previous bipolar system than balancing at sea in East Asia today. The European continent had few geographical barriers that could prevent invasion. The stopping power of water in East Asia and the natural geographical barriers on the East Asian mainland make invasion and expansion more difficult and increase security in contemporary East Asia. The United States and NATO were inferior to the Soviet Union in conventional military power in the European theater. The West feared Soviet expansion across the European continent. At the same time, the Soviet Union sought to secure its western borders from another attack from the West. Arms racing, including a nuclear arms race, ensued, and alliances were formed. But this scenario is different from that of the current situation in East Asia, where the United States has military superiority in the maritime domain and China dominates the East Asian mainland. The stopping power of water also serves to protect U.S. allies from potential Chinese military expansion while simultaneously protecting China from any invasion from the sea and allowing it to secure its continental borders. Geopolitical factors mitigate threat perceptions and provide fewer incentives to pursue strong balancing behaviors at the origins of a new bipolar system concentrated on maritime East Asia.

Nevertheless, in contrast to the previous bipolar system, which saw stability and peace in the relationship between the United States and the Soviet Union, the second argument (chapter 6) hypothesizes a higher likelihood of limited war between the superpowers in the new bipolar era than during the previous bipolar period. A new bipolar system with superpower rivalry concentrated in maritime East Asia will be more unstable[73] and more prone to war and conflict than the bipolar system concentrated on continental Europe during the Cold War.[74] Since large bodies of water create significant power-projection problems for attacking forces, decision makers might risk a limited war or a battle at sea in maritime East Asia, calculating that escalation to a full-scale invasion or major war is less likely when the superpowers are not located on the same landmass, which of course was the case in Europe under the last bipolar system.[75]

If the Soviet Union had invaded West Germany or Western Europe, it could easily have escalated into a major, even nuclear, war, especially since the United States was inferior to Soviet conventional forces on the ground in Europe. If China were to invade Taiwan or sink U.S. naval ships in a confrontation in the South or East China Sea, the risk of such aggression escalating into a major or nuclear war would still be lower than it was in Europe because the armed forces of China and the United States are separated by a sea, not a land, border. Geographical factors with a potential for provoking war in East Asian waters foster instability and make war at sea more likely than war on the European continent during the previous bipolar system.[76]

In contrast to that system, with stability at the center in Europe and instability at the periphery or "third world," I argue in chapter 7 that U.S.-China relations are set to be more unstable at the center in East Asia and more stable at the periphery. The two superpowers are unlikely to engage in the type of proxy war that characterized the Cold War. A status quo, with spheres of influence and clearly marked red lines or "trip wires," as Schelling succinctly described them, effectively stabilized Europe during the previous bipolar era. The stakes in crossing the East-West divide and challenging the status quo were so high that Europe remained stable. Superpower rivalry and conflict instead migrated to other regions.

The contested waters in East Asia where the two superpowers will mainly interact in the new bipolar system comprise a geographical space where trip wires and red lines are less clear, the status quo is contested, spheres of influence are challenged, and security buffers are lacking. Rivalry and confrontation will therefore more likely be concentrated in maritime East Asia, not the peripheries. Instability in the new power center in East Asia will deter the United States and China from pursuing the type of global confrontation that characterized U.S.-Soviet behavior during the previous bipolar era. Nonetheless, the return of bipolarity will have important implications globally, and the second part of chapter 7 examines how a U.S.-China bipolar system affects international politics by focusing on U.S. grand strategy, transatlantic relations, European security policy, Sino-Russian relations, institutions, and nontraditional security challenges.

The concluding chapter rehearses the book's core arguments. The polarity debate is revisited, and the chapter elaborates on how this book refines structural-realist theory and develops a new geostructural-realist theory. It points to new research areas opened by the bipolarity argument and shows how geostructural realism can predict future balancing and stability under a potential new polarity. It discusses how a bipolarity perspective can enhance our understanding of how global power shifts shape states' interaction. It is essential that we improve our understanding of how superpowers behave in a new bipolar system and how systemic constraints will shape state behavior. When the risk of war is higher at the center in East Asia in the new bipolar U.S.-China system than it was in the previous bipolar system concentrated in Europe, then we obviously need to know more about the risk factors before we can mitigate them. It is important to know why the patterns of behavior in the new bipolar system of the twenty-first century are different from the strong balancing and confrontational behaviors that characterized the previous bipolar system of the Cold War in the twentieth century.

Part I

PAST AND PRESENT
POLARITY

Chapter 2

EXPLAINING AND UNDERSTANDING POLARITY

What can we do to determine the relative power of states and establish which states count among the top ranking? What criteria can be used to conclude whether the polarity of the international system changes? In addition to methodological clarification, there is also a need for theoretical guidance. Contending that the current international system is bipolar is more useful after examining how systemic effects on states are different under unipolar, bipolar, and multipolar systems. That is the task of this chapter, which is divided into four parts. The first part defines power and discusses how polarity can be measured. The second part focuses on the conditions for establishing polarity shifts. The third part seeks to explain the meaning of the term *bipolarity*.[1] The final part examines why polarity matters and how shifts in the distribution of capabilities shape state behavior.

DEFINING POWER AND MEASURING POLARITY

Structural realists define power in terms of material resources and consider power as a means to an end. Mearsheimer provides the most straightforward definition: "Power, as I define it, represents nothing more than specific assets or material resources that are available to a state."[2] Material capabilities are things states use to pursue their goals. "Power is a means, and the outcome of its use is necessarily uncertain," wrote Waltz.[3] He emphasized material capabilities when counting the top-ranking states but also included factors such as "political stability and competence," which are more difficult to measure than military, economic, or other material resources.[4] Mearsheimer distinguishes carefully between power as material capability and as outcome.[5] Waltz was more ambiguous, defining power in his early work "as the capacity to produce an intended effect"[6] while later stating that "an agent is powerful to the extent that he affects others more than they affect him." Nevertheless, Waltz stressed that how power is distributed and what its effects are need to be kept distinct: "The extent of one's power cannot be inferred from the results one may or may not get."[7]

Other scholars have also warned against equating power with outcomes. The first of Wohlforth's "rules of power analysis" concerns the "problem with conflating power-as-resources with power-as-influence."[8] Although U.S. power could not solve all international problems under unipolarity, and there were limits to what the United States and the Soviet Union could accomplish during the previous bipolar system, they did not cease to be superpowers. The world remained unipolar even though the United States could not defeat the Taliban in Afghanistan or stabilize Iraq after Saddam Hussein was removed from power in 2003. The world did not become multipolar because the communists in North Vietnam and the Afghanistan Mujahedeen could contend in war with the United States and the Soviet Union during the previous bipolar system. As Wohlforth argues, defining power as the ability to solve a particular global problem "does not have bearing on the polarity of the international system."[9] Most contributions to an edited volume examining contemporary international relations, polarity, and IR theory define "power in terms of material capabilities rather than in terms of influence or outcomes." As such, these scholars "are interested in how a unipolar distribution of power affects the grand strategies of the unipolar state, the responses of weaker and secondary states, and the overall patterns of the global system."[10] Similar attentiveness to the distribution of power is adopted here.

According to Waltz, we can measure state power and how power is distributed in the international system according to how the top-ranking powers "score on *all* of the following items: size of the population and territory, resource endowment, economic capability, military strength, political stability and competence."[11] Similar methods of measuring polarity and the distribution of capabilities have been used in seminal IR works.[12] Most of Morgenthau's "elements of national power" are incorporated in Waltz's definition, including geography, natural resources, industrial capacity, military preparedness, and population. However, Morgenthau also included national character and morals and the quality of diplomacy and government in his assessment.[13] Since the former elements are relatively easier to measure than the latter, this study focuses primarily on Waltz's definition.

According to structural realists, states in the system are defined according to how they stand in relation to one another and are placed differently based on their relative power, not against an absolute scale.[14] By examining their combined capability score, we can separate states into superpowers, great powers, major powers, and minor powers.[15] The number of superpowers or great powers that exist within the international system can be defined according to the distribution of capabilities across units or states in the system. As Waltz explains, states' individual capabilities are measured according to their combined score on the aforementioned six factors, but their ranking relative to other states or the distribution of capabilities "is not a unit attribute, but rather a system-wide concept."[16]

More recent studies have used Waltz's method as a starting point, and the metrics of national power used in his definition have not been abandoned by alternative approaches.[17] While this study draws mainly on Waltz's method for measuring capability distribution in the international system, it agrees with Posen's observation that even though "political scientists strive for objective measures of relative power, they are elusive,"[18] and it recognizes that other scholars propose alternative ways to assess power.[19]

Leading Chinese scholars such as Hu Angang and Yan Xuetong have written extensively on the metrics used to assess comprehensive national power and have provided various estimates and conclusions on China's power status.[20] Their measurements yield results very similar to those produced using Waltz's combined six factors. Yan notes that there remains disagreement over the measurements, causing differences in the estimation of China's combined capabilities. The large number of factors used in the various measuring methods, he determines, have not led to an "improvement in the accuracy of measuring China's current power status."[21] Resembling Morgenthau's and Waltz's methods of gauging national power and the distribution of capabilities, Yan stresses that China's power status is relative and must be compared to that of other states. He further notes that even if the term "comprehensive national power" was coined in the post–Cold War era, the method of measuring national power by assessing a combination of factors has been around for ages.[22]

Power relations between two or more nations should not be measured simply at a particular moment in history but must "be projected into the future," as Morgenthau noted.[23] Capabilities may be imminent or latent, and patterns of behavior can deviate from structural constraints and distribution of capabilities.[24] This book provides a "picture of the moment" as a baseline for conducting a structural analysis of the current distribution of capabilities, but at times it also considers future distributions in order to seek a more dynamic analysis of trends.[25] This is especially so inasmuch as certain factors, such as natural resources, demography, and geography, do not change much; technology may even improve resource-extraction and food-production rates. It is more difficult to project long-term future trends in terms of economic development, military capability, political stability, and competence, not to mention factors such as national morale and character and quality of government and diplomacy.

Measuring Distribution of Capabilities and Polarity

T. R. Fox introduced the term *superpower* in 1944. He considered the international system at the time to be multipolar.[26] In the aftermath of the Second World War, it became clear to most observers that Britain lacked the combined capabilities of a superpower. This book uses the term "superpower" only when referring to unipolar or bipolar systems and describes the most powerful states in a multipolar system as great powers. The bipolar power distribution in the aftermath of the Second World War marked something new. The United States and the Soviet Union were distinctly superior to all other states and much more powerful than the great powers of the preceding multipolar period. Accordingly, the unprecedented bipolar systemic distribution of capabilities defined these two poles as superpowers. This shift had a radical effect upon, and transformed, the operation of the balance of power. As Morgenthau argued, this led to the disappearance of a balancer or holder of the balance, and Waltz contended that a system of two is more stable than a system of three or more.[27]

How capabilities are distributed tells us what type of international system exists at a given time. In a multipolar system, there are three or more great powers whose capabilities are roughly equal. Each great power is substantially more powerful than any other state in the system. In a bipolar system, there are two superpowers whose capabilities dwarf those of any other state in the system.[28] In a unipolar system, one superpower is unambiguously more powerful than any other state.[29] The global international system, at least since the developments of nation-states in the aftermath of the French Revolution or even since the 1648 Peace of Westphalia, was multipolar until the Second World War, bipolar during the second half of the twentieth century,[30] and unipolar after the Soviet Union's collapse in 1991.

Fox argued in 1944 that the United States, Great Britain, and the Soviet Union would be the Big Three, or powers of first ranks, "in war as they will be in peace."[31] Morgenthau recognized Great Britain as a great power at the end of World War II but argued in 1948 that in the aftermath of the Second World War, "British power has declined to such an extent as to be distinctly inferior to the power of the United States and the Soviet Union, the only two great powers left at present."[32] In Morgenthau's revised and enlarged second edition of *Politics Among Nations*, published in 1954, he added, concerning the decline of the relative power of Great Britain, that the United States and the Soviet Union, "in view of their enormous superiority over the power next in rank, deserved to be called superpowers."[33] In considering how we can establish whether polarity has changed and how we can define superpowers, there are lessons to be drawn from comparing Morgenthau's first and second editions of *Politics Among Nations*.

First, Morgenthau did not use the term "superpower" in his first edition. This suggests that measuring and establishing top-ranking status is difficult but necessary for determining polarity. When he used the term "superpower" to describe the combined capabilities of the United States and the Soviet Union in the 1954 second edition, Morgenthau had clearly come to the conclusion that these two powers had acquired capabilities superior to those traditionally attributed to great-power status in the past. The usage of the term "superpower" helped distinguish a bipolar system from a multipolar one.

Second, while Morgenthau pointed to the importance of measuring the combined capabilities required for top ranking, in his second edition he also highlighted the gap between the top- and next-ranking states. The United States and the Soviet Union were not only top-tier powers because of their preponderant capabilities but also because of their relative superiority over Great Britain, the third-ranking power. The asymmetric power balance between the United States and the Soviet Union did not change in any significant way in the aftermath of the Second World War, but while the Soviet Union remained inferior to the United States in combined capabilities, they were sufficient to give it top ranking. It was the decline in Great Britain's relative power and the shifts in the distribution of capabilities between the second-ranking superpower and third-ranking great power that transformed the international system from multipolar to bipolar between 1945 and 1950. This shift urged Morgenthau to define the United States and the Soviet Union as superpowers in his second edition of *Politics Among Nations*. This is an important but often underemphasized point in the current polarity debate, which correctly focuses on whether China's combined capabilities are sufficient for top-ranking status but neglects the equal importance of measuring the power gap between China and the power next in rank for determining the polarity of the contemporary international system.

Third, Morgenthau stressed that Britain had lost its ability to affect decisively the balance of power. It had disappeared as the balancer.[34] Similarly, it can, for example, be argued today that whether India bandwagons with China or the United States will not fundamentally change the bipolar balance of power and that no third power can take China's place in the top ranking. Should China collapse in the near future, then the international system will return to unipolarity.

Distribution of Power Versus Power Attributes of States

As pointed to in the introduction, many would argue that China has not become a superpower, because China's overall economic, military, and political clout is not on parity with the United States and because it falls short of being a global superpower or even a regional hegemon.[35] Such views do not emphasize the importance of defining a superpower and polarity in terms of distribution of capabilities; do not compare the distribution of capabilities when the superpower concept was introduced in the 1940s and 1950s with the current distribution of capabilities; do not assess the power gap between the second- and the third-ranking power; and neglect that, similar to the Soviet Union, China does not need to obtain power parity with the United States to become a superpower or pole in a new bipolar system.

From a structural-realist perspective, if we want to find out if the international system is unipolar, bipolar, or multipolar, and if it is composed of superpowers(s) or great powers, we should examine the distribution of capabilities within the international system, not the attributes of states. That is, polarity and top ranking do not depend on whether states are regional hegemons, have global power-projection capability, have recent experience with successfully fighting wars, possess nuclear weapons and have nuclear second-strike capability, and have allies.

The United States was a regional hegemon in the Western Hemisphere as early as before World War I, but it was not defined as a pole or superpower in a bipolar or unipolar system. Instead, it was a great power in a multipolar system. The distribution of capabilities in the international system up until the Second World War was such that there were more than three great powers with roughly equal combined capabilities, irrespective of the fact that the United States was a regional hegemon. The Soviet Union never obtained regional hegemony during the previous bipolar system. It only controlled Eastern Europe, while the United States was the dominating power in Western Europe, and they both competed over influence in a divided Germany at the center of Europe. However, the Soviet Union was still defined as a superpower because the distribution of capabilities in the post–World War II period was bipolar. Contemporary China is not a regional hegemon like the United States, and it has not obtained power parity with the latter, but it can be defined as a superpower in a new bipolar system because of today's distribution of capabilities.

Despite that the United States, Japan, and Great Britain had global power-projection capability prior to World War II, they were not superpowers, because other states, such as Germany, France, and the Soviet Union, were considered as powerful, although they lacked global power projection. Britain had global power-projection capabilities throughout most of the nineteenth and twentieth centuries, but it was not a superpower. The Soviet Union did not have global power-projection capabilities at the start of the previous bipolar era. It had limited naval capabilities in the 1950s and only developed an aircraft carrier in the late 1970s. The Afghan-Soviet war did not give the Soviet Union any superpower credentials, and it only fought a few proxy wars overseas throughout the Cold War. Still, the Soviet Union was defined as a pole and a superpower because the distribution of capabilities in the post–World War II era was such that there were only two top-ranking powers.

China has a relatively stronger navy compared to the United States than the Soviet Union did at the start of the previous bipolar system, and the PLAN operates globally. China is not fighting wars overseas, but we cannot rule out that China might participate in proxy wars in the decades to come, similar to how the Soviets gradually became involved in conflicts globally during the previous bipolar system. China has sustained the escort mission in the Gulf of Aden for a decade, participated in the Syrian chemical weapons disposal in 2014, and conducted and participated in military exercises and carried out port visits globally. It is a permanent member of the UN Security Council and contributes the most to UN peacekeeping operations. China is clearly more of an economic superpower on a global scale than the Soviet Union ever was. It is a leading foreign investor and an important market to countries all over the world. China sells arms globally and has contributed to states' nuclear-weapons programs (Pakistan's in particular, but also Iran's and North Korea's). It has advanced global cyber capabilities and a strong space-based program. But even if China is more involved in global affairs than the Soviet Union in the 1950s, none of these factors defines China as a superpower. Structural realism does not define polarity and superpower(s) according to the particular capabilities a state may or may not have. It is China's combined and relative score on Waltz's six factors for measuring distribution of capabilities that defines polarity and superpower status.

Although it remains unlikely, if the distribution of capabilities is such that China is the only pole or superpower by the mid-twenty-first century, it does not have to acquire global power-projection capabilities similar to those of the United States during the previous unipolar era to be defined as the only superpower. It is the distribution of capabilities in 2050 that will determine the polarity of the international system, not whether the top-ranking powers have developed, for example, certain revolutionary military capabilities. It is by examining this distribution that we will know whether we have one or two superpowers or three or more great powers in a unipolar, bipolar, or multipolar system at that time.

One might think that China's lack of war-fighting experience and the fact that China has not waged war since 1979 means that it cannot be defined as a superpower. However, willingness to use military force, and even being victorious in war, does not define a superpower. Based on Russia's use of force in Ukraine in 2014 and its involvement in the war in Syria, some suggest that Russia must be considered a pole in a contemporary multipolar system. Conversely, Russia's use of force might be perceived as a sign of weakness: a response to NATO's eastward expansion and a calculation to use force before Russia's relative power evaporates further. Given China's formidable land power, it does not need to use force to prevent anything similar to NATO's expansion on the East Asian mainland. The United States would find it very difficult to challenge Chinese security by, for example, expanding its alliances to countries such as Vietnam, Myanmar, Laos, Cambodia, or Nepal.

More importantly, if we only consider some examples of the use of military force during the first years of the previous bipolar system, we can conclude that this cannot be a defining characteristic of a superpower or a factor determining polarity. The newly founded PRC fought the leading superpower, the United States, to a standstill in the Korean War in 1950–1953. Few, however, suggested afterward that China was a superpower or that the international system had shifted to multipolarity because the PLA had pushed back the United States militarily on the Korean Peninsula. During the same period, France was fighting the First Indochina War halfway around the world, but even with such a display of global power-projection capability it was not considered a superpower or a pole in the international system. Last but not least, in 1956 France and Great Britain colluded with Israel in the Suez War against Nasser's Egypt, defeating the Egyptian army, but their military adventure only showed to the world that they were clearly no longer top-ranking powers.

Neither can the possession of nuclear weapons and second-strike capability be the defining characteristic of a superpower. The United States had a nuclear capability for some years while the Soviet Union did not, during the period 1945–1949, but the Soviet Union could still be considered a superpower. When other states obtained nuclear weapons during the Cold War, they did not become superpowers; nor did it bring about a polarity shift. Moreover, after the collapse of the Soviet Union, Russia was no longer a superpower and is still not a superpower, and the distribution of capabilities shifted from bipolarity to unipolarity, even though Russia maintained a strong global second-strike nuclear capability.

It is often pointed out that the United States has many allies and China nearly none.[36] From a structural-realist point of view, however, it is the distribution of capabilities that matters. The entire point of being a superpower is that you do not need to depend on your allies. In addition, as Morgenthau and Waltz pointed out, the European countries did not significantly add to U.S. power in the bipolar balance; they provided access to Europe.[37] Similarly, Japan does not significantly augment U.S. power but instead allows for forward presence. It can also be argued that U.S. global commitments and alliances, such as in Europe and the Middle East, are a liability rather than strength when the United States is confronted with a peer competitor in East Asia.

Polarity and the definition of a superpower are relative. As this book emphasizes, we can only know the structure of the international system and whether it is composed of superpowers or great powers by examining the distribution of capabilities in the international system, not by examining the attributes and characteristics of states alone. The United States remains a superpower today, and despite their asymmetric power relationship, China's relative power rise in terms of the shifting distribution of capabilities suggests it can be elevated from great-power to superpower ranking.

How many top-ranking powers there are within the international system shapes balancing behavior and stability, but when there are one or two superpowers, there are also other great powers and major powers in the world.[38] The United States and the Soviet Union were superpowers during the Cold War era, and Britain, France, and China could be considered great powers. The United States was the only superpower in the post–Cold War unipolar system; China and Russia could be considered great powers; and Germany, France, Britain, Japan, and India could be considered major powers during that period.[39] The United States and China are the superpowers of the new bipolar system; Russia and India can now be considered great powers; and France, Britain, Germany and Japan major powers.

Weighing the Components of Power

Unlike Morgenthau,[40] Waltz did not single out one particular component of national power, and there is no consensus regarding how the six items in Waltz's definition should be weighted. At times, ranking "involves difficulties of comparison and uncertainties about where to draw lines." Capabilities can only be measured "roughly": conclusions about polarity are ultimately a judgment call.[41]

It has been argued that preponderance in military power will be the defining factor in determining the durability of the post–Cold War unipolar system and not "whether, how, and when other economies—namely China's—will surpass the U.S. economy."[42] Monteiro argues that "a unipolar world will endure for as long as one state has preeminent military capabilities, [and] it is impossible to understand the dynamics that may lead to the end of unipolarity by looking at economic power." But how long a superpower can endure as a preeminent military power depends on its economic strength. The previous bipolar era taught us that it was not the Soviet Union's lack of military power that ended the bipolar system but the Soviet Union's economic weakness. Despite the gap between latent power and military power, there is compelling evidence that economic strength underpins military power and that wealth constitutes an important factor of latent power.[43]

Monteiro not only accentuates the United States' preponderant military power but predicts that unipolarity will continue as long as the unipole sustains its superior global power-projection capability.[44] If IR scholars had followed such a definition at the origins of the previous bipolar system, then Morgenthau and others could never have considered the international system in the aftermath of the Second World War as bipolar, since the Soviet Union was far from having global power-projection capability comparable to the United States.[45] Britain, the third-ranking power, had more global power-projection capability at the starting point and even throughout most of the Cold War period compared to the Soviet Union,[46] but its economic power was not sufficient to sustain its military power or superpower position. Because Britain lacked the *combined* capabilities to match the United States and the Soviet Union, the international system shifted from multipolarity to bipolarity in the aftermath of the Second World War.

All of Waltz's six factors are important, but the most important item in the combined capability score is the economic base of a state's power.[47] The Soviet Union's inability to stay in the race during the Cold War because of its relatively weaker economy and Great Britain's loss of top-ranking-power status because of its much weaker economy (despite retaining global power-projection capability) support this argument. The Soviet Union had to spend twice as much on defense in terms of percentage of GDP to compete with the United States. This was a heavy burden, and it led Waltz to question the durability of the U.S.-Soviet bipolar system.[48] Waltz could not foresee the rise of the PRC in 1979 but insisted that China "may mobilize the nation in order to increase production rapidly while simultaneously acquiring a large and modern military capability. . . . It is doubtful that she can do either, and surely not both, and *surely not the second without the first.*"[49] China cannot obtain top-ranking status, and the United States cannot sustain its top-ranking position, without a strong economic base. All six factors matter, but economic capability matters the most.

Evaluating Economic Strength

Determining economic power is far from straightforward. Much of the debate comes down to whether there should be an emphasis on qualitative over quantitative factors, and the current debate regarding U.S. qualitative superiority over China's quantitative advantages is reminiscent of the comparison between the qualitative and quantitative capabilities of the United States and the Soviet Union.[50] Unipolarists tend to argue that traditional power measures exaggerate the importance of gross size and volume while underplaying per capita wealth and technological superiority.[51] Beckley, in his critique of multipolarists and proponents of U.S. decline, warns us that national power is not synonymous with GDP. He stresses the importance of "surplus wealth" and points out that since 1991, "the average Chinese citizen is more than $17,000 poorer relative to the average American."[52] This is an important observation, but unipolarists should be careful not to move the goalposts and undermine the "rules of power analysis." Wohlforth criticized multipolarists for exaggerating China's economic rise by drawing on purchasing power parity estimates (PPP). Instead, he maintained, gross domestic product (GDP) figures in 2005 clearly showed continued

U.S. primacy.[53] In the following decade, as China's remarkable economic growth continued, China's nominal GDP surpassed 60 percent of U.S. GDP,[54] and PPP estimates of China's economy showed it had become the world's largest, unipolarists point more and more to China's low per capita GDP level to support their claims.[55]

There is not only disagreement about whether nominal GDP, per capita GDP, or GDP measured in PPPs best reflect a country's economic strength.[56] Trade (measured as the sum of goods exported and imported) and creditor status are frequently used indications of economic strength. China has become the world's largest trading nation. This status can be used by China to trade its way to power by leveraging countries by offering or denying them access to its market and by investing overseas.[57] Hirschman described how large and growing trade relations influence states' attitude toward the state upon which their economic interests depend.[58] Arguing that economic power in the absence of military power cannot determine small-state alignment, Ross, on the other hand, finds that secondary-state economic dependence on a great economic power is an *insufficient* force to compel small-state realignment.[59] Others point out that the U.S.-China trade balance is smaller when measured in value-added terms and that China's trading power and real productive capacity are overstated. China is often where the final assembly of manufactured goods takes place, but much of the value added in manufactured goods comes from earlier stages of production in other countries.[60]

Assessments of China's role as a major creditor show similar divergence. In the eyes of many, China's almost $3 trillion in foreign reserves[61] and its role as a leading financier enhances its economic power, which it can use to launch the Belt and Road initiative and establish institutions such as AIIB, which challenge the Bretton Woods system and the current U.S.-led international economic and political order.[62] It can decide to fund states in need, and according to former secretary of state Hillary Clinton, the United States is pondering "how do you deal toughly with your banker?"[63] Currently, China is the largest foreign creditor, with about $1.4 trillion of U.S. government debt, and the yuan has been included in the International Monetary Fund's reserve-currency basket. Conversely, the trend according to some reports is that the demand for U.S. Treasuries is now so robust that even if China sells most of its holdings of U.S. Treasuries, it would matter little.[64] China also faces the challenge of increasing capital flight,[65] which affects its capacity to influence developing countries through over-seas investments and its ambitions to develop alternative institutions that might challenge the U.S.-led international institutional order.

Irrespective of perceptions of economic strength, the United States is still the most central actor in the network of global finance and capital markets, the status of the dollar continues to be strong and remains the official dominant currency reserve for most states, and the dollar has the largest share in international banking and foreign-exchange markets.[66] While it is acknowledged that the United States has accumulated great wealth in part by borrowing from abroad, China's level of public debt, especially at the local and provincial level, and corporate debt has increased dramati-cally since the financial crisis, when the Chinese government introduced economic-stimulus programs.[67] Conversely, according to some analysts, China's total debt, including local government debt, shadow banking debt, and property market downturn, are manageable.[68] China's leaders have sufficient resources to tackle economic problems, the challenges have been identified,[69] and Xi's reform agenda, although still in its initial stages, is making some progress in rebalancing China's economy toward a "new normal."[70]

Economists are unlikely to arrive at any consensus as to how China's economy and economic power should be measured, not to mention China's future economic development. Taken together, a mixed picture emerges when it comes to measuring economic power. Moreover, economic strength is only one of the six factors in Waltz's method of measuring the distribu-tion of capabilities. Caveats and nuances apply to all of the items. The main task of the next chapter is to demonstrate that the underlying distribution of capabilities has shifted to bipolarity while simultaneously providing a balanced approach that shows awareness of counterarguments when measuring China's resources, geography, competence, political stability, and military and economic strength. The remaining parts of this chapter will consider the difficulties in establishing how much more powerful the top-ranking powers need to be before polarity changes and will discuss the various meanings of bipolarity and why polarity matters.

ESTABLISHING POLARITY SHIFTS

It is not clear, Wagner has pointed out, "how *much* more powerful they [the two superpowers] have to be."[71] Polarity is transformed only by changes in organizing principle (anarchy) and consequential changes in the number of top-ranking states.[72] But when the theory of neorealism was being developed, the structure of the international system had only changed once.[73] There were only two systems to consider; no one had foreseen a unipolar system. The shifts in the distribution of capabilities following the Second World War[74] and the collapse of the Soviet Union made it easier to make judgments about polarity shifts, but certainly not without difficulties. Today it is more difficult to establish exactly if and when a polarity has changed and if and when the international system has moved from unipolarity to bipolarity. There are no hegemonic or great-power wars to reconfigure the international distribution of capabilities, and the United States is not likely to collapse like the Soviet Union. The transition to bipolarity is therefore more gradual than the previous polarity shift from multipolarity to bipolarity and from bipolarity to unipolarity.

As Posen writes, "polarity is not synonymous with equality."[75] While China does not need to obtain power parity with the United States for the international system to become bipolar again, there is no formula or definition to say whether China's combined score needs to be, in metaphorical terms, 60, 70, 80, or 90 percent of combined U.S. capabilities or how large the power gap between China and the power next in rank needs to be. In a bipolar system, the gap between the second- and the third-ranking power should be larger than that between the first- and second-ranked power.[76] For example, if China's combined capabilities are 60 to 70 percent of the United States', then the respective combined capabilities of Russia, India, Japan, Germany, or any other state China is measured against should not be more than 60 percent of China's.

It has been suggested that one should focus on the conditions under which polarity is more or less likely to change rather than predicting the timing of the shift.[77] This is sound advice. The criteria this book applies in order to determine whether polarity has shifted from unipolarity to bipolarity are:

1. Rank based on the combined capability score on Waltz's six items. That is, I assess whether China is now a top-ranking nation based on an estimate of the narrowing power gap between China and the United States, keeping in mind that power parity is not a requirement for top ranking.
2. The gap between the second- and third-ranking power—Russia, India, Japan, Germany or any other state one might conceivably argue could contend for top ranking on the combined six factors. If this gap is larger than that between the first- and the second-ranked power, then the system is probably bipolar.
3. A historical comparison based on the previous bipolar system. If the current distribution of capabilities resembles that at the start of the previous bipolar system, then the current international system is very likely bipolar.

The bipolar system of the twenty-first century is likely to be as durable as the last bipolar system. The danger of one superpower toppling the other through war is low. Both superpowers are on different continents and protected by the stopping power of water; invasion is therefore unlikely.[78] The rises and falls of the great powers have historically been slow, and even if economic and technological bases of power may change more rapidly, it is unlikely to alter the standing of the United States and China as top-ranking powers. It was easier to become a top-ranking power when there were more great powers and they were smaller in size. With the superpower club now populated by a few and bigger states, gaining membership has become more challenging.[79] While China's remarkable economic growth and rise in power over the last decades have not given it power parity with the United States, it has shifted the distribution of power and made it more likely that China will avoid collapse and remain at the top than that any other major power will catch up with either of the two superpowers in the coming decades.

Fox's and Morgenthau's writings, in addition to observations made during the Second World War and soon afterward, show that it takes some time before a polarity shift is acknowledged.[80] John Herz argued that most postwar plans had "been based on the expected emergence (or rather, continuance) of a multipolar world. . . . Concentration of overwhelming strength in only two of the victorious nations was something which, at least in the case of one of them [the United States], occurred quite unexpectedly and almost against the inclinations and policies of that country."[81]

It did not become clear that the international system had shifted to bipolarity until the late 1940s, although the Second World War showed that the combined capabilities of the United States and the Soviet Union had outmatched those of Great Britain. It may take five to ten years before the return to a state of bipolarity is generally acknowledged. And even if it is generally agreed that the international system has returned to bipolarity, there are likely to be voices calling for the emergence of a multipolar system, as was the case during the previous bipolar system.[82]

THE MEANING OF BIPOLARITY

The meaning of bipolarity has never been clearly specified. In Wagner's survey of the literature on post–World War II international politics, he found that the word "bipolarity" has at least four distinct meanings: (1) a condition in which states are polarized into hostile coalitions, (2) a condition in which there are only two states capable of a strategy of global deterrence, (3) a system of only two states, and (4) a system in which power is distributed in such a way that two states are so powerful that they can each defend themselves against any combination of other states. However, as Wagner recognized, some of these are not appropriate definitions of bipolarity,[83] and such different usages of the term "bipolarity" have been rejected.

First, a bipolar distribution of capabilities is different from the formation of two blocs in a multipolar system.[84] If a multipolar system with three or more great powers polarizes and splits into two blocs or alliances, it will still be different from a bipolar system. The configuration of alliances or blocs in a multipolar system can change, while it will remain the same in a bipolar system.[85]

Second, Waltz consistently distinguishes in his work between structural forces and unit-level factors.[86] Nuclear weapons are not included in Waltz's definition of structure (anarchy and distribution of capabilities among like units/states), and nuclear weapons do not equalize states' combined capabilities.[87] Nuclear weapons cannot by themselves be used to explain polarity.

Third, according to Wagner, one interpretation of the distinction between bipolarity and multipolarity is that "a bipolar system is one containing only two states."[88] This is also a misguided view. It is rather that the superpowers are less dependent on other states under bipolarity than multipolarity.[89] To describe the world as bipolar does not mean that either superpower can exert positive control everywhere in the world. The powers of the United States and the Soviet Union were predominant but not absolute.[90]

Fourth, as discussed above, this meaning comes closest to establishing what bipolarity means. What was distinctive about the post–World War II international system was the bipolar distribution of capabilities. Bipolarity is a structure in which two states' capabilities are so great that they determine the balance of power solely between them. By the late 1940s it was clear there were two superpowers substantially more powerful than all the others measured according to the combined distribution of capabilities. This bipolar system was distinct from previous multipolar systems with three or more great powers.

Bipolarity Is Not Cold War or Geography

Wagner's emphasis on geography is important.[91] Lacking any "stopping power of water"[92] and given Europe's geographical terrain, it was the Soviet Union's land power and its threat to overrun Western Europe that fueled strong balancing and created the distinctive Cold War characteristics of the previous bipolar era. However, it is essential not to conflate bipolarity with the Cold War or Soviet land power. The new bipolar system in the twenty-first century has so far not produced anything similar, and there may not be a Cold War, despite a bipolar distribution of capabilities in the international system. Indeed, as this book maintains, there are more differences than similarities between the two bipolar systems.

Whether unipolarity, bipolarity, or multipolarity becomes the dominant international system of the twenty-first century cannot be settled according to whether a state occupies most of the Eurasian continent. Polarity and ranking are determined by how capabilities are distributed within the international system, not geography. Russia has been a leading land power on the Eurasian continent for centuries. The Russian empire of the eighteenth and nineteenth centuries, spanning 22 million square kilometers at its geographical zenith, was as large as the Soviet Union.

The Russian army went further west when it entered Paris in 1814 than the Soviet Red Army did when it defeated Nazi Germany in Eastern and Central Europe during the Second World War. However, because of the distribution of capabilities within the international system, Russia did not become a superpower, even though the Russian army pushed back the French army and became the dominant land power in Europe. Conversely, the Soviet Union was considered a superpower after advancing to Berlin in 1945 even though it did not go as far west as the Russian army earlier had and even though it was confronted by American, British, and French armies on the European continent.

Resembling the contemporary spheres of influences in East Asia, after 1814, Russia became the dominant power on the European continent and much of Eurasia, and Britain was preeminent on the seas, dominated global finance, and became the master of the Industrial Revolution.[93] Why, then, did the international system not become bipolar during the nineteenth century? Primarily because the power gap between the two empires and the next-lower-ranked state was "perilously close." As Wohlforth writes, France's "power and status were close enough to those of the two top dogs that either could rationally view Paris as a revisionist bent on hegemony for itself."[94] The Second World War, however, fundamentally changed the distribution of capabilities. The power gap between the top-ranking states and Britain was enormous and led to a new bipolar system. Similarly, China's unprecedented rise has now changed the distribution of capabilities and returned the international system to bipolarity.

Fox was attentive to how geopolitics shapes great-power politics. He noted that until the twentieth century the great powers were all European powers. In the post–World War II era, the majority of powers of first rank were no longer located within continental Western Europe.[95] Not only was the distribution of power different from how it was in the past, but the superpowers were also geographically more separate. This geopolitical fact improves somewhat the prospect for stability and peace, argued Fox,[96] and affects systemic constraints differently than in the past. The Cold War confirmed Fox's propositions.

The number of superpowers and great powers that exist in the international system at any one time depends on the distribution of capabilities across units, not their geographical position. Waltz's method is still the most suitable and sufficiently comprehensive definition against which to measure the distribution of capabilities in the international system, defining polarity and establishing whether the top-ranking powers are superpower(s) or great powers.

WHY POLARITY MATTERS

An international system with one or two superpowers has properties that distinguish it from an international system with three or more great powers. Determining polarity is important because it allows one to make predictions about stability and patterns of state behavior.

Polarity and Stability

Noting that "there are no objectively correct answers," Jervis considered various definitions of stability in the international system: from peacefulness to the speed and consequences of change, from the outcomes and causes of war to the standpoint of individual actors, the relative ease with which one system could be transformed into another, and "the system's ability to ward off or cope with radical change."[97] Waltz defined stability exclusively in terms of durability in his later work, arguing that international systems have been remarkably stable while maintaining that a system of two is more stable than a system of three or more.[98] Stability does not equate with peace or durability, but a system is relatively more stable when there are no wars among the top-ranking powers. The analysis here follows Wohlforth's interpretation: peace and durability are separate but core elements of a stable system.[99]

In a bipolar world, the superpowers mainly rely on their own military capabilities, not the capabilities of allies. They largely balance each other by internal means instead of by combining external and internal balancing. In a multipolar system with more than two powers, changing alliances and shifts in alignment provide an additional means of balancing. This added flexibility is a crucial difference between bi- and multipolar systems because the balance of power operates on a very different basis.[100] When the superpowers are less dependent on allies, it reduces the fear of abandonment and makes defections more tolerable. Uncertainty regarding who will help whom in the event of war and who will oppose an aggressor is reduced in a bipolar system.

External balancing is less precise than internal balancing. When the superpowers predominantly rely on their own capabilities, their balancing efforts become more reliable, since they can more easily calculate their own strength and are less likely to misjudge the strength and reliability of the other superpower.[101] Greater clarity about potential threats and a lower risk of miscalculation in a bipolar system makes war among the top-ranking powers less likely. Stability increases as the number of poles decreases,[102] and the problem of chain-ganging is avoided. Buck-passing dilemmas are also much less likely to arise in bipolarity. Balancing under bipolarity is therefore more efficient.[103]

Multipolar Systems

Other scholars have argued that multipolar systems have lasted and preserved peace for as long as the Cold War bipolar system existed. There were lengthy periods in the nineteenth century—from 1815 to 1852 and 1871 to 1913—when there were no wars between any European great powers. The durability of these two periods of relative multipolar stability compare favorably with the "long peace" of the Cold War.[104] Kissinger writes how equilibrium and legitimacy provided stability and order at various periods during the European balance of power since the Peace of Westphalia, but he recognizes that the multipolar system lost its flexibility in the two decades leading up to the First World War.[105] Proponents of multipolar stability contend that in multipolar systems there are more great powers to deter and offset any great power with regional hegemonic ambitions. They also believe that intense rivalry and conflict develop between the two superpowers under bipolarity but that multipolar systems can spread tension across more great powers. As Deutsch and Singer predicted, under multipolarity, "the frequency and intensity of war should be expected to diminish."[106]

While Aron noted that a "system which covers the planet differs, by nature, from a system of Greek city-states or European states,"[107] such an interpretation suggests that the multipolar international system during the nineteenth and early twentieth centuries included several wars between the great powers and between great powers and major powers, including the Greek War of Independence (1821–1832), the two Opium Wars (1839–1842, 1856–1860), the Sino-French War (1884–1885), the Sino-Japanese War (1884–1885), the Spanish-American War (1898), the intervention in China by the Eight-Nation Alliance during the Boxer Rebellion in the summer of 1900, and the Russo-Japanese War (1904–1905). Power imbalances are more likely, and there will be more opportunities for great powers to fight one another if they gang up against a third power in a multipolar system.

The Peacefulness of Unipolarity

The post–Cold War global distribution of capabilities has been unambiguously unipolar in the 1990s and the early years of the new century. The system has been prone to peace, and any counterbalancing against the United States has been limited. Wohlforth contended that "unipolarity is the least war prone of all structures" and that the United States' unprecedented preponderance of power suggests that unipolarity will last for many decades more.[108] The unipolar system has been the most peaceful international system.[109] There has not been a war between the United States and any other great power or major power or a war between the great powers and major powers during unipolarity. There was no war between the two superpowers during the twentieth-century bipolar system, but the superpowers fought another great power, China, and China fought India, another major power. Multipolar systems have seen wars between all the great powers and major powers. The new configuration of power suggests that the unipolar system will be sustained for less than three decades. Accordingly, unipolarity remains the least durable of the systems. The lack of durability undermines the stability of a unipolar system, since systemic stability encompasses both peacefulness and durability.

By focusing their analyses on the relative stability of bipolar and multipolar systems, structural realists fall short of accounting for unipolarity. Despite that Waltz questioned whether the Soviet Union would be able to stay in the race during the Cold War,[110] anticipated the emergence of unipolarity, and accepted that both bipolarity and unipolarity represented a better system than multipolarity for managing problems in international affairs, he remained reluctant to use his ideas to explore what a new unipolar system would look like and what consequences it would have for international politics—and for his theory.[111] Instead, he refused to amend, modify, or adopt his theory and insisted that one could "take-it-or-leave-it."[112] Waltz consistently argued against unipolarity by maintaining that balances will form over time and that the international system tends toward balancing. "Multipolarity is developing before our eyes," and it is emerging in accordance with the balancing imperative," he maintained in the 1990s.[113]

Mearsheimer shares this view and argues that the post–Cold War system has been multipolar, not unipolar, since Russia and China have been great powers. Mearsheimer characterizes contemporary East Asia as an unbalanced multipolarity, arguing that Russia qualifies as a great power in the region.[114] This is a questionable conclusion. Mearsheimer does not update his examination of polarity in the 2014 revised second edition of his *The Tragedy of Great Power Politics*. He stops in 1990.[115] This is unfortunate, as he provides no evidence to substantiate his argument regarding multipolarity in the post–Cold War era. The fact that East Asia has been the most peaceful region in the world during the post–Cold War era does not square well with Mearsheimer's argument that "unbalanced multipolarity is by far the most war-prone and deadly distribution of power."[116] East Asian stability over the last thirty-five years is more convincingly explained by Ross's emphasis on regional bipolarity and "the geography of peace" argument or by Wohlforth's unipolar-stability thesis.[117]

When comparing Russian and Chinese demography, economic development, military modernization, and cross-border migration in the Far East, Russia has few of the attributes of a great power in East Asia. Indeed, Ross concludes that "the Russian Far East is Russian because of Chinese forbearance."[118] The consequence of the decline of Russia, he argues, is that "Russia increasingly affects Chinese security the way that Canada affects U.S. security. For China, Russia is an underpopulated northern neighbor that requires minimal strategic attention to maintain Chinese border security."[119] Russia can rely on nuclear deterrence to safeguard its sovereignty in the Far East, but nuclear capability is not enough to define Russia as a pole in the international system. If this were the case, then the previous bipolar system could not have ended when the Soviet Union collapsed, since Russia maintained a strong nuclear second-strike capability. If U.S.-China rivalry were to unfold within an unbalanced multipolar system, then it would be even more likely to culminate in war and tragedy.[120] But the contemporary distribution of capabilities in the international system is bipolar, which from a structural-realist perspective is the set of systemic conditions most conducive to stability.

Nuclear Peace and Stability

Some critics of the bipolar-stability thesis have pointed out that the long peace during the Cold War is better explained by the role of nuclear weapons than by the systemic distribution of capabilities.[121] When great powers possess nuclear weapons with second-strike capabilities, it could undermine the logic of balance-of-power theory.[122] Conversely, some contend, if nuclear weapons have such a devastating effect, the probability of their deployment will be very low, allowing security competition, conventional military balancing, and balance-of-power politics to persist.[123]

The emphasis on the nuclear revolution has been advanced by many.[124] Some of the most sophisticated analyses of the implications of nuclear weapons for conventional war have been conducted by scholars who recognize that bipolarity fosters stability.[125] Waltz acknowledged that nuclear weapons strongly affect international politics, maintaining that nuclear states become more cautious in their interaction, which has contributed to international peace and stability.[126] Nonetheless, as Waltz has stated repeatedly, causes at both the structural and unit levels make the world more or less peaceful and stable.[127] Given Waltz's preoccupation with third-image factors, it is not surprising that he concluded that the effects of bipolarity mattered in the late 1940s when the Soviet Union had not developed nuclear weapons and the United States had few atomic bombs. "Nuclear weapons cannot by themselves be used to explain the stability— or the instability—of international systems."[128] While this is still a very short period of time to test the bipolar-stability thesis against the role of nuclear weapons, it can be argued that polarity matters for stability even in a nuclear world.

As we have seen, the bipolar-stability thesis rests on the assumption that two superpowers can deal better than three or more great powers with security dilemmas, miscalculations, arms racing, internal and external balancing, and the fear of abandonment and defection. A smaller number at the top favors stability.[129] A bipolar system is likely to be more stable than a multipolar system even when the top-tier powers possess nuclear weapons. If a new multipolar system emerges with three or more great powers possessing nuclear weapons, then such a multipolar system is likely to be more unstable and war prone than a bipolar system with only two superpowers with a nuclear capability.

At the same time, chapter 6 will argue that geopolitics could trump both the bipolar-stability argument and the assumption that nuclear weapons have radical transformative effects on the risk of war between states. The rivalry and contest for hegemony in East Asia are in the maritime domain, where a battle at sea could largely be confined to East Asian waters and not pose a direct existential threat in the form of a land invasion, possibly warranting the use of nuclear weapons. This might increase the risk of a limited war or sea battle between the two superpowers in the twenty-first century.[130]

Polarity and Patterns of Behavior

Establishing whether a new bipolar or multipolar system emerges is not only important in order to make predictions about the stability of the international system and great-power politics. Defining polarity also matters because the superpower(s), great powers, and other states behave differently within different international structures. Behavior follows from the changed position of the top-ranking powers and the new structure of the international system. The United States and the Soviet Union acted differently from Britain and France following the emergence of a bipolar system in the post–World War II era because the latter two were not superpowers. As Waltz writes, "the most telling illustration of the difference is seen in the mutual dependence of allies before and during World War II and in the relative independence of the two alliance leaders since, along with the dependence of their associates on them."[131]

The 1956 Suez Case

President Eisenhower could refuse to support France and Britain during the Suez crisis in 1956 because the shift from multipolarity to bipolarity meant that alliances were no longer, in Kissinger's words, the rigid alliance system that before the First World War was a "matter of life and death." In his explanation of how the multipolar system had lost its flexibility before the First World War, Kissinger said it was since "a switch in alliances might spell national disaster for the abandoned side, each ally was able to extort support from its partner regardless of its best convictions, thereby escalating all crises and linking them to each other."[132] It was precisely such an outcome Eisenhower could avoid during the Suez crisis.

The blockade of the Suez Canal and sabotage of pipelines delivering oil to the Mediterranean led to oil shortages and pressures on Western Europe in 1956. Anticipating that this could happen again in the event of war, American and British officials worked out plans to ship oil from the United States. Eisenhower, however, retained the right to decide when to activate those plans: "Those [Britain, France and Israel] who began this operation," he said, "should be left to work out their own problems—to boil in their own oil so to speak."[133] The president, who felt "double-crossed"[134] and presented with a fait accompli by British and French collusion in and support of Israel's invasion of Egypt, could also put more pressure on its closest allies by financial means. There is no strong evidence that the United States sponsored a run against the pound sterling by threatening devaluation. Nonetheless, the United States did not have to sabotage the pound to influence Britain; the United States merely had to refuse to support it.[135] After being refused assistance by U.S. Treasury Secretary George Humphrey on November 6, 1956, the British chancellor of the exchequer Harold Macmillan warned the Cabinet that "in view of the financial and economic pressures, we must stop [or he could] not anymore be responsible for Her Majesty's Exchequer."[136]

Comparing the situation in which the United States could dissociate itself from the British and French military adventure in the Suez in a bipolar system with the situation in which Germany felt compelled to support Austria-Hungary in a multipolar system of rigid blocs during the 1914 July Crisis that led to the First World War, the United States, according to Waltz's analysis, could continue to focus its attention on its major adversary—the Soviet Union—while disciplining its allies. The ability of the United States and the inability of Germany to pay a price measured in intra-alliance terms was striking, in Waltz's opinion.[137] This illustrates one important characteristic of bipolarity: power is distributed in such a way that two states are so powerful that they can defend themselves against any combination of other states and make calculations based mostly on their own national interests and independent of their allies.[138] As Christensen points out, the analogy is relevant to the alliance system in contemporary East Asia: "The United States does not rely on, say, the Philippines for survival, as Germany did with Austria-Hungary or France with Russia prior to World War I."[139]

Polarity continues to matter in international politics and shapes state behavior. The United States and China, the two superpowers in the current bipolar system, are similarly less constrained by intra-alliance considerations; "through their own preponderant weight they determine the balance of power between them,"[140] to quote Morgenthau again. The return of bipolarity is the single most important factor that will shape the superpowers', great powers', and the major powers' behavior in the first half of the twenty-first century.

Chapter 3

CONTEMPORARY U.S.-CHINA BIPOLARITY

By drawing on the method of measuring and counting poles in the international system elaborated on in the previous chapter, this chapter contends that China has increased its combined score across all dimensions of power sufficiently to have reached top ranking, even though China has not obtained power parity with the United States. This chapter's analysis examines the power gap between the United States and China on the different combinations of capabilities to establish that China can be elevated from great-power to superpower status, if only barely. I show, according to one of the three criteria used to determine the distribution of capabilities in the international system, that is, the power gap between the first- and second-ranked power, how China has become a pole in a new bipolar international system. The next step, undertaken in chapter 4, will be to examine the last two criteria and demonstrate both that no third power is able to challenge the top two and that the distribution of capabilities at the start of the contemporary bipolar system is roughly similar to the distribution at the origins of the previous bipolar system.

China's rise has been phenomenal. "Never before in the history has a state risen so far, so fast, on so many dimensions of power."[1] China's economy was smaller than that of the Netherlands in 1980, but in 2014, China's GDP *growth* was roughly equal to that of the entire Dutch economy.[2] The following analysis is not based on using China's current rates of economic growth to project China's future growth. Instead, it is assumed that China will manage about half of the 2016 official economic growth rate of 6.5 percent over the next two decades.

It is further assumed that this economic growth, which is not a best-case scenario for China's economy but instead represents a considerable slow-down in economic growth, will allow China to keep its position in the top ranking, generate enough funding to continue to expand and modernize its military, maintain high levels of R&D spending and promote innovation, and sustain the CCP's monopoly of power and ability to contain challenges to social stability. To assess top-ranking status, we will look at China's economy, military, population, geography, resource endowment, political stability, and competence rates. Each aspect will be examined separately in the following seven sections.

ECONOMIC POWER

Historically, forecasts and projections have tended to underestimate China's extraordinary economic growth over the last three decades, surprising even the most bullish analysts. The U.S. economy is still larger than China's if we measure GDP at market exchange rates (MER), but China is narrowing that gap at a remarkable rate. China's nominal GDP currently accounts for more than 60 percent of that of the United States.[3] This contrasts sharply with the early 1990s, when U.S. nominal GDP was about fifteen times larger than China's, or in 2000, when it was approximately eight times larger.[4]

Based on World Bank and IMF datasets, China now accounts for roughly 15 percent of global GDP in MER, up from about 4 percent in 2000, whereas the United States accounted for 31 percent in 2001 and about 23 percent in 2017. Datasets developed by other economists, such as Arvind Subramanian at the Peterson Institute for International Economics and Angus Maddison, show that U.S. and Chinese shares of global GDP are roughly the same, at about 18 percent.[5]

It has been argued that economic power is better measured in terms of per capita income and that the United States has increased its lead across most indicators by amounts that exceed China's total capabilities.[6] In 2015, according to the World Bank, China's per capita GDP (in PPP current international $) was US$13,572, and the comparable figure for the

United States was approximately US$52,704. The gap in GDP per capita between the United States and the Soviet Union in 1950 was almost 1:4, roughly similar to the contemporary gap between the United States and China. Moreover, the Soviet Union's GDP in MER was never more than about 50 percent of the U.S. GDP.[7] China's GDP in MER has surpassed 60 percent of the U.S. GDP in MER.

There is a proviso, however, noted by the U.S. National Intelligence Council in *Global Trends 2030*. While MER-based measures are important for trade and financial analysis, purchasing power parity (PPP)–based measures are also an indicator of economic strength.[8] Economists disagree on how to measure PPP in a way that accommodates the fact that prices in China are low. PPP-converted GDPs measure what one can buy in each country to compare the relative size of the economies. However, PPP measurements are tied to domestic consumption and do not measure either the U.S. or Chinese ability to buy things from global markets. Most analysts now believe China's GDP has surpassed that of the United States and become the world's largest economy based on PPP-based measures.[9] Nonetheless, here the argument that China is a top-ranking economic power is based on nominal GDP figures.[10]

The debate is often about whether absolute differences or relative distribution and capability ratios are most important. Is it more important that China, over the course of 1991 to 2011, narrowed the ratio of U.S. to Chinese GDP from 15:1 to 2:1 or that the U.S. economy is still roughly US$7 trillion larger than China's? Is it more important that the ratio of American per capita GDP to Chinese per capita GDP fell from 67:1 in 1991 to 5:1 in 2013 or that the gap in per capita incomes in real terms widened by US$19,000 during the same period?

Beckley answers this by comparing a Ph.D. student living on US$20,000 per year who lands a job as a professor earning US$80,000 a year with a banker earning US1$ million per year and receiving a US$200,000 bonus, raising her annual income to $1.2 million. "The ratio of the banker's income to the scholar's dropped from 50:1 to 15:1," he writes, "yet the scholar is now US$140,000 poorer compared to the banker than he was as a graduate student."[11] But if this ratio continued to drop for only another three years, then the professor would be earning more than the banker.[12] This is the trend in the contemporary economic balance between the United States and China, and it has shifted the distribution of economic capabilities.

Joffe, building on Beckley's analysis, acknowledges that "higher growth will eventually beat lower growth," but whichever way one plays the numbers, "the upshot is that it will take many, many years for China to best the United States." Remember, however, that the argument positing the return of bipolarity does not depend on China achieving power parity with the United States. China has already surpassed the Soviet Union's relative economic strength during the previous bipolar era and is now closing the economic gap with the United States even in absolute terms. According to Joffe, in the mid-1990s, when China was growing at roughly 10 percent, it added $200 billion to its GDP in one year. The American economy, growing at a mere 3 percent, added $360 billion per annum to its GDP. Similarly, according to Joffe, in 2012 China added $450 billion to its $7 trillion economy by growing at 7 percent, while the United States added $480 billion to its $16 billion economy growing at 3 percent.[13]

Following Joffe's method, if we assume China's economic growth was 5 percent in 2015, toward the low end of reasonable estimates (the official growth rate was 6.9 percent), it adds $550 billion to an $11 trillion economy. The U.S. GDP growth in 2015 was 2.4 percent, which added $432 billion to an $18 trillion economy. China is now narrowing the economic gap in both absolute and relative terms, even if it is likely to take another decade or two before the Chinese economy surpasses the U.S. economy based on MER. When considering the various measurements of economic power, the absolute size of the economy, regardless of per capita GDP, provides for large government revenues that can be allocated to defense and innovation. In this respect, assuming domestic stability, absolute GDP is the critical factor in measuring the bases of power.

China reportedly surpassed the United States in 2012 to become the world's largest trading nation.[14] In terms of output, China is now the world's top manufacturing country, taking the title from the United States, which held it for more than a century.[15] However, despite the redistribution of trade and that the large part of the production and manufacturing of goods are being transferred to China, it is mostly the assembly of the final products or the last stage of the supply chain that has relocated to China. As the WTO writes, the production of the core components often remains within the original country. Thus, most of the content of the products, and their economic value, are still being developed and produced outside China, in the United States, Europe, and developed countries in East Asia.

Caveats that acknowledge the issue of "value added," question the concept of "country of origin," and provide new measurements of international trade should therefore be taken into account.[16]

Equally important, if not more significant than trade data, is China's market power in trade relations. Export to the Chinese market is critical to many countries and companies today, and this enhances China's economic power. China is the world's largest holder of foreign reserves, a major investor in the world, and a major recipient of foreign direct investments (FDI).[17] As Allison puts it regarding the relative rankings of China and the United States, in 1980, China had 10 percent of America's GDP as measured by PPP, 7 percent of its GDP at current US$ exchange rates, and 6 percent of its exports, and the foreign currency held by China was just one-sixth the size of America's reserves. By 2014, those figures were 101 percent of GDP, 60 percent at US$ exchange rates, and 106 percent of exports, and China's reserves were twenty-eight times larger than America's.[18] Economically, China is obviously more powerful than in the past: its share of the world economy has increased considerably, and it can now be ranked in the top tier in terms of economic capability.

CHINA'S ECONOMIC CHALLENGES

China's leaders have recognized that the economic model that has provided double-digit growth in the past is becoming unsustainable. Since Hu Jintao's report to the Eighteenth Party Congress in 2012, Chinese leaders have argued that China must recalibrate its economy. Reforms seek to rebalance economic growth from one based on exports and investments in infrastructure, real estate, and heavy industry to a more service-oriented economy where domestic consumption and innovation increase their share of the economy, state-owned enterprises are transformed, and more entrepreneurship can flourish. The fundamental imbalance in China's economy is the low GDP share of consumption. China's economic growth has for too long relied on repressing household consumption to make modernizing investments. In consequence, China's growth has been driven mainly by the need to keep investment rates at an extraordinarily high level.[19] This dependence on investments has further snowballed into a significant increase in debt. To rebalance the economy, China needs to increase consumption's share of GDP. Rising domestic consumption is linked to the challenge of building a welfare system that allows households to spend more rather than save their money for child care, education, healthcare, and pensions. Challenging reforms are also needed to tackle corruption, restructure state-owned companies, adopt new financial and monetary policies, and prevent further environmental degradation.

President Xi Jinping continues to push ahead with economic reforms and has sought to implement the economic-reform agenda announced at the Third Plenum of the CPC's Eighteenth Party Congress in 2013.[20] The Five-Year Plan for National Economic and Social Development adopted by the Fifth Plenary Session of the Eighteenth Communist Party of China (CPC) Central Committee on October 29, 2015, resolved to maintain medium to high growth and prioritized the reform of the economic system.[21]

These high rates of economic growth cannot be sustained. The main question posed by economists today is whether China will be able to slow its growth to a more sustainable pace. At the same time, even some of the bearish estimates and projections of China's future economic growth suggest that China will retain its top-ranking position and continue to narrow the economic power gap with the United States, albeit at a slower pace.

With the growth rate expected to edge lower in the years ahead, recent projections of China's economic growth seem to have been too optimistic. The IMF, World Bank, and the majority of private analysts are now, in contrast to only a few years ago, much more bearish and are busy lowering their estimates of China's growth potential. One study that considered various revised forecasts developed a multiscenario working model of Chinese growth to 2020. China, the authors write, can hope to deliver 6 percent annual growth by 2020—if it does it right. But if the reforms fall short, "the story is more dire and China can only look forward to 1–3% GDP growth six years from now."[22]

Larry Summers and Lant Pritchett have suggested, in what has been referred to as a bearish or more cautious economic forecast (the World Bank and the IMF's forecasts are less pessimistic), that China's economy will grow at an average rate of "only" 3.9 percent annually for the next two decades.[23] If we assume a hard landing (average growth of 5.2 percent from 2014–2020) and a crisis scenario (average growth of 4.2 percent from 2014–2020), using the multiscenario working model devised by the Rhodium Group, and combine it with Summers and Pritchett's cautious

estimates, then China's annual economic growth is projected to be about
4–5 percent in the period 2014–2020, 4 percent in 2020–2025, 3.5 percent in
2025–2030, and 3 percent in 2030–2035.[24] These projections are lower than
the targets proposed by the Chinese government and the IMF and World
Bank forecasts. Nevertheless, even when we rely on such bearish projections, China can catch up economically with the United States, assuming
the U.S. economy will grow at roughly 2 percent over the same period,
which is a high estimate, since the U.S. economy is likely to be affected
negatively by a crisis or hard landing in China.

Despite the economic slowdown and crisis in the Chinese stock market in the summer of 2015, which led to headlines about "the great fall of
China," China's economy is now so large that even a 5 percent growth
rate in 2015—a low estimate—would add more to world output than the
14 percent expansion China posted in 2007, according to the *Economist*.[25]
China's economy is not collapsing, and its economic growth is likely to
remain strong in absolute and relative terms over the coming years.

Nonetheless, China's extraordinary economic growth presents Chinese
leaders with more challenges than declining GDP growth.[26] China's rising
debt is causing alarm in many circles. The Chinese economy, they say, is
addicted to stimulus and investment. The debt-to-GDP ratio has changed
from 100 percent of GDP in 2007 to about 280 in 2015, inflating the risk in
the real estate and credit sectors.[27] At the same time, economists point out
that state debt in China has only reached 55 percent of GDP, substantially
lower than in much of the West; China's government therefore has plenty
of financial elbow room to weather a crisis.[28]

China needs to rebalance its model of economic growth and manage its
economy so that its growth doesn't slow too rapidly, and decision makers
cannot delay making certain adjustments for too much longer. Chinese
leaders will be forced to make difficult decisions that will entail some cost
to near-term growth and require measures that entail some vulnerabilities
and risks. In raising household income, the cost of production is likely
to rise, and China will lose competiveness abroad. In exchange, domestic
consumption is likely to increase as households benefit from the rebalancing project. The benefits are likely to be healthier economic growth and
a lowered risk of a debt crisis.[29] If China rebalances successfully, it can
sustain medium to high growth, providing higher incomes and growth
in the longer term.

We have learned over the last two decades that it is difficult to estimate and project China's future economic growth. But despite uncertainty in this respect, we do not need to extrapolate from China's growth to determine its future economic power. As of today, China has vaulted into the top rank in terms of economic strength even though it has not obtained power parity with the United States. Relatively, the United States is less economically powerful in comparison than it was in the 1990s and 2000s, and China has outpaced all other contenders for top-ranking status in terms of economic strength.

MILITARY STRENGTH

China's military budget has grown by about 10 percent annually for about two decades, while military expenditure has remained fairly steady at 2 to 2.2 percent of GDP. As the Pentagon and other observers have noted, the official Chinese budget does not include several major categories of expenditures, such as the procurement of foreign weapons and equipment.[30] SIPRI estimated China's defense spending in 2014 at US$216 billion, 64 percent higher than the official Chinese figure. In 2016 and 2017, China announced that it would keep its defense spending to a single-digit-percentage increase, respectively 7.6 and 7.0 percent, amounting to US$147 billion and US$151 billion. According to SIPRI's estimate of a 64 percent higher budget than official figures, China's defense spending in 2016 was about US$225 billion. China's share of world military spending rose to 13 percent in 2016, up from 9.5 percent in 2012, 6.6 percent in 2010, and 4 percent in 2005, according to SIPRI.

Comparative numbers by SIPRI show that U.S. military expenditure declined from a high in 2010 of US$749 billion to a low in 2015 of US$598 billion. In 2016, U.S. military spending saw its first increase since 2010, amounting to US$606 billion, and the new Trump administration has called for a further increase in defense spending.[31] According to SIPRI, the U.S. share of world military expenditures has decreased from 48 percent in 2005 to 43 percent in 2010, 39 percent in 2012, and 36 percent in 2016.

Currently, U.S. military spending is about two to three times that of China. This contrasts sharply with 2000, when the U.S. defense budget was more than ten times that of China (US$311 billion versus US$30 billion), not to mention the early 1990s, when the U.S. defense expenditure was more than twenty times higher.

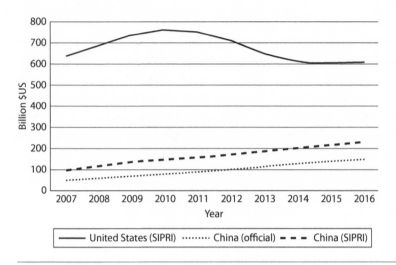

FIGURE 3.1 U.S. and Chinese defense spending, 2007–2016.

Source: SIPRI Military Expenditure Database.

China's large absolute GDP and low defense spending as a percentage of GDP provide opportunities for increasing defense spending in the future and suggest that China will be able to continue narrowing the gap in military power. And when comparing military spending, it is useful to take PPP measurements into consideration: the cost of producing military equipment and of training soldiers in China is much lower than the comparable cost in the United States. For example, "a U.S. soldier costs approximately US$18,000 a year to put in the field, while his Chinese counterpart probably costs no more than US$2,000." Whatever the actual figures may be, the key point is that "the Chinese military has much more money to spend on fewer troops than it did 15 years ago."[32] A roughly 10 percent annual increase in defense expenditures over the last two decades has contributed to a cumulative effect on China's defense budget and spending.[33]

Conversely, it is argued that the United States has accumulated stocks of military equipment, technological sophistication, and organizational and management skills that suggest that it will sustain its military advantage over China even after China, sometimes toward the mid-twenty-first century, arrives at a larger economy and higher annual defense expenditure than the United States.[34] Brooks and Wohlforth remind us that military capability is generated over years and decades and that defense spending understates the extent of the global military gap between the United States and its nearest rivals.[35] Another scholar has emphasized that modernization matters and that "raw numbers do not mean as much in measuring military power as technological sophistication."[36]

China still faces challenges in modernizing its armed forces, and it remains uncertain whether the PLA would be able to fight and win a war against a modern opponent in the twenty-first century.[37] Currently, China and the PLA do not possess global power-projection capabilities that can contend with U.S. capabilities around the world. However, in the post–Cold War era, China has not prioritized developing "the capabilities necessary to wage high- or even medium-intensity warfare beyond China's immediate vicinity"[38] or sought to match U.S. defense spending. China's military expenditure as a percentage of GDP has remained about half of the United States' for the last two decades. Instead, China has sought to learn from the mistakes of the Soviet Union and emphasized domestic economic development and reforms, while at the same time sustaining a robust military buildup.

Recent trends, most significantly stated in the 2015 white paper *China's Military Strategy*, suggest that China seeks to develop capabilities to defend national security interests globally and operate as a world-class maritime power.[39] Discussing recent developments in China's maritime forces and strategy, one leading observer of the PLAN points to a shift whereby China has developed new strategies, doctrines, and capabilities and conducted several operations, missions, and training exercises to enhance China's readiness to carry out overseas contingency operations. "The emphasis on far-seas training is a strong indicator of the PLAN's desire to better prepare for and routinely conduct the long-distance deployments currently conducted by the small task group assigned to the Gulf of Aden counterpiracy patrols."[40] This has led some to emphasize that the United States should take seriously the maritime challenges from a "risen China" rather than a "rising China." With the rapid emergence of an increasingly global PLAN, the Center for a New American Security (CNAS) argues that the era whereby the United States has enjoyed largely uncontested blue-water naval supremacy will soon end.[41]

The United States is still ahead of China in military capabilities, but as the findings of a recent comprehensive RAND report show, China is closing several military gaps. In fact, the net change in capabilities is still moving in China's favor.[42] If another Taiwan Strait crisis erupts today, the PLA will be much more able to contest the sea, subsea, air, land, and space around Taiwan than it was during the 1995/1996 crisis.[43] China's military modernization has improved the quality of its armed forces. The PLA and its four branches, the Army, Navy, Air Force, and Second Artillery, are more advanced technologically and in terms of combat capability. The PLA is also conducting more realistic training exercises.

The RAND and CNAS reports concur with the findings of the 2015 U.S. Office of Naval Intelligence in confirming the "significant strides" taken by the PLA(N) since 2009 in operationalizing and modernizing its forces.[44] Similar views on China's military modernization are expressed in the U.S. Department of Defense 2015 *Asia-Pacific Maritime Security Strategy* report.[45] Leading experts on the PLAN see the development and deployment of a strong Chinese navy,[46] one that is increasingly modern, regionally powerful, and able to pose a significant "challenge in the Western Pacific to the U.S. Navy's ability to achieve and maintain control of blue-water ocean areas in wartime—*the first such challenge the U.S. Navy has faced since the end of the Cold War.*"[47] Figure 3.2 shows the current trend.[48]

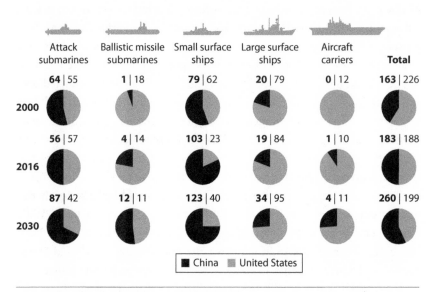

FIGURE 3.2 U.S. and Chinese navies, 2000–2030.

Note: Attack submarines include nuclear- and diesel-powered vessels; small surface ships include frigates, littoral combat ships, and mine ships; large surface ships include cruisers and destroyers.

Source: Center for a New American Security, International Institute for Strategic Studies, Bloomberg.

With increased capabilities, the PLA Navy now operates in closer proximity to U.S. carrier battle groups, harassing U.S. Navy ships and planes. It has increasingly resisted U.S. surveillance activities within its exclusive economic zone. China has also channeled increased resources into coast guard and maritime surveillance agencies that can better safeguard its interests and enforce its interpretation of the international law of the sea. These capabilities go far beyond what the Soviet navy had in the maritime domain at the origins of the previous bipolar era in the late 1940s and early 1950s.

American allies provide bases and support, facilitating a forward U.S. military presence and contributing to its global power-projection capability, but these allies cannot simply be added to the United States' combined military capabilities. It remains uncertain whether most of Washington's allies would support the United States militarily in an armed conflict with China. And as long as so many states rely on the United States for their own security, and as long as U.S. forces are still needed globally to ensure security and stability, its global security commitments might become a liability in a conflict with China. The global power-projection capabilities of America's allies in Europe are diminutive in comparison, and they are preoccupied with Russia and instability in the Near East and Africa. They would hardly pick a fight with China in East Asia.

China's military modernization, consolidation of power on Asia's mainland, and expanding naval capabilities suggest that, as Morgenthau professed with the previous bipolar system in mind, the "defection of an ally or the addition of another could no longer overturn the balance of power and thus materially affect the ultimate outcome of the struggle."[49] China and the United States are capable of avoiding defeat in a conventional war with any state or even a coalition of states. This places China and the United States in a league of their own. The United States still has a larger share of overall military capabilities, but China excels in its combined capabilities sufficiently to reach the top tier.

POPULATION

China's population, at almost 1.4 billion, is the largest in the world, and it has always provided an important power base for the country's economic strength and military capability. It offers the People's Liberation Army (PLA) more soldiers to defend Chinese territory. This allowed inferior Chinese "volunteers" to outnumber and outcompete U.S. troops on the Korean Peninsula in the 1950s. China and the PLA also confronted and forced the Soviet Union, another superpower, into retreat from its borders in the 1960s and successfully defeated India's military forces in 1962. Its large population has allowed China to emerge victorious from years of war and to survive blockades, embargoes, hunger, and other catastrophes. Undoubtedly, China has the population to "put up a good fight" and "avoid defeat" in war.[50] Morgenthau's argument that no country can remain or become a first-rate power if it does not belong to the more populous nations of the earth is still true.[51] Population size, together with economic strength, remain the essential ingredients and the two most important components for generating military power among the top-ranking states.[52]

China's "one billion workers"[53] and huge market have attracted investors and stimulated unprecedented economic growth in recent decades. But China is also host to an aging population, rising pension payouts, gender disparity, and a shrinking labor force, all of which could undermine China's economic prospects and leave the country in the "middle-income trap."[54] China could grow old before it grows rich. Demography is becoming a liability and is likely to slow China's growth. Moreover, China is becoming old at a much earlier stage in its development cycle. Against this backdrop, Brooks and Wohlforth contend that the United States, with its high fertility rate and as a popular destination for immigration, will maintain a comparative advantage in the decades to come.[55]

All projections agree that China's population will continue to grow for another decade, but there are marked differences in estimates of its peak population, which range from 1.35 to 1.67 billion between 2023 to 2050, given disagreement about the present fertility level in China and the effects of the government's relaxation of the one-child policy. The working-age population will shrink when the population stops growing, but depending on policy measures introduced by the government, the size of China's working-age population will range between 780 and 1,100 million in 2050. But even a reduced working-age population will remain enormous in terms of absolute size, as a proportion of the world's population, and in comparison to that of many developed and developing countries.[56] In addition, some argue that the impending robot revolution in China suggests that the Chinese manufacturing industry will remain strong and competitive despite a decline in the working-age population.[57]

The imbalance in sex ratio at birth has resulted in a deficit of young females and a marriage squeeze.[58] The single-child generation will affect the country's socioeconomic development and traditional family support system, putting pressure on social stability and order. The Chinese government has initiated policies and large reforms to tackle these challenges.[59] The one-child policy has been relaxed to boost fertility, with the total fertility rate increasing from 1.6 births per woman in 2009 to 1.7 births in 2010–2012.[60] The Thirteenth Five Year plan has now abolished the one-child policy and is aimed at "improving public services for reproductive health, maternal and child health, nurseries and kindergartens."[61] However, there is a strong negative correlation between fertility rates and GDP per capita growth. Some researchers argue that the current fertility rate is perhaps 1.4–1.6, which is consistent with the thesis that the fertility decline can be attributed to economic growth.[62]

Additionally, rising costs of living and education in cities and growing concerns about pollution might also lead to fewer children. The government has proposed raising the legal retirement age from fifty-five to sixty for women and sixty to sixty-five for men.[63] Another response to the relative decline in the working-age population is to improve labor productivity by increasing efficiency in the labor market, allocating labor between sectors better and raising the educational level of the Chinese people.[64] As discussed, the government aims to rebalance the economy, with a stronger focus on domestic consumption and services. Improvements to healthcare, education, pension systems, and social security can provide a new growth market for the new model of economic growth.[65] China has opportunities to cope with future population-related socioeconomic changes.[66]

GEOGRAPHICAL SIZE

As a continental power, China has the capability to compete for regional hegemony based on its geographical size.[67] China has showed that it has the strategic depth necessary to survive a military clash with another great power or superpower. It resisted and survived the Japanese occupation during World War II, just as the Soviet Union withstood the invasion by another great power, Nazi Germany.[68]

Conversely, China's geographical position traditionally has been considered a relative disadvantage. China shares a land border with fourteen countries and an additional five states at sea. Four of its neighbors on the Asian continent possess nuclear weapons. Stability along its borders has been a major concern for Chinese leaders throughout its history. China also faces the challenge, confronted by most traditional land powers, of being constrained by its defense of continental interests as it seeks to develop naval power, expand its interests in the maritime domain, and challenge the maritime order and naval status quo.[69] In comparison, the United States has the benefit of bordering only two states and no great powers and being insulated from Eurasia by the Atlantic and Pacific oceans.[70]

At the same time, for most of China's neighbors, including Russia and India, bordering China is more of a problem for them than it is for China. Today China is much stronger than its neighbors, which permits it to focus on developing strong naval capabilities.[71] Indeed, the PRC has never been more secure along its borders than it is today. Being responsible for the survival and security of their nation, China's leaders may not allow themselves to be too sanguine about China's border security. Nonetheless, none of China's neighbors would even think of invading China. This was not the case even a few decades ago. China now occupies an advantageous position on the map of Central-East Asia, and its land borders at this junction in time seem to offer more opportunities than danger.[72] This is mainly a result of the relative shift in the systemic distribution of capabilities.

Geostructural conditions have changed China's security environment on the Asian mainland fundamentally, allowing China to expand its interests and influence over land and sea. China's position on the map in the 1960s was the same as today, but China's strategic environment was hardly favorable; it was at war with India to the southwest, embargoed by and in conflict with the United States in Southeast Asia and the Taiwan Strait, and confronted by the Soviet Union to the north. The recent shifts in the distribution of capabilities and the relative and absolute rise in China's power have now turned China's geographical location and long borders from a liability to an advantage and strength as China seeks to expand its dominance in East and Central Asia and challenge the United States in East Asian waters. There are few examples in modern history of a land power being as secure as China is as it seeks to maintain its dominance at land and challenge the dominant sea power. The PRC's ambitious Belt and Road initiative,[73] which emphasizes the land-based "silk road" economic belt and the oceangoing maritime silk road, suggests that China is taking advantage of its favorable geographical environment and growing capabilities.[74]

NATURAL RESOURCES

China is rich in energy sources, food production is high, and mineral resources are robust, as are several other resources of commercial importance.[75]

Energy Security

China's rapid economic growth has been accompanied by an enormous rise in energy demand. Remarkably, and probably unprecedented in history, China's energy consumption grew fivefold from 1978 to 2009, and between 2005 and 2010, China's total electricity capacity doubled.[76] In 2010, China became the largest energy consumer in the world, surpassing the United States. In 2013, it was reported that China had gone from exporting oil in 1993 to surpassing the United States as the world's largest net oil importer.[77] Despite this extraordinary rise in energy demand, almost 90 percent of China's energy mix is still satisfied by domestic supplies.[78]

China's energy mix is favorable in terms of energy security, but its heavy reliance on coal is not environmentally sustainable, and China is searching for alternative energy sources. The importation of hydrocarbons from abroad is likely to increase, together with domestic gas production and hydro and nuclear power. Investments in alternative energy sources such as solar and wind power are massive, but it remains to be seen if clean energy sources will substantially increase their share of China's energy mix. Sustainability is a major issue when it comes to China's natural resources and will affect how China's resource endowments are measured. Even if China's net oil imports continue to grow and if domestic energy production were to fall to 80 percent of its total energy consumption in the years ahead, China's energy security can be sustained by domestic energy production. Abundant coal reserves are an important element in China's energy security. The possibility of creating synthetic oil from these reserves could provide vital insurance in times of emergency or war.[79]

Oil is China's second-largest source of energy, accounting for about 20 percent of its total energy consumption.[80] In 2016, China was the world's fourth-largest producer of oil (after the United States, Saudi Arabia, and Russia), accounting for about 7 percent of global production.[81] It is projected that China's oil production over the next decade will be above 4 mbd. China's dependence on foreign oil exceeded 50 percent between 2007 and 2009, and it now imports about 60 percent of its oil needs. But contrary to conventional and popular wisdom that emphasizes the so-called Malacca Dilemma,[82] China does not face any such concerns.

Were China confronted with a wartime contingency and a direct blockade of its seaborne oil supply routes, which only the U.S. Navy could enforce, and only in a wartime scenario, China's war-fighting capability would not be hampered.[83] In fiscal year 2004, the U.S. military, fighting wars in Iraq and Afghanistan as well as maintaining normal operations, used approximately 395,000 bpd of oil.[84] China produces domestically more than ten times more oil than the United States needed to wage two wars and conduct military operations around the world. In 2015, China had a massive refining capacity of about 14 mbd.[85]

Since China's current and future oil imports reflect current automobile use, and since car sales are increasingly consumption rather than industry driven, China's energy security is not significantly challenged; personal car use can be curtailed, as it was during the 2008 Summer Olympics in Beijing and is regularly in many large cities. And if China found itself at war with the United States the Chinese people, it is reasonable to assume, would be willing to tighten their belts and reduce energy consumption. Additionally, China has hedged against a wartime scenario and a blockade of seaborne energy supplies by laying cross-border petroleum pipelines with Russia and Central Asia.

When it comes to China's energy security, pipelines (Central Asian and Russian) are more likely to be "safer" in wartime threat scenarios and more "unsafe" in peacetime risk scenarios, while SLOCs are "safer" in peacetime risk scenarios and more "unsafe" in wartime threat scenarios. The key is that by maintaining both (pipelines and seaborne energy/building a large state-owned tanker fleet) in combination with other measures, such as building a strategic petroleum reserve, increasing the production of nuclear energy, and maintaining a high degree of self-sufficiency through coal and—although to a much lesser extent—hydro and gas, China is hedging against any disruptions to its energy supplies and bolstering its energy security.[86]

Food and Water Security

Food and water security has been a major concern for China. The country has to feed roughly 20 percent of the world's population with only about 11 percent of the world's arable land and roughly 7 percent for the world's freshwater resources.[87] China's food crisis during the Great Leap Forward between 1959 and 1962 remains a lesson for Chinese leaders in terms of the importance of food security. China has in recent years managed to increase its food production, decrease the number of undernourished people from 21 to 12 percent, and is self-sufficient in major crops, such as wheat and rice, and livestock, such as bovines and poultry.[88]

As a result, after several thousand years, hunger as a social problem has largely been eradicated, and the government continues to issue guidelines that guarantee maintaining farmland at a level that sustains food security.[89] As Morgenthau acknowledged when discussing the role of food and natural resources in influencing the power of nations, self-sufficient or nearly self-sufficient countries have a great advantage over those that are not and are obliged to import the foodstuffs they do not grow themselves, or face starvation. "Self-sufficiency in food has . . . always been source of great strength," Morgenthau avers.[90] China scores higher on this power measurement today than it did in the past. When the most populous country in the world is able to feed its population, such a development contributes in elevating China to top-ranking power status.[91]

The future, however, presents a number of challenges. Farmland and water resources are shrinking and increasingly polluted. The population is still growing (albeit more slowly) and is consuming more meat. This has a significant knock-on effect on grain demand, since more grain is needed to produce the beef, pork, and poultry.[92] Rapid urbanization and rising prosperity stimulate meat consumption and simultaneously create an exodus of rural labor into cities, limiting China's ability to expand its meat production further. But while all this will indeed increase China's dependence on imports in the coming years,[93] it is important to note that meat production is not the same thing as food security. Insufficient production of meat may cause domestic instability, but it does not threaten starvation, as was the case in past decades. Surviving on meat is not a requirement in food-security terms. Moreover, estimates and projections about China's food scarcity may have underestimated the importance of genetically modified food production to curb dependency on imports.

Roughly 60 percent of China's water resources are used in agricultural production.[94] Industry-driven economic growth, urbanization, and higher living standards have increased water consumption. China's average availability of fresh water is only one-third of global levels, and groundwater quality in both rural and urban areas is often bad.[95] Water shortages already affect major cities in China, and increasingly polluted water supplies endanger public health and economic growth.[96] In 2004, Elizabeth Economy noted how the government was having to pursue "expansive river diversion and pollution remediation projects" but found few improvements ten years on: water resources were continuing to decrease, and the widespread pollution of groundwater and rivers continued to increase.[97]

Clearly, Chinese leaders face daunting challenges in managing scarce water resources and combating deteriorating water quality, but according to some, China is improving its resource management.[98] Constraining water demand, improving efficiency in the usage of scarce water supplies, recycling more water in the industrial sector, and fining and punishing polluters more strongly are some of the important measures the government has initiated and can enforce with greater dexterity in the future.[99] The Chinese government has invested in large projects to transfer water from central and southwestern China to augment the flow of the Yellow River to meet water demand in the Beijing-Tianjin region.[100] However, these are very costly projects that cannot solve the water problem in the long term if demand, consumption, and efficiency issues are not tackled. Bureaucratic fragmentation and regional rivalries remain impediments to the central government's policy responses to address water-quality issues, and this shows that a deeper and more systematic reform of governance systems and institutions are needed.[101]

Minerals

China ranks third in the world in terms of mineral reserves. Its national reserves of rare-earth elements are larger than the (known) combined total in the rest of the world. However, on a per capita basis, China's known mineral reserves are less than half the world average.[102] With China's double-digit growth in the consumption of mineral resources, shortages of mineral resources and security of supplies will increasingly preoccupy Chinese decision makers. Nonetheless, China's total amount and relative share of important minerals place it in the top rank.

In sum, despite being the world's most populous country and the world's most energy hungry, China is able to feed its population and is almost self-sufficient in food and energy production. After taking power in 1949, the Communist Party was forced to maintain a high degree of self-reliance as a result of the Western embargo, diplomatic isolation, and the split with the Soviet Union. Nonetheless, during the previous bipolar period China contended with the superpowers and shaped their behavior. China has now improved its energy production, increased food security, and has a strong base of mineral resources. Taken together, this tells us that China scores among the top rankers with respect to resource endowments.

POLITICAL STABILITY

Will China's Communist Party sustain its rule, or will it collapse? According to many, the destabilizing forces are overwhelming. Debt, corruption, pollution, rising levels of income, and asset inequality all are undermining the CCP's legitimacy, pushing China's economic elite to flee abroad and forcing President Xi to intensify political repression, signifying the CCP's leaders' deep anxiety and insecurity.[103] The collapse of the CCP has been predicted by many over the years,[104] but its system of one-party control and leadership has survived. The Chinese state, in the opinion of some, is not fragile. On the contrary, the regime is strong, increasingly self-confident, and lacks any organized opposition.[105] Examining the power of China's current leader, two prominent observers arrive at different assessments. On the one hand, President Xi is described as the most powerful leader in China since Mao;[106] on the other, Chinese leaders are said to have become progressively weaker in relation to one another and to society.[107] The scholars Minxin Pei and David Shambaugh argue that without "fundamental and far-reaching political reforms, China's economy will stagnate, and the regime may well collapse."[108] Conversely, another recent study based on two large surveys in China suggests that the CCP has done a good job in improving its approval rating and sustaining popular support.[109]

A middle-ground perspective is provided by leading scholars' contributions to a volume discussing China's new leadership. Few anticipate the collapse of China or the fall of the CCP, but China's leaders face a different and more complex set of challenges.[110] It is difficult to know whether Xi's reforms and anticorruption campaign will be successful and whether they will weaken or strengthen his position within the party. Few observers have knowledge of the inner workings of the Communist Party or the black box of decision making within the Politburo. And political predictions are notoriously difficult. Strong controversy over the future political stability in China will remain. What we know is that the CCP has remained in power and overseen unprecedented growth in the economy over the last three decades. Such an accomplishment would have been impossible without political stability. The CCP's resilience has been strong, and it can be argued that China still scores relatively high on political stability.[111]

The CCP and the PLA find themselves in a boat that cannot be rocked and hanging from a "stability rope" that cannot be cut. The PLA is probably still willing to use force to maintain CCP power and stability. There is little to indicate that China's civilian and military leaders would be better off with another revolution or civil war. The Bo Xilai and Zhou Yongkang cases only serve to illustrate Xi's and the CCP's continued control of the PLA and domestic security apparatus.[112] Xi has also initiated a major reorganization of the PLA and proclaimed a reduction of 300,000 PLA personnel, bringing the size of the active-duty PLA down to two million.[113] It would be unlikely that Xi would have initiated such steps were he not confident in his abilities to control the PLA.

We cannot foresee the future. What we do know is that the CCP remains in power. Durability is a defining characteristic of stability. The CCP has survived major internal crises and demonstrated its political stability. The history of the PRC has included significant conflicts, and Chinese leaders have been willing to use force to retain control. A one-party state is likely to prioritize its own survival, even at the expense of people's livelihoods and China's national interests. The PRC is ethnically homogenous, with the Han ethnic group constituting about 92 percent of the population. The CCP leadership can draw on China's history as an ancient civilization with traditions dating back several thousand years. As Terrill points out, China can boast of a political governance of its core territory longer than that of any other nation in the world.[114] All of these factors foster stability.

COMPETENCE

Competence and innovation constitute a source of state power. High-income countries are dominating research and development, but of late China has been climbing up the technology ladder.[115] Production is no longer limited to low-tech and low-end manufacturing. In the early 1990s China's R&D progress and innovation were practically negligible, but since then the overall trend, as the UN Educational, Scientific, and Cultural Organization (UNESCO) and the UN World Intellectual Property Organization (UNWIPO) note, is unmistakable: China has increased and the United States has decreased its relative share of world GDP, gross domestic expenditure of research and development (GERD), researchers, and publications.[116] China's GERD as a percentage of GDP (GERD/GDP) reached 1.98 percent in 2012, more than tripling since 1995 and surpassing the twenty-eight member states of the European Union, whose aggregate GERD/GDP was at 1.96 percent.[117] China has continued to stay ahead of the European Union.[118]

As science becomes increasingly internationalized, China is playing a key role in the change in the sources of global scientific publications. China increased its share of world scientific publications from about 10 to 20.2 percent in the period 2008–2014; the U.S. share declined from 28.1 to 25.3 percent during the same period.[119] China is now the second-highest producer of research output in the world.[120] China has also increased its world share of researchers from 16.7 to 19.1 percent from 2009 to 2013.[121] China annually graduates four times more students than the United States in STEM subjects (science, technology, engineering, and mathematics), which provide the core competencies driving modern economies.[122] China is also a leader in emerging fields such as nanotechnology and renewable energy.[123]

Cong Cao points to some outstanding achievements of Chinese scientists and engineers since 2011 in areas such as basic research, strategic high technology, deep-ground drilling, supercomputing, and aerospace. Furthermore, several gaps in technology and equipment have been filled in recent years, and China has taken a great leap forward in the medical sciences.[124] According to the *Economist*, "the common perception that China is incapable of innovation needs re-examining. China is moving up the value chain and China's new entrepreneurs are coming up with entirely new industries."[125] Moreover, reports suggest that China now outspends the United States on the later stages of R&D, those that turn discoveries into commercial products.[126]

The growth trend in R&D spending, patent and trademark applications, and scientific publications indicates an increasing capacity to innovate, but the issue of quality is still a problem.[127] The number of patents and trademark applications may not necessarily be reflective of an ability to innovate, and high levels of R&D spending may not actually produce much innovative output.[128] As the UNESCO *Science Report 2015* shows, there is a difference between patent applications and patents submitted. China's world share of patents submitted to the U.S. Patent and Trademark Office (USPTO) has remained low, increasing from 1.1 to 2.7 percent in the period 2008–2013. Trends in triadic patents worldwide show a contraction in the U.S. world share and an increase in China's, but China's share stood at only 3.6 percent in 2013, up from 0.5 percent in 2002.[129]

Beckley urges us to be careful before using R&D spending, numbers of graduating scientists and engineering students, and scientific publications as yardsticks because the rush to increase quantity is reducing the quality of China's education, research, and innovation.[130] Shaped by the political system, the educational system and research environment in China lack the freedom of exploration and critical thinking that allow innovation to thrive and prosper. China still scores poorly in terms of the number of scientific citations.[131]

After examining the "believers" versus the "doubters," Steinfeld concludes that while the "diametrically opposed schools of thought" actually agree on the main facts, they are completely at odds about what those facts mean. And no amount of additional aggregate data—whether regarding patent output, numbers of new inventions, types of products introduced, or really anything else—is likely to persuade one side of the other's claims, he writes. China's innovation is thriving, Steinfeld adds, thanks to an emerging system of globalized R&D that has forged "a symbiotic relationship between multinational and indigenous Chinese producers."[132] Despite these caveats, it is reasonable to assume that China's overall score on competence, whether developed indigenously or via multinational corporations and globalization, places the country in contention for a spot among the top-ranking nations.

CONCLUSION: CHINA'S BID FOR TOP RANKING

One issue runs through my assessment of China's rise in power, the shifting distribution of capabilities, and the narrowing of the power gap between China and the United States: quality versus quantity. On the seven dimensions of power we have attempted to measure, we still cannot resolve the quality-versus-quantity issue, and it remains embedded in the debate between "believers" and "doubters." One wonders whether China's high-growth economy can be said to be strong when it remains inherently unhealthy and unsustainable. Would China be economically stronger if growth was only 3 percent and the economy much healthier? Similarly, would China be stronger if it had a leaner, meaner, and more modern PLA and a smaller population, say, about 700 million, roughly half of its current population, able to flourish on the country's own natural resources? But a smaller population could not have produced the same GDP, had the same military capabilities, or made the same investments in R&D. China would not have been able to narrow the power gap with the United States or widen the power gap with other states as quickly as it has. The adage that quantity has a quality all its own applies to the rise of China and its rivalry with the United States.

Economies are never perfect. When we look at China's economic growth, we find many deficiencies and challenges, but they need to be put into perspective and compared with those facing other major economies. The U.S. economy has recently recovered from one of its most devastating financial crises. But while its economy now seems healthier and able to fuel sustainable growth, there is also political dysfunction[133] and deficiencies in fiscal policy, challenges related to healthcare and immigration, and rising rates of private debt and deficits in the U.S. balance of payment.

The Russian economy is in recession and facing so many problems that it is vastly inferior to China's. Japan suffers from stagnant growth, and the huge debt the government is absorbing will be difficult to manage with a rapidly aging population. The major powers in Europe are still struggling with slow growth in the aftermath of the debt and financial crisis, the recent refugee crisis is threatening to undermine some of the core foundations of the European Union, and most European countries face demographic challenges. India's economy is, relatively speaking, much smaller than China's, and it is questionable whether the high levels of economic growth needed to narrow the gap with China can be sustained. All the major economies, especially Russia, India, and Japan but also the United States and a number of European states, will be affected if the Chinese economy slows down or makes a hard landing, and it therefore remains to be seen how it will affect the distribution of capabilities and China's relative power status.

China's economic growth rate has dropped from about 10 percent to roughly 6 percent in only a few years, and it is unlikely that China will be able to sustain even 6 percent growth. However, this does not mark the end of China's rise.[134] The growth might be slower, but it potentially could be healthier. Since the absolute size of China's economy is now so large, even a 3–4 percent growth rate in the years ahead would be strong and something most other major economies would envy. In 2007, when China was growing at record-high 14 percent, it added $490 billion to a $3.5 trillion economy. If China was growing at the official 6.9 percent in 2015, it would add $759 billion to an $11 trillion economy (even 5 percent growth, which would have been $550 billion in growth, would have been more in absolute numbers than in 2007). The argument here has never been that China will overtake the United States and rule the world.[135] China does not even need to obtain power parity with the United States to reach a top-ranking slot. China's nominal GDP is now more than 60 percent of the United States'. If China maintains 4 percent growth and the United States grows at 2 percent, then China will continue to narrow the gap between it and the United States, and widen the gap between it and any other great or major power, in terms of economic strength.

China, like most states, is constantly in transition and seeking development. There is evidence that China is both strong and weak; depending on whether you're looking at nominal GDP, GDP measured in PPP, or per capita GDP, it can be contended that China is either a superpower or a developing state. The evidence marshaled above suggests that China has vaulted into the top ranking. China's overall capability score remains lower than that of the United States. Nonetheless, asymmetry is to be expected, as the system will never be perfectly bipolar in the sense of China and the United States scoring equally on all the items that can be used to measure the distribution of capabilities. China's combined score on the seven factors examined in this chapter place it in the top ranking. As we will see in the next chapter, the Soviet Union never scored as high as the United States in 1950 or at any time during the Cold War on the combined capabilities that define a pole. The power gap between the Soviet Union and the United States in 1950 is roughly similar to the uneven distribution of power between the United States and China today.

Chapter 4

DISTINGUISHING TOP-RANKING STATES
AND COMPARING BIPOLARITY

The narrowing power gap between the United States and China is only one aspect of the shift in the distribution of capabilities in the international system. China's rise and the relative decline of the United States explain why the international system is no longer as unbalanced as during the unipolar era of the 1990s and first decade of this century. However, we cannot know whether the international system has become bipolar or multipolar before we examine the power distribution between China and the other great powers contending for place among the top-ranking nations. If we base our analysis on IR scholars' customary definitions of pole and polarity, multipolarity—a system in which three or more great powers have roughly equal capabilities—is nowhere to be seen in the current international system. No great or major power measures up to China's combined score. China is catching up with the United States more rapidly than any other great power is catching up with China, which is why the international system has evolved into bipolarity, not multipolarity.

The modern state system has been bipolar only once. Establishing whether the current international system has changed from unipolarity to bipolarity not only involves measuring scores on all the elements of power and counting the poles by examining the distribution of capabilities within the current international system; it also requires a comprehensive assessment that compares the distribution of capabilities at the starts of the old and new bipolar systems. This is challenging because it is difficult to measure the different combinations of capabilities of states during a particular period, not least because how the different elements are weighted changes over time.[1] Nonetheless, if the current distribution of capabilities at the start of a new bipolar era is roughly similar to that at the start of the previous bipolar era, this lends support to the overall thesis that the international system has returned to bipolarity. This chapter first examines how China surpassed the powers next in rank by a broad margin and then compares the current and previous distribution of capabilities.

CHINA AND THE POWERS NEXT IN RANK

Territorial size and geographical location will always be crucial markers when we want to determine membership of the league of top-ranking nations. Population was the core of military power in previous centuries, but it is no longer as important today for measuring military strength. Still, manpower does matter. A militarily strong state such as Israel, with a population of about 8.5 million, cannot become a superpower. Military force is the final arbiter in world politics, and military power has been crucial in establishing which states qualify as top rankers in the past and in defining the United States and the Soviet Union as superpowers in 1950. But military power also depends on the economic base, which again is linked to a nation's resource endowment, political stability, competence, and innovation.

China and the Great Powers

Russia's and India's economic capabilities are dwarfed in comparison with China's. China's and India's GDPs were roughly the same in 1978; the Soviet Union's was more than four times larger in the late 1970s than China's. The size of the Chinese economy in 1990 was about 1.5 times that of India and roughly half the Soviet Union's, and in 1993, China's and Russia's economies in nominal GDP were roughly the same. In 2016, China's GDP was ten times larger than Russia's and more than five times larger than India's.[2] Crucially, the economic gap between China and Russia and India is growing in China's favor every year. Even though China's economic growth is beginning to slow, dropping from double-digit growth to 7 and 6 percent in 2015–2016, growth in Russia has declined quickly, and India enjoys roughly the same growth level as China. It seems illogical to argue for a transition to multipolarity and not bipolarity when India has about one-fifth and Russia one-tenth of China's nominal GDP while China has reached more than three-fifths of the U.S. nominal GDP.

Russia's economy began to shrink in 2014. With falling oil prices and Western sanctions imposed in the aftermath of the annexation of Crimea and the Ukraine war, Russia's economy continued to contract in 2015 and fell into recession. Because Russia's and India's economies are much smaller than China's, they will need to post double-digit growth figures for one or two decades to have any chance of catching up with China or to obtain a GDP that is more than 60 percent of China's GDP, similar to the economic gap between China and the United States today. This will be highly unlikely for Russia, and it remains to be seen if India can manage to sustain such growth. The "rise of India" has failed to meet expectations.[3] The economic gap between China and India is still likely to grow in China's favor every year for the next five to ten years, despite India having a larger-percentage GDP growth than China in 2015 and 2016. In addition, if the Chinese economy faced a crisis or even a hard landing, it would become increasingly difficult for Russia to obtain and India to maintain high growth rates because the slowdown in the Chinese economy would likely affect India's and Russia's economies also. China still outperforms most other large economies even if its growth rate is expected to edge lower in the near and medium term, and it will remain enormously superior in economic terms over the power(s) next in rank over the coming decades.

China's military expenditure is nearly four times that of Russia. SIPRI estimated in 2016 that China's and Russia's defense spending amounted to $225 billion and $70 billion, respectively. As long as China and Russia both possess a nuclear second-strike capability, China's superior conventional forces give it an edge in terms of military power. China looms over Russia in terms of demographics and economic and military power in the Far East and is replacing Russia as the dominant power in Central Asia. There are about 6 million Russians living in the Far East, mostly elderly. More than 100 million Chinese live in the three provinces across the border, and the border is patrolled largely by the Chinese, not the Russians. If China actively encouraged migrants to cross into Russia, it would create an immigration challenge for Russia much larger than the one that enveloped Europe in 2015 and 2016.

Geography is another important factor in the asymmetric Sino-Russian power relationship. The Russian Far East is four thousand miles to the east of Moscow, and Russia lacks both the infrastructure and capabilities to maintain military preparedness in the region. The harsh and inhospitable climate of Siberia and the Russian Far East reinforces the challenges Russia needs to overcome in projecting military power into the region. These demographic, geographic, and climatic factors do not constrain China, which has a populous and relatively well-developed industrial and infrastructure base to the south.[4]

China demonstrated its military superiority over India in 1962 and continues to remain stronger than India militarily. According to SIPRI, India's defense budget in 2016 was $55 billion less than a quarter of China's. Indeed, as one observer has noted, India's "sense of encirclement" is growing in step with the rise of relative Chinese capabilities.[5]

In terms of size, Russia's relatively small population and weaker infrastructure and India's smaller territory and poorer infrastructure mean that both score lower than China. Russia's population is about ten times smaller than China's. The Russian population is growing, although at a very small rate and mostly driven by immigration. Over the next few decades, the population will probably shrink; according to some estimates, the drop will be from 142 million in 2014 to only 107 million by 2050.[6]

India will be the youngest country in the world in a few years and is currently experiencing a youth bulge. Comparing India's median age of twenty-nine in 2020 with China's thirty-seven at that point, India's youth population is often called a "demographic dividend" that could turn India into the biggest consumer market with the biggest labor force in the world.[7] However, despite potential demographic advantages, India faces large hurdles in educating its youth to become skilled workers and in creating enough jobs to employ them. India still has a long way to go in developing the potential of its enormous population, and the caste system remains a socioeconomic constraint. If India is unable to create jobs for its workers, the huge demographic dividend might turn into a liability and increase social instability.

China had an infant-mortality rate of 9 per 1,000 in 2015, as opposed to Russia's 8 and India's 38. Life expectancy in China in 2013 was 75, 71 in Russia, and 66 in India.[8] The literacy rate is 96 percent in China, 99 percent in Russia, and 72 percent in India.[9] Similar to China, India is also grappling with a low sex ratio. Moreover, by midcentury, India is likely to have turned into an aging population.[10]

Russia is the only power contending for a top-ranking place that can compete with China in terms of combined natural resources. Nonetheless, Russia remains a "petrostate"[11] and vulnerable to fluctuations in the international oil and gas market. Current sanctions imposed on Russia by the European Union and the United States after Russia's annexation of Crimea and aggression in Ukraine have had both immediate and long-term consequences for Russia's economic growth. India cannot match China's resource endowments. Despite having an economy that is five times smaller than China's, India is much more dependent on imported fossil fuels (oil, gas, and coal). Net oil import dependence rose to 80 percent in November 2016, and India managed to satisfy 63 percent of its natural gas demand through indigenous production.[12] In contrast, China is the world's largest producer of fossil fuels and satisfied 65 percent of its crude oil demand with imports. Even with an economy much larger than India's, China is far less dependent on imported fossil fuels. If India is going to sustain high economic growth in the coming decades, then its import dependence on fossil fuels is likely to increase. India scores lower than China in terms of food and water security, and a larger percentage of its population is undernourished.[13] China is a leading producer of metals and minerals, although India has strong reserves and might catch up.

The World Bank's governance indicators rank China higher than Russia and India in terms of "political stability and absence of violence." Taken together, China's average score for the period 1996–2013 on the bank's six dimensions of governance—voice and accountability, political stability and absence of violence, government effectiveness, regulatory quality, rule of law, and control of corruption—is higher than India's and Russia's.[14] In terms of competence, China scores higher than either Russia or India and has consistently outspent India and Russia on R&D, both in terms of percentage of GDP and in absolute numbers over the last two decades.[15] China has a higher research output, in terms of the number of scientific publications and researchers. It produces far more college graduates per year and has become a leader in awarded patents and trademark applications. India and Russia remain smaller players in global trade and manufacturing, and China receives much more FDI (foreign direct investment). Russia has traditionally had an advantage in military technology and signed significant arms deals with both India and China. Nonetheless, China has surpassed India's military technological competence, and new advances are bringing China's defense industrial base on parity with Russia's capabilities.[16]

Developments in Central Asia in the post–Cold War era provide an example of China's enhanced combined capabilities. Traditionally, the region was a Russian stronghold, and Moscow still retains considerable influence. The United States established military bases in Central Asia and conducted its longest war ever in Afghanistan. India also has an interest in developments in Central Asia. Nonetheless, most observers will agree that China, without Russia's Commonwealth of Independent States or the U.S. military presence in Central Asia, during the last two decades has increased its influence in the region faster than any of the others.[17] China has used trade, energy deals, investments, military exercises, the SCO, and President Xi's development of the Silk Road Economic Belt to change the balance of power in Central Asia, into one of greater importance to China and while reducing the roles of the United States, Russia, and India. China has become the most attractive partner for most Central Asian governments and has demonstrated how its rising power affects the balance of power and state alignments.

China and the Major Powers

Other major powers, such as Japan, Germany, France, and Britain, do not measure up in terms of combined capabilities. In 2015, the Chinese economy was almost three times as large as Japan's, more than three times as large as Germany's, and more than four times as large as France's or Great Britain's.[18] The major powers are unlikely to see the necessary rate of growth to catch up economically with China, and the gap in economic strength is likely to continue to widen in China's favor.

China is a leader in R&D as well, surpassing R&D spending in Japan and the leading European states. Japan and Germany, and probably Great Britain and France, might have a qualitative edge over China in technology and innovation. France, Great Britain, Japan, and Germany also score higher on political stability, although the CCP has been in power in the PRC roughly as long as the Federal Republic of Germany and the postwar Japanese constitution have existed. Even if these major powers scored higher on these two factors it would not be enough to match China's combined capabilities. When we add population, geographic extent, natural resources, military power, and economic strength, then China's combined score becomes much higher.

Geographically, China is much larger than Japan, Germany, France, and the United Kingdom individually—and combined—and they all lack the strategic depth to counter a potential military invasion from another great power or superpower. Despite that China's population is more than ten times larger than Japan's, more than fifteen times larger than Germany's, and more than twenty times larger than France's or the United Kingdom's, it has a higher food self-sufficiency rate than Japan and United Kingdom. Moreover, China outmatches those major powers when it comes to self-sufficiency in terms of energy[19] and scores as high or higher on minerals and other natural resources. China's defense budget is roughly four times Great Britain's and France's and about five times larger than Germany's and Japan's. Moreover, Great Britain, Japan, Germany, and France depend on the United States for defense and security, hardly an attribute of a great power or superpower. Their combined capabilities are far below what is required for superpower ranking and do not match China's military capabilities.

In the previous multipolar systems prior to the two world wars, the United States could rely on European and Asian powers to maintain the regional balance of power. When they eventually could not sustain the balance of power between themselves, the United States was compelled to intervene. If the international system had been multipolar today, with three or more roughly equal great powers, then the United States could theoretically have relied on Japan, Russia, and India to balance China. However, in the new bipolar system with two superpowers, it is only the United States that can balance China's hegemonic aspirations in East Asia.

Over the last several years, China has pulled ahead of all the other powers that might have been considered for a place at the high table. Figures 4.1 and 4.2 convincingly illustrate the move toward bipolarity in economic strength. China is a top-ranked power on all the measurements of states' aggregated power, including military, population, geography, resource endowments, political stability, and competence. Not only has China achieved this position by closing the power gap with the United States; it has now achieved superiority over the power next in rank for designation as a superpower.

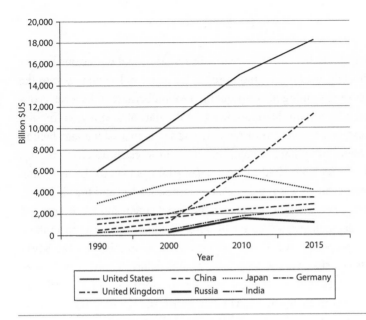

FIGURE 4.1 Nominal GDP, 1990–2015.

Source: IMF, World Economic Outlook Database, November 2015.

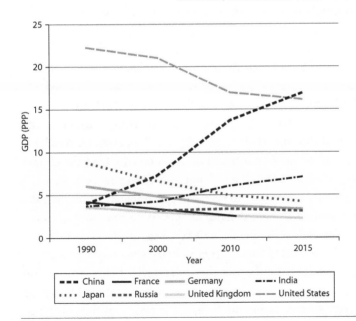

FIGURE 4.2 GDP based on the share of global purchasing power parity (PPP), 1990–2015.

Source: IMF, World Economic Outlook Database, November 2015.

PERFECT BIPOLARITY?

Economic capability became an essential feature during the previous bipolar period. Ultimately, the Soviet Union proved incapable of keeping up with the United States or sustaining its top-ranking position because of its weak economy. The most important difference between the start of the previous bipolar system in 1950 and the return of bipolarity today is that China lags behind the United States in military strength but is about to catch up economically. Although the Soviet Union had a higher defense budget than the United States in 1950, economically it was much weaker. Chinese leaders and the CCP have undoubtedly learned from the mistakes of the Soviet Union and are determined to avoid a similar collapse. When establishing whether China is a top-ranking nation and superpower, we should not expect China to follow in the Soviet Union's footsteps, since we and they know it led to failure. It remains to be seen whether the Chinese government can manage to steer China onto a different path and succeed in their ambitions in the years and decades ahead. China has chosen a different path when it comes to defense spending and overseas military interventions, for instance, but it can still be regarded a superpower based on the distribution of capabilities in the international system.

U.S.-Soviet Distribution of Capabilities

The size of the Soviet economy was less than that of the United States, and throughout the Cold War the Soviet Union remained inferior to the economic power of the United States (see fig. 4.3).[20] In absolute numbers, in 1950 and 1980 the Soviet Union spent more on defense than the United States, whereas in 1960 and 1970 the U.S. figures were higher (see fig. 4.4).[21] As a result, the Soviet Union had to spend proportionately more than the United States to sustain its high defense budget. With roughly half of the U.S. GDP, the Soviet Union spent about twice as much of its GDP on defense than did the United States. This military spending was a heavy burden. Waltz noted that by the late 1970s the Soviet Union would find it hard to "stay in the race," and he questioned whether it could keep up given its relatively weaker economic base.[22] It is clear that the combined distribution of capabilities in the early 1950s favored the United States and that the power gap was sustained throughout the Cold War.

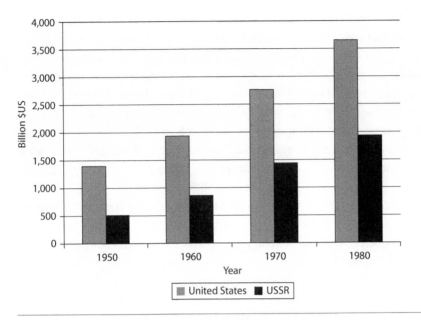

FIGURE 4.3 U.S. and Soviet GDP during the Cold War, 1950–1980.

Source: Charles Wolf Jr., Gregory Hildenbrandt, Michael Kennedy, et al., "Long-Term Economic and Military Trends, 1950–2010" (Santa Monica: RAND, April 1989).

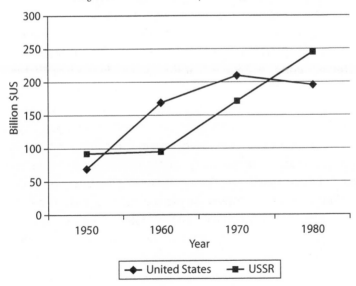

FIGURE 4.4 U.S. and Soviet military spending during the Cold War, 1950–1980.

Source: Charles Wolf Jr., Gregory Hildenbrandt, Michael Kennedy, et al., "Long-Term Economic and Military Trends, 1950–2010" (Santa Monica: RAND, April 1989).

The Soviet Union had a larger population than the United States,[23] but its population included a number of large ethnic groups seeking independence, thus contributing to political instability.[24] The Soviet Union was larger than the United States, but the former's lack of infrastructure prevented it from taking full advantage of its vast territory.[25] With the world's longest land border, the Soviet Union was throughout most of the Cold War preoccupied with security in the areas bordering Soviet territory. The country had strong resource endowments, but so did the United States, and the latter had a higher efficiency rate in agricultural production. The United States also scored higher on political stability.

The United States was ahead on measures of competency and innovation, outspending the Soviet Union on R&D, but the Soviet Union had leading scientists in some areas and was able to compete in many scientific and technological fields.[26] Graham has concluded that despite some spectacular achievements in fields such as physics and the Soviet space program, Soviet science and technology achievements were generally disappointing, not least in view of the mammoth size of the Soviet science establishment, especially to Soviet leaders. And everywhere within the science establishment, Graham has pointed out, "creativity fell to low levels," the root cause of these weaknesses being "organizational, political, and social."[27]

Some have questioned whether the international system was bipolar given the asymmetric power relationship between the United States and the Soviet Union.[28] Porter maintains that the quantitative and qualitative power gap between the United States and the Soviet Union suggests that the disparity in power "between the two superpowers was far greater than any other disparity between the strongest power and its strongest rival, or group of rivals, since the modern state system came into existence in the seventeenth century."[29] By focusing on the power gap between the United States and the Soviet Union, Porter pays insufficient attention to the importance of the power gap between the two top-ranking powers and the power next in rank in defining the international system. Porter's argument also disregards that the power parity between the top- and second-ranking power is not essential to defining the international system as bipolar. If we, on the other hand, use the distribution-of-capabilities method of analysis, the Soviet Union can be said to have been a superpower in a bipolar system.

Political scientists and historians have largely conceded that the second half of the twentieth century was a bipolar system.[30] The historian Kennedy notes that although the American "superpower" was vastly superior, in the new bipolar strategic landscape following the Second World War "only the United States and the USSR counted."[31] Another historian, Gaddis, has cautioned how retrospective judgments neglect the perceptions of policy makers at the time, "who clearly saw their world as bipolar."[32] Most other historians and political scientists would agree that the international system in the years following World War II evolved into a new bipolar system.

Comparing Bipolar Distribution

When we compare the 1950 distribution of capabilities with the contemporary period, we note several differences. In 1950, both the Soviet Union and China outnumbered the United States in terms of population, the Soviet Union had a larger territory than the United States and China, all three had strong resource endowments, the Soviet Union and China scored lower on political stability than the United States, and the competence gap between the Soviet Union and the United States in 1950 was not much different from the advantages the United States enjoys today over China.[33] Today, contemporary China has a well-developed infrastructure, and the gap between it and the United States is no larger than it was between the Soviet Union and the United States in 1950.[34] By the end of Xi's presidency in 2022, the CCP will have ruled China about as long as the Communist Party ruled the Soviet Union. But historical comparisons of political stability are not straightforward. How can we know whether China today is more politically stable than the Soviet Union in 1965 or 1987? No one knows for certain, but given the CCP's sustained control of China, there are reasons to suggest that China scores as high today, relatively speaking, as the Soviet Union did in 1950 on political stability.

Thus, the major differences lie in military strength and economic capabilities. Contemporary U.S. military expenditures are probably about two to three times higher than China's and may remain so for many years. However, the Soviets never experienced an economic boom comparable to China's over the last three decades. Strikingly, contemporary China is rapidly catching up with U.S. military spending, although China spends half as much of its GDP on defense compared to the United States. According to the World Bank, in the period 2010–2014 the United States spent between

4.5 and 3.5 percent of its GDP on defense, whereas China spent about 2 percent on average in the same period.[35] If China were to spend twice as much of its GDP on defense as the United States (as did the USSR during the Cold War), which would be roughly 8 percent, then China today would be spending more on defense than the United States in absolute numbers. Still, if China were to spend 8 percent of its GDP on defense, it would not be spending more on its military as a share of GDP than the Soviet Union in 1950, and it would be spending less than Soviet military expenditures as a share of GDP throughout the Cold War.[36]

At its peak, the Soviet Union's nominal GDP was no more than 50 percent of that of the United States. China has already surpassed this level. Economically, the gap between the United States and the Soviet Union in 1950 and throughout the Cold War was larger than it is between China and the United States today. The Soviet Union accounted for about 13 percent of global GDP in MER in 1950, whereas China today accounts for close to 16 percent. Comparative GDP per capita data show similar gaps between the two top-ranked states. In 1950, U.S. GDP per capita was $9,500, whereas Soviet GDP per capita was $2,800. In 2014, according to the World Bank, China had a per capita GDP (in PPP) of $13,216; the comparable figure for the United States was $54,629. As Chung notes, "we are reminded of the sobering fact that the Soviet Union, whose per capita income indicators did not fare well, managed to compete with the United States for more than four decades."[37]

With a much stronger economic base than the Soviet Union, China is more likely to be capable of "staying in the race" in the contemporary bipolar system. China's has more latent power available to build military forces than did the former Soviet Union, and China will likely be capable of competing with the United States.

Comparing Top-Ranking Powers and the Rest Under Bipolarity

In 1950, according to a RAND study, the Soviet Union had a GDP of $492 billion, whereas that of the United Kingdom was $251 billion and of France, $172 billion. The Soviet GDP was therefore almost twice as large as that of the third-ranking power, the United Kingdom.[38] Angus Maddison's dataset on the world economy shows that the United States accounted for about 27 percent of global GDP in 1950; the Soviet Union, about 10 percent (13.5 percent if the Eastern European countries are included); the United Kingdom, 6.5 percent; Germany, 5 percent; France, 4 percent; India, 4 percent; and Japan, 3 percent.[39] Japan and Germany were outliers, having been defeated in World War II, but their economies quickly recovered during the Cold War, and by the early 1980s Japan had surpassed the Soviet Union as the world's second-largest economy.

Maddison's dataset further shows that the U.S. share of global GDP in 2008 was roughly 18.6 percent, whereas China's was 17.4 percent; India, 6.7 percent; Japan, 5.6 percent; Germany, 3.3 percent; the United Kingdom, 2.8 percent; France, 2.7 percent; Russia, 2.5 percent; and Brazil, 2.4 percent.[40] Accordingly, by drawing on Maddison's data, we see how the economic power gap between number 2 in 1950, the Soviet Union, and number 3, the United Kingdom, was much smaller than the economic difference between today's number 2, China, and number 3, India. Also based on Maddison's data, the difference between the current numbers 1 and 2 is smaller than it was in 1950. The Conference Board's data on the distribution of world output corroborate Maddison's statistics, showing that the United States in January 2013 accounted for 18.2 percent of global GDP and China 16.4 percent, whereas India accounted for 6.3 percent and Japan 5.6 percent.[41]

Conversely, when compared with other datasets, these numbers seem bullish for China, especially so for India, and bearish for the United States, Japan, and the European powers. According to the IMF, in 2015 the U.S. share of the world nominal GDP was roughly 24.4 percent, whereas China's share was 15.5 percent; Japan, 5.5 percent; Germany, 4.6 percent; the United Kingdom, 3.9 percent; France, 3.2 percent; India, 2.9 percent; and Russia, 1.6 percent.[42] This shows that in terms of economic strength the gap between the United States and China (24.4 versus 15.5) is less than between the United States and the Soviet Union in 1950 (27 versus 13.5) and that the gap is larger between China and the third-ranking power today (15.5 versus 5.5) than it was in 1950 (13.5 versus 6.5). In addition, if we look at world GDP based on PPP, economically, the modern international system has never been more bipolar than it is today. The economic data will produce differences of opinion, and economists seldom agree on how to measure shares of world GDP. Despite the lack of consensus, there is evidence to suggest that the gaps between the top-ranking powers and the great and major powers today are similar to what they were under the previous bipolar system.

Soviet military spending in 1950 was US$91 billion; the United States spent US$69 billion; the United Kingdom, US$23 billion; and France, US$11 billion.[43] So the second-ranked power had defense expenditures three times greater than those of the third-ranked power. SIPRI ranks China second in terms of world military spending in 2016, accounting for 13 percent of the world total. Russia was ranked third, with a 4.1 percent share of global military spending. Therefore, China's share of world military spending is more than three times as large as the third-ranked power.[44] In short, the power gap in military terms between the top-ranked powers in 1950 was less than today, but the gap between the second- and third-ranking power was not that different from the distribution of military capabilities today. In terms of territorial size, population, and resource endowments, the United States, Soviet Union, and China have been in the top rank since 1950, and there are no significant differences between the superpowers in 1950 and the superpowers today compared with the great and major powers in the past and present.

Comparing Behavior Under Bipolarity

Statistics and military budgets aren't everything. The Soviet Union was not feared and regarded as a superpower in 1950 because of its military budget but because it had proved itself a formidable military power during World War II. The United States not only has a larger defense budget than China today, but it has demonstrated an unprecedented capability to wage war all over the world. Nevertheless, China managed to push back two military superpowers ranged along its borders in the early 1950s and late 1960s, despite a relatively weak economy and only marginal defense spending in comparison to the United States and Soviet Union. Although Waltz notes that ranking states does not require us to predict their success in war,[45] the PLA would fight the U.S. military better on the Korean Peninsula today than it did in 1950: when Chinese "volunteers" entered the Korean War in 1950, they did so without critical air support.[46] Today the airspace above Beijing and northeastern China is one of the world's best defended. Nor did China have a navy in 1950. If it faced resistance from the PLA Air

Force, Navy, and Second Artillery today, a U.S. amphibious operation on the Korean Peninsula, similar to the September 1950 Inchon amphibious operation at the height of the Korean War, would be much more difficult and unlikely to be as successful as in the past.

The PLA is more superior to Indian forces today than it was in 1962. Chinese forces would perform even better against Russian troops today than they did against Soviet troops in 1969 and would be more prepared for a new military campaign against Vietnam today than they were in 1979. Contemporary China is as militarily dominant, if not more, on the Asian mainland as the Soviet Union was in Europe in 1950. Europe was divided, and NATO needed to be able to put up a good fight against the Soviet Union in 1950 and during the Cold War. In comparison, who could put up a good fight against China on the Asian mainland today? In comparison to the Soviet Union, who had to contend with the United States and NATO in Europe and China in the Far East, China does not face any powers today that are equally threatening or challenging along its borders. Relatively, China is as, or probably more, secure and dominant along its borders as the Soviet Union, and the PLA is as formidable a land power in today's bipolar system as the Soviet Union's Red Army was during the previous bipolar system.

Even though the Soviet Union rivaled the United States in defense spending in 1950, it did not dominate the European continent, nor was it militarily superior to China and the PLA in northeastern Asia. Russia is less capable of defending its own territory in the Far East against Chinese dominance today than it was during the Cold War. Russia's response to China's conventional military superiority in East Asia today is nuclear deterrence. Contemporary Russia is in no position to deter the PRC by conventional military means, as it was able to do during the standoff along the Sino-Russian border in the 1960s. This is similar to how the United States was forced to rely on nuclear deterrence when confronted by a superior land power on the European continent in the 1950s. Few contemporary great powers would be able to stop China from moving into Central Asia, and China also has a strong sphere of influence on the Korean Peninsula and in Indochina. The PLA is today as capable of causing harm on mainland Asia as the Soviet military was of inflicting harm on the European continent in 1950.

Chinese naval power and global power-projection capabilities are dwarfed in comparison with contemporary U.S. military might, but the

PLA has developed "anti-access and area-denial" military capabilities, which would compromise U.S. deployment and military operations in East Asian waters in a conflict in the Taiwan Strait, the East and South China Seas, or on the Korean Peninsula. China has developed considerable submarine capabilities, and its fleet has become more modern and capable of patrolling blue-water seas.[47] China today has more naval power than the Soviet Union had at the start of the previous bipolar era, and it has a stronger navy relative to the United States than the Soviet Union had in 1950.

China does not need to "go global"[48] before the international system can be defined as bipolar and China considered a superpower. Britain had more global power-projection capability in the late 1940s and early 1950s than the Soviet Union, but the Soviet Union was considered to have "enormous superiority over the power next in rank."[49] The Soviet Union did not have the global power projection to pursue its interventionism in Angola, Somalia, Cuba, Ethiopia, South Yemen, or Afghanistan at the start of the previous bipolar era. Instead, the Soviet Union gradually emerged as a world power from the end of hostilities in World War II to the first years of the 1960s.[50] China is reluctant today to use military force abroad and lacks the capabilities to sustain operations far from its home territory or waters, although it has sustained its antipiracy operations and escort missions in the Gulf of Aden since early 2009,[51] sent a naval escort to assist with the disposal of Syria's chemical weapons,[52] and participated in a number of military exercises around the world.

China's decision in 2011 to send the missile frigate *Xuzhou* to assist, facilitate, and provide security for the evacuation of more than 35,000 Chinese workers based in Libya suggests that China's growing global portfolio of interests will push it toward more interventionism. It now seeks to build military capabilities commensurate with its growing power in order to perform "far seas operations."[53] The 2015 Chinese defense white paper and President Xi's statements envision a more global role for China's military and emphasize the development of naval power and global power-projection capabilities.[54] Five Chinese naval ships—an amphibious ship, a replenishment vessel, and three surface combatant ships—sailed in the Bering Sea off Alaska in September 2015, demonstrating the increasing global presence of the Chinese Navy.[55]

We should therefore not be surprised if, within a decade or two, China becomes militarily involved in Africa, the Middle East, Central Asia, or

Latin America, echoing Soviet adventures in the 1960s and 1970s. However, as will be explained in chapter 7, since China is likely to prioritize efforts on changing the status quo in East Asia, which will fuel instability and rivalry with the United States in East Asian waters, China is less likely to get itself entangled in proxy wars and conflicts in other regions.[56] Potential Chinese intervention in conflicts in other regions will probably assume a form different from the Soviet Union's interventions on the periphery, which were often designed to further the communist cause and were facilitated by decolonization and power vacuums emerging in the post–World War II era. China will have fewer power vacuums to expand into, and it is less likely to be driven by the goal of spreading communism or other ideological agendas. However, nationalism and a growing portfolio of national interests in need of protection, such as overseas Chinese workers, investments, and assets, may push China toward some military activism abroad, although its primary focus is most likely to be in maritime East Asia.

The current Chinese economy outperforms the Soviet economy of 1950 and is more competitive than the Soviet economy compared to the U.S. economy. The PLA is as capable of causing harm on mainland Asia as the Soviet military was of inflicting harm on the European continent in 1950. This places China among the top-ranking nations, just as the Soviet Union was considered a member of the top rank in 1950.

THE NEXT STEP

The first part of the book has demonstrated that the current international system has returned to bipolarity: (1) The power gap between the United States and China has narrowed significantly to place China in the top ranking despite the asymmetric U.S.-China power relation; (2) no other states match China's power in the aggregate, and in the current international system no third power is able to challenge the top two; and (3) the contemporary distribution of capabilities is roughly similar to the previous bipolar era. The next step is to shift the focus from measuring the distribution of capabilities and demonstrating that the international system is bipolar to showing how and why a new bipolar system shapes and shoves U.S.-China relations and international politics.

The second part of the book will examine the distinct patterns of behavior and effects we can observe and expect from a system whereby two states (superpowers) are much more powerful than all the others. Building on structural realism, the following analysis will show why a bipolar system is different from a system with one dominating superpower (unipolarity) or a system with three or more great powers (multipolarity) in three core realms: balancing, stability, and global and regional effects. It will compare and contrast U.S.-Soviet strategic competition during the Cold War (especially the early Cold War) with contemporary U.S.-China strategic competition at the origins of a new bipolar era. I will argue that Waltz's neorealism, the previous reigning theory about how a bipolar system works, does not apply directly to the current situation because each bipolar system is different given its specific geopolitical features.

In chapters 5 and 6, I will develop predictions about balancing and stability through a comparative analysis of two bipolar systems. Primarily as a result of distinct geopolitical factors, I contend that strong balancing will be postponed and that the risk of a limited war is higher in the new bipolar system than in the previous U.S.-Soviet one. In chapter 7, I will show that the rest of the world is beginning to behave as if a bipolar system existed: The United States is pivoting toward the Asia-Pacific region, East Asia is becoming more polarized, Japan is reinvigorating its foreign and security policy, India is developing a new "look East" policy, European states are compelled to take more responsibility for their own security and stability, Sino-Russia relations are shifting, and many states are orienting toward China in terms of trade and multilateral forums (for example, the AIIB). I will argue that China plays a vastly more predominant role than any other player except the United States in shaping contemporary international affairs because China is the only power that can bid for regional hegemony (in East Asia) and challenge U.S. power preponderance. No other state in any other region of the world is in a similar position.

By contending that geopolitics trumps structure, I will develop a geostructural-realist theory that can account for the different effects and patterns of behavior between similar bipolar systems. Nonetheless, other secondary factors, such as economic interdependence, an existing international institutional order, the lack of ideological rivalry, and the fact that the two superpowers today possess nuclear second-strike capability, contribute to explaining why the superpowers behave differently in different bipolar systems.

Finally, because the contemporary polarity shift is slower and more gradual compared to the polarity shifts following World War II and the collapse of the Soviet Union, it is likely that it will take more time before systemic effects will shape and shove policy makers' choices and scholars' observations. World War II made it clear that there were only two top-ranking states, and the rivalry on the European continent allowed for the bipolar effects to become very strong at the start of the previous bipolar system. The collapse of the Soviet Union left the United States alone at the top. U.S. primacy was unquestionable, and it shaped the United States' and other states' patterns of behavior directly in the early years of the post–Cold War era (for example, the Gulf War and U.S. intervention in Somalia and Bosnia). The contemporary polarity shift is less abrupt and more of a transition. This contributes to explaining why patterns of behavior appear different and adds to our understanding of why the rest of the world behaves differently in the new bipolar system in contrast to the previous one.

Part II

SYSTEMIC EFFECTS

Patterns of Behavior and Stability

Chapter 5

STRONG BALANCING POSTPONED

The return of bipolarity raises the questions, first, of whether we will witness an exercise in balancing similar to that of the starting point of the previous bipolar system and, second, whether there will be a new Cold War. A neorealist would expect a change in the systemic distribution of capabilities from unipolarity to bipolarity to alter behavior and outcomes. "Structural thought conceives of actions simultaneously taking place within a matrix. Change the matrix—the structure of the system—and expected actions and outcomes are altered," argued Waltz.[1] A roughly similar bipolar distribution of capabilities provides compelling structural incentives for the United States and China to pursue strong balancing. The pressures of competing for survival in a self-helped system encourage competitors, according to Waltz to seek "sameness," and, based on the theory, states would be expected to engage in balancing behavior.[2] Neorealism is not a deterministic theory, but it does suggest the presence of strong structural incentives that are likely to compel and constrain the United States and China to act like the United States and the Soviet Union acted previously. As Jervis pointed out, Waltz "stressed the continuity of international politics as long as structure remains the same."[3]

U.S.-China rivalry today does not resemble the internal balancing and arms racing of the 1950s, and in the coming decade, this bilateral relationship is unlikely to be as prone to strong balancing and confrontation as was the U.S.-Soviet relationship. This chapter seeks to explain the lack of strong balancing in U.S.-China relations and compares U.S.-China balancing behavior with that of the United States and Soviet Union at the emergence of the previous bipolar system. It distinguishes between limited, moderate, and strong balancing. Shifts in the distribution of capabilities affect balancing behavior, but geopolitics can postpone, moderate, or intensify balancing, which shows that there are degrees of balancing.

Not all balancing is the same. A country's general-armament program is different than participation in an arms race. This suggests that we can differentiate between strong and moderate balancing. Strong balancing involves arms racing and alliance formation. For example, the great powers pursued strong balancing under the pre–World War I multipolar system. Strong balancing was defined in terms of internal balancing during the previous bipolar system. The current systemic effects of a shift from unipolarity to bipolarity have not sparked strong balancing. If China had doubled or quadrupled its defense spending and spent close to 5 or 10 percent, rather than 2 percent, of its GDP on defense, many would argue that China was pursuing internal strong balancing. Since China is not taking such steps, we need to adopt a more nuanced view on balancing. China's contemporary nuclear buildup, missile deployments, and defense spending pale in comparison with the arms race of the 1950s and 1960s between the United States and the Soviet Union. Thus it is not helpful to label both types of pattern as simply balancing. The United States' and China's balancing today is much more moderate in scale.[4]

Differentiating between moderate and limited balancing helps us describe how a country goes about increasing the number and strength of its weapons. China's internal balancing is a far cry from the arms race and strong balancing of the Cold War, but its military buildup is an important factor in any analysis of the distribution of capabilities in the international system and of the balance of power in East Asia. While China has not increased its defense spending as a percentage of GDP, it has spent more money on armaments. Annual increases in defense expenditures by about 10 percent for two decades have provided the PLA with a substantial budget rise in absolute size and allowed China to accumulate military capabilities that now allows it to secure its interests more forcefully and more robustly balance against the United States.

China also seems willing to maintain its high defense spending despite the slowdown in its economic growth, and since China's economy is now so large, when China allocates about 2 percent of GDP to defense, it provides the PLA with a much larger budget than when China spent 2 percent of GDP on defense five to ten years ago. In addition, China's 2015 White Paper is the first one to focus on maritime concerns and issues. It signals a shift in Beijing's security preoccupation from the traditional Chinese continental focus to the maritime domain. This shift in defense posture is important. If China moves its strategic orientation and forces from the west to the east or from its land borders to the maritime domain, then such a strategic reorientation can be considered internal balancing. These trends suggest that China is putting more emphasis on internal balancing.

The United States is not close to following the internal strong balancing it pursued against its peer competitor during the Cold War. However, the 2011 announcement by the Obama administration that it intended to pivot and refocus its strategic priority on strengthening the U.S. military presence in the Asia-Pacific marked an adjustment and shift in U.S. balancing tactics compared to previous administrations' emphasis on reinforcing the U.S. military presence in East Asia in the 1990s and first decade of the new millennium. This change in priority was important in itself but became even more significant by coinciding with austerity measures and declining defense budgets. Sustaining or even increasing the U.S. military presence in East Asia given a climate of shrinking defense budgets is evidence of more balancing, even though it is not strong balancing. The Trump administration seeks to continue increasing U.S. military spending, but it has not laid out a strategy for where the United States will place its increased capabilities and what they will be used for. Geostructural conditions are likely to compel the United States to sustain and increase its presence in the Asia-Pacific to balance a rising China.

Although China and the United States have refrained from pursuing the strong balancing that characterized relations between the Soviet Union and the United States, there has been a tendency toward more balancing, which a distinction between limited, moderate, and strong balancing can capture. U.S.-China relations and the East Asian region have experienced a shift from unipolar limited balancing to moderate bipolar balancing as China has increased its relative power. Geopolitics is the key factor accounting for the lack of contemporary strong balancing and the "sameness effect," but other factors, such as limited ideological rivalry, economic interdependence, an established international institutional order, and nuclear weapons, are helping postpone strong balancing. These additional unit-level factors have a moderating effect on arms racing in U.S.-China relations. Contemporary East Asia is not shaped by the relative power shifts that shaped Europe during the second half of the twentieth century, nor does the security environment in East Asia pose the type existential threat that warranted strong balancing in the past.

EXPLAINING DIFFERENT BALANCING BEHAVIORS
UNDER SIMILAR STRUCTURAL CONSTRAINTS

Current developments in East Asia and in U.S.-China relations are gradually meeting the criteria of the balancing proposition. Realists are correct in arguing that the United States and China are incorporating balancing elements in their strategies and that China's military buildup is motivated by a desire to counter U.S. military dominance in East Asia.[5] But interaction between China and the United States since the end of the Cold War has not satisfied the predictions of structural realism, and the return of bipolarity has not sparked strong balancing behavior by the two top-ranking powers.

The following analysis uses geopolitics to explain why contemporary strong balancing has been put on hold even though it is expected given the structural conditions. I argue that Waltz's theory is incomplete because he could not compare bipolar systems and neglected geopolitics. Rivalry on land is more intense and differs from rivalry at sea.[6] The security competition and fear implicit in the relations between the United States and the Soviet Union were much stronger on the European continent during the previous bipolar system. Balancing and patterns of behavior are different under these two instances of bipolarity, in large part because of different geopolitics.

Geopolitics and Balancing

U.S. China policy is guided in the bipolar system of the twenty-first century by the same balance-of-power politics that prevailed in U.S. Soviet policy during the Cold War—the goal being preventing the other super-power from becoming a regional hegemon. However, geography and the "stopping power of water" make it relatively easier for the United States to counterbalance China's contemporary naval ambitions in East Asian waters than it was to preserve a balance of power when confronted by the Soviet Red Army on the European continent. This is not because the Soviet Union was more powerful than contemporary China or because the United States is relatively more powerful than China in comparison to the Soviet Union. The systemic distribution of capabilities between the two bipolar systems is roughly similar. China today is as formidable a land power as the Soviet Union was in its day, but while regional hegemony in Europe can largely be obtained through land power, regional hegemony in East Asia requires both land and sea power.[7]

East Asia remains geopolitically divided between China's superiority and sphere of influence on the East Asian mainland and the United States' superiority and sphere of influence in maritime East Asia. As a result of the shifting systemic distribution of capabilities, China is now increasingly challenging U.S. naval supremacy and seeking to alter the regional status quo, causing tension and conflict. In the 1990s and the first decade of this century, when the power gap between China and the third-ranking power was not as great—and the gap between China and the United States was unambiguously in the favor of the latter—China was not able to challenge the regional security order in East Asia. China's rise; the relative decline of the United States, Russia, Japan, and India; and the shift from unipolarity to bipolarity in the systemic distribution of capabilities now allow and compel the PRC for the first time in its history to challenge the regional balance of power.[8] Nonetheless, the United States can rely on its superior conventional naval forces to balance China's regional hegemonic ambitions. This contrasts with the start of the previous bipolar system, when Washington had to balance a militarily superior Soviet Union on the European continent in order to sustain the regional balance of power. Strong balancing followed in Europe, but such balancing has been postponed for the time being in East Asia today.

Immediately after World War II, the United States could rely on its exclusive possession of the atomic bomb to counter Soviet conventional-force superiority in Europe. However, with the August 1949 Soviet atomic test, Moscow gained the advantage. As Gaddis points out, President

Truman and most of his advisors believed "it was the United States, as a technologically rich but manpower-poor country, that was operating from a position of weakness, since of necessity it relied more heavily than did the Soviet Union on weapons of mass destruction to maintain the balance of power."[9] These geographical and military conditions encouraged the creation of formal military alliances and prompted the arms race of the early Cold War years, including nuclear arms, reflecting Washington's response to Soviet conventional military superiority on the ground in Europe.

Since China dominates the East Asian mainland, different geographical conditions apply in the new bipolar system concentrated on East Asia. The superpowers are not confronting each other on land but at sea. In contrast to the Cold War, when continental Europe was the power center and critical to the balance of power between the superpowers, maritime East Asia is the new power center. This new geopolitical space where rivalry and military confrontation are concentrated in the twenty-first century allows for new security dynamics and balancing behavior. The stopping power of water in East Asia limits Washington's and Beijing's power-projection capabilities, makes it difficult for the superpowers to challenge each other's respective spheres of influence, and makes both states less vulnerable to a first strike. Bodies of water create significant power-projection problems for attacking armies.[10]

In contrast to the "European continental system,"[11] homeland invasion and territorial conquest are less likely to occur among the major regional actors in maritime East Asia.[12] Amphibious invasions have always been difficult, and current technology trends make maritime East Asia "defense dominant."[13] Thanks to satellites and long-range detection technologies, attackers are unlikely to achieve surprise. Antiship missiles and strong air and ground forces make it dangerous to move naval forces near an enemy's coast. Water barriers constrain the PLA from expanding into maritime East Asia and potentially invading Japan, a key U.S. ally. Similarly, the United States would find it very difficult to invade China. A potential attack by the Soviet Red Army on Western Europe during the early Cold War years posed an existential threat to European states and a much larger challenge to U.S. credibility than protecting U.S. maritime allies in today's East Asia does. This situation heightened fear and tensions in Europe because the threat could only be deterred with nuclear weapons. Geopolitics postpones similar security dynamics in contemporary East Asia. East Asian geopolitics produces less fear and subdues strong balancing even with the return of bipolarity.

Not only was the United States forced to rely on nuclear deterrence in Europe, but in an age without intercontinental ballistic missiles, Washington had to depend on the use of air bases and a militarily strong foothold on the European continent to fight a war against the Soviet Union.[14] We should therefore not be surprised by the absence of strong balancing behavior in contemporary U.S.-China relations, given that the two superpowers do not have large militaries located on the same landmass with a common border but instead are separated by water,[15] and also given that the United States can rely on its conventional naval superiority to balance China naval ambitions. Moreover, the United States sought to deter the Soviet Union from attacking its allies in Europe, many of which bordered the Soviet Union and Warsaw Pact countries. In contrast, the United States has no allies in East Asia directly bordering China, and most are protected by the stopping power of water. Because of geography, the United States and its allies neither fear nor feel threatened by a Chinese invasion as Western Europe feared and felt threatened by the Soviet Red Army. The proximity in Europe of the two adversaries' armies and a "sort of common border" cannot be underestimated.[16] Despite a roughly similar bipolar distribution of capabilities, the incentive for strong balancing is not as compelling in contemporary East Asia as it was in Europe during the previous bipolar era.

The Role of Power Vacuums

Geographical conditions in Europe precipitated arms racing and the creation of formal military alliances to deter an existential threat during the early Cold War years. Orthodox historians have maintained that the Soviet Union caused the Cold War through a mix of expansionism, uncompromising ideology, and Stalin's personality. Accordingly, the origins of the Cold War in Europe were driven by fears of the Soviet Union's land power and its ambition to establish spheres of influence and regional hegemony. Washington was forced to respond. Soviet expansion altered the balance of power in Europe and compelled the United States to restore it. Conversely, revisionist Cold War historians have contended that the United States was not simply reacting to Soviet aggression but was itself a "self-consciously expansionist power in search of prosperity and security."[17] Some sort of synthesis was developed by the postrevisionist historians, who considered both superpowers to be at fault, but with an additional emphasis on the agency of European countries that sought to "invite" and "at least to some extent" promote a strong American role in postwar Europe.[18]

Irrespective of who was to blame for the Cold War in Europe, there is no geopolitical power vacuum to fill in contemporary East Asia comparable to the geopolitical space that opened up on the European continent with the defeat of Germany in World War II. This accounts for the different patterns of balancing behavior. Historical lessons and the experiences of land invasions from the West had taught the Soviet leaders that strong land power and a buffer zone in Eastern Europe were essential to Soviet security in the aftermath of the Second World War. In contrast, China has consolidated its power on the East Asian mainland, and the country has never been more secure from external threats since the establishment of the PRC. China's dominating land power and the stopping power of water give China security from any invasion from sea or land. Less fear and fewer threat perceptions serve to restrain balancing measures.[19]

With few geographical barriers on the European continent, there was a strong fear in the West that the Soviet Red Army would march into West Germany and overrun Western Europe within weeks. As Walter Lippman wrote in 1947,

> the westward expansion of the Russian frontier and of the Russian sphere of influence, though always a Russian aim, was accomplished when, as, and because the Red Army defeated the German army and advanced to the center of Europe. . . . It is the threat that the Red Army may advance still farther west—into Italy, into western Germany, into Scandinavia—that gives the Kremlin and the native communist parties of western Europe an abnormal and intolerable influence in the affairs of the European continent.[20]

Kennan also stressed the importance of this geopolitical transformation "to all thinking about the Soviet problem."[21] The military strength of the Soviet Union was not seen as an immediate threat prior to the Second World

War. World War II changed all this completely, with the Soviet Union filling the power vacuum in Eastern and Central Europe after defeating Nazi Germany.[22] No such geopolitical dynamic or power vacuum is present in contemporary East Asia.

East Asia: A Land-Sea Region

The patterns of behavior at the start of the Cold War bipolar system are different from those in the era of U.S.-China bipolarity. These observations strengthen and add to the argument that structural realism largely draws on European experiences and that the theory is Eurocentric. It has been argued that the concentration of power on the European continent triggered counterbalancing coalitions throughout history, while the preponderant naval power of the United States has not provoked similar balancing behavior. Attentiveness to the distinction between a "global maritime system" and a "relatively autonomous continental system" shows that states are more inclined to balance against land powers than sea powers. The "Eurocentric bias in the balance of power theory . . . fails to recognize that the strong tendency toward counterhegemonic balancing in the European system during the last five centuries has not been replicated in the global maritime system."[23] While agreeing with Levy and Thompson that we need to distinguish between land and sea powers and between the global maritime system and a European continental system, we also need to distinguish between regions.[24]

East Asia is not a relatively autonomous continental system, as is Europe, but instead a relatively dynamic regional land-sea system. If France, Germany, or Russia had occupied the entire European continent, they would have achieved regional hegemony. Geographically, China today controls an area as large as the entire European continent, from the Urals to Portugal and from Gibraltar to Norway's North Cape. The geographical sizes of China, Europe, and the United States are roughly similar, close to ten million square kilometers. That said, China is far from being a regional hegemon. To obtain such a position, it would have to control maritime East Asia and its vital SLOCs, similar to how the United States came to control the North American continent and then the region's adjacent waters and the Caribbean Sea. Distinctive geopolitics leads to different balancing.

Geographical Terrain

The terrain of Europe and that of mainland East Asia are also different. The European continent is relatively flat, with few natural barriers in comparison to mainland East Asia, where Chinese expansion is constrained by jungles and mountains to the south, the Himalayas to the southwest, deserts to the west and northwest, permafrost in the north, and water to the east.[25] The relatively flat geographical terrain in Europe was not an obstacle to potential land expansionism on Moscow's part, contributing to insecurity in Western Europe. This flat terrain also created insecurity in Moscow and compelled Soviet leaders to seek security buffers in Eastern Europe. As Morgenthau noted, "there exists, then, no natural obstacle to invasion on the western frontier of Russia, either on the part of the Soviet Union or on the part of the Soviet Union's western neighbors."[26]

Structural realists have long argued that the international system tends toward balance and that balancing against the United States is just a matter of time in the post–Cold War era.[27] But this thesis was never sufficiently developed. The proposition relied too much on neorealist theory and its foundation in European experiences, and it underestimated the importance of geography and regional differences. Had Germany, France, or Russia in the post–Cold War period shifted the distribution of power in the international system toward bipolarity and similarly experienced the phenomenal economic growth of China and its attendant increased military and civilian capabilities, it is likely that, based on its geography and historical experiences, Europe would have witnessed strong balancing and back-to-the-future scenarios, as some realists predicted in the early 1990s.[28] For instance, it is highly unlikely that the United States would have rebalanced to the Asia-Pacific (1) had the Russian economy been ten times larger and its defense spending more than twice of what it is today and (2) had China's GDP been only 6 percent of the U.S. economy, that is, similar in size to Russia's economy today. But that is not the case. China's economy is more than 60 percent of that of the United States'.

Contrary to the belief that structure has universal applicability, a roughly similar bipolar systemic distribution of capabilities does not produce similar effects. Put differently, at times, "geography trumps structure."[29] The post–World War II Eurocentric bipolar system produced strong internal balancing. The contemporary bipolar system concentrated on East Asia has not produced similar behavior. The unique geographical conditions of East Asia, its terrain, and the importance of the stopping power of water postpone contemporary strong balancing in East Asia. Geopolitics is a necessary explanatory factor in accounting for different patterns of behavior when comparing the bipolar systems of the twentieth and twenty-first centuries, but at least four other unit-level factors shaping U.S. and Chinese balancing behavior should be considered when explaining why contemporary strong balancing has been postponed in East Asia even as the international system returns to bipolarity.

ADDITIONAL UNIT-LEVEL FACTORS

The lack of economic interdependence and an international institutional order, strong ideological rivalry, and the role of nuclear weapons are factors that scholars maintain have shaped strong balancing during the Cold War–era bipolar system. Some of these factors are also said to be vital in distinguishing U.S.-China rivalry in the contemporary globalized and interdependent system from the great-power politics of the nineteenth and twentieth centuries.[30] This book focuses on how structural changes alter balancing behavior, stability, and security dynamics but seeks to add geopolitics to structural realism in order to explain different systemic effects when analyzing bipolarity. However, structural and unit-level causes interact. The rest of this chapter considers the explanatory power of certain additional unit-level factors in explaining why strong balancing has been postponed in contemporary U.S.-China relations and establishes a hierarchy of causes that distinguishes between the systemic and the unit level of analysis.

Economic Interdependence and Globalization

In contrast to the Cold War, when the Soviet Union and the United States had limited trade relations and interaction, China is today a major force in the world economy, and interaction between the United States and China includes extensive political, economic, institutional, cultural, and military exchanges and cooperation. As the previous bipolar system was characterized by economic independence and strong balancing between West and East, China's interconnection with the global economy and Sino-U.S. economic interdependence may well have moderated strong balancing in U.S.-China relations.

It is often argued that economic interdependence and cultural exchange promote cooperation and prevent confrontation in Sino-U.S. relations.[31] Accordingly, the more extensive contacts and trade that take place between countries make war and strong balancing more costly and therefore less likely.[32] In considering the effects of economic interdependence on the balancing behavior of different states, it is useful to distinguish between interdependence, dependence, and independence.

Interdependence, understood as mutual dependence, is likely to foster more stability than dependence. Interdependence constrains the actions of the United States and China and promotes stability because both are expected avoid undermining their trade relationships. China's growing economic clout makes balancing against it less likely. At the same time, the historical evidence of the years prior to World War I and the period between 1919 and 1939 show that an open, liberal, and interconnected world economy can be undone "through the actions of states responding to recession through increased protectionism"[33] and that arms racing, alliances, and wars cannot be prevented by economic interdependence or extensive cultural and diplomatic interaction alone.[34] Some of the most friction-creating issues in contemporary Sino-U.S. relations are related to the economy and Chinese trade, especially as the United States grows increasingly concerned about relative, not only absolute, gains in its trade relations with China. However, despite the emphasis on economic interdependence in U.S.-China relations, in 2015 only about 8 percent of American exports, worth about 0.7 percent of GDP, go to China. Conversely, about 17 percent of China's exports, worth about 4 percent of GDP, go to the United States.[35]

Hveem and Pempel remind us that focusing on trade per se "does not take into account the increased complexity of today's international economic relations."[36] Cross-border trade in products is only a minor portion of the modern global economic activity of complex transnational production networks. As Christensen stresses, "crude measures of trade do not capture the newer forces of globalization" that are based on transnational production networks.[37] U.S. companies rely on the Chinese market and have outsourced much of their manufacturing operations to China. Economic growth in both countries is tied to pressures of globalization and the effects of a capitalist-oriented system.[38] The novelty of today's interdependence and globalization, argues Steinfeld, lies in how companies are pulled "into complex production hierarchies" and how so many different kinds of industries organize production on a worldwide basis.[39]

China's Economic Ties with Regional States

The Soviet Union relied on the threat and use of military of force in the shape of the Red Army to advance and safeguard its economic and security interests. This is why Cold War crises became so intense and dangerous. Given China's economic position in a globalized economy, it has more tools and leverage at its disposal in its foreign and security policy, enabling signaling at lower levels of tension and conflict management, including the willingness to compromise, at lower levels of violence.[40] China does not need to threaten to use military force or undertake a strong military buildup to advance and safeguard its interests. It can rely instead on its economic power to influence both its neighbors and, increasingly, countries in the Middle East, Africa, Latin America, and Europe, in a way that the Soviet Union never could. This affects the way in which a given kind of polarity shapes the workings of the international system. The use of economic strength can influence the operations of bipolarity in ways not seen in the Soviet case.

This might account for the lack of strong balancing in U.S.-China relations and within East Asia. China can use its growing economic strength to undermine U.S. interests and relationships with allies and use sanctions, protectionism, embargos, boycotts, investments, and its huge market as leverage. This may increase tensions and friction between the United States and its allies and incite balancing behavior in Sino-U.S. relations while avoiding, nonetheless, the strong balancing and arms race of the previous bipolar era. China is now the largest export market for most East Asian states, and the GDP of many of them depends on these exports. Ross, however, has demonstrated that economic power in the absence of military power cannot determine small-state alignments.[41] Singapore, Malaysia, and

Australia depend on exports to China for economic stability and growth at home, but they have sought closer strategic and military ties with Washington following Beijing's growing assertiveness and relative power shift. Security concerns and U.S. superiority in maritime East Asia rather than economic considerations and Chinese market power have shaped their alignment preferences.[42]

China, Globalization, and Market Forces

According to some, access to strategic resources rather than ideology will lie at the heart of U.S.-Sino rivalries in the future, with the new "great game" most likely being played out in Africa.[43] China's actions abroad are not "missionary . . . seeking to spread an ideology or a system of government," Kaplan notes, but are instead "propelled by [China's] need to secure energy, metals, and strategic minerals." Accordingly, China's activities overseas should be understood as a core national interest, that is, economic survival. China simply has "no choice in the matter." Kaplan further thinks that "China's worldwide scouring for resources brings it into conflict with the missionary-oriented United States, as well as with countries such as India and Russia."[44]

Survival of the CCP and the PRC is, of course, a core national interest to Chinese leaders. However, competition for natural resources and petroleum reserves overseas does not threaten China's economic survival. Its core national interests do not require safeguarding natural resources in Africa, the Middle East, Central Asia, Latin America, Europe, or the Arctic, resources China largely buys on the international petroleum and commodities market. China's core national interest is to safeguard its sovereignty and territorial integrity in East Asia and corresponding waters.[45]

China has not developed a strategy to "secure" overseas resources while adapting to its increasing reliance on imported natural resources and petroleum. China has primarily relied on the international market, trade, and globalization to provide for its resource needs. China does not have the power-projection capability to protect Chinese companies' production and resource extraction overseas or to safeguard the sea lanes of communication that transport resources back to China. Instead of "securing" and "locking up" resources overseas and shipping them back home, mercantilist fashion,

China has sought to manage the risks associated with its growing reliance on overseas resources and to hedge against peacetime risk scenarios, such as environmental disasters, terrorism, piracy, accidents, embargoes, sanctions, and conflict or wars that do not directly involve China but may cause shocks in the international petroleum and commodities market. Even in a wartime scenario, China's domestic energy supplies, high self-sufficiency, and hedging strategies provide for China's energy security.[46]

This pattern of behavior distinguishes current U.S.-China relations from U.S.-Soviet economic *in*dependence, limited economic cooperation, and global confrontation and rivalry. There is little evidence to suggest that China and the United States will be pulled into a "new great game" of proxy wars to safeguard strategic resources. Supposedly, in order to safeguard and promote its overseas petroleum interests and balance the United States, China could have supported Saddam Hussein when the United States invaded Iraq in 2003. Instead, China remained reserved. Through investments and collaboration in joint ventures with leading Western oil companies after the war, Chinese oil companies had become the largest external actor in the Iraqi upstream oil market by 2010.[47] Instead of balancing the United States, Beijing collaborated with Washington to impose several rounds of sanctions on Iran between 2006 and 2010—while simultaneously trading and investing in Iran. This did not lead to any confrontation and conflict between China and the United States. China is now the largest consumer of oil from Saudi Arabia, one of the United States' closest allies in the Middle East, without raising the risk of Sino-American confrontations or balancing actions. China has become a leading trading partner with Central Asian states, even taking market shares from Russia and allowing Central Asian republics to diversify away from their traditional dependence on the Russian petroleum sector, without undermining its strategic partnership with Russia.

Mutual independence provided stability during the Cold War. The extent to which the Soviet Union and the United States were independent of each other, wrote John Lewis Gaddis in 1986, "the fact that there have been so few points of economic leverage available to each, the fact that two such dissimilar people have had so few opportunities for interaction," created in itself a structural support for stable relations between the two countries, irrespective of the actions of the respective governments.[48] Economic independence might have contributed to peace and stability during the Cold War, but it did not prevent strong balancing in the form of arms racing and alliance formation.

It is tempting to conclude that independence contributed to strong balancing in the previous bipolar system and that interdependence explains the moderate balancing in the contemporary bipolar system. But the historical record is not clear on the relationship between interdependence, balancing, and conflict. At times, economic interdependence has been insufficient to prevent strong balancing and constrain conflict and wars. Economic interdependence is not sufficient to trump the importance of geopolitics. Without East Asia's unique geopolitics and the stopping power of water, the United States and China may well have taken strong balancing measures despite their economic interdependence. If China continues to close in on the United States powerwise, more successfully masters the geographical challenges in turning itself into both a leading land and sea power, and more forcefully challenges the United States and its allies in East Asian waters, the United States will likely respond by strong balancing, boosting defense spending, and seeking to contain China despite economic interdependence and close diplomatic, cultural, and educational ties.

An Established World Order

Any international institutional order is established, maintained, and changed by the rise and fall of superpowers and great powers. Hegemonic wars have traditionally changed an order, with a new governance of the system arising from the new distribution of power and new structural conditions.[49] The Concert of Europe following the French Revolution and the Napoleonic Wars, the League of Nations following World War I, the United Nations and the Bretton Woods system following World War II, and the "one-hub global system"[50] following the end of the Cold War are all examples of new institutional orders established under the modern international state system. The transition from a unipolar to a new bipolar system has not been shaped by a hegemonic war that reordered international institutions. The United States has not been removed from its superpower position, as was the Soviet Union after its collapse. The old mechanisms for overturning international orders, as Ikenberry points out, just do not work today.[51] Instead, China is closing in on the United States and widening the gap between it and the next-strongest power through a peaceful process of power change.

In contrast to the Soviet Union, which had its own economic bloc with a Soviet socioeconomic system and political structures, China has tied itself to the liberal capitalist system and has been unwilling to undermine the basis of its economic growth and prosperity by challenging the existing institutional world order.[52] Chinese leaders recognize that China's phenomenal economic growth is a result of the post-Mao economic reforms instituted by the December 1978 third plenum of the Eleventh Central Committee of the Chinese Communist Party, which saw China embrace "Markets over Mao,"[53] including liberalization of trade, foreign direct investments, and the rise of a large private sector in the economy.[54] China has sought integration with the global economic system and world order dominated by the United States.[55] China's "joining" of international regimes and the liberal international order has been "remarkable," even though China simultaneously has worked to influence and shape the way regimes work and the international order evolves.[56]

The superpowers will increasingly compete in a new bipolar system, but the existence of an international institutional order alleviates global confrontation and rivalry between China and the United States. The cost of changing the international institutional order would be high insofar as the existing order is not in ruins, China lacks an alternative world order, and as China benefits more from integration with the existing order than from undermining it.[57] In the absence of a hegemonic war, which shaped the post–World War II bipolar period and a new world order, U.S.-Chinese interaction in the new bipolar system has evolved on more amicable terms. Gilpin's "law of uneven growth" has yet to move the world toward another round of hegemonic conflict.[58] The changed distribution of capabilities and the resultant polarity shift from unipolarity to bipolarity may have brought about a more balanced international system, but it has not spawned a new international institutional order. It has pushed China and the United States toward balancing but not strong balancing. Simultaneously, we cannot conclude with Ikenberry that nuclear deterrence and the dominance of democracies have "eliminated" the "traditional mechanism for order destruction and building."[59]

A Changing World Order

The contemporary American-led liberal institutional order is increasingly challenged by China's attempts to take advantage of the existing order and reconfigure it to fit its rising-power status and growing interests.[60] According to Gregory Shaffer and Henry Gao, China has become "a serious rival to the U.S. and Europe in the development and enforcement of international trade law."[61] Shifts in the distribution of capabilities are shaping how the rising power views the costs and benefits of changing the international institutional order. With an enhanced power position, and in accordance with Gilpin's predictions of rising powers, China has started to challenge the status quo "as the perceived potential benefits begin to exceed the perceived cost of undertaking a change in the system."[62] China has recently been willing to risk its benign security environment by more assertively securing its interests and antagonizing its neighbors and the United States.[63]

While China has yet to develop a robust strategy to replace the current world order or confront and challenge the United States globally, there are clear signs that it is ready and willing to challenge and balance U.S. primacy and promote an alternative international institutional order, including the establishment of the China-led Asian Infrastructure Investment Bank (AIIB), the Shanghai-based BRICS New Development Bank, China's ambitious Belt and Road initiative, China's leadership in the Shanghai Cooperation Organization (SCO), and its increased collaboration with Russia in opposing the United States in the UN Security Council.

It is not just the East Asian states that look to China for economic development. This is also the case for many states in Central Asia, Europe, the Middle East, Africa, Oceania, and Latin America. China rivals the United States in influence in Southeast Asia, Central Asia, and Africa.[64] China has become an important economic and diplomatic partner for states in the Middle East[65] and Latin America and is developing ties with American allies in Europe.

The new Silk Road Economic Belt and Twenty-First Century Maritime Silk Road Initiative[66] involves the construction of infrastructure and linking of economic relations across Central Asia and South Asia, enhancing cooperation and developing intraregional markets with China in a leading role.[67] China's ambitious strategy has the potential to become a new land-and-sea-based order that challenges the U.S. maritime order. Based on high-speed railway links between China and Europe, the strategy is an illustration of Mackinder's "heartland" thesis,[68] launched at a time when the United States was pulling out of Afghanistan and downsizing its presence in Central Asia and the Middle East. As one leading Chinese international affairs scholar has put it, China should "March West" all the way to Europe and participate in development projects "that will reshape China's geostrategic vision as well as the Eurasian landscape."[69]

However, China is not simply a land power; it is a hybrid. Although China is predominantly a continental power pursuing an interior strategy, it is also a maritime power with a strong determination to develop sea power.[70] China controls a huge littoral of East Asian waters and has a large maritime and shipping sector with one of the world's largest merchant fleets, and, being one of the three largest shipbuilders in the world, it is much more dependent on SLOCs and seaborne trade than previous continental powers.[71] Thus, China's economic belt on the Eurasian landmass is likely to have routes through Pakistan, Myanmar, Bangladesh, Afghanistan, and Iran, which will link the continental strategy with China's Maritime Silk Road ambitions. China's port calls and investments in port infrastructure around the Indian Ocean and in Southeast Asia boost China's commercial interests and trading system while complementing its overseas military presence by providing logistic support. Additionally, China has expressed a growing interest in the Arctic region. As the climate warms, the Arctic ice cap is retreating, creating commercial, strategic, diplomatic, military, and resource-harvesting opportunities.[72]

Geographically, the Indian Ocean and the Arctic Ocean are the southern and northern flanks of the Eurasian landmass. A stronger Chinese presence in these regions in the decades ahead, through investments in shipping and infrastructure along the Northern Sea Route and the Maritime Silk Road, will enhance China's Belt and Road initiative. Since China remains a huge littoral state, it might add three oceanic frontiers to Mackinder's "heartland" in Eurasia and potentially overcome some of the challenges in controlling the heartland envisioned in the past. This could provide China with a favorable geopolitical position and an opportunity to "command the world islands"—Asia, Europe, and Africa—in the twenty-first century, thereby creating a new and alternative order via its geoeconomic ambitions. China could in the twenty-first century rise to a position in which it dominates Eurasia and the sea lanes in Asian waters and Indian Ocean.[73] If successful, the Belt and Road initiative could mark a new geopolitical era.

However, there are several challenges to this long-term strategy. Eurasia lacks an order similar to that upheld by the United States in the maritime domain, and China has not developed any international institutional order similar to the American-led liberal order to promote its ambitions on the Eurasian continent.[74] To advance its influence and provide stability for its trade routes, China might need to develop a new order on the Eurasia landmass, but it is not clear how China will overcome resistance from the great powers Russia and India and other states that might resent China's growing influence, including the stronger Islamic countries and societies. It also remains to be seen whether the new trade routes are commercially viable and whether China can sustain economic growth to maintain the necessary investments in infrastructure throughout Eurasia. China may face a strategic overstretch as it seeks to become both a dominating land and sea power but still need to focus on domestic reforms and modernization. Finally, China's Belt and Road initiative might face so much geopolitical tension and conflict in Eurasia and in East Asian waters that it might undermine China peaceful rise.

Ikenberry considers the international system as unipolar in arguing that in "the decades ahead, as China rises, the world could well turn into a bipolar system—but one with only one global hub."[75] However, by geopolitically combining its land and sea power and its growing economic power, China could develop an alternative "hub" and world order. The current U.S.-led international order could shrink into largely a maritime "hub" and no longer a global "hub" if there is an alternative "hub" on the Eurasian continent, China's Maritime Silk Road, and China's dominating role in free-trade agreements in the Asia Pacific to challenge it. China is clearly trying to capitalize on the power vacuum created by the Trump administration's withdrawal from the Trans-Pacific Partnership and the Paris climate agreement. U.S. retrenchment, growing isolationism, and an "America first" strategy could allow China to position itself as a leader of a new or alternative international "hub" and order.

The main point here is not to speculate about whether China will succeed in its ambitions but to emphasize how developments are consequences and effects of the shift in the distribution of capabilities and a new bipolar system. Unit-level factors and the election of Trump in the United States matter, of course, but China could never have filled any power vacuum or pursued its ambitious Belt and Road initiative without the contemporary power shifts. The existing international institutional order helps mitigate strong balancing at the start of a new U.S.-China bipolar system. However, the shift from a unipolar to a bipolar system and the relative rise of China and relative decline of the United States and other great and major powers allow China to challenge the existing international institutional order, balance against the United States, and promote a new regional and potential new world order. If China continues to strengthen its relative power, increased balancing may eventually lead to strong balancing irrespective of the existing international institutional order.

Ideology and Credibility

The sharply divided anticommunist/procapitalism and procommunist/ anticapitalist polarities of the Cold War years were based on incompatible ideologies.[76] Liberalism and communism were mutually exclusive. Communists believed capitalism would inevitably be replaced by communism and that any coexistence of the two systems could never be permanent.[77] Ideological beliefs assured Soviet leaders that the capitalist powers, led by the United States, would sooner or later be minded to seek war with the Soviet Union to circumvent political frustrations and difficulties to which capitalism is supposedly prone.[78] Ideology shaped American foreign policy in a similar fashion.[79] The ideological rivalry stoked arms racing, shaped alliance formations, and committed the United States and the Soviet Union to an aggressive stance. As Hobsbawm writes, "both sides thus found themselves committed to an insane arms race to mutual destruction."[80]

Conflicting ideologies constrain U.S.-China relations, but ideological confrontation does not fuel balancing as it did during the previous bipolar era. The persistence of conflicting ideologies and divergent views about good governance and human rights do not resemble the deep-seated ideological hostilities that helped kickstart the Cold War and the strong balancing and containment in U.S.-Soviet relations. The mix of cooperation and conflict in contemporary U.S.-China relations is worlds apart from the Red Menace scaremongering, propaganda campaigns, apocalyptic rhetoric, and arms race of the Cold War.[81] The Cold War was a struggle for the balance of power but also a contest between competing and "in many ways mutually exclusive ideational blueprints for constructing international political orders."[82] The Cold War literature has shown the close links between Chinese, Korean, and Russian communist regimes in the late 1940s and early 1950s. The ideological affinities of Mao, Stalin, and Kim shaped strong balancing and the evolution of the Cold War in Europe and East Asia.[83] Archives will show to what extent Chinese, Russian, and North Korean leaders' interests and ideologies converge today, but few consider Russia's aggression in Ukraine or Chinese assertiveness in East Asian waters as a worldwide communist or authoritarian conspiracy.[84]

Additionally, as the international system returns to bipolarity, it is not accompanied by the socioeconomic transformation unleashed by the Second World War. East and West not only based their ideologies and worldviews on incompatible assumptions, but the chaos following the collapse of the Axis powers created a power vacuum in Europe and Asia, with communist infiltration threatening a political revolution in many countries. The danger feared by the Truman administration in the initial stages of the Cold War "was that the Europeans were so dispirited, discouraged, and demoralized by the war's destruction that they might turn to communism out of desperation for a 'quick fix' to their economic difficulties."[85] The Truman Doctrine, announced in 1947 to assist anticommunist regimes, emphasized that the "greatest danger presented to us by Soviet policy is still its attempt to promote internecine division and conflict within our system of alliances and within our body politics." As Kennan further noted,

> there are great areas of softness and vulnerability in the non-communist world, [thus] the problem of containment is basically a problem of the reactions of people within the non-communist world . . . the things that need most to be done to prevent the further expansion of Soviet power are not, so far as we are concerned, things we can do directly in our relations with the Soviet Government; they are things we must do in our relations with the peoples of the non-communist world.[86]

The United States needs to manage its alliances in the face of China's growing assertiveness and coercive diplomacy, but contemporary East Asia is neither chaotic, nor in ruins, nor devastated by war. East Asian countries today are not desperately seeking economic and security aid. Instead, most

U.S. allies are stable and prosperous democracies, part of the regional U.S. alliance system, and protected by the stopping power of water. In contrast to the situation in Europe and Asia in the post–World War II period, there is little fear that East Asian states in desperation will fall into the "China bloc." In the 1940s, when the Soviet Union was spurring Communist Party activity in Europe, European communist parties won more than 20 percent of the votes in elections and participated in governing coalitions. There are few political opposition parties in China's neighboring states that obtain such electoral support and simultaneously seek to bring their countries into the fold of China's authoritarian ideological camp, thereby fostering ideological confrontation between China and the United States. Put differently, Beijing and Washington are not at loggerheads over the hearts and minds of the "non-China bloc." Less ideological hostility helps account for the absence of contemporary strong balancing in U.S.-China relations.

THE ROLE OF NUCLEAR WEAPONS

Even if the international structure "shapes and shoves," one unit-level variable that undeniably affects great powers' strategic behavior is the possession of nuclear weapons.[87] Some have questioned whether China has a nuclear second-strike capability, but the consensus among most scholars is that once China went mobile, it had second-strike capability.[88] Technological developments such as the development of long-range precision guided weapons and the U.S. ambitions for a missile defense, in addition to the Joint Concept for Access and Maneuver in the Global Commons (JAM-GC) and the so-called third offset, which focuses on machine, drone, and network-centric warfare, are forcing the Chinese to modernize and adjust their nuclear-defense posture.[89] Biddle and Oelrich, however, have emphasized that land-based and road-mobile missile launchers are very hard to strike and that the defense has an advantage over the offense.[90]

An authoritative assessment of China's nuclear forces in 2016 points out that China has deployed twenty-five DF-31As in four brigades. The DF-31A is a solid-fueled, three-stage, road-mobile ICBM designed to target most of the continental United States. The total numbers of ICBMs are estimated to be between fifty and seventy-five. In addition to the DF-31A, China has about ten DF-5As and thirty DF-5Bs, some carrying multiple warheads.[91] China has also made improvements in developing SSBNs. The Pentagon now reports that four Jin-class SSBNs are in service and that a fifth is being built. The PLAN reported in 2013 that it conducted a successful at-sea launch of the JL-2 missile. It is not clear whether the JL-2 has been tested to its full range of 7,000-plus kilometers, but it is believed that warheads have already been produced for the forty-eight JL-2s that the four existing SSBNs can carry. According to the Pentagon, this provides China with its first viable sea-based nuclear detterent.[92] The JL-2 missile has insufficient range to target the continental United States from Chinese waters, but China is already developing its next generation of SSBNs, the Type 096, with missiles able to reach most if not all of the continental United States.[93]

The fact that both the United States and China have nuclear second-strike capabilities at the start of a new bipolar system is likely to have a different effect on balancing than when neither superpower possessed such capabilities. However, Washington and Moscow pursued strong balancing in the early 1980s after achieving second-strike capabilities, in which case second-strike capability should not be taken as an impediment to strong balancing.

Sustaining the balance of power in Europe during the Cold War forced the United States to confront the Soviet Red Army on the European continent. It could not rely on naval superiority. These geographical factors instigated the creation of formal military alliances and an arms race during the early Cold War, including nuclear arms, reflecting Washington's response to Moscow's conventional military (army) superiority.[94] The Soviet atomic test and development of the hydrogen bomb and intercontinental missiles eroded U.S. nuclear supremacy. With both sides developing second-strike capability and mutually assured destruction, an imbalance in conventional forces was replaced by a nuclear terror balance that effectively stabilized the European continent.

In contemporary East Asia, the United States can rely on conventional weapons and naval supremacy to deter China from expanding into a regional hegemon. While Beijing and Washington seek to modernize and expand their nuclear capabilities, there is no arms race, since nuclear deterrence has already been achieved. Second-strike capability, the stopping power of water, and the difficult terrain of the Asian mainland provide strong guarantees for survival and fewer incentives for strong balancing.

Nuclear weapons do not preclude strong balancing or war between nuclear powers, but a nuclear second-strike capability will likely inspire more caution and moderation on the part of the superpowers and great powers than in the past.[95] Once a great power develops nuclear weapons, it will make sense to rely on asymmetric strategies instead of competing in spiraling, conventional, zero-sum arms races. Moreover, entering a formal alliance with a great power in order to balance another great power or coalition of states may be dangerous, the more so when nuclear weapons are part of the equation. If, say, contemporary China and Russia established a close alliance and one of them decided to use tactical or strategic nuclear weapons, the other would risk entrapment in a horrendous nuclear showdown.[96] This predicament was not an issue when the Sino-Soviet Treaty of Friendship, Alliance, and Mutual Assistance was signed in February 1950.

Nuclear weapons do not eliminate balancing and balance-of-power politics,[97] but they may weaken the incentives and postpone strong balancing. Together with geographical conditions, the spread of nuclear weapons deters strong balancing in the U.S.-China relationship in this new bipolar era.

CONCLUSION

Eventually, we have been told, strong U.S.-China balancing behavior and intensive security competition will set in.[98] The unbalanced system of the unipolar era has been replaced by a more balanced bipolar system, and balancing tendencies can be observed in U.S.-China relations. Although the behavior of China and the United States in recent years is gradually fulfilling the predictions of structural realists, the application of the theory is not straightforward. We can develop the argument about the tendency toward balance in the international system further. Neorealism "cannot say when 'tomorrow' will come," writes Waltz, "because international-political theory deals with pressure of structures on states, not with how states will respond to the pressures."[99] A state can escape the "sameness effect" of the system or refuse to conform to successful practices of the past even though such behavior risks disadvantaging the state in the competition among states under anarchy.

Structural constraints may be successfully resisted, for example, as the diplomatic skills and virtuosity of Bismarck allowed him to do from 1871 to 1894. After three wars against Denmark in 1864, Austria in 1866, and France in 1870–1871, the German Empire under Prussian leadership was established in 1871. This shifted the balance of power at the center of Europe. Bismarck managed to prevent the unification of Germany from generating actions of strong balancing and starting a war, something few would have thought possible beforehand.[100] While Goldstein has noted that the comparison should not be pushed too far, he finds China's current grand strategic challenge to be "closer to that of Germany during the last two decades of Bismarck's leadership." China's peaceful rise or development could be seen as another example of how structural effects can be successfully resisted. A polarity shift is likely to trigger more polarization and make it more difficult to manage and sustain U.S.-China relations, which in the 2000s were more cooperative than conflictive.[101]

This suggests that there are degrees, different intensities, and different patterns of balancing behavior even within similar structural conditions. Critics and those seeking to modify neorealism see more variability and change both at the systemic and domestic level.[102] In explaining different balancing behaviors under the multipolar system before the two world wars, Christensen and Snyder emphasized the need to broaden international structures (anarchy and polarity) to include perceptions and misperceptions of the offensive or defensive advantages and of the security-dilemma variables of geography and technology.[103] Similarly, Walt sought to modify neorealism by developing the balance-of-threat theory, which adds geographical proximity, offensive capabilities, and offensive intentions to states' aggregate power.[104]

The superpowers and other states have responded differently to the structural pressures of the bipolar system in the twenty-first century than they did in the twentieth. The balancing behaviors of the two bipolar systems are different in a way that does not correspond with what we would expect from neorealist theory. As long as the structure remains roughly similar, the structural "sameness effect" should be strong, especially when comparing two bipolar systems in which the superpowers mainly rely on internal rather than external balancing, but questions still loom about the content and intensity of balancing, questions that neorealism is unable to answer satisfactorily. Geostructural realism captures the presence of structural opportunities and constraints and why balancing is increasing, but it also explains why balancing changes as the power center in the new bipolar system moves from continental Europe to the land-sea region of East Asia and as rivalries and the balance of power move from land to sea.

The stopping power of water and the nature of East Asian geopolitics mitigate the effects of relative power shifts, moderate the challenge posed by a rising China to the regional balance of power, produce less fear, and dampen threat perceptions, with the result that strong balancing is delayed. Additional factors mediate and reinforce the postponement of strong balancing. There would possibly have been more balancing were there a strong ideological rivalry, less economic interdependence, and a fragile international institutional order—and if the superpowers did not both have a second-strike nuclear capability. Nonetheless, these additional factors remain secondary and geopolitics primary in explaining why strong balancing has been postponed in the new bipolar system.

If we imagine a scenario involving (1) the removal of the main islands of Japan to the Yellow and East China Sea, (2) Japan suddenly sharing a long land border with China, and (3) U.S. troops in Japan stationed along the Sino-Japanese border, that would describe a geopolitical configuration more similar to the East-West divide in Europe. Under such geostructural conditions, the current bipolar system would more likely resemble the strong balancing in Europe at the start of the last bipolar era, irrespective of today's economic interdependence, an established international institutional order, limited ideological rivalry, and the existence of a second-strike nuclear capability. Moreover, the unit-level causes discussed cannot adequately explain the shift from limited unipolar balancing to moderate bipolar balancing. Geostructural realism instead explains increased balancing to be a result of the shifting distribution of capabilities while showing how the unique geographical conditions of East Asia, including the geographical terrain of the East Asian mainland and the respective U.S. and Chinese maritime and continental spheres of influence, shape the degree of balancing and are putting contemporary strong balancing in East Asia on hold despite the return of bipolarity.

Chapter 6

U.S.-CHINA RELATIONS AND THE RISK OF WAR

A system of two superpowers is likely to be more stable than a system of three or more great powers. The return of bipolarity matters if we want to gauge the possibility of war between the United States and China over the course of the twenty-first century. While neorealism presupposes the sameness of features across systems of similar polarity, we know that multipolar systems in the past have been alternately stable and war prone. Waltz's theory says nothing about the fact that bipolar stability is *relative*. A bipolar system concentrated on one region will be more or less stable than a bipolar system concentrated on a different region, according to geostructural realism.

A major war between two superpowers possessing nuclear weapons remains unlikely.[1] China and the United States are deterred by the costs of nuclear exchange.[2] Nonetheless, that there will be a limited war directly involving the United States and China in maritime East Asia is more likely than the risk of war emerging from superpower rivalry in continental Europe during the previous bipolar system. Chapter 5 argued that the competition between the United States and China will not reprise the U.S.-Soviet pattern of strong balancing, because the two contemporary rivals are separated by a vast body of water, which diminishes the U.S. threat to China and the Chinese threat to American allies in Asia. However, precisely because a major war is less likely between China and the

United States, and given the complexity of the East Asian strategic landscape, this chapter argues that limited war is more likely to occur than it was in the Soviet-U.S. case. The geographical conditions that postpone strong balancing in contemporary U.S.-China relations increase instability and the likelihood of a limited war involving the superpowers in maritime East Asia.

The land-sea regional geopolitics of East Asia is more dynamic and unstable than the static European geopolitics of the Cold War. If the militaries of either the Warsaw Pact countries or the North Atlantic Treaty Organization (NATO) crossed the East-West divide in Europe during the Cold War, it would probably have triggered a major war, one posing an existential threat and risk of nuclear war. The stakes of inadvertent escalation were so high that they effectively stabilized the European continent. In contrast, the contested areas in East Asia today are in the maritime domain,[3] where a battle at sea could largely be confined to East Asian waters and not pose a direct existential threat in the form of a land invasion. Decision makers might risk a limited war or battle at sea in maritime East Asia, calculating that the possibility of a major war is less likely. The risk of escalation to the use of nuclear weapons is, therefore, less likely; this might paradoxically increase the risk of limited conventional war at sea.

As Osgood explains, a limited war is a war in which the belligerents do not expend all of their resources at their disposal in a specific conflict. A limited war is distinct from a major or unlimited war, in which a state mobilizes all of the resources of society to fight a war. Examples of limited wars are the U.S. involvement in the Korean War and the Vietnam War and the Soviet Union's involvement in the Soviet-Afghan War.[4] A limited war is not as destructive as a major war, but the stakes in a battle at sea between the United States and China will be enormous, regardless, because it will be a contest for regional hegemony in East Asia.[5]

Schelling has written on how geography and physical configurations have helped define the limits to war.[6] A shooting war between the United States and China will clearly come with the added risk of escalation.[7] The main point here, however, is not to speculate about the potential risk of escalation after a limited war erupts. It is an open-ended question: no one can know how a conflict might escalate once the superpowers start shooting at each other. Somewhere in the sequence of events, things could get out of hand. Precisely what would happen is a debatable point. The situation will be both dynamic and uncertain.[8] Geopolitics and water barriers may prevent a major war in East Asia, but they also raise the risk of a limited war between the two superpowers.

The following analysis is divided into two parts. The first part examines how geopolitics makes East Asia more unstable and war prone than Europe was during the previous bipolar system. It focuses on how the stopping power of water can contain a limited war at sea, how China's sea-power ambitions challenges the status quo, how spheres of influences are undermined, how different security buffers heighten the risk of a limited war, and how geographical factors might persuade Chinese leaders to take risks in the belief that China can overcome the asymmetry in U.S.-China power relations in a short, sharp war. When we compare the bipolar systems, we find that the risk of a limited war in Europe was low because of the extreme risk of escalation to all-out war. The risk of a limited war in East Asia is higher because the chances of a war escalating to all-out war are lower. The second part of this chapter contends that the role of nuclear weapons, combined with the number of maritime flashpoints but lack of tripwires, is more likely to trigger crisis and limited war in contemporary East Asia under the current new bipolar system.

GEOGRAPHY AND THE RISK OF A LIMITED WAR

There is a fundamental geopolitical difference between the post–World War II rivalry of the superpowers on the European continent and their early-twenty-first-century contest at sea in East Asia. After Germany's division and the establishment of NATO and the Warsaw Pact, Europe was split into two blocs. By the 1950s, a third world war was seen as the likely outcome of either side invading the other. The Soviet armed forces, which only a few years before the Cold War had defeated Nazi Germany's Wehrmacht in the greatest series of land battles in human history, posed an overwhelming threat to U.S. forces in Europe and U.S. allies in Western Europe. Its inability to match and prevail over Soviet conventional army forces in Europe compelled the United States to introduce the principle of "massive retaliation": a conventional or tactical nuclear Soviet attack on Western Europe or West Berlin would trigger massive retaliation against the Soviet Union with nuclear weapons.[9] This, according to former Secretary of State John Foster Dulles, would force the Soviet Union to "weigh the consequences of invoking nuclear war."[10] The strategy of massive retaliation sought to deter the possibility of limited war in the 1950s by threatening all-out war.

The use of military force by the PLA in East Asian waters is unlikely to pose an existential threat of the same magnitude. Washington can instead rely on its not insignificant conventional forces in a limited war at sea against China in East Asia. It has not developed any strategy akin to "massive retaliation" to deter China and the PLA. U.S. military superiority in the maritime domain and the stopping power of water prevent China from launching an all-out conventional attack on U.S. forces. Although China might use nuclear weapons if invaded and Beijing occupied, it is much less likely, almost inconceivable, that Chinese leaders would risk a nuclear war with the United States because some of its naval ships had been sunk. Similarly, it is not likely that the United States would use nuclear weapons in a confrontation with China. Even should it lose multiple ships, it could remain confident that the Chinese navy could not control East Asian waters and become a regional hegemon within the next decade. In contrast, if the Soviet Red Army attacked and destroyed U.S. forces in Western Europe, the United States was much less confident in its ability to prevent the Soviet Union from gaining the throne as regional hegemon in Europe.

The lower risk of nuclear war in East Asia increases the risk of conventional war at sea. In contrast to continental Europe, the stopping power of water in East Asia makes China, the United States, and U.S. maritime allies less concerned about survival and existential threats. Under these conditions, decision makers in the United States and China might be willing to risk war to solve maritime disputes in East Asia or risk launching a first strike against an opponent's navy, calculating that a full-scale invasion or all-out war would be less likely than if the superpowers were located on the same landmass. Realist writers have emphasized how preventive war is "a natural outgrowth of the balance of power" and of the conditions between a status quo and a revisionist power.[11] Chinese observers have also expressed concern that "the United States might use a local conflict as a pretext to carry out a 'Copenhagen,' a preventive attack, on China's rising naval capabilities."[12]

Geopolitics can be added to the discussion of what makes a preventive war more likely. In the coming decades, Washington might initiate a war in maritime East Asia to forestall a realignment in the regional balance of power and prevent China from developing sufficient capabilities to attack U.S. forces. A future preventive war might also resemble the situation that obtained between a rising and a status quo power in the twentieth century, for example, when Japan attacked U.S. military targets at Pearl Harbor. Chinese leaders, motivated by a desire to achieve regional hegemony, might risk a crippling attack on U.S. forces in order to undermine the U.S. forward naval presence in East Asia. Sino-American competition and rivalry in maritime East Asia will take place in a geographical space more conducive to war than continental Europe.[13]

This argument complicates the view that since East Asia is a seascape, with water separating the dominant power from the rising power, geopolitics becomes an impediment to invasion and that therefore the risk of conflict will be somewhat diminished. "It is because of the seas around East Asia that the twenty-first century has a better chance than the twentieth of avoiding great military conflagrations," writes Kaplan.[14] Water barriers in East Asia create significant power-projection problems for attacking armies, and a limited war at sea does not have to evolve into a major war or bring about as much devastation as a land war on the Eurasian continent. However, a battle at sea between the U.S. and Chinese navies would be a battle for regional hegemony in East Asia and could involve vast military encounters. Water may prevent a third world war, but it also makes an extensive limited war between the superpowers in the first half of the twenty-first century more likely.

When Land Powers Go to Sea

Other geographical conditions heighten the risk of limited war and will shape the relationship between the two twenty-first-century poles. There are few periods in modern history during which a secure, dominating land power could focus on developing naval power and eventually sea power, as China has done today.[15] Most of the Soviet Union's coastline was either frozen or effectively closed off from the seas (the Baltic, Black, and Caspian, and the Sea of Japan), and the Soviet Union was thus mainly a land power concerned with its continental borders. Russia and then the Soviet Union had to maintain separate fleets in the Pacific Ocean, the North Atlantic, and the Baltic and Black seas, and this made it difficult to concentrate naval power or have its fleets support one another. The Soviet Union gradually became more of a global-security actor after the arms deal with Nasser's Egypt in 1955 and by the mid-late Cold War period had developed a strong navy, but it remained preoccupied with security on the European continent, stability and control within the Soviet bloc, Chinese threats along its borders in Asia, and the Soviet-Afghan conflict.

Contemporary China, on the other hand, is a land power that dominates the East Asian mainland, and it has never been more secure from external threats than it is today. It is unthinkable that any of China's neighboring states are considering invading China from its borders. The development of an increasingly more sanguine security environment was recognized with Deng's "strategic decision" back in 1985, which "codified a more relaxed estimate of the probability of a massive Soviet thrust into China from the north and northwest."[16] As Finkelstein has noted, what Deng predicted in 1985—that China's *fundamental security* would be assured—by 2001 had indeed come to pass.[17] This strategic shift accentuated China's eastern coastline as the bedrock of an internal process of modernization and reform, but the change in China's strategic orientation also elevated the importance of maritime security challenges in the mindset of China's civilian and military leaders and "improved the PLAN's ability to obtain resources within the PLA."[18]

In his speech on September 3, 2015, commemorating the seventieth anniversary of China's victory in World War II, President Xi announced a downsizing of the PLA army by 300,000 troops. The stated aim was to modernize the PLA and enhance its war-fighting capabilities;[19] increase the relative importance of the navy, air force, and Second Artillery among the armed services; and enhance the PLA's ability to prevail in a nearby maritime crisis and to fight and win a "local war under informatized conditions." The shift also signals China's determination to enhance further its ability to engage in high-intensity combat in both the near seas (Yellow, East, and South China) and, gradually, the far seas, rather than maintaining a strong priority on traditional threats along its land borders.[20] China's 2015 defense White Paper indicates that China has decided to devote increased resources to its navy, stating that "the traditional mentality that land outweighs sea must be abandoned, and great importance has to be attached to managing the seas and oceans and protecting maritime rights and interests."[21]

Without peer competitors on the Asian mainland, China can afford to take greater risks in confronting the United States in East Asian waters. In addition, since China controls a huge littoral of East Asian waters, its geography provides greater access to the seas and vital SLOCs than the Soviet Union enjoyed in its day. Geography gives China a unity of naval power. The PLA can more easily bring together its northern, eastern, and southern fleets. As Spykman noted in 1942, a "modern, vitalized, and militarized China" will be "a continental power of huge dimensions in control of a large section of the littoral," of what he described as "the Asiatic Mediterranean [the Yellow, East and South China seas]." China's "geographic position will be similar to that of the United States in regard to the American Mediterranean [the Caribbean Sea]."[22] Once China has secured its continental borders and become relatively more powerful, it would be natural, as a huge littoral state dependent on SLOCs for trade, to go to sea[23] to seek control of the maritime geographical space in its region. This geopolitical development can hardly be reversed as China grows more powerful. At the same time, China's neighbors and the United States are naturally alarmed by this geopolitical shift and will therefore seek to balance China's ambitions. The result of the United States and the PLAN increasingly interacting at sea will be the intensification of rivalries and the heightened risk of a limited war.

Conflict often erupts when land powers go to sea.[24] But as history tells us, nearly all continental powers have failed in war against the dominant sea power, in large part because they were constrained by exposure to a continental frontier and forced to maintain security along their land border: the Spanish Armada was defeated by the British in 1588, but Spain was simultaneously involved in several land wars in Europe; the fleet of Napoleonic France was destroyed at the Battle of Trafalgar in 1805,[25] while France was simultaneously contending with several rivals on the European continent; Russia's naval ambitions were dashed during the Crimean War, although naval power and sea power ambitions[26] remained of secondary importance to the tsars of Russia; Keiser Wilhelm's sea-power aspirations never paid off; and imperial Japan's sea-power ambitions were constrained by the resources needed to occupy large parts of mainland East Asia during World War II.

Spykman's geopolitical analysis led him to a controversial but farsighted and bold conclusion, which he arrived at *during* the Second World War:

> When China becomes strong, her present economic penetration in that region will undoubtedly take on political overtones. It is quite possible to envisage the day when this body of water will be controlled not by British, American, or Japanese sea power but by Chinese air power.... It will be difficult to find public support in the United States for a Far Eastern strategy based on these realities of power politics.... Public opinion will probably continue to see Japan as the great danger, long after the balance has shifted in favor of China and it has become necessary to pursue in the Far East the same policy that we have pursued in regard to Europe. Twice in one generation we have come to the aid of Great Britain in order that the small off-shore island might not have to face a single gigantic military state in control of the opposite coast of the mainland. If the balance of power in the Far East is to be preserved in the future as well as in the present, the United States will have to adopt a similar protective policy toward Japan. The present inconsistency in American policy will have to be removed. It is illogical to insist that Japan accept a Chinese empire from Vladivostok to Canton and at the same time to support Great Britain in her wars for the preservation of buffer states across the North Sea.[27]

More than seventy years later, this analysis manages to capture the geopolitical rivalry of the twenty-first century, but in comparison to the Soviet Union, contemporary China has more secure borders and better access to the sea and is geographically more centrally placed in East Asia, with more favorable internal lines of communication to support its naval fleets and defend its territory. Geopolitics facilitates China's maritime expansion, allows China to challenge the status quo in East Asia, produces geopolitical friction between China and the United States, and increases the risk of limited war.

Status Quo, Buffer Zones, and Spheres of Influence

China is not a status quo power to the extent that the Soviet Union was after World War II, when Moscow was largely content with the geopolitical situation in Europe. This also explains why the risk of a limited war in East Asia is higher than it was in Europe during the Cold War. The Soviet Union advanced to Berlin during the Second World War, and in the post–World War II years established a new security buffer in Eastern Europe by controlling the eastern parts of a divided Germany in the heart of Europe. Despite its revolutionary and ideological hostility toward the West, once the Soviet armed forces came to control eastern and central parts of Europe, the Soviet Union became a status quo power and had few aspirations to expand further in Europe. A land invasion of the Soviet Union via Eastern Europe seemed unlikely, and the Soviet Union remained a status quo power in Europe throughout the Cold War.

In contrast, China aims to establish a new security buffer within its near seas or the first island chain and compete with the United States in the latter's sphere of influence in maritime East Asia. China lacks capabilities to safeguard its sovereignty, maritime security, and economic interests today but is modernizing its military and developing anti-access and area-denial capabilities to contend with the United States in the maritime domain. In the future, China will seek to dominate its nearby waters and more forcefully protect its SLOC. The stopping power of water provides a de facto security buffer between U.S. maritime and Chinese continental spheres of influence, but China is now challenging this status quo and looking to create a new regional security order.

There are at least two reasons why establishing a new security buffer, which consolidated stability in Europe during the Cold War, will be difficult if not impossible in East Asia. First, maritime East Asia's geography makes it hard for China to establish a clear security buffer. The East-West divide on the European continent provided a security buffer between the Soviet Union and the United States during the Cold War. U.S. and USSR troops faced each other directly but were not defending their own sovereignty. They were defending their allies or buffer nations. China and the United States, on the other hand, now sail within shouting distance in waters where the latter used to be free to maneuver its navy in response to vital national security interests whenever necessary but where today China's maritime sovereignty and security interests are considered equally important by Beijing.

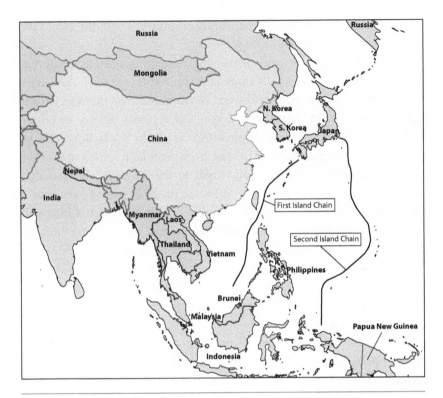

FIGURE 6.1 First Island Chain.

Source: Norwegian Military Geographic Service.

Second, it is simply harder to establish a security buffer at sea than on land. The sea cannot be conquered and occupied. Land intrusions can be repelled and territory retaken and restored. This is much more difficult at sea. It is inherently more challenging to uphold the status quo at sea than on land. For instance, during the standoff with Soviet forces in Europe, the United States did not face the "salami-slicing" tactic the Chinese government is using to challenge the status quo in East Asian waters today. Contemporary Chinese behavior is more difficult to deter, since it does not threaten military invasion and includes the use of China's maritime surveillance ships, coast guard, and maritime militia.[28] Although these ships are deployed in coordination with the leadership of the CCP and the PLA, they belong to civilian agencies. And since the United States is unlikely to deploy its coast guard in these waters, it either has to let China assert its interests to the detriment of its neighbors or intervene with the U.S. Navy and risk escalation, accidents, and conflict.[29]

There was much more agreement about the status quo in Europe during the Cold War than there is in contemporary maritime Asia.[30] The Soviet Union helped set the terms at the end of the Second World War, carved out its spheres of influence, and shaped the regional balance of power in Europe. Today, China is rising within a system it did not shape at its origins. The separation of Taiwan from mainland China and other outstanding territorial claims add weight to the longstanding view that contemporary China's spheres of influence in the region do not reflect China's traditional regional dominance, which suggests that China will challenge the status quo.[31] The Soviet Union did not claim territory in Western Europe or within Washington's sphere of influence. China, on the other hand, has claims to sovereign territory in maritime East Asia, in what has long been part of the U.S. sphere of influence. This will increase instability in ways that were unseen in Europe and heighten the risk of crisis and limited war.

The United States was dependent on a strong military foothold on the European continent in order to deter and balance Soviet land power credibly, maintain the status quo, and preserve its sphere of influence. Therefore, the United States developed a broad strategy of containment and a significant forward military presence on the European continent. China cannot advance in maritime East Asia as the Soviet Union could have done to expand its power over the European continent. China is not the superior power in the maritime domain, and, as mentioned, it is much more difficult to hold and control large bodies of water. Although China challenges the regional status quo through its land reclamation in the disputed South China Sea and by occupying and seeking to control reefs, islands, and rocks in the East and South China seas, it does not threaten the regional balance of power as the Red Army would have done had it marched into West Berlin and farther into West Germany or Western Europe. The United States remains today the dominant power in East Asian waters and can, if it wishes, at any time in the near future actively resist Chinese expansion in those waters. Pushing the Red Army out of West Germany, for example, would have been a much more difficult task.

While Chinese leaders and the PLA acknowledge U.S. primacy in East Asian waters, increased capabilities, a belief in asymmetric strategies, and a recognition of the dynamic security environment allow China to test the waters and challenge the status quo, increasing the risk of conflict and limited war.

Related to the issue of a new buffer zone and status quo is the importance of recognized spheres of influence. The power vacuum caused by the fall of Nazi Germany in Europe initially created tension between Soviet and U.S. troops as they strove to fill the vacuum, but spheres of influence were soon established, which stabilized the European continent for the duration of the post–World War II period. Percentage agreements and demarcation lines were drawn up in 1943–1945, and although they were disputed in some areas early on, they eventually became the red lines later described by Churchill as the Iron Curtain. U.S. and Soviet troops in Europe knew exactly where the East-West divide was in Europe. Soviet tanks could not venture across this border without risking war. Neither the United States nor the Soviet Union officially admitted to any "spheres" during the Cold War, but both respected the other's right to a sphere of influence, and neither directly challenged the other's sphere.[32]

The Soviet Union was quietly allowed to control its zone in East Germany forcibly. When the West remained passive to the clampdown sparked by the 1956 Hungarian revolution, it confirmed its policy keeping out of the region of Soviet domination.[33] In return, Soviet armed forces did not intervene when the United States exercised its predominance in Western Europe.

Spheres of influence can undoubtedly preserve stability and peace, and not only in Europe. East Asia has remained the most peaceful region in the world for more than three decades largely as a result of the geography of peace that saw China dominate mainland East Asia, even while the United States maintained maritime superiority.[34] However, China's navy is unremittingly encroaching on the U.S. sphere of influence in maritime East Asia and confronting the U.S. Navy and its allies in these waters. The contest and rivalry at sea in maritime East Asia are not similar to the zero-sum game in Europe. If the Soviet Union had expanded farther west on the European continent, there would have been less geographical space for the United States to seek to counterbalance the Soviet Union. It will be many years before China can control East Asian waters, and anyway, China's maritime expansion does not resemble the zero-sum game played out in Europe during the previous bipolar era. In addition, the Chinese occupation and control of reefs, rocks, and island in the East Asian waters do not amount to the control of the strategically vital piece of territory that was Germany, in the heart of Europe, by the USSR. The stakes are likely not as high in confrontations over relatively insignificant reefs and rocks in East Asian waters as they were over territory in Europe. Nonetheless, the United States has an enduring interest in maintaining the balance of power and preventing China from becoming a regional hegemon in East Asia. This allows for a more unstable and dynamic security situation in which spheres of influences and the status quo can be challenged to a much larger extent than in Europe during the early Cold War years.

The Soviet navy challenged its U.S. counterpart at sea during the Cold War, but the two adversaries did not interact militarily within each other's respective vital spheres of influence on the European continent. U.S. tanks were not operating within East Germany or West Berlin, and Soviet armed forces did not maneuver within the borders of NATO countries. Now, East Asian waters are the main power center and theater of military operations. It has already resulted in several crises and incidents, including the Taiwan Strait crisis of 1995/1996, the EP-3 crisis of 2001, the USNS *Impeccable* incident of 2009, the USS *Cowpens* incident of 2013, the P-8 incident of 2014, and the USS *Lassen* freedom-of-navigation operation in the South China Sea. More of these incidents can be expected, and they increase the risk of limited war between the United States and China.

Geopolitics, Asymmetry, and the Risk of Limited War

Chinese civilian and military leaders have noted the inferiority of China's armed forces as compared to the U.S. military. The phrase "two incompatibles" refers to the PLA insufficiencies in "winning local wars under informatized conditions" and their ability to carry out the "historical missions." Blasko, however, also notes that "should the situation require and the PLA be ordered by its CCP leaders, the Chinese armed forces will make use of whatever progress it has made to date and devise plans appropriate to its current conditions to accomplish the mission assigned."[35] By relying on asymmetric strategies and new equipment, China can, as Christensen succinctly pointed out more than a decade ago, pose "problems without catching up."[36]

Geographical conditions will be very influential in determining the like-lihood of conflict between China and the United States, and many writers have pointed to various factors that could trigger a conflict or undermine crisis management.[37] Christensen warns in his careful analysis against overemphasizing the United States as the only global military power and downplaying China's ability to obtain parity. In a crisis or conflict, China could take advantage of the fact that the United States has global security commitments, that its forces are spread out and operating in more than one theater, and that U.S. forces face difficulties in overcoming the "tyr-anny of distance."[38] In contrast to the United States, which will need to deploy ships based in the United States and elsewhere in the world, China can benefit from having all its naval facilities in the region and its ships spending less time in transition to and from deployments or maintenance. The United States is seeking to manage such challenges by home-porting more ships in allies' facilities, but as Ross notes, there are limits to this.[39]

China would be fighting in its own region and determined to defend sovereignty claims, where most of the potential points-of-conflict areas are very close to China geographically and all very far from the United States.[40] China can therefore mobilize more rapidly, operate from dozens of hard-ened mainland bases, and, taking advantage of its more favorable interior lines of communication, commit more forces to a conflict, concentrate its military forces in one theater, and sustain them longer and more easily. In this vein, Montgomery argues, "when geography enters the equation, the situation looks much less favorable for the United States than its advantage in military spending and military reach would seem to suggest."[41] Others have pointed out how China "might attempt a fait accompli strategy to gain political or military control of the situation before the United States can respond effectively."[42] China's military modernization gives its air, sea, missile, and cyber forces the ability to threaten the U.S. military and pose problems in ways that were unattainable a decade or two ago.[43]

Regional Hegemonic Ambitions

The geography of East Asia makes it necessary to be both a land and a sea power to gain supremacy in the region. China will need to control East Asian waters if it is to establish regional hegemony. This is similar to how the United States first became the dominant land power in North America (following the American Indian Wars and Civil War) and then challenged Britain's naval supremacy in the Western Hemisphere over the second half of the nineteenth century. By the turn of the twentieth century, when the United States had gained control of the Caribbean Sea and American waters, it had become a regional hegemon.[44] China is looking ahead to a new Long March, with the ambition to establish regional dominance or hegemony by 2049.[45] When asked whether China aspires to displace the United States as the top power in Asia, Lee Kuan Yew, a former prime minister of Singapore and longtime China watcher, answered: "Of course. Why not . . . how could they not aspire to be number one in Asia and in time the world?"[46] However, geopolitical factors and the bipolar distribution of power make it inherently more difficult for China to become a regional hegemon than it was for the United States, and the rivalry and power transition are more likely to end in a limited war.

China's peer competitor, the United States, is a well-established regional hegemon in the Western Hemisphere and is likely to retain that position in the twenty-first century. Great Britain was not a regional hegemon when the United States established itself as one. Britain's island status gave it an advantage when it sought maritime supremacy, but confronted with potential regional hegemons in Europe (Germany), the Western Hemisphere (United States), and East Asia (Japan) in the late nineteenth and early twentieth century, Britain had to give priority to sustaining the multipolar balance of power in Europe, leaving an opening for the United States. Britain could not risk war with the United States, as it was confronting more pressing security challenges closer to home. Moreover, despite its naval superiority over the United States, Britain could have done little to defend Canada.[47] The United States today does not face the same type of threat from China and is consequently more determined to prevent China from attaining regional hegemony, even if it means going to war.

The United States is blessed with regional hegemony and a geography that makes it impregnable, and these geopolitical factors are reinforced by the contemporary bipolar distribution of capabilities. The United States is confronted by only one peer competitor or superpower, China, not three or more great powers, as Great Britain was. Russia, or any other European or Asian power, cannot challenge the contemporary balance of power in Europe or in Asia.[48] In contrast to Britain in a multipolar system in the nineteenth and twentieth centuries, the United States does not need to concern itself with the balance of power within its own region or any other regions besides East Asia in the new bipolar system of the twenty-first century. It can primarily concentrate its power on preventing China from dominating East Asia and sustaining the balance of power in that region. This suggests that China's aspirations for regional hegemony and a potential future power transition in East Asia are more likely to result in conflict and a limited war than the peaceful U.S.-UK power-transition case suggests.

Today's geostructural conditions are not only different from the U.S.-UK power-transition analogy under multipolarity; they also contrast with the previous bipolar era. If the Soviet Union had sought regional hegemony, then sea power would have been insufficient. Regional hegemony in Europe demands control over the European continent. The development of Soviet naval power did not threaten the regional balance of power in Europe. Conversely, China's naval aspirations and developments are crucial for the contest over regional hegemony in East Asia. The stakes in the more uncontrollable environment at sea are higher in East Asian waters than in the maritime domain during the previous bipolar period.

In sum, the contested area at sea in East Asia in the new bipolar system, where the two superpowers mainly will interact, is a geographical space where a limited war between the superpowers can be largely contained to the maritime domain, where the status quo and spheres of influence are challenged, where security buffers are lacking, and where geopolitics provides the rising land power with opportunities to challenge the dominant sea power, but where polarity and geopolitics allow the United States to concentrate on balancing China's regional ambitions. This makes a bipolar system concentrated on East Asia and U.S.-China relations more prone to limited war than the previous bipolar system.

NUKES, TRIPWIRES, AND MARITIME FLASHPOINTS

China's Nuclear Strategy

The longstanding view of Chinese leaders on the role of nuclear weapons in an armed struggle reinforces the possibility of a limited conventional war.

Since its first nuclear test in 1964, China's nuclear policy has emphasized deterrence, no first use, retaliation, and a "lean and effective" nuclear force. Chinese leaders have consistently believed that the nature and purpose of nuclear weapons are "as tools for deterring nuclear aggression and countering coercion, not as weapons to be used in combat to accomplish discrete military objectives."[49] China's no-first-use policy has therefore reflected a strategic belief that a small nuclear force is "sufficient for deterrence so long as it could survive a first strike and retaliate."[50]

Mutual second-strike capability promotes strategic stability and decreases the probability of a major war between two nuclear states, but since the risk of unlimited war is minimized, the risk of limited war increases. If nuclear war were to lead to mutual destruction, notes Jervis, then neither side should start an all-out war, which becomes unthinkable and unwinnable. However, "this very stability allows either side to use limited violence because the other's threat to respond by all-out retaliation cannot be very credible."[51] Snyder calls this the "stability-instability paradox."[52]

The U.S.-China Stability-Instability Paradox

Acquiring a secure second-strike capability is likely to increase Chinese leaders' confidence in risk taking. To the extent that Chinese leaders assert that escalation to nuclear war can be avoided and that the threshold in moving from limited to major war will remain large, they may become more willing to take risks, making a limited war more likely. This may allow, as Goldstein has noted, for a "stability-instability paradox" to emerge in Sino-U.S. relations, which "suggests that stability at the highest level of general nuclear war increases instability at lower levels by making lesser conflicts seem safe to fight."[53] This paradox points to instability at the conventional level, but it is also important to acknowledge that the dynamics of strategic stability that existed between the United States and the Soviet Union is different from contemporary Sino-U.S. stability both because of geopolitics and the role of nuclear weapons in their bilateral relationship. Geopolitics reinforces the stability-instability paradox, since U.S.-China rivalry and the danger of limited conventional war at sea in maritime East Asia is higher than on land during the previous, Eurocentric bipolar system.

The United States, Christensen has observed, "now faces a conventionally inferior potential adversary with nuclear weapons, so the hawkish and dovish logics of the Cold War, somewhat ironically, are turned on their heads in the post–Cold War world."[54] The United States remained inferior in conventional warfare to the Soviet Union in Europe in the early years of the previous bipolar era. U.S. deterrence had to rely on nuclear weapons. This made the threat of nuclear war more credible and served to strengthen stability in Europe. Because of the stopping power of water and because the U.S. military does not need to fight the PLA on the East Asian mainland to maintain a regional balance of power, the United States remains not only superior to China in nuclear capability but also at the conventional level. This makes a limited war more likely, since the U.S. threshold for using military force may not include the use of nuclear forces. Moreover, Chinese leaders counting on their second-strike capability to prevent all-out nuclear war and on their belief in a clear firebreak between conventional and nuclear conflict could interpret this situation such that they might be willing to risk a conventional first strike or a limited war at their own choosing, believing such adventurism would not spark a major or nuclear war. Soviet leaders in the 1950s, and even after Washington introduced its flexible response and countervailing strategy in the 1960s, could not rule out to the same extent that the United States would not use nuclear weapons in a limited war.[55]

We should consider the role of both the nuclear and conventional weapons that both countries possess, but the "prospect for stability in a Sino-American crisis looks bleak when only conventional forces are considered."[56] A potential conventional military conflict between two nuclear-armed states must meet a stiffer test than if states with only conventional military capabilities are considered, but the geopolitical factors, the "stability-instability paradox," and China's nuclear policy and second-strike capability make it necessary to focus on the risk of a limited conventional war between China and the United States.

Added to this is another difference: some key U.S. allies in Europe questioned America's credibility and willingness to wage nuclear war, risking the devastation of its own territory, for the sake of Western Europe. As a result, France and Britain sought their own limited nuclear deterrent against the Soviet Union. Conceivably, this added nuclear capability stabilized Europe and helped discourage the Soviet Union from attacking

Western Europe. No U.S. allies in East Asia have developed nuclear weapons. Thus, if Chinese leaders are questioning U.S. resolve, they are less likely to be deterred by the capabilities of U.S. allies in the region. Unlike the situation in Europe, it is more likely that China could act more recklessly than the Soviet Union and risk a limited war with non-nuclear U.S. allies in East Asia.

Tripwires and Maritime Flashpoints

According to Schelling, deterrence involves setting the stage by announcing and rigging the "tripwire."[57] However, "words rarely do it," noted Schelling. "To have told the Soviets in the late 1940s that, if they attacked, we were obliged to defend Europe might not have been wholly convincing." Stationing U.S. troops in Europe was not primarily to "defend against a superior Soviet army but to leave the Soviet Union in no doubt that the United States would be automatically involved in the event of any attack on Europe." "Tripwire" was Schelling's term for troops that could be run over by the Soviet Army. He asked: What can seven thousand American troops stationed in Berlin do? And answered: "Bluntly, they can die. They can die heroically, dramatically, and in a manner that guarantees that the action cannot stop there."[58] U.S. commitments were clearly marked red lines, frontiers the Soviet did not dare cross. And the commitments were credible because they were "inescapable."[59] The western sector of Berlin offered, as Schelling put it, "no graceful way out if we wished our troops to yield ground," and West Berlin was "too small an area in which to ignore small encroachments."[60]

The United States is not similarly committed in East Asian waters today. "There is much less clarity about the delimitation of U.S. and Chinese vital interests beyond their homelands, especially in the Western Pacific," notes Goldstein.[61] It is also more difficult to draw red lines at sea. There is no East-West divide, Berlin Wall, or Checkpoint Charlie in East Asian waters. There are no tripwires or inescapable commitments. Instead, U.S. commitments regarding potential flashpoints in the South China Sea, the East China Sea, and the Taiwan Strait are less clear.

Maritime Flashpoints

During a standoff between China and the Philippines over the Scarborough Shoal in 2012, the United States acted with restraint and was reluctant to escalate the conflict. China took control of the shoal, and the United States de facto accepted the outcome. Washington has stated that the U.S.-Japan Security Treaty does cover the disputed Senkakus islands. Supporting its most important regional ally, Japan, in the dispute with China over the Senkakus is important to maintaining U.S. credibility. Nonetheless, the islands remain relatively insignificant in determining the balance of power in the region, and the United States might not be willing to defend these rocks at all costs. If Beijing, which is determined to protect its sovereignty claims, questions U.S. resolve, it might undermine U.S. deterrence. As Schelling warns us, if an opponent expects the adversary to "be under strong temptation to make a graceful exit,"[62] deterrence is no longer as credible. This increases the risk of conflict. Ambiguity can be exploited in a crisis that is geographically closer to China than the United States and over an issue perceived by Beijing to be of more vital importance to the former than the latter.[63] The lack of a massive-retaliation doctrine that threatens to escalate a limited war to a nuclear war, the scarcity of tripwires in maritime East Asia, ill-defined U.S. commitments, and the absence of a European East-West divide all will increase the temptation during a crisis on the Chinese side to resort to force, possibly sparking a limited war with the United States.

Ambiguity has served U.S. Taiwan policy and promoted stability in the Taiwan Strait for decades, but in contrast to Berlin during the Cold War, the Taiwan issue leaves "loopholes through which to exit."[64] The U.S. commitment to the defense of Taiwan might be strong, and it has deterred the mainland from invading the island, but the tripwire is not equivalent to the U.S. commitment to defend West Berlin and Western Europe. For instance, the United States has no troops stationed on the island and has no official policy of massive retaliation if Taiwan is invaded by mainland China. Washington's commitment to defend Taiwan is comparatively more escapable than the commitment to defend West Berlin during the Cold War. This undermines the credibility of U.S. deterrence in a Taiwan conflict and increases the risk of a limited war.

Except for the survival of the CCP and the PRC, no single issue in China's internal affairs/foreign affairs has preoccupied Chinese leaders more than seeking unification of mainland China and Taiwan. Their determination has resulted in numerous crises and the use of military force in the past, and Chinese leaders are likely to consider all means necessary in the future to preserve the status quo and eventually seek reunification. Taiwan is not a formal ally of the United States, and it remains uncertain whether U.S. commitments to the defense of Taiwan are as strong as they are to formal allies in the region. The regional balance of power will not fundamentally change if the PRC gained control of Taiwan, but the shift would alter the power equilibrium and give China a major strategic advantage in its pursuit of regional hegemony.

A more modernized PLA with improved anti-access/area-denial military capabilities enhances China's ability to deter any U.S. military intervention in a conflict in the Taiwan Strait and boosts Chinese leaders' belief in the likely success of a military invasion of Taiwan. Several reports suggest that Washington is becoming increasingly concerned with China's growing military capabilities and regional ambitions; some scholars argue that preventing the PRC from controlling Taiwan is of growing strategic importance.[65]

To others, however, Taiwan is not worth fighting for.[66] U.S. supremacy in East Asian waters is not eroded by China overtaking Taiwan, preserving strong economic ties with China is more vital than going to war with China over Taiwan, and Taiwan is not worth the danger of nuclear war. However, a U.S.-China limited war in the Taiwan Strait would not be a war just for Taiwan but for maintaining the regional balance of power, preventing China from dominating East Asia, and preserving U.S. credibility within the region, especially toward its maritime allies.[67]

China will not become a regional hegemon if it controls Taiwan, but it will be much more difficult for the United States to maintain a regional balance of power if the PRC gained control of the island. Economic interdependence has not prevented conflicts and wars between the great powers in the past, and a nuclear second-strike capability may not be enough to prevent a limited, non–existentially threatening war. Instead, preventing a limited war in the Taiwan Strait requires conventional military deterrence, which will be increasingly difficult for the United States to maintain as China continues its military modernization.

Neither the United States nor the Soviet Union had sovereignty claims over Berlin to the degree the PRC claims Taiwan as part of China, a claim recognized by most states in the world. The East-West divide produced guaranteed tripwires on the European continent. If either NATO or the Warsaw Pact crossed the threshold and invaded the other side, both would be committed to repelling the intruders and restoring the original boundary, even by means of massive retaliation. A limited war in the Taiwan Strait, even if it included targeting mainland China and U.S. regional bases, could presumably be contained within the maritime domain without the risk of a major war. This makes war originating in maritime East Asia more likely than war on the European continent, with the Taiwan issue remaining the most contentious and dangerous one in U.S.-China relations.

The maritime flashpoints include the question of Taiwan, disputes over island sovereignty, diverging views on the law of the sea, struggles over maritime natural resources, and control of sea lanes.[68] Undoubtedly, similar issues fueled tensions and security dynamics in Europe during the Berlin Blockade of 1948–1949 and the uprisings in Hungary in 1956 and in Czechoslovakia in 1968. However, Cold War conflicts were largely contained and deterred by Soviet land power and nuclear weaponry. NATO was forced to watch as the Red Army crushed opposition within its sphere of influence. Tensions increased during these crises, but stability was maintained. Unlike Cold War Europe, there is no clear divide in East Asian waters. Instead, China is challenging the status quo, and Washington is being pulled into conflicts concerning various regional disputes and flashpoints.

CONCLUSION

The substantive argument developed here is that while the risk of major war between the two superpowers remains low, there is a relatively higher risk of a limited war between them than was the case between the United States and Soviet Union during the previous bipolar era. Geopolitics provides the primary explanation for the heightened risk of a limited war, but the different roles of tripwires and sovereignty issues also contribute to increased instability. The superpowers did not come to blows over maritime sovereignty disputes, SLOCs, and natural resources behind the Iron Curtain and within respective spheres of influence in Europe during the Cold War. The United States and the Soviet Union refrained from launching destabilizing military operations within the adversary's respective sphere of influence in continental Europe. While agreeing with Lind that geography and current technology trends make East Asia "defense dominant,"[69] Christensen's point that there are important "potential spiral dynamics in the region" remains valid.[70] Maritime East Asia lacks the Cold War boundaries and tripwires in Europe, and China's growing military capabilities allow it to operate militarily within the U.S. sphere of influence. Increased Chinese military activity in East Asian waters allows for more friction, instability, and conflict than was the case in Europe.

A limited war involving the United States and China in East Asian waters would be very dangerous and would include a great risk of escalation.[71] It is impossible to predict the sequence of events and potential escalation after the outbreak of a limited war. The controversial development by the Pentagon of AirSea Battle (ASB), a U.S. military operational concept to defeat and disable China's growing anti-access/area-denial capabilities, may escalate into something more if strikes are conducted against military sites inside China, especially if nuclear forces are targeted. It has been reported that the ASB operational concept has been dropped by the Pentagon, but that this is only in name. The new Joint Concept for Access and Maneuver in the Global Commons (JAM-GC) focuses on including U.S. land forces into the wider concept.[72] Accordingly, the U.S. military will continue to develop capabilities to defeat threats to access and counter emerging Chinese capabilities that could hold a risk to forward-deployed U.S. forces. This may include targeting weapons launchers and military facilities on the Chinese mainland.[73] A limited war between the United States and China will clearly risk escalation.

At the same time, Admiral Greenert and General Welsh have pointed out that "strikes against installations deep inland are not necessarily required in Air-Sea Battle because adversary C4ISR may be vulnerable to disruption, weapons can be deceived or intercepted, and adversary ships and aircraft destroyed."[74] Alternatives to the ASB concept that eschew direct attacks on Chinese territory have been advanced,[75] and some experts on the PLAN have suggested that the U.S. military can disrupt China's A2/AD capabilities, for example, the antiship ballistic missile (ASBM), by "breaking the ASBM's kill chain."[76] U.S. surface ships can hide and operate in ways that make it harder for the PLA to detect, identify, and track them. The navy can also improve systems for jamming, spoofing, and confusing ASBMs in flight and develop weapons for destroying ASBMs as they approach their intended targets.[77]

There is a higher risk of a limited war between the superpowers of the twenty-first century than in the twentieth century, since a limited war at sea in East Asia is more likely to be contained and the risk of it escalating into a major or nuclear war is lower than the risk posed by a land war and invasion on the European continent during the Cold War. As Goldstein has pointed out, "the risk of a serious Sino-American confrontation exists despite, and perhaps is underappreciated because of, the absence of the zero-sum, life-and-death struggle between two archrivals that characterized Soviet-American relations."[78] Since geography and the stopping power of water allow China and the United States to be superior in conventional military forces within their respective spheres of influence, nuclear war and the threat of invasion are not the greatest dangers. Instead, maritime disputes and other sources of friction could more easily spark a limited war between China and the United States. The risk of a preventive war, for example, a military attack by the United States that cripples the PLAN or an attack by the PLA on U.S. forces in the region, is higher than was ever the case of the United States attacking the Soviet Union in Europe during the Cold War.

Chapter 7

THE RETURN OF BIPOLARITY

Global and Regional Effects

U.S.-China rivalry and confrontation in East Asia in the twenty-first century have not resembled the confrontation and strong balancing that marked U.S.-Soviet relations in Europe at the origins of the previous bipolar system. The first part of this chapter argues that the distinct balancing pattern also distinguishes U.S.-China relations from U.S.-Soviet relations globally. For the foreseeable future, the United States and China are less likely to be adversaries in proxy wars and pursue the confrontational pattern of behavior that the United States and Soviet Union pursued on a global stage during the Cold War.

Notwithstanding the moderate global rivalry and confrontation, the return of bipolarity shapes and shoves international politics. The second part of the chapter examines how the global power shift is likely to compel the United States to continue its rebalancing efforts toward East Asia and pivot toward the Asia-Pacific. This has four important implications. First, U.S. allies in Asia are strengthening their defense ties with the United States. Nonaligned states, such as India, are improving their defense capabilities and developing closer ties with the United States to safeguard their security interests. Second, as a consequence of the U.S. pivot to the Asia-Pacific, U.S. allies in Europe are compelled to assume more responsibility for their own security or risk facing increased strategic challenges and higher security risks. Third, Russia can take advantage of Washington's

Asia-Pacific pivot and the reluctance of European states to raise defense spending and cooperate more strongly in security affairs. Finally, the return of bipolarity will affect institutions, conflict resolution, the management of nontraditional security challenges, and the maintenance of the current world order.

INSTABILITY AT THE CENTER, STABILITY ON THE PERIPHERY

Within a bipolar world, wrote Waltz, "there are no peripheries." The bipolar structural conditions suggest that any global event will involve the interests of the two superpowers, which are compelled to intervene across the world to safeguard their interests. A "loss to one could easily appear as a gain to the other, a conclusion that follows from the very condition of a two-power competition," argued Waltz.[1] However, the sameness effect and the zero-sum thinking that neorealist theory expects are not evident in U.S.-China interaction in world affairs today. Similar factors that prevent strong balancing in U.S.-China relations and heighten the risk of war in East Asia explain the different patterns of behavior by the United States and China as they compete for influence globally.

In contrast to the previous bipolar system, which experienced stability at the center in Europe and instability at the periphery, or "Third World," contemporary U.S.-China relations are set to be more unstable at the center in East Asia and more stable at the edges. Preoccupation with confrontation, instability, and conflict in maritime East Asia is likely to prevent U.S.-China rivalry from growing as intense in other regions of the world as were U.S.-Soviet relations.

Avoiding Proxy Wars and Global Confrontation

After Europe was stabilized into two blocs and spheres of influence during the early Cold War, the superpowers' rivalry and conflict moved instead to other regions. The Korean Peninsula, Indochina, the Middle East, Africa, Latin America, and Central Asia became theaters for the struggles and proxy wars of the two superpowers. In the new bipolar system, disputes in East Asia, from the Korean Peninsula and the East

China Sea to Taiwan and the South China Sea, remain unsettled. These concerns at China's "core" will help prevent superpower rivalry from spreading to other regions. Contemporary China remains preoccupied with its regional ambitions in East Asia, where it is challenging the existing status quo and spheres of influence, protecting its sovereignty claims in maritime East Asia, expanding its presence at land and at sea (for example, the Belt and Road initiative), and seeking to establish a security buffer at sea by emphasizing the development of anti-access and area-denial capabilities. The Soviet Union, on the other hand, was a status quo power in Europe whose sovereignty claims were satisfied, had established a security buffer in Eastern Europe, and had de facto gained recognition for its sphere of influence on the European continent. The Soviet Union could therefore allow itself to challenge the United States more forcefully on the global stage.

The Egyptian-Czech arms deal of 1955, orchestrated by the Soviet Union, marked the first major transfer of arms by the Soviet Union to a Third World country during the Cold War. It was perceived in the West as an ominous development that sharpened Cold War rivalry, threatened insta-bility in the Middle East, and signaled that arms transfers would become an important dimension in the foreign policy of the superpowers toward allies and nonaligned states.[2] The Soviet Union had demonstrated its ability to advance its interests on the global stage and to compete directly with the United States concerning a nonaligned state's security, directly affecting stability in the Near East.

Conceivably, China could have supplied more arms to U.S. adversaries in a number of conflict zones around the world. In order to keep the United States even more preoccupied with the wars in Iraq, Afghanistan, and Syria, thereby slowing a U.S. rebalancing and pivoting exercise to the Asia-Pacific, China could have supplied insurgency groups in Iraq, the Taliban, and the Islamic State operating in Syria and Iraq with weapons or economic aid. China could also have given stronger support to Gaddafi's regime in Libya, assisted Russia in pushing back NATO and the European Union in Eastern Europe, and aligned more closely with the various countries in Africa and Latin America that are in conflict with the United States. However, the distribution of capabilities had not shifted to bipolarity at that time, and instability in contemporary East Asia restrains China from pursuing such a strategy.

The United States could retaliate against such a policy by strengthening its support, arms sales, and transfers to countries such as Taiwan, South Korea, Japan, the Philippines, Vietnam, Myanmar, and India, possibly undermining China's security in the region most vital to China's interests. This tit-for-tat strategy was much less of a policy option during the Cold War. The East-West divide gave the United States with few options to retaliate, for instance, against the Egyptian-Czech arms deal. It could not have sold arms to Eastern European countries and thereby threatened the Soviet Union's vital security interests. Moscow retained control within its buffer zone and sphere of influence in Europe. Moreover, in contrast to 1950, the trade in arms is today much more of a marketplace and less prone to provoke superpower confrontation or conflict as it did during the Cold War.

It took the Soviet Union some years from the transition from a multipolar to a bipolar system (1945–1950) and the start of a bipolar system in 1950 to initiate a wider global strategy of confronting the United States and drawing nonaligned states into its orbit, as the Egyptian-Czech arms deal in 1955 signaled. The Soviet Union lacked power-projection capability to maintain any forward military presence globally, but it used its geographical outreach to support its allies in the Korean War, challenge the United States in Iran in the early 1950s, and establish a foothold in the Middle and Near East by the mid-1950s. China reaches into and dominates Northeast, Southeast, and Central Asia and outflanks India on the subcontinent through its land power on the Tibetan plateau and ties with Pakistan, Afghanistan, Bangladesh, and Myanmar. Even so, China lacks the geographical reach of the Soviet Union. This constrains China from pursuing a more active global strategy of confronting the United States on the Eurasian landmass or further abroad.

It remains to be seen if China, in five or so years, will embark upon a global strategy of confronting the United States. China would be no match for the United States in a military clash sited far from East Asia, but its power-projection capabilities are stronger than the Soviet Union's at the start of the previous bipolar era. If it chooses, China can support countries and groups resisting or in direct conflict with the United States around the globe. However, China is more likely to prioritize its regional ambitions and challenge the status quo in East Asian waters. By advancing to Berlin, the Soviet Union had obtained its core security goals and could allow itself to promote a worldwide communist movement. China, on the other hand, will be preoccupied with security in its own region and less interested in confronting the United States globally. China's leaders have learned the lessons of the collapse of the Soviet Union and are determined to avoid its mistakes. This reinforces the argument that China will prefer to prioritize domestic stability and security within its own region rather than following in the footsteps of the Soviet Union's global ambitions.

The Role of Power Vacuums

There are fewer power vacuums to fill and less geographical space for China's global interests to expand into. This explains why U.S.-China rivalry and conflict on the global stage are evolving more gradually and why China is more likely to focus on safeguarding and expanding its interests in East Asia. The shift from multipolarity to bipolarity in the post–World War II period saw traditional great powers, such as France and Britain, lose their top-ranking position, opening the way for colonial revolutions, decolonization, civil wars, and power vacuums. The aftershocks of World War II "allowed the superpower rivalry to ripple across the world."[3] With the British and French power in decline during and after World War II, European powers lost their hold on colonies in Asia, Africa, and Latin America. The new superpowers took the opportunity to move into the global power vacuum.[4]

The two new post–World War II superpowers embarked on an intense decades-long rivalry to fill the power vacuums and gain influence in the numerous new states that were appearing. Colonial revolutions and decolonization created, in the words of Morgenthau, "a moral, military, and political no-man's land neither completely nor irrevocably committed to either side." The faith of the new "uncommitted nations,"[5] whether they aligned themselves politically and militarily with the United States or the Soviet Union, sparked superpower rivalry on the global stage and created the two blocs and nonaligned movement of the Cold War.

Today, no empires are dissolving; there are no comparable colonial revolutions worldwide or power vacuums to fill. There are failed states and power vacuums in the contemporary world, but the instability in parts of Africa, Latin America, the Near and Middle East, and Afghanistan is not comparable with the instability in the aftermath of World War II and the decline of the traditional great powers. There is less geopolitical space for the superpowers to be pulled into and fewer newly developed states where the new superpower can compete for influence globally.

Stability in Europe and power vacuums globally gave the Soviet Union an opportunity to compete globally with the United States despite the asymmetric power relationship between the Soviet Union and the United States. Instability in East Asia and smaller power vacuums globally prevent China from emulating the Soviet Union, at least until China achieves more power parity with the United States.[6] This line of reasoning challenges the argument that, as "during the Cold War, a bipolar system in which war between the United States and China is too costly will lead to policy decisions that seek conflict resolution elsewhere."[7] The new bipolar system has new characteristics.

There will always be a mix of competition, confrontation, and cooperation in superpower and great-power relationships. Contemporary U.S.-China relations are more cooperative than U.S.-Soviet relations during the Cold War. The United States and China will support different states or groups in various conflicts, pursue different agendas within international organizations, compete for influence globally, and in some cases confront each other. Waltz argues that three factors—the absence of peripheries, the range and intensity of competition, and the persistence of pressure and crisis—are the most important characteristics of the two-power competition in the bipolar system since World War II.[8] The importance of geopolitics, however, shapes distinctive forms of behavior under twenty-first-century U.S.-China bipolarity and diffuses the zero-sum game of the Cold War period.

The geopolitical security order in Europe during the previous bipolar era was static. The security order in contemporary East Asia is dynamic and affects China's strategic choices; the geostructural conditions provide an opportunity to contend for regional hegemony in East Asia but constrain China's global ambitions. There will likely be less confrontation globally between the superpowers in the bipolar era of the twenty-first century than there was during the Cold War. Conversely, the geostructural conditions in Europe tempered the Soviet Union's ambitions for regional hegemony and pushed it into global confrontation and rivalry with the United States.

Nonetheless, as noted in chapter 5, this does not suggest that other factors do not remain important. The fact that the Soviets had little economic influence beyond their own bloc while China has extensive economic influence globally is an important difference between the two bipolar systems and likely to shape patterns of behavior and influence stability. The lack of contemporary strong ideological confrontation between the superpowers is also likely to constrain their global rivalry. Since China remains committed to the existing international institutional order, its ambitions and initiatives to develop an alternative order and institutions whereby Beijing has a more prominent role are likely to be more gradual than the Soviet Union's revolutionary approach. New technology and connectivity are facilitating interaction among states and people in unprecedented ways. New advanced weapons systems and cyber warfare will shape military conflict in the twenty-first century, and the role of nuclear weapons is different today compared to the origins of the previous bipolar system. All these factors matter and will shape and shove a new bipolar system. However, simply pointing to a number of factors that will influence superpower rivalry in the twenty-first century is insufficient. We need to establish some hierarchy of causes. Thus, this book contends that geopolitics is the single most important factor explaining different stability and patterns of behavior in a new bipolar system.

SHIFTING DISTRIBUTION OF CAPABILITIES AND GLOBAL IMPLICATIONS

The previous bipolar era profoundly shaped international politics. Regions, states, institutions, corporations, and individuals were affected by the Cold War. While the return of bipolarity might not lead to another Cold War, the current shift in the distribution of capabilities in the international system will affect international affairs.

U.S. Grand Strategy: Rebalance and Pivot to the Asia-Pacific

U.S. national security interests have always benefitted from the internal division of its two transoceanic flanking regions.[9] The United States benefited from European rivalries during the early years of the republic and throughout the nineteenth century, and it could count on power balancing among great European and East Asian powers to prevent a great power from becoming a regional hegemon.[10] The United States replaced Britain as the holder of the European balance of power during World War I, and after another cycle of isolation, neutrality, intervention, and war, the United States prevented the domination of both Europe and Asia by regional hegemonic powers during World War II.

In the post–World War II period, the United States had to participate directly in "the preservation of a balance of power in Europe and in Asia."[11] The United States had learned that "there can be security only in balanced power" and that "constant attention and adjustment"[12] was required when prioritizing between the flanking regions to maintain the balance of power within the regions. The primary interest of the United States during the early years of the previous bipolar system was in maintaining the balance of power in Europe.[13] World War II left the Soviet Union with the physical control of an area in the center of Europe at a time when no other great powers were able to contend for regional hegemony.[14]

After the fall of the Soviet Union in 1991, the United States adjusted its defense posture. It began to downsize its military presence in Europe and increase it in East Asia, especially following the Taiwan Strait crisis of 1995/1996.[15] With no other great powers capable of challenging U.S. supremacy, the United States also became more preoccupied with human-itarian interventions—"saving strangers"—during the 1990s.[16] The terrorist attacks of September 11, 2001, shifted the focus onto the war on terrorism. Nonetheless, since the wars in Afghanistan and Iraq to a large extent were financed by a supplementary budget, much of the enormous U.S. defense budget in the early years of the new century continued to be allocated to maintaining and increasing the U.S. military presence in the Asia-Pacific.[17]

The announcement of the U.S. pivot in 2011 revitalized and reinforced the process of rebalancing. The rebalancing in the mid-late 1990s and early years of the new century was a response to the collapse of the Soviet Union and China's early rise. The pivot sought to adjust the U.S. defense posture after the wars in Afghanistan and Iraq and to address power shifts and the emergence of China as the only peer competitor of the United States. In other words, the pivot explicitly prioritized the Asia-Pacific region in U.S. grand strategy, unlike the prioritization of the war on terrorism under the Bush administration. The United States never "left" East Asia under the

Bush administration, however.[18] As China became more assertive following the 2007–2008 financial crisis, it created an additional "demand signal" from the region, that is, a call for a stronger U.S. presence to counterbalance China's enhanced power and assertiveness. The Obama administration responded to these signals.[19] There had also been demand signals during the Taiwan Strait crisis, but the contemporary shift in the distribution of capabilities made this factor even more important when the pivot was announced.

In contrast to the rebalancing of the 1990s and the early years of the new century, the pivot was also a timely response to the situation following the financial crisis, and the Obama administration sought to renew economic growth by integrating more strongly with the fastest growing region in the world. Questions were also being raised about U.S. primacy for the first time in the aftermath of the financial crisis. Thus, an important difference between the rebalancing and the 2011 pivot is that the United States now had to prioritize its resources more carefully than during U.S. rebalancing at the height of the "unipolar moment" in the 1990s and the early years of the new century. As former Secretary of State Hillary Clinton wrote:

> As the war in Iraq winds down and America begins to withdraw its forces from Afghanistan, the United States stands at a pivot point. Over the last 10 years, we have allocated immense resources to those two theaters. In the next 10 years, we need to be smart and systematic about where we invest time and energy, so that we put ourselves in the best position to sustain our leadership, secure our interests, and advance our values. One of the most important tasks of American statecraft over the next decade will therefore be to lock in a substantially increased investment—diplomatic, economic, strategic, and otherwise—in the Asia-Pacific region. The Asia-Pacific has become a key driver of global politics.[20]

One month later, President Obama spoke in similar terms when he addressed the Australian parliament:

> After a decade in which we fought two wars that cost us dearly, in blood and treasure, the United States is turning our attention to the vast poten-tial of the Asia-Pacific region. . . . Here, we see the future. As the world's fastest-growing region—and home to more than half the global economy . . .

as President, I have, therefore, made a deliberate and strategic decision—as
a Pacific nation, the United States will play a larger and long-term role in
shaping this region and its future.[21]

Obama emphasized in his remarks that in a time of austerity, the Asia-
Pacific would be a "top priority" and that the reduction in the defense
budget would not "come at the expense of the Asia-Pacific." "My guidance
is clear," Obama continued. "As we plan and budget for the future, we
will allocate the resources necessary to maintain our strong military presence in this region. . . . So let there be no doubt: In the Asia-Pacific in the
twenty-first century, the United States of America is all in."[22]

It has been argued that cuts in the defense budget under the Obama
administration undermined the pivot to the Asia-Pacific.[23] However, in a
time of general austerity and budget cuts, the U.S. military forces in the
Asia-Pacific have been maintained in numbers and increased in capability,
as Obama promised in 2011.[24] This prioritizing of the Asia-Pacific suggests
that the pivot is being sustained and reinforcing the previous rebalancing,
although developments may not be proceeding as quickly as the Obama
administration envisaged in 2011. As Deputy Secretary of Defense Robert O.
Work stated in September 2014, "the Asia-Pacific rebalance is real as part
of a broader reexamination of our global posture. We might not be able
to go as fast as we would want because of budgetary pressure. We might
not be able to have as many forces as we would otherwise like. . . . But
the Asia-Pacific rebalance continues apace."[25] The United States remains
committed to security and stability in Europe, the Middle East, and other
regions such as Africa, the Americas, and the Arctic, but the emphasis and
priority is likely to be the Asia-Pacific region.[26] Despite a number of wars
and conflicts beyond that region, especially in the "arc of instability" from
North and Central Africa to the Middle East and Afghanistan, along with
Russian aggression in Ukraine and its growing assertiveness in Europe,
the U.S. rebalance and pivot to the Asia-Pacific have not been reversed.

Speeches and words have been followed up by action. U.S. military
capacity in maritime Asia has been enhanced.[27] In 2015, the more modern
USS *Ronald Reagan* replaced the USS *George Washington* at the Yokosuka
base in Japan. The modernized guided-missile cruiser USS *Chancellorsville*
and USS *Benfold*, an Aegis-capable destroyer, also arrived in Japan in 2015
to boost the Seventh Fleet.[28] This is a continuation of a trend that builds on

the rebalancing efforts of the 1990s and of the George W. Bush administration, although the emphasis on the Asia-Pacific during a period when the overall U.S. defense budget was declining suggests that the United States was prioritizing balancing China's growing power. An additional Aegis-capable destroyer will be deployed to Japan in 2017, and all three of the new DDG-1000 stealth destroyers will be home-porting with the Pacific fleet.

An additional nuclear attack submarine has been based in Guam, and a rotational deployment of littoral combat ships in Singapore enhances U.S. operations in the region's littoral waters. This is complemented by forward-stationing the most capable air assets, including F-22s, continuous deployment of B-2 and B-52 strategic bombers, additional tilt-rotor aircraft for the Marine Corps and Special Forces, and, in 2017, the first forward-stationing of F-35s to Iwakuni, Japan.[29] Even if these measures come on top of the substantial increase in U.S. forward military presence in the region during the rebalancing in the 1990s and 2000s, the pivot still marks a new priority in U.S. force posture and strategy. As Commander of the U.S. Pacific Command Admiral Harry B. Harris Jr. puts it, "everything that is new and cool that the United States is developing is going to the Pacific."[30]

The United States will probably remain committed to its two flanking regions, but since the balance of power is only being challenged in one region, East Asia, the contemporary power shift is likely to constrain the United States from strengthening its presence in Europe and the High North in the years to come and instead compel the United States to prioritize East Asia. Geopolitics matter in this assessment. U.S.-China rivalry in a new bipolar system will primarily be in the maritime domain. Balancing China's regional ambitions in maritime East Asia demands a strong U.S. air and naval presence. The primary challenge from Russia is on the ground in Europe. While its naval capabilities pose a threat, that threat remains secondary to the continental theater. Thus, U.S. ground forces might maintain a light footprint in Europe, but U.S. naval and air forces are likely to be concentrated in the Asia Pacific.

Over the next five years, according to the 2015 Asia-Pacific Maritime Security Strategy, the U.S. Navy will improve its ability to maintain a more regular and persistent maritime presence in the Pacific by increasing the number of ships assigned to the Pacific Fleet outside of U.S. territory by approximately 30 percent. "By 2020, 60 percent of naval and overseas air assets will be home-ported in the Pacific region."[31] Moreover, the

Obama administration's pivot was not only about military-force posture. The Obama administration stressed that its was a multifaceted strategy consisting of diplomatic, economic, military, institutional, and political engagement.[32] The United States has been more active in regional institutions, summits, and forums, for example, acceding to the ASEAN Treaty of Amity and Cooperation, stationing a U.S ambassador to ASEAN in Jakarta, and elevating the U.S.-ASEAN relationship to a strategic partnership.[33]

The United States is most likely to continue to prioritize the Asia-Pacific region even though the Trump administration has not presented a new strategy for the region. Shifts in the distribution of capabilities and a new bipolar system, along with the balance of power in the regions flanking the United States, strongly suggest that the United States will prioritize sustaining and increasing its presence in East Asia in the years to come. China's GDP and defense spending is today about the same as all other states in its region combined. Conversely, no state is in a position to dominate the European continent, the Middle East, or Africa. East Asia is the only region where the United States needs a strong forward presence to maintain a balance of power. Geostructural conditions will be predominant in shaping U.S. foreign policy and defense posture in a new bipolar system.

U.S. Allies and Nonaligned in Asia

As China becomes more powerful and increases its share in the distribution of capabilities within the international system, neighboring states are developing strategies to enhance their own security. They feel compelled to realign closer to one of the poles, creating significant dilemmas for makers of foreign policy. Power shifts compel smaller states to reconsider their defense, security, and foreign-policy alignments. Regional states are spending more on defense, and some have sought to establish a counterweight to China's rise and assertiveness by strengthening their ties with the United States.[34] Some have improved relations with the rising power; others remain reluctant to take sides and prefer to continue with a hedging strategy.[35]

U.S. treaty allies in maritime East Asia have done the most to resist the rise of China. Japan has strengthened its defense postures and alliance cooperation with the United States. Under Prime Minister Shinzō Abe, Japan is in the process of reinterpreting its pacifist constitution and upgrading the role of its self-defense forces to allow for participation in collective self-defense. The Japanese military has strengthened its deterrent capabilities with improved surveillance capabilities and expanded arms deployments in the East China Sea.[36] In August 2016, the Abe administration requested a record defense budget for 2017 of 5.16 trillion yen ($51 billion), and the defense budget has increased each of the last five years.[37] In addition, the U.S. basing structure in Japan has undergone changes in recent years, whereby Japan and the United States have sought to reduce the U.S. military's visible "footprint" but at the same time significantly upgrading the capabilities of American forces based in Japan.[38]

Japan has moved toward an upgraded security role and strategic diplomacy that would most likely have been unfeasible only a decade ago. It has developed strategic partnerships with countries on China's perimeter, including the Philippines, India, Vietnam, and Australia.[39] While restrictions on offensive weapons remain in place, Japan's ongoing national security reforms, which allow for a more active role for Japan's modernized armed forces, boost U.S. counterbalancing of China's rise. "Japan," Prime Minister Abe has announced, "is back."[40] Speeches and words, however, do not make Japan a great power, and Japan's security-enhancing measures have so far been relatively limited in scope. The abovementioned measures bolster Japan's capabilities, but Japan lacks the underlying resources to enable balancing in the contemporary U.S.-China bipolar system. Nonetheless, China's rise has produced a multifaceted Japanese strategic response to prevent China from posing a significant threat to Japanese security. It has energized Japan's ambitions to play a more prominent role in East Asian security affairs and presented a rationale for enhancing Japan's military capabilities, alliances, and diplomatic and strategic partnerships.

The defense and security measures initiated by the Philippines, another U.S. treaty ally, are not as significant and ambitious as Japan's. The Philippines has protested strongly against China's assertiveness and challenged the PRC's maritime claims in the South China Sea before an impartial arbitration tribunal.[41] It has initiated "the highest-ever increase in spending for military modernization in over two decades."[42] However, with limited military capabilities and financial resources, the Philippines is in no position to balance China or safeguard its interests in territorial disputes with China in the South China Sea. In addition to appealing to international law and boosting defense, Manila has consolidated its alli-

ance with the United States and strengthened its defense cooperation with
Japan. It signed the Enhanced Defense Cooperation Agreement (EDCA)
with the United States in April 2014, the first substantial bilateral defense
agreement since the end of the Cold War.[43] The agreement allows the
United States to station troops and equipment on Philippine territory
but not set up a permanent base.[44] However, the election of President
Duterte in 2016 has led to a cooling of U.S.-Philippine relations, even
though it remains to be seen whether Manila can establish more amicable
ties with Beijing and push the Philippines toward a more independent
foreign-policy stance.[45]

In May 2015, the Philippines and Japan held their first-ever joint South
China Sea exercise. This was followed by another that coincided with joint
U.S.-Philippine drills in the South China Sea in June the same year.[46] The
Philippines and Japan have also initiated talks on defense-equipment
transfers and visiting-forces agreements involving the exchange of military
defense equipment and technology as well as educational and personnel
exchanges. These steps, according to the Philippine defense secretary Vol-
taire Gazmin, "would have been unthinkable previously."[47] The Philippines
has also strengthened defense cooperation with Malaysia and Australia.[48]

Other U.S. treaty allies, including South Korea and Australia,[49] have
bolstered defense cooperation with the United States but simultaneously
showed reluctance to challenge China. South Korea has one of the most
difficult dilemmas. China became South Korea's largest trading partner
more than a decade ago, and its economy is increasingly dependent on
the Chinese. South Korea has enhanced cooperation with China to manage North Korean belligerence and seeks both to accommodate Chinese
interests and maintain its defense cooperation with the United States.[50]
But South Korea remains reluctant to improve defense ties with Japan.
China is also Australia's largest trading partner and New Zealand's largest
export market, but neither country depends on China for its security or
is directly involved in territorial and sovereignty disputes with China.
Geostructural conditions suggest that South Korea, in close geographical
proximity to China and more dependent on it for economic prosperity,
stability, and security, is more likely to drift toward China.[51] Australia
and New Zealand are more likely to sustain the alliances with the United
States but will seek to maintain hedging strategies that allow for cooperation with China.

Similar effects can be observed in the behavior of non-U.S. treaty allies. Most consequential, India is gradually moving closer to the United States[52] and the latter's regional partners.[53] Southeast Asian states prefer not to take sides, but the return of bipolarity is pushing the region toward polarization and making hedging more difficult. While Vietnam and the United States have improved their cooperation and defense ties,[54] China's military superiority over countries in Indochina suggests that states on the Southeast Asian mainland are more likely to bandwagon with China. Southeast Asian maritime states have more maneuverability but are more likely to align with the United States.

The indirect competition[55] over the alignments of smaller regional states has been the primary focus of U.S.-China rivalry in East Asia, rather than direct U.S.-China competition in bilateral arms races and defense spending. This has been a contributing factor in postponing the strong balancing of the new bipolar era. The ongoing competition for alignment, with East Asian spheres of influence under constant challenge, contrasts with Europe's Iron Curtain and East-West divide. China remains the dominant power on the East Asian mainland, and the United States maintains supremacy in the maritime domain; however, no status quo or equilibrium of the type that prevailed in Europe in the previous bipolar era is in sight in contemporary East Asia. Competition and instability will prevail.[56] This constrains the U.S.-China rivalry from going global and suggests that the new superpowers primarily will be concerned with instability and competition in East Asia.

The return of bipolarity shapes patterns of behavior and stability. The rise of China and the corresponding power shift are (1) the core drivers behind Japan's aspirations to become a "normal" great power and enhance its defense capabilities and security, (2) the reason why the Philippines is reinvigorating its alliance with the United States and developing unprecedented defense cooperation with Japan and other regional states, (3) important reasons for the dilemmas facing South Korea's defense and security alignment, (4) a central reason why Australia is adjusting its defense and security policy, (5) the main drivers behind India's "Act East policy," and (6) the major factor shaping the alignment and realignment of Southeast Asian states. East Asia would have looked very different without China's rise. The bipolar distribution of power is reshaping the region in new and unprecedented ways.

European Security and Transatlantic Ties

The shift of global power from West to East and the rise of China have contributed together with wars in the Middle East and Afghanistan to Washington's decision to downsize its military presence on its European flank. In 2013, Admiral James Stavridis, then head of U.S. European Command, informed the House Armed Services Committee in his defense-posture statement that U.S. forces in Europe had been reduced by more than 85 percent and basing sites by 75 percent since the end of the Cold War.[57] In 2014, Air Force General Philip Breedlove, former Supreme Allied Commander Europe and chief of U.S. European Command, called for a halt to the drawdown in Europe in order to counter the renewed military threat from Russia.[58]

In response to Russia's latest land grab in Crimea and involvement in the civil war in Ukraine, the United States has sought to reassure its NATO allies with Operation Atlantic Resolve.[59] Instead of deploying permanent forces to Europe, the new American strategy keeps a rotational presence of forward-deployed soldiers and seeks to increase the forward prepositioning of equipment to enhance the ability to reinforce Europe rapidly.[60] The NATO summit in Warsaw in 2016 agreed to build further on this approach by establishing in Eastern Europe an enhanced forward presence of multinational forces. This includes the rotational presence of four multinational Allied battalions in the three Baltic States and Poland; rotational deployment of a U.S. armored brigade combat team, headquartered in Poland; and the formation of the Very High Readiness Joint Task Force.[61]

Washington's downsizing of its military forces in Europe since the Cold War has so far not led to any robust European military buildup.[62] Because the Second World War drove the transition from multipolarity to bipolarity, the ensuing power vacuum and exhaustion of Great Britain's resources forced the United States to take responsibility for containing the Soviet Union's ambitions in both Europe and East Asia. The current shift from unipolarity to bipolarity has not been associated with similar power vacuums and dynamics, but European states remain prosperous and capable of taking more responsibility for their own defense and stability.

The GDP of each major power in Europe—Germany, France, Great Britain, and Italy—is larger than Russia's. Indeed, Russia's nominal GDP in 2016 was about the size of Spain's. The defense spending of any dual combination of Germany, France, or Great Britain would be larger than Russia's.[63] The combined conventional military forces of European NATO members are much larger than Russia's armed forces. Compared to East Asia, the difference is more striking. China's GDP is larger than all East and Southeast Asian states combined, as is China's defense budget. China's GDP and defense spending would match all these countries even if we added India and Russia to the equation. The PLA has more army, navy, air, sea, and missile capabilities, and a larger maritime surveillance agency or coast guard, than all the East and Southeast Asian states combined. Neither Russia, nor any other great or major power, can challenge any regional balance of power as China can. China is the only power with regional hegemonic aspirations, and it is developing capabilities to match those ambitions.[64] The rise of China compels the United States to concentrate its forces in East Asia.

Europe's NATO members have the resources to respond to the new bipolar system, and the German chancellor Angela Merkel has stated that "we in Europe have to take our fate into our own hands . . . [and] Europe can't rely on others,"[65] but it remains to be seen if Germany and the other European countries have the resolve to do so. Currently, the United States is spending roughly twice as much on defense in percentage of GDP than its European allies. The United States accounts for about three-quarters of NATO members' combined defense spending. This is basically Europe taking a free security ride and is incompatible with sustained transatlantic security cooperation. Washington expects its European allies to invest more in European security and their own defense. As it stands, however, European countries are unprepared to meet security challenges in their own neighborhood.

NATO's Deterrence Credibility

The historian Gaddis described Kennan's strategy for how the United States should maintain a balance of power at the start of the previous bipolar system. The United States may not pursue Kennan's containment strategy in the first period of the new bipolar system, but Kennan's emphasis on "the necessity, imposed by limited means, of establishing hierarchies of interests, of differentiating between the vital and the peripheral,"[66] is likely to guide the United States.[67] Europe and individual European states are lower on the priority list in Washington today than during the Cold War.

Such developments will have major implications for European defense and stability. NATO's eastward expansion during the unipolar era is leaving European states with more responsibilities with the advent of the new bipolar system concentrated on East Asia. This is a great disadvantage in light of Russia's recent actions. Most of the new NATO members in Eastern Europe are relatively weak. Lippmann's 1947 warning about containing "the Soviet Union by attempting to make 'unassailable barriers' out of the surrounding border states" is now more relevant than ever. "They are admittedly weak," noted Lippmann. "A weak ally is not an asset. It is a liability. It requires the diversion of power, money, and prestige to support it and to maintain it. These weak states are vulnerable. Yet the effort to defend them brings us no nearer to a decision or to a settlement of the main conflict."[68]

Compared to the previous bipolar system, the United States has a smaller military presence in Europe, and NATO has fewer resources but more responsibilities. And although Russia is threatening to expand, this is unlike the threat posed by the much more powerful Soviet Union. Russia's assertiveness and ambitions for control, for example, of the Baltic states do not present the same overarching security challenge as the Soviet Union did when contending for the control of Germany in the heart of Europe. Moreover, Russia is a revisionist power in Europe today; the Soviet Union, with its control of East Germany and a security buffer in Eastern Europe, was a status quo power. U.S. allies once questioned whether the United States would risk a nuclear war with the Soviet Union over Germany; today one might ask whether the United States would risk a nuclear war with Russia over Estonia, Latvia, or Lithuania. There are major differences between these two challenges, and they affect the credibility of NATO and U.S. defense commitments to Europe.

The stakes are not as high in Europe today as they were in the past; the Baltics are not Germany, and Russia is not the mighty Soviet Union. But the risk of conflict is increasing because NATO's deterrence is not as credible as it was during the Cold War. NATO's eastward expansion, combined with considerable defense cuts in Europe, the downsizing of U.S. forces in Europe, and uncertainty about the Trump administration's commitment to the NATO alliance, leaves allies wary and undermines NATO's Article 5. Accordingly, European states must take more responsibility for their own defense and stability or face higher security risks under the new bipolar system.

National, Collective, and Out-of-Area Defense

The previous unipolar system not only allowed for NATO expansion but also for out-of-area operations. Without a peer competitor or fear of superpower war, the United States was less constrained and freer to wage war against minor powers.[69] Not only was the only superpower free to roam, but smaller European states could participate in and wage wars in the Balkans, Iraq, Afghanistan, Libya, and Syria, behavior that for many European states was unthinkable during the previous bipolar system but possible in the shadow of U.S. primacy.

In a new bipolar system, European states and NATO are not only being pushed to take more responsibility for national and collective defense of an alliance that has moved its borders to Russia's surroundings, but European states are also forced to take more responsibility for out-of-area operations, such as security in Europe's "southern flank"—northern Africa and the Levant—and to manage nontraditional security challenges in their proximity or face higher security risks.[70] The new U.S.-China bipolar system is forcing European states to make tough choices between their national defense requirements, collective defense responsibilities, and participation in out-of-area operations. There is likely to be increased pressure in all areas in the wake of U.S. military retrenchment. European states will be torn between prioritizing national defense and traditional security concerns, illustrated by Russia's aggression in Ukraine; collective defense through NATO, the EU, or the UN; and new security challenges that will require a more proactive European stance on terrorism and other nontraditional security risks. European NATO allies also differ in their views on whether the main threats and challenges are to the south, the east, or even in to the high north. Prioritizing between limited resources and working out an appropriate division of labor will be a major challenge for European states and the transatlantic security community in the new bipolar era.

Diverging Views of China's Rise

Contending with a rising China and a resurgent Russia not only requires an adjustment to the transatlantic burden-sharing arrangement and compensating for the U.S. military drawdown in Europe. It also involves overcoming challenges in the difference between European and American approaches to China. The transatlantic relationship is struggling to work out military, security, economic, and diplomatic issues in relation to China's rise.[71] Differences in approaches to China reflect the fact that the United States, European states, and the European Union are unequal powers and distinct actors in international politics. Unlike European states, the United States maintains alliances and significant strategic and political interests in Asia given its regional and global defense and security responsibilities. While both the United States and European states see opportunities and challenges in China's growing market and economic power, the United States is more concerned about China's growing military power. European states are primarily not the ones having to face a potentially more threatening, aggressive, and expansionist China.

For the first time since the establishment of NATO, there is no longer a predominant common threat or challenge to the transatlantic alliance. In the aftermath of Russia's aggression in Ukraine, the refugee crisis sparked by the Arab spring and the wars in Libya and Syria, and the wave of terrorist attacks across European capitals, few European countries are thinking primarily about the challenges and threats from China. While some European NATO allies were reluctant to join the war on terrorism and some declined to support the United States in its war against Iraq, the war on terrorism provided a common threat and challenge to NATO during the first decade of the new century, and European NATO allies contributed militarily in Afghanistan. Few European states are willing or able to contribute militarily to any U.S. balancing of China today and in the years to come. This is likely to constrain the alliances across the Atlantic in the new bipolar era.

Strong transatlantic ties were forged when the United States and its European allies shared a common and overwhelming threat in the Soviet Union. The transatlantic alliance was sustained in the unipolar period as European NATO allies contributed to in- and out-of-area operations. The growing threat from Russia fosters new cohesion and commitment to collective defense and in-area operations. The dilemma, however, is that the alliance no longer shares a primary threat. If European states take more responsibility for European security and stability, it could relieve the United States of the primary burden of maintaining stability in Europe. This might allow the United States to keep a light footprint in Europe and more effectively pivot toward the Asia-Pacific, particularly China. While the proposition is still premature, it could make transatlantic defense and security cooperation more sustainable and boost Europe's role in regional and world affairs.[72] If Europe expects the United States to maintain its role as Europe's security guarantor for the foreseeable future at the same time as the United States is confronted with a peer competitor in East Asia, a region to which European states have no capabilities or willingness to contribute, then transatlantic ties are most likely to wither in the coming decades.

The Western alliance will need to cooperate in economic affairs and in upholding the international order, in which it has invested so heavily. But Europe's growing economic dependency on China and the U.S. request for higher European defense spending have the potential to compromise transatlantic relations. In 2017, China had become Germany's most important trading partner. As Germany simultaneously is pushed to take more responsibility for its own security and invest in a military buildup, ties between Germany and the United States are likely to diminish almost irrespectively of the personal chemistry between the leaders of the two powers.[73] If Germany spends 2 percent or more of its GDP on defense in five years—not an unlikely scenario but still not very much defense spending for a major power—Germany is still likely to have the highest defense spending in Europe by a large margin. This, in combination with strong economic ties to China, would strengthen Germany's independence and prominent role in Europe, which also suggests that transatlantic ties could wither.

The diverging threat perceptions of a rising China is the principal cause of strains in working out a common China policy in transatlantic relations, but the growing economic ties between China and European states are an important indicator of divergence, alerting us to the possibility that European states and the United States could take different paths in their relations with China. New geostructural conditions pose a major challenge to transatlantic ties.

Russia: Taking Advantage of Power Shifts

In a new bipolar system, Russia might lean toward one of the two poles or seek an independent role.[74] Moscow would prefer the latter, but Russia remains too weak to play any decisive role in the contemporary bipolar balance of power. Russia is most likely to lean toward China but will seek to take advantage of the U.S.-China rivalry to promote Russian interests.[75] Nor can we rule out whether Russia and China will drift apart, with Russia choosing to move closer to the United States in the coming decades.

The Sino-Russian strategic partnership has advanced in recent years. Ross argues that common interests in resisting U.S. power in their respective theaters drove the Sino-Soviet alliance in the 1950s and will likely be the basis of enhanced Sino-Russian strategic stability in the twenty-first century.[76] Sino-Russian cooperation allows Russia to prioritize its sphere of influence in Eastern Europe and the Caucasus and China to focus on its strategic shift onto the maritime domain while maintaining cooperation in Central Asia. The strategic partnership could develop into a formal alliance and continental bloc that would control the "heartland" and challenge the U.S.-led maritime bloc and alliance system. Increased tension between a democratic and an authoritarian camp could reinvigorate Cold War thinking.[77] Sustained transatlantic cooperation would be needed to balance a stronger Sino-Russian partnership, but the United States cannot give equal attention to its two flanking regions. As long as European states remain unprepared to meet such a security challenge, it will give Russia more opportunities.

The Sino-Russian strategic partnership will not be one of equals. China will be in the driver's seat, which Moscow will dislike. Russia will seek to avoid becoming too dependent on China. There is a strategic rationale in cooperating that allows China and Russia to confront the United States on its two flanking regions. However, Russia has little to offer China in a conflict in East Asia, and China has little influence over NATO's eastward expansion and Russia's core security concerns. The Sino-Russian strategic partnership in the unipolar era was founded on mutual suspicion and apprehension about U.S. primacy. This rationale is undermined by the return of bipolarity. The new bipolar distribution of capabilities, the Sino-Russian power transition, and growing asymmetry in the bilateral relationship fuel suspicions in Moscow about China's strategic interests.

Coupled with the historical legacy of mistrust, animosity, and diverging cultural traditions, the Sino-Russian strategic partnership may be unsustainable.

While Russia's aggression in Ukraine and assertiveness toward NATO suggest the proposition is unlikely, another possibility that cannot be ruled out as an effect of the shifting distribution of capabilities is that the United States and Russia might be pushed toward a partnership or closer ties as a result of China's growing might. Russia has a realist view of world affairs, shares U.S. concerns about a rising China, and focuses on traditional security issues and great-power politics. Russia's geographical position and inroads into Central Asia make Russia a potential strategic partner for the United States in counterbalancing China. As Walt pointed out more than a decade ago, "a revitalized Russia would be more useful ally against a rising China" than European allies, "which is a good reason why the U.S. should not humiliate Moscow by expanding NATO ever eastward."[78] Increased Russian leverage in a U.S.-China bipolar system could challenge the relationship between the United States and its NATO allies, just as closer economic ties between China and Europe and European states' reluctance to join the U.S. counterbalancing of China's rise could undermine transatlantic relations.

The example of China's alliance with the Soviet Union, isolation after the Sino-Soviet split, and rapprochement with the United States during the previous bipolar system shows that it will be very difficult to predict Russia's strategic behavior in the coming decades. Nonetheless, a new bipolar system presents an opportunity for a resurgent Russia to strengthen its presence in Eastern Europe and the Middle East. It can take advantage of the Washington's military drawdown in Europe and the Middle East and European states' reluctance to boost defense spending and participate in out-of-area operations, and it can test NATO's credibility and willingness to defend new NATO members in Eastern Europe. Russian military exercises close to the border of Eastern European NATO members, combined with strategic overflight, intelligence operations, cyber attacks, and propaganda campaigns, will increasingly contest the individual national defenses of NATO members and the alliance's commitment to collective defense and cooperation. It remains to be seen whether European states in the short and medium term will be able to boost their defense capabilities and whether NATO will have the capabilities to deter Russia.

Sanctions imposed by the United States and the European Union in response to the annexation of Crimea and aggression in Ukraine have, together with lower oil prices, weakened the Russian economy. However, the recession has so far been less severe than the recession that hit the Russian economy following the financial crisis in 2007–2008.[79] Russia bounced back from the last crisis only to launch its aggression in Ukraine. Sanctions have deepened and reinforced the slump in the economy in 2014–2015, but more important in the longer term is the effect that sanctions could have on cooperation and economic interdependence between Russia and Europe. If a trend toward less integration, declining trade, limited collaboration, and the abandonment of any partnership continues, then Russia will have less to lose from confronting the European Union and NATO. Russia's turn eastward and the signing of large petroleum deals with China, coupled with growth in Russian petroleum exports to Northeast Asia, are additional factors that give Russia more leverage in its dealings with the West and increase the risk of conflict.

Nontraditional Security Challenges, Institutions, and World Order

Shifts in the distribution of capabilities will affect the United States and China more than nontraditional security challenges. It remains to be seen if international politics will shift from order to disorder in the absence of U.S. primacy.[80] The return of bipolarity promises more stability than if the international system had returned to multipolarity. Instability at the power center in East Asia makes U.S.-China confrontation at the periphery less likely. The new bipolar system might avoid the devastation of the Cold War era, during which the superpowers supported proxies in civil wars.[81] Since rivalry and confrontation between the superpowers are mainly at sea, the risk of a limited war is higher, but the superpowers in the twenty-first century might thereby avoid the far more destructive wars of the previous multipolar system, where the great powers clashed on land.

The United States is likely to become a more restrained and selective superpower,[82] less willing to uphold the current global order and provide collective goods as it becomes increasingly concerned with superpower rivalry. With the United States preoccupied with the regional balance of power in East Asia, Ross warns us that the rise of China will bring about the demise of U.S. global "unipolarity" and result in less, not more, secu-rity.[83] The U.S. pivot to the Asia-Pacific is likely to continue apace, and there is likely to be more uncertainty and possibly even power vacuums in Europe, the Middle East, and Africa, with corresponding security concerns and instability. Nonetheless, conflict and disorder on the periphery are less likely to resemble the destruction of the previous bipolar period: the superpowers are unlikely to be as strongly involved in proxy wars because the status quo is being challenged at the power center in East Asia. More-over, the United States is unlikely to abandon the current international institutional order, and China is currently committed to largely sustaining that order, even though Beijing is seeking to reconfigure it and gradually develop an alternative international institutional order through the Belt and Road initiative. Finally, the bipolar system is likely to compel and constrain the United States from undertaking some of the military interventions and destabilizing wars it pursued during the unipolar era. A more restrained and selective United States, focused on balancing China at the new power center in East Asia, is going to be less able to roam freely.

Growing U.S.-China rivalry and China's more recent assertiveness will have spillover effects on global and regional institutions and multilateralism and potentially undermine cooperation. The return of bipolarity is likely to marginalize the United Nations, as it did during the previous bipolar period. From 1948 to 1989, the UN Security Council passed only eight resolutions invoking Chapter VII, which refers to members' responsibility to "maintain or restore international peace and security." From 1990 to 2011, 511 such resolutions were passed, more than sixty times the Cold War figure, and the number of troops deployed for UN peacekeeping operations more than quintupled in that timeframe.[84] Moreover, alternative institu-tions and an emerging new order will gradually challenge the U.S. liberal order and the Bretton Woods system.

China has been working closely with regional institutions to become socialized into multilateralism and the established international order. While it continues to promote its peaceful development strategy, with growing relative power it has now become more assertive and is gradually moving away from the principles that has guided its peaceful rise since Deng Xiaoping. Principles such as securing China's position and showing restraint, rising within the existing order, never seeking leadership and maintaining a low profile, noninterference in other countries' internal affairs, and biding time and hiding capabilities have now transformed into a more active and assertive strategy, reflected in the Belt and Road initiative. China's expansion in Eurasia and at sea can hardly be reversed, as China grows more powerful. However, it is natural that the United States and China's neighbors would become alarmed by this geopolitical development. Thus, it is becoming more difficult for China to reassure neighbors of its benign intentions. China is clearly taking on a stronger leadership role and seeking to establish an alternative international institutional order. The Belt and Road initiative is also gradually forcing China to abandon noninterference as China increasingly seeks to safeguard investments and Chinese overseas workers in numerous infrastructure projects abroad. In addition, China can no longer bide its time and hide its capabilities.

China's recent behavior in the South China Sea contradicts the code of conduct to which it agreed when it was relatively weaker in the early years of the new century. ASEAN has been an important forum for regional cooperation, and China has promoted its strategy of peaceful development there. In the last few years, however, this leading regional organization has become more polarized. Members have often been divided by their alignment with China or the United States, and the superpowers have increasingly used the institution to advance their diplomatic and strategic objectives. In 2012, no communiqué was released by the ASEAN ministers in Cambodia, owing to divergent views on the aggressive activities of China in the disputed waters of the South China Sea. U.S. Secretary of State Hillary Clinton used her remarks at the ASEAN Regional Forum in 2010 to challenge China's activities in the South China Sea.[85] Such developments coincided with the transition from a unipolar to a bipolar system, and one can expect that ASEAN will become more polarized and marginalized in the new bipolar system.

A return to superpower rivalry will shape the potential for cooperation on a number of global issues. Challenges related to the environment, economic stability, terrorism, proliferation of weapons of mass destruction, and a number of other transnational issues will be more difficult to manage when the superpowers increasingly engage in traditional balance-of-power and confrontational politics toward each other. Shifts at the structural level help explain why the United States is modifying its counterterrorism operations and intervening less in humanitarian affairs. The United States is becoming more reluctant to take the lead in costly humanitarian-intervention operations and will want to avoid being bogged down in military operations against terrorists, extremists, and authoritarian regimes in Syria, Iraq, Libya, and Mali now that it is being challenged by a peer competitor in East Asia.[86] Superpower rivalry in the twenty-first century will condition how and to what degree nontraditional security threats such as terrorism and extremism, piracy, and cyber attacks will increase and flourish or be managed and contained.

When the superpowers pursue more confrontational policies under bipolarity than unipolarity, then such a pattern of behavior is likely to constrain trade negotiations, compromise climate agreements, undermine energy security, and weaken development aid work. If global challenges are to be overcome and lasting solutions implemented, then there is a need to understand the new superpower dynamics. As the return of bipolarity compels the United States toward a preoccupation with U.S.-China regional competition, U.S. contribution to global stability is likely to erode. The return of bipolarity will have important bilateral, regional, and global effects.

CONCLUSION: A NEW BIPOLAR SYSTEM
AND ITS CONSEQUENCES

Systemic effects and the importance of polarity continue to have a "profound impact on international politics."[87] Superpower rivalry is again beginning to preoccupy the United States. A new bipolar system centered on East Asia and U.S.-China relations is compelling the United States to ramp up its military presence in the Asia-Pacific, maintain a moderate presence in Europe, modify its war on terrorism, and adjust its role in humanitarian interventions and participation in constabulary tasks (the antipiracy mission in the Gulf of Aden being one example of the latter). International organizations are becoming marginalized and the idea of multilateralism less persuasive. China is behaving more assertively, and its increased relative power has sparked its ambitious Belt and Road initiative. Japan is changing its defense posture and seeking to become a more normalized power. European states are being pushed to take more responsibility for their own security.[88] Russia is gaining more maneuverability in the shadow of superpower rivalry. The security environment in East Asia and Europe is becoming more polarized.

Structural realism, however, cannot explain and predict how states will respond to structural shifts and new pressures and possibilities. Such knowledge requires state- and agency-level analyses that account for the making of foreign policy and leaders' motivations.[89] Additional causal factors and analytical levels are needed to explain how and why China's neighbors will align and realign in response to the emergence of the new bipolar system. Structural realism provides a starting point[90] for examining how the return of bipolarity is likely to shape European security and transatlantic ties, Russian assertiveness, and a new international order. Geostructural realism can explain why stability and balancing are different when comparing two bipolar systems. It takes us one step further in explaining and predicting balancing behavior and stability and structural effects. But similar to structural realism, it can only describe and understand the new pressure states are subject to, not how states adapt to new structural conditions. The foreign policies that states will pursue, how institutions will respond, and the extent to which new security actors will prosper and proliferate under the new structural conditions require an examination of second- and first-image factors.

Chapter 8

CONCLUSION: GEOSTRUCTURAL REALISM

Kenneth N. Waltz argued that simply adding a variable to a theory is not enough to plug a gap in a theory. "To add to a theory something that one believes has been omitted requires showing how it can take its place as one element of a coherent and effective theory."[1] This book shows how geopolitics can take its place as one element that complements structural realism, enhancing its explanatory and predictive power. I have termed such a reconfigured theory "geostructural realism." In chapters 5, 6, and 7, I showed that the return of bipolarity and its systemic effects do not entirely correspond with the predictions of structural realism. By adding geopolitics to neorealist theory we can better understand and explain why structural change and the return of bipolarity have not led to the expected actions and outcomes. The geostructural-realist theory developed here, in contrast to neorealism, allows us to predict whether a new bipolar system in the twenty-first century will be more or less stable than the bipolar system of the twentieth century and accounts for different balancing behavior between bipolar systems.

The first step, however, was to demonstrate that the contemporary distribution of capabilities in the international system is indeed bipolar. I used three criteria to examine the polarity shift. First, I measured the power gap between the United States and China, concluding that it had narrowed to the extent that allowed China to vault into top-ranking status. Second, I considered the widening power gap between China and other great powers contending for top ranking, concluding that no third power is capable of challenging the top two. Third, I compared the current distribution of capabilities with those at the origins of the previous bipolar system, concluding that it was roughly similar.

If the theory is good, Waltz argued, then "we will see the kind of behavior and record the range of outcomes the theory leads us to expect."[2] The features of the previous bipolar system were strong balancing, stability, and strong competition and rivalry at the periphery. The contemporary bipolar system is characterized by moderate balancing, instability, and limited competition and rivalry at the periphery. Parsimonious neorealist theory needs geopolitics to account for these different structural effects.

This should not surprise us. Events never happen under the same circumstances.[3] The axiom that history never repeats itself exactly would leave us to believe that the Cold War will never return. Nonetheless, explanations and understandings of international politics often arise from comparing and differentiating events and political situations. We must, in Morgenthau's view, learn to distinguish between the similarities and differences of two political situations.[4] Geostructural realism accounts for similarities and differences in distributions of capabilities and their outcomes and records the kind of behaviors and consequences we would expect to see as the international system reverts to bipolarity.

CONTEMPORARY BIPOLARITY

If we examine the international system from a bipolarity perspective, with the United States and China as the two poles or superpowers, we arrive at different explanations and predictions about China's rise and the present and future effect of this rise on the nature and intensity of security competition in Asia and world affairs. The current polarity debate is essentially about whether China is reaching power parity with the United States; the conclusion so far is either that unipolarity persists, that the current international system is in transition to multipolarity, or that a new multipolar system has already emerged.[5] However, in this book I have argued that China, by virtue of its current combined capabilities, has moved from great-power to superpower status, even though it has only "barely"[6] made it to the top position together with the United States. Its status as a superpower and pole in a new bipolar system does not depend on whether it obtains power parity with the United States, becomes a regional hegemon, or develops global power projection; its status is instead defined according to the contemporary distribution of capabilities.

Discussing whether China has obtained power parity with the United States is important but will not in itself tell us whether the polarity of the system is changing from unipolarity to bipolarity or to multipolarity. The state of power parity is not sufficient to determine whether the international system has returned to bipolarity, something the asymmetric power relationship between the United States and the Soviet Union during the previous bipolar system demonstrates. Equally important is that China can be defined as a superpower in view of its superiority over the power next in rank.

The Gap Between Number 2 and Number 3

The power gap between the second- and third-ranking power is now so great that it marks the origins of a new bipolar system. This allows us to reexamine the widely anticipated arrival of multipolarity. Multipolarity, where three or more great powers have roughly equal capabilities, is nowhere in sight in the current international system.[7] Participants in the contemporary polarity debate have overlooked the importance of the power gap between the second- and the third-ranking power in determining the polarity of the current international system. This was the crucial issue that preoccupied Morgenthau and other observers at the start of the previous bipolar system when they examined how the big three—Britain, the United States, and the Soviet Union—had dropped to two. Similarly, the power gap between the second- and the third-ranking power was vital when considering the international system in the aftermath of the hegemonic wars of the Napoleonic era. Britain, the dominating sea power, and Russia, the dominating land power, were more powerful than any other great power in 1814. However, their superiority over the third-ranking power, France, was not sufficient to shift the distribution of capabilities from a multipolar to a bipolar system.

The return of bipolarity has important implications. It challenges the widespread assumption that U.S.-China relations are ripe for tragedy based on analogies of great-power rivalry under multipolar systems.[8] From a

structural-realist point of view, bipolarity and multipolarity are two fundamentally different starting points for analysis. Instead of comparing U.S.-
China relations to great-power rivalry and wars in the past, from a bipolar
perspective we can start with the analogy of the "long peace" between the
superpowers during the Cold War. While my analysis has shown that geopolitics makes the contemporary bipolar system more prone to instability
and a limited war than the previous bipolar system, geostructural realism
is not a deterministic theory. China and the United States might move
from a peaceful rise to a "long peace."[9]

Comparing Bipolar Systems

Examining the extent to which the current distribution of capabilities
approximates the distribution at the start of the last bipolar system has
been an important third factor in establishing whether the contemporary
international system has returned to bipolarity. The power gap between
the two leading states today, the United States and China, and the third-
ranking power is similar to that between the two top-ranked superpowers
and the great powers in 1950. No states other than the United States and
China are within reach of the top position, and for the foreseeable future
no third state will be capable of developing a combined capability comparable to either the United States or China. Consequently, these observations
suggest that if one agrees that the international system was bipolar in 1950,
it is hard to deny that it is bipolar today.

It is important not to conflate bipolarity with the Cold War. The post–
World War II system became bipolar because all other powers were distinctly inferior to the United States and the Soviet Union. The fact that the
Soviet Union was a dominating power on the Eurasian continent shaped
the Cold War but did not make the system bipolar. Russia has dominated
the Eurasian continent in the past without changing the system from multipolarity to bipolarity. The international system shifted to bipolarity because
the distribution of capabilities changed during and after the Second World
War. The Soviet Union's westward expansion during the Second World
War pushed the bipolar system toward a cold war by bringing the Red
Army to the doorstep of Central and Western Europe, allowing the Soviet
threat to dominate the European continent and requiring the injection of

U.S. power into Western Europe. A land border divided Europe, strong balancing ensued, and stability in Europe allowed for superpower rivalry, conflict, and confrontation at the periphery.

The contemporary bipolar system does not share the Cold War characteristics of the previous bipolar period, in large part because of different geopolitics. China is not a Eurasian power like the Soviet Union or Russia. However, since the United States has no strong military presence on the Asian mainland, China dominates this geographical space more strongly than the Soviet Union dominated a divided European continent. China and the United States are confronting each other at sea, not on land. The regional balance of power will largely be decided in East Asian waters. The geopolitical differences explain the different characteristics of the two bipolar systems: why the stopping power of water postpones strong balancing; why the current bipolar system is more unstable, with a higher risk of war at the power center in East Asia; and why the superpowers are less likely to pursue rivalry and confrontation in other regions.

Structural realists acknowledge the role played by both structure- and unit-level factors in international politics. Contemporary stronger economic interdependence, an international institutional order, less ideological rivalry, and the role of nuclear weapons are factors that help explain why the patterns of behavior typical of the two bipolar systems are different. Structural realism leaves some things aside in order to concentrate on others, and this book has mainly focused on adding geopolitics to the structural factors in neorealism. It has also sought to establish a hierarchy of causes. The shift in the distribution of capabilities is the primary cause of increased U.S.-China balancing, and geopolitics is the main factor explaining why contemporary strong balancing is postponed and why there is a higher risk that the superpowers will be involved in a limited war in maritime East Asia. Geostructural realism allows us to predict that in some respects the new bipolar system is likely to be more unstable and shape superpower balancing differently than the previous bipolar system.

Power Change Versus Power Transition

The preoccupation with power parity has not only neglected that a top-ranking position in a bipolar system does not require power parity but has also stimulated a premature analysis that applies power-transition theory[10] to U.S.-China relations. Power-transition theory is inadequate in explaining the new power dynamics in East Asia, which is characterized by power *change*, not transition.[11] In contemporary East Asia, the rising power, China, has not gone to war to change the status quo, and the existing leading power, the United States, has not launched a preventive war to preserve it. The United States remains the most powerful state within the international system, and China's power in East Asia has not surpassed that of the United States. Power has been redistributed between the United States and China, and the relative power shift continues, but there has not been a power transition between China and the United States. The rise of China has not reached the point where there is a heightened risk of a power-transition war.

In addition, power transition and growing asymmetry in China's relations with its neighbors, Russia, India, and Japan, have not contributed to any wars. East Asia has been the most peaceful region in the world for more than three decades, despite power transitions within the region and China's phenomenal rise. It is the redistribution of power in the system and the shift from unipolarity to bipolarity that is behind the tendency toward balancing and compelling China to challenge the status quo. The heightened risk of war in U.S.-China relations is more an effect of power changes and geographical factors than power transition.

BUILDING ON STRUCTURAL REALISM

Neorealism explains change across systems, not within roughly similar systems. Geostructural realism opens up for a theory that can account for shifts in the distribution of capabilities, the better to compare and analyze similar polarities and their effects.

A More Balanced System

Several studies have explained why the world has remained "out of balance" in the post–Cold War period.[12] Waltz argued that the international system is seldom in balance or equilibrium. Instead, his theory expects that "a balance, once disrupted, will be restored one way or another."[13] As such, it was maintained that "no contradiction exists between saying that international political systems tend strongly *toward* balance but are seldom *in* balance."[14] The shift from unipolarity to bipolarity and the asymmetric power relationship between the United States and China confirm neorealism's proposition that balances of power recurrently form and that the international system tends toward balance "one way or another."[15] The unbalanced unipolar system has been balanced by a new bipolar system, but Waltz's prediction in the post–Cold War era that "multipolarity is developing before our eyes" has proved to be misguided.[16] In other words, neorealism becomes validated when the international system is no longer unipolar irrespective of whether bipolarity or multipolarity reemerges; the predictions about a shift to multipolarity in the 1990s and 2000s, however, have turned out wrong. Without providing any decisive conclusion, Waltz asked: "Should delay in completing a balance be taken as evidence contradicting balance of power theory?"[17] The answer is no, but it shows that structural realism as a theory is incomplete.

The return of bipolarity fosters more stability than if the international system had shifted to multipolarity. The long peace of the previous bipolar system suggests that U.S.-China bipolarity might avoid the tragedy of great-power politics under multipolarity. However, neorealism cannot answer whether bipolarity in the twenty-first century will be more stable than it was in the twentieth century. By complementing structural realism with geopolitics, in this book I have argued that a bipolar system concentrated on maritime East Asia in the twenty-first century is likely to be more unstable and prone to limited war than the bipolar system concentrated on continental Europe was in the twentieth century. In addition, instability at the power center in East Asia is likely to foster more stability at the periphery than during the previous bipolar era, since the superpowers are likely to be less involved in proxy wars. These are important propositions when considering the debate about the potential for rivalry and conflict in U.S.-China relations in the first half of the twenty-first century. Geostructural realism accounts for why stability and patterns of behavior are different between two bipolar systems.

The Degree and Intensity of Balancing

China's rise and the corresponding shifts in the distribution of capabilities have not only contributed to a more balanced system and reshaped the prospect for stability. China and the United States are increasingly, if only gradually, balancing against each other. However, the balancing of the superpowers under bipolarity in the twenty-first century does not resemble the balancing under bipolarity in the twentieth century. Strong balancing remains postponed.[18] Instead, the shift from unipolarity to bipolarity has accentuated a change from limited to moderate balancing in U.S.-China relations. By complementing neorealism with geopolitics, geostructural realism can better explain the patterns of balancing behavior and predict that strong balancing will be postponed until China obtains more power parity with the United States than the Soviet Union achieved. However, like structural realism, geostructural realism cannot say how long the process will take.[19] Geostructural realism explains why the superpowers' pattern of behavior at the start of a new bipolar system is different from the behavior at the start of the previous bipolar system. It can also explain why contemporary strong balancing is delayed even though neorealist theory predicts sameness of balancing under roughly similar structural conditions.

Future Polarity Shifts and Geostructural Realism

Geostructural realism can provide theoretical guidance to future studies of the stability and patterns of behavior of a potential unipolar system with China as the only pole, a multipolar system concentrated on Asia rather than Europe, or bipolar systems with the two superpowers located on the same continent. For example, by combining polarity and geopolitics we can predict whether a unipolar system with China as the only pole or superpower in the second half of the twenty-first century is likely to be more or less stable than the post–Cold War U.S. unipolar system. Other than the United States, there are no superpowers or great powers in the Western Hemisphere. During the unipolar era, the United States was separated from other great powers by the Pacific and Atlantic Oceans. Its power preponderance therefore posed less of a threat to any other great power.[20]

If China was to become the only superpower in a new unipolar system in the future, it is likely to border another great power, and its power preponderance would potentially cause a more rapid shift toward balancing and relatively more instability than the previous U.S. unipolar system. Since Waltz's theory did not consider the effect of geopolitics, predictions based on neorealism could not account for why the unipolar system saw limited balancing against U.S. primacy, which sparked the so-called soft-balancing debate.[21] Geostructural realism can potentially predict and explain why the trend toward balancing will evolve more rapidly in a hypothetical China-dominated unipolar system and why balancing is likely to be more prominent and stronger than during the previous unipolar system.

Similarly, if a multipolar system reappears in the future, it is likely to be less stable than a bipolar one, but geostructural realism would expect a multipolar system concentrated on Europe to be more unstable than a multipolar system concentrated on Asia. Neorealist theory does not allow us to make such predictions. Asia's terrain and China's geographical size suggest that a potential multipolar system concentrated on Asia would have different dynamics than the previous multipolar system concentrated on Europe or a potential future multipolar system concentrated on Europe. The most obvious point is that the potential great powers in such a multipolar system, China, India, Russia, Japan, and the United States, will geographically be much further away from one another and separated by more formidable natural barriers, including the Himalayas, permafrost, desert, and oceans, than the great powers in Europe during previous multipolar systems. That there are fewer states on the Asian mainland compared to the European continent is also likely to foster more stability.

Furthermore, while it is highly unlikely that Russia or Germany will become poles in a bipolar system in the twenty-first century, it is likely that a new bipolar system concentrated on Europe, with the two superpowers located on the same continent, would be more unstable and prone to strong balancing than in the past and in comparison with the current bipolar system or a potential China-India bipolar system in the future. If Russia and Germany had experienced anything similar to the rise of China, they would almost certainly have been revisionist powers seeking to expand on the European continent. Without the geopolitical space that allowed the Soviet Union and the United States to expand their spheres of influence and establish a new status quo during and after the Second World War, this would probably have been the most unstable bipolar system. Since it is relatively easier to expand, invade, and occupy territory over a relatively flat European continent than across the Himalayas or an ocean, another bipolar system concentrated on Europe—especially if it were composed of two continental European superpowers—would likely be more unstable than the previous bipolar system and the contemporary bipolar system concentrated on East Asia. In the same vein, the Himalayas would most likely have a moderating effect on strong balancing in a potentially new China-India bipolar system in the second half of the twenty-first century.

Such geostructural realist predictions and reasoning build on Fox's observation that the prospect for stability was enhanced when none of the leading powers following the Second World War were located within Western Europe.[22] By refining Waltz's theory and developing geostructural realism we can better explain and predict contemporary and future superpower and great-power politics. Clearly, a new U.S.-China bipolar international system will shape international politics. Structural realism, complemented by geopolitics, has now returned as a more prominent explanatory theory after providing less understanding and explanation of state behavior during the unipolar post–Cold War period. The geostructural-realist theory developed here will provide an important starting point for those seeking to understand the new superpower rivalry and its effect on international politics in the twenty-first century.

NOTES

1. INTRODUCTION: A NEW BIPOLAR SYSTEM

1. Kenneth N. Waltz, "The Stability of a Bipolar World," *Daedalus* 93, no. 3 (Summer 1964): 881–909; Kenneth N. Waltz, *Man, the State, and War: A Theoretical Analysis* (New York: Columbia University Press, 1959); and Kenneth N. Waltz, *Theory of International Politics* (1979; Long Grove, Ill.: Waveland, 2010).

2. Barry R. Posen, "From Unipolarity to Multipolarity: Transition in Sight?" in *International Relations Theory and the Consequences of Unipolarity*, ed. John G. Ikenberry, Michael Mastanduno, and William C. Wohlforth (Cambridge: Cambridge University Press, 2011), 317–341, 321.

3. Chapter 4 examines Russia's and India's combined capabilities scores and argues that they contend for third-ranking position. I also argue that neither Germany nor Japan matches China's power in the aggregate.

4. The phrase "stopping power of water" is from John J. Mearsheimer, *The Tragedy of Great Power Politics*, 2nd ed. (New York: Norton, 2014), esp. chap. 4. Mearsheimer argues that the stopping power of water prevents the most powerful states from becoming global hegemons because of the difficulties in conquering and holding distant territories separated by water. Aside from a new preface and a new conclusion, Mearsheimer's revised edition of *The Tragedy* book is similar to the first. I refer to the second edition throughout this study. However, many other studies before Mearsheimer's see water as a barrier that can isolate a conflict, constrain power projection, sustain spheres of influence, and uphold a status quo. See Thomas C. Schelling, *The Strategy of Conflict* (Cambridge, Mass.: Harvard University Press, 1980), 74–77; William T. R. Fox, *The Super-Powers: The United States, Britain, and the Soviet Union—Their Responsibility for Peace* (New York: Harcourt, Brace & World, 1944), 22; Nicholas J. Spykman, *America's Strategy in World Politics: The United States*

and the Balance of Power (New York: Harcourt, Brace & World, 1942; Hamden, Conn.: Archon, 1970), 446–472; Nicholas J. Spykman, *The Geography of the Peace* (New York: Harcourt, Brace and Company, 1944; Hamden, Conn.: Archon, 1970); and Robert S. Ross, "The Geography of Peace: East Asia in the Twenty First Century," *International Security* 23, no. 4 (Spring 1999): 81–118.

5. This book emphasizes a "more or less" instead of an "either/or" perspective to balancing. Superpowers and great powers have always balanced by internal and external means, but the intensity and degree of balancing differ and are shaped by both systemic and unit-level factors. In differentiating between intensity and degree of balancing, we can speak of strong, moderate, and limited balancing. The early period of the previous bipolar system witnessed strong balancing, and the current bipolar system is characterized by moderate balancing, which can be differentiated from the limited balancing of the unipolar post–Cold War era. For further discussion, see chapter 5.

6. East Asia has become the new power center in world politics because this is where power is concentrated, and East Asia is the only region where a new regional hegemon might emerge. The two contemporary superpowers are mainly contending for the balance of power in East Asia, similar to when the United States was preoccupied with preventing the Soviet Union from becoming the regional hegemon in Europe during the early Cold War years.

7. This phrase is borrowed from Ross, "The Geography of Peace," 82. Ross takes the title of his article from Spykman, *The Geography of Peace.*

8. Of the more than 1,000 papers presented at the fifty-fourth, fifty-fifth, fifty-sixth, and fifty-seventh annual International Studies Association conferences in 2013, 2014, 2015, and 2016, none had either the word "bipolarity" or "bipolar" in its title (search by subject "bipolarity" and "bipolar" in the annual conventions PDF programs). Nor did more than a few papers have "unipolarity" or "multipolarity" in their titles. This might suggest polarity is not an interesting or important research topic. Conversely, most scholars, researchers, and Ph.D. students might have accepted or been unwilling to challenge the unipolarity thesis developed in the 1990s and 2000s and authoritatively subscribed to by leading scholars in various contributions to Ikenberry, Mastanduno, and Wohlforth, eds., *International Relations Theory.*

9. One of China's leading U.S.-China experts, Yan Xuetong, argues in a short article that bipolarity is a more likely outcome than multipolarity. See Yan Xuetong, "A Bipolar World Is More Likely Than a Unipolar or Multipolar One," *China-US Focus Digest,* April 20, 2015, http://www.chinausfocus.com/foreign-policy/a-bipolar-world -is-more-likely-than-a-unipolar-or-multipolar-one/. Another short article by Judy Dempsey notes "the emergence of a new bipolar world," but there is no comprehensive examination of the contemporary distribution of capabilities, the role of geopolitics, or the implications for Waltz's structural-realist theory. See Judy Dempsey, "The United States and China: The Return of a Bipolar World," *Carnegie Europe,* November 12, 2012, http://carnegieeurope.eu/strategiceurope/?fa=49969. Although Noah Feldman, *Cool War: The Future of Global Competition* (New York: Random House, 2013), examines the close cooperation between the United States and China in economics and sees in their intense security and great-power rivalry the emergence of a new "cool war," it does not consider the effects of bipolarity or provide

any in-depth analysis of the importance of geopolitics. Mark O. Yeisley, "Bipolarity, Proxy Wars, and the Rise of China," *Strategic Studies Quarterly* 5, no. 4 (Winter 2011): 75–91, has pointed to the likelihood of bipolarity and the risk of U.S.-China proxy wars but offers no comprehensive analysis of the return of bipolarity.

10. Waltz, *Theory of International Politics*, 98.
11. Waltz, *Theory of International Politics*, 98–99.
12. Fox, *The Super-Powers*; Hans J. Morgenthau, *Politics Among Nations: The Struggle for Power and Peace*, 2nd ed. (New York: Knopf, 1954), 324–326.
13. Waltz, *Theory of International Politics*, 98.
14. Posen, "From Unipolarity to Multipolarity," 321.
15. Charles Krauthammer, "The Unipolar Moment," *Foreign Affairs* 70, no. 1 (1990–1991): 23–33; Charles Krauthammer, "The Unipolar Moment Revisited," *National Interest* 70, no. 5 (2002–2003): 5–17; Michael Mastanduno, "Preserving the Unipolar Moment: Realist Theories and U.S. Grand Strategy After the Cold War," *International Security* 21, no. 4 (Spring 1997): 44–98; Samuel P. Huntington, "The Lonely Superpower," *Foreign Affairs* 78, no. 2 (March–April 1999); Aaron L. Freidberg, "Ripe for Rivalry: Prospect for Peace in a Multipolar Asia," *International Security* 18, no. 3 (Winter 1993–1994): 5–33; Charles A. Kupchan, "After Pax Americana: Benign Power, Regional Integration, and the Sources of Stable Multipolarity," *International Security* 23, no. 3 (Fall 1998): 40–79; Richard N. Haass, "The Age of Nonpolarity: What Will Follow U.S. Dominance," *Foreign Affairs* 77, no. 2 (May–June 2008): 44–56; Ikenberry, Mastanduno, and Wohlforth, eds., *International Relations Theory and the Consequences of Unipolarity*; and Michael Beckley and Joshua R. Itzkowitz, "Correspondence: Debating China's Rise and U.S. Decline," *International Security* 37, no. 3 (Winter 2012–2013): 172–181.
16. Kenneth N. Waltz, "The Emerging Structure of International Politics," *International Security* 18, no. 2 (Fall 1993): 44–79; Kenneth N. Waltz, "Evaluating Theories," *American Political Science Review* 91, no. 4 (December 1997): 915; John J. Mearsheimer, "Back to the Future: Instability in Europe After the Cold War," *International Security* 15, no. 1 (Summer 1990): 5–56; Christopher Layne, "The Unipolar Illusion: Why New Great Powers Will Rise," *International Security* 17, no. 4 (Spring 1993): 5–51. Christopher Layne, "The Unipolar Illusion Revisited: The Coming End of the United States' Unipolar Moment," *International Security* 31, no. 2 (Fall 2006): 7–41.
17. William C. Wohlforth, "The Stability of a Unipolar World," *International Security* 24, no. 1 (Summer 1999): 5–41; Stephen G. Brooks and William C. Wohlforth, *World Out of Balance: International Relations and the Challenge of American Primacy* (Princeton, N.J.: Princeton University Press, 2008); G. John Ikenberry, Michael Mastanduno, and William C. Wohlforth, "Introduction: Unipolarity, State Behavior, and Systemic Consequences," *World Politics* 61, no. 1 (January 2009): 1–27; Birthe Hansen, *Unipolarity and World Politics; A Theory and Its Implications* (London: Routledge, 2011). See also John G. Ikenberry, ed., *America Unrivaled: The Future of the Balance of Power* (Ithaca, N.Y.: Cornell University Press, 2002); and Ethan B. Kapstein and Michael Mastanduno, eds., *Unipolar Politics: Realism and State Strategies After the Cold War* (New York: Columbia University Press, 1999).
18. Fareed Zakaria, *The Post-American World* (New York: Norton, 2008); Barry R. Posen, "Emerging Multipolarity: Why Should We Care?" *Current History* 108, no.

721 (November 2009), 347–352; Robert Kagan, *The Return of History and the End of Dreams* (New York: Knopf, 2008); and National Intelligence Council (NIC), *Global Trends 2030: Alternative Worlds* (Washington D.C.: December 2012).

19. Randall L. Schweller, *Maxwell's Demon and the Golden Apple: Global Disorder in the New Millennium* (Baltimore, Md.: Johns Hopkins University Press, 2014), 20–21, 50, 52, 54, 55, 64, 83, 91; Donette Murray and David Brown, eds., *Multipolarity in the Twenty-First Century: A New World Order* (London: Routledge, 2012); Posen, "From Unipolarity to Multipolarity." The leaders of Brazil, Russia, India, China, and South Africa (the BRICS group of emerging economies) often refer to an emerging multipolar world. The "multipolar" discourse is used prominently by the Chinese government. When presented with the return-of-bipolarity argument developed here, leading Chinese IR scholars noted that few studies in China have examined why China would be better off in a new multipolar system than a bipolar system. Interviews at Peking, Tsinghua, and Renmin University, Beijing, December 2015.

20. Christopher Layne, "This Time It's Real: The End of Unipolarity and the *Pax Americana*," *International Studies Quarterly* 56, no. 1 (March 2012): 203–213; Christopher Layne, "U.S. Hegemony in a Unipolar World: Here to Stay or Sic Transit Gloria?" *International Studies Review* 11, no. 4 (2009): 784–787; Arvind Subramanian, "The Inevitable Superpower: Why China's Dominance Is a Sure Thing," *Foreign Affairs* (September/October 2011); Mearsheimer, *The Tragedy*.

21. Layne, "This Time It's Real," 205.

22. Stephen G. Brooks and William Wohlforth, *America Abroad: The United States' Global Role in the Twenty-First Century* (Oxford: Oxford University Press, 2016); Nuno P. Monteiro, *Theory of Unipolar Politics* (Cambridge: Cambridge University Press, 2014); William C. Wohlforth, "How Not to Evaluate Theories," *International Studies Quarterly* 56, no. 1 (March 2012): 219–222; Michael Beckley, "China's Century? Why America's Edge Will Endure," *International Security* 36, no. 3 (Winter 2011/2012): 41-78.

23. Stephen G. Brooks and William Wohlforth, "The Rise and Fall of the Great Powers in the Twenty-First Century: China's Rise and the Fate of America's Global Position," *International Security* 40, no. 3 (Winter 2015/2016): 15–16, 53.

24. John G. Ikenberry, Michael Mastanduno, and William C. Wohlforth, "Introduction: Unipolarity, State Behavior, and Systemic Consequences," in *International Relations Theory and the Consequences of Unipolarity*, ed. John G. Ikenberry, Michael Mastanduno, and William C. Wohlforth (Cambridge: Cambridge University Press, 2011), 1–32, 11.

25. Morgenthau, *Politics Among Nations*, 324.

26. Henry Kissinger, *World Order* (New York: Penguin, 2014), 366–367.

27. John J. Mearsheimer, "China's Unpeaceful Rise," *Current History* 105, no. 690 (April 2006): 160–162; Jonathan Holslag, *China's Coming War with Asia* (Cambridge: Polity, 2015); Christopher Layne, "China's Challenge to U.S. Hegemony," *Current History* 107, no. 705 (January 2008): 13–18; Mearsheimer, *The Tragedy*.

28. Graham Allison, *Destined for War: Can America and China Escape Thucydides's Trap?* (New York: Houghton Mifflin Harcourt, 2017); Christopher Coker, *The Improbable War: China, the United States, and the Continuing Logic of Great Power Conflict* (London: Hurst & Company, 2015); Kissinger, *World Order*. Chong and Hall have

critically reflected on the 1914 analogy and pointed to important alternative lessons. Nonetheless, their study works within a multipolar analogy and does not consider the bipolar-stability thesis. It also disregards the importance of geopolitics in assessing lessons for contemporary East Asia and U.S.-China relations. Ja Ian Chong and Todd H. Hall, "The Lessons of 1914 for East Asia Today: Missing the Trees for the Forest," *International Security* 39, no. 1 (Summer 2014): 7–43.

29. John Lewis Gaddis, "The Long Peace: Elements of Stability in the Postwar International System," *International Security* 10, no. 4 (Spring 1986): 99–142.

30. As Snyder and others have noted, there are varieties of structural realism. Snyder sees Kenneth Waltz's neorealism and the "English school" as the main divide; Brooks delineates between neorealism and "postclassical realism." This study draws mainly on Waltz's neorealist structural theory but also on varieties of defensive and offensive realism, neoclassical realism, and classical or traditional realism. Most structural realists with affinities to Waltz share the view that a bipolar system is more stable than a multipolar one. Glenn H. Snyder, "Mearsheimer's World—Offensive Realism and the Struggle for Security: A Review Essay," *International Security* 27, no. 1 (Summer 2002): 149–173; Stephen G. Brooks, "Dueling Realisms," *International Organization* 51, no. 3 (Summer 1997): 445–477; Waltz, *Theory of International Politics*.

31. Waltz, "The Stability of a Bipolar World."

32. Kissinger, *World Order*, 367.

33. Waltz, *Theory of International Politics*, 67, 167–169; Thomas J. Christensen and Jack Snyder, "Chain Gangs and Passed Bucks: Predicting Alliance Patterns in Multipolarity," *International Organization* 44, no. 2 (Spring 1990): 137–168.

34. Josep S. Nye, *Is The American Century Over?* (Cambridge: Polity, 2015), 47; Graham Allison, "The Thucydides Trap: Are the U.S. and China Headed for War?" *The Atlantic*, September 24, 2015, http://www.theatlantic.com/international/archive/2015/09/united-states-china-war-thucydides-trap/406756/.

35. Raymond Aron, *Peace and War: A Theory of International Relations* (London: Weidenfeld and Nicolson, 1962), 149.

36. Allison, "The Thucydides Trap"; Allison, *Destined for War*. See also Nye, *Is the American Century Over?* 44.

37. Allison ("The Thucydides Trap") writes that the "preeminent geostrategic challenge of this era is not violent Islamic extremists or a resurgent Russia. It is the impact of China's ascendance," and he emphasizes that the BRICS group are no match compared to China's economic strength.

38. Allison, *Destined for War*, xi–xiv.

39. Mearsheimer, *The Tragedy*, chap. 9.

40. Kissinger, *World Order*, 367.

41. Thomas J. Christensen, *The China Challenge: Shaping the Choices of a Rising Power* (New York: Norton, 2015), esp. chap. 2 and p. 290. For a nuanced and comprehensive analysis of U.S.-China economic interdependence, see Helge Hveem and T. J. Pempel, "China's Rise and Economic Interdependence," in *China in the Era of Xi Jinping: Domestic and Foreign Policy Challenges*, ed. Jo Inge Bekkevold and Robert S. Ross (Washington, D.C.: Georgetown University Press, 2016), 196–232.

42. James Steinberg and Michael E. O'Hanlon, *Strategic Reassurance and Resolve: U.S.-China Relations in the Twenty-First Century* (Princeton, N.J.: Princeton University

Press, 2014); Lyle Goldstein, *Meeting China Half Way: How to Defuse the Emerging U.S.-China Rivalry* (Washington, D.C.: Georgetown University Press, 2015).

43. Waltz, *Theory of International Politics*, 70–71; Waltz, "Evaluating Theories"; and Thomas J. Christensen and Jack Snyder, "Progressive Research on Degenerate Alliances," in *Realism and the Balancing of Power*, ed. John A. Vasquez and Colin Elman (Upper Saddle River, N.J.: Prentice Hall, 2003), 66–73.

44. Waltz, *Theory of International Politics*, 128; Waltz, "The Emerging Structure."

45. Brooks and Wohlforth, *World Out of Balance.*

46. Waltz, "The Emerging Structure"; Waltz, "Evaluating Theories." Neorealism could not say how long the process would take, and Waltz's own predictions in the 1990 and 2000s that a multipolar system was emerging turned out wrong.

47. Waltz, *Theory of International Politics*, 128; Øystein Tunsjø, "U.S.-China Relations: From Unipolar Hedging Toward Bipolar Balancing," in *Strategic Adjustment and the Rise of China: Power and Politics in East Asia*, ed. Robert S. Ross and Øystein Tunsjø (Ithaca, N.Y.: Cornell University Press, 2017), 41–68.

48. Robert Jervis, *System Effects: Complexity in Political and Social Life* (Princeton, N.J.: Princeton University Press, 1997), 103.

49. Christensen and Snyder, "Chain Gangs and Passed Bucks."

50. That is even more likely when, in contrast to Snyder and Christensen's comparative analysis of multipolar systems in Europe, the new bipolar system is concentrated on a different region than the previous bipolar system.

51. Waltz, *Theory of International Politics*, 71–72, 122–123, 174–175; Kenneth N. Waltz, "Reflections on *Theory of International Politics*: A Response to My Critics," in *Neorealism and Its Critics*, ed. Robert O. Keohane (New York: Columbia University Press, 1986), 322–345; Kenneth N. Waltz, "International Politics Is Not Foreign Policy," *Security Studies* 6, no. 1 (1996): 54–57.

52. Waltz, *Theory of International Politics*, 128; Waltz, "Reflections," 330–337.

53. Waltz, *Theory of International Politics*, 72.

54. On the primary importance of internal balancing even within a multipolar system, see Joseph M. Parent and Sebastian Rosato, "Balancing in Neorealism," *International Security* 40, no. 2 (Fall 2015): 51–86.

55. Waltz, *Theory of International Politics*, 118, 128, 163.

56. Waltz, "Reflections," 329.

57. Waltz, *Theory of International Politics*, 71; Waltz, *Man, the State, and War.*

58. Geography is a unit-level factor when fixed to state boundaries, for instance, when we compare states' geographical size, which is one component of Waltz's combined factors that we can use to measure states' power and the distribution of power in the international system.

59. Prominent writers within the former strand are Alfred Thayer Mahan, Halford J. Mackinder, Robert Strausz-Hupé, and Nicholas J. Spykman. The work of Karl Haushofer, Friedrich Ratzel, and Rudolf Kjellén falls more within the geopolitik tradition.

60. Phil Kelly, *Classical Geopolitics: A New Analytical Model* (Stanford, Calif.: Stanford University Press, 2016), 8.

61. Barry Posen's seminal article "Command of the Commons: The Military Foundations for U.S. Hegemony," *International Security* 20, no. 1 (2003): 5–46, convincingly demonstrated how the United States had obtained primacy in the global commons

in the post–Cold War era. However, Posen now acknowledges that U.S. command of the commons has become more contested, especially because of China's increased military capabilities. See Barry Posen's keynote and other scholars' contributions to the conference "The Command of the Commons: A Ten-Year Reassessment," organized by the Bush School of Government & Public Service and Haifa Research Center for Maritime Strategy, Texas A&M University, November 29–30, 2016.

62. I thank one anonymous reviewer for summarizing and stressing the importance of these geopolitical factors.

63. Jack S. Levy and William R. Thompson, "Balancing on Land and Sea: Do States Ally Against the Leading Global Power?" *International Security* 35, no. 1 (Summer 2010): 7–43.

64. Thomas C. Schelling, *Arms and Influence* (New Haven, Conn.: Yale University Press, 1966), 47.

65. On the challenges inherent with the distance a military must travel, see Fox, *The Super-Powers*, 22; Kenneth E. Boulding, *Conflict and Defense: A General Theory* (New York: Harper and Row, 1962), 230–231, 245–245.

66. See, for example, the works of Hans J. Morgenthau, George F. Kennan, Paul Kennedy, Henry Kissinger, John J. Mearsheimer, Stephen M. Walt, Robert D. Kaplan, and Robert S. Ross.

67. Mearsheimer's emphasis on revisionist states seeking to maximize power or on developing an offensive structural-realist theory is not discussed in depth. Instead, the focus is on what Snyder calls the "subtheory of offensive realism," that is, how geography can enrich structural analysis and balance-of-power theory. See *The Tragedy*, esp chap. 4; and Snyder, "Mearsheimer's World," 162.

68. Ross, "The Geography of Peace"; Robert S. Ross, "Bipolarity and Balancing in East Asia," in *Balance of Power: Theory and Practice in the Twenty-First Century*, ed. T. V. Paul, James J. Wirtz, and Michael Fortmann (Stanford, Calif.: Stanford University Press, 2004), 267–304; Jack Levy, "Power Transition Theory and the Rise of China," in *China's Ascent: Power, Security, and the Future of International Politics*, ed. Robert S. Ross and Zhu Feng (Ithaca, N.Y.: Cornell University Press, 2008), 11–33; Stephen M. Walt, *The Origins of Alliances* (Ithaca, N.Y.: Cornell University Press, 1990).

69. Levy, "Power Transition Theory," 21; Ross, "The Geography of Peace"; Ross, "Bipolarity and Balancing in East Asia"; Robert S. Ross, "The Rise of the Chinese Navy: From Regional Naval Power to Global Naval Power?" in *China's Global Engagement: Cooperation, Competition, and Influence in the Twenty-First Century*, ed. Jacques deLisle and Avery Goldstein (Brookings Institution, 2017), 207–234; Christopher Layne, *The Peace of Illusions: American Grand Strategy from 1940 to the Present* (Ithaca, N.Y.: Cornell University Press, 2006).

70. Waltz, *Man, the State, and War*; Waltz, *Theory of International Politics*.

71. Waltz, *Theory of International Politics*, chap. 5.

72. Harrison R. Wagner, "What Was Bipolarity?" *International Organization* 47, no. 1 (Winter 1993): 77–106.

73. In this context, stability refers to the absence of wars and conflicts involving the superpowers. Systemic stability is discussed in terms of both peacefulness and durability.

74. Øystein Tunsjø, "The Cold War as a Guide to the Risk of War in East Asia," *Global Asia* 9, no. 3 (Fall 2014): 15–19.

75. Tunsjø, "The Cold War as a Guide." Mearsheimer develops a similar argument in the last chapter of his revised *The Tragedy* (394–399). However, the way Mearsheimer arrives at this argument is different from how it is developed in this book. For example, Mearsheimer views U.S.-China relations within a structure of unbalanced multipolarity.

76. As chapter 6 will discuss, such a limited war might include strikes on the Chinese mainland and potentially U.S. regional bases as well as potential warfare in orbit and cyberspace. However, it is unlikely to escalate to a major war, including a U.S. invasion of the Chinese mainland or a nuclear war.

2. EXPLAINING AND UNDERSTANDING POLARITY

1. Harrison R. Wagner, "What Was Bipolarity?" *International Organization* 47, no. 1 (Winter 1993): 77–106.
2. John J. Mearsheimer, *The Tragedy of Great Power Politics*, 2nd ed. (New York: Norton, 2014), 57.
3. Kenneth N. Waltz, *Theory of International Politics* (1979; Long Grove, Ill.: Waveland, 2010), 192.
4. Waltz, *Theory of International Politics*, 131.
5. Mearsheimer, *The Tragedy*, 57–60. Accordingly, power should not be conflated with control or the common definition by Dahl that measures power in terms of the ability to get people to do what one wants them to do when otherwise they would not do it. Robert A. Dahl, *Who Governs: Democracy and Power in an American City* (New Haven, Conn.: Yale University Press, 1961).
6. Kenneth N. Waltz, *Man, the State, and War: A Theoretical Analysis* (New York: Columbia University Press, 1959), 205.
7. Waltz, *Theory of International Politics*, 192. This contrasts with Hart's emphasis on three approaches to the observation and measurement of power: (1) control over resources, (2) control over actors, and (3) control over events and outcomes. Jeffrey Hart, "Three Approaches to the Measurement of Power in International Relations," *International Organization* 30, no. 2 (Spring 1976): 289–305.
8. William Wohlforth, "Unipolar Stability: The Rules of Power Analysis," *Harvard International Review* (Spring 2007): 44–48.
9. Wohlforth, "Unipolar Stability," 45–46. Beckley follows Wohlforth in defining power "in terms of resources rather than influence." Michael Beckley, "China's Century? Why America's Edge Will Endure," *International Security* 36, no. 3 (Winter 2011/2012): 56.
10. John G. Ikenberry, "The Liberal Sources of American Unipolarity," in *International Relations Theory and the Consequences of Unipolarity*, ed. John G. Ikenberry, Michael Mastanduno, and William C. Wohlforth (Cambridge: Cambridge University Press, 2011), 216–251, 216.
11. Waltz, *Theory of International Politics*, 131.
12. See Spykman for a similar emphasis on a combination of factors that conditions the formation of foreign policy, Mahan's six attributes that determine states' capacity to become sea powers, Morgenthau's "elements of national power," and Aron's "space, number and resources." Nicholas J. Spykman, *The Geography of the Peace* (New York:

Harcourt, Brace and Company, 1944; Archon, 1970), 7; Alfred T. Mahan, *The Influence of Seapower on History, 1660-1783* (Boston, 1890); Hans J. Morgenthau, *Politics Among Nations: The Struggle for Power and Peace*, 2nd ed. (New York: Knopf, 1954), 53, 93-154; Raymond Aron, *Peace and War: A Theory of International Politics* (London: Weidenfeld and Nicolson, 1966), 177-278. See also Harold Sprout and Margaret Sprout, *Foundations of International Politics* (Princeton, N.J.: Van Nostrand, 1962); and Klaus Knorr, *The Power of Nations* (New York: Basic Books, 1975).

13. Morgenthau, *Politics Among Nations*, 2nd ed., 186.

14. Waltz, *Theory of International Politics*, 97; Morgenthau, *Politics Among Nations*, 2nd ed., chap. 10, esp. 142-143; John G. Ikenberry, Michael Mastanduno, and William C. Wohlforth, "Introduction: Unipolarity, State Behavior, and Systemic Consequences," in *International Relations Theory and the Consequences of Unipolarity*, ed. John G. Ikenberry, Michael Mastanduno, and William C. Wohlforth (Cambridge: Cambridge University Press, 2011), 1–32, 6.

15. This distinction between states' power is similar to Handel's superpowers, great powers, middle powers, small powers, and micro-states. See Michael I. Handel, *Weak States in the International System* (London: Frank Cass, 1981). Nuno P. Monteiro, *Theory of Unipolar Politics* (Cambridge: Cambridge University Press, 2014), 42–48, 46, distinguishes among great powers, major powers, and minor powers. Although states sometimes "punch above their weight," his distinction between major and minor powers is based on their nuclear-weapon capabilities and is confusing. Japan and Germany are categorized as minor powers together with Austria and the Philippines, while North Korea and Pakistan are major powers together with China and Russia. This clouds the definition and mischaracterizes how power is distributed in the international system.

16. Waltz, *Theory of International Politics*, 98.

17. In his authoritative statement on unipolarity, Wohlforth draws explicitly on Waltz's definition, but he also modifies and refines it. See William C. Wohlforth, "The Stability of a Unipolar World," *International Security* 24, no. 1 (Summer 1999): 5–41, 10; William C. Wohlforth, "The Perception of Power: Russia in the Pre-1914 Balance," *World Politics* 39, no. 3 (April 1987): 353–381. Ashley J. Tellis, Janice Bially, Christopher Layne, and Melissa McPherson, *Measuring National Power in the Postindustrial Age* (Santa Monica, Calif.: RAND, 2000), write that wealth, innovation, and conventional military power are the most important resources for measuring national power. Jae Ho Chung's edited volume *Assessing China's Power* (New York: Palgrave Macmillan, 2015) explores four dimensions to measure the multiple capabilities of a great power, namely, economic, governance related, military, and external/soft. Hopf defines a pole according to the distribution of military capabilities, population figures, and government revenues. Ted Hopf, "Polarity, the Offense-Defense Balance, and War," *American Political Science Review* 85, no. 2 (June 1991): 475–493, 478–479. These measurements can all be incorporated into Waltz's six factors. Nye's emphasis on soft power and alternative definition of power do not disregard a definition of power that focuses on states' relative capabilities in terms of large population, territory, natural resources, economic strength, military force, and social stability. See Joseph S. Nye, *The Future of Power* (New York: PublicAffairs, 2011), 8, 25. Several other studies also draw on Waltz's definition; Ikenberry et al., eds., *International Relations Theory*;

Monteiro, *Theory of Unipolar Politics*; Mearsheimer, *The Tragedy*; Charles L. Glaser, "Why Unipolarity Doesn't Matter (Much)," *Cambridge Review of International Affairs* 24, no. 2 (June 2011), 135–147.

18. Barry Posen, "From Unipolarity to Multipolarity: Transition in Sight?" in *International Relations Theory and the Consequences of Unipolarity*, ed. John G. Ikenberry, Michael Mastanduno, and William C. Wohlforth (Cambridge: Cambridge University Press, 2011), 317–341, 320.

19. Developing on Dahl's "coercive influence of power" definition, several studies have emphasized the multiple faces of power, including agenda setting and belief changing. See Peter Bachrach and Morton S. Baratz, "Two Faces of Power," *American Political Science Review* 56, no. 4 (December 1962): 947–952; Steven Lukes, *Power: A Radical View*, 2nd ed. (London: MacMillan, 2005). Stephen G. Brooks, *Producing Security: Multinational Corporations, Globalization, and the Changing Calculus of Conflict* (Princeton, N.J.: Princeton University Press, 2005), highlights how changes in the global production and the role of multinational corporations affect power and the global security environment. Joseph J. Nye coined the soft-power term "the ability to affect others through co-optive means of framing the agenda, persuading, and eliciting positive attraction in order to obtain preferred outcomes." Joseph S. Nye, *Soft Power: The Means to Success in World Politics* (New York: PublicAffairs, 2004), x, 11.

20. Yan Xuetong, "The Rise of China and Its Power Status," *Chinese Journal of International Politics* 1 (2006): 5–33; Hu Angang, *China in 2020: A New Type of Superpower* (Washington D.C.: Brookings 2011).

21. Yan, "The Rise of China," 8–9.

22. Yan, "The Rise of China," 10–12, 15.

23. Morgenthau, *Politics Among Nations*, 2nd ed., 140. This is also an important aspect in Yan's ("The Rise of China") examination of China's comprehensive national power.

24. Posen, "From Unipolarity to Multipolarity," 320.

25. Morgenthau's emphasis on the "dynamic, ever changing character of the power relations between nations" and Gilpin's focus on the continuous "redistribution of power in the system" provide guidance when assessing the current shift in the distribution of capabilities, but the approach here is more inspired by Waltz in measuring the top ranking among states today. See Morgenthau, *Politics Among Nations*, 2nd ed., 146; Gilpin, *War and Change*, 186; Waltz, *Theory of International Politics*, 131.

26. William T. R. Fox, *The Super-Powers: The United States, Britain, and the Soviet Union—Their Responsibility for Peace* (New York: Harcourt, Brace and Company, 1944), 12.

27. Morgenthau, *Politics Among Nations*, 1st ed., chap. 19; 2nd ed., chap. 22. Kenneth N. Waltz, "The Stability of a Bipolar World," *Daedalus* 93, no. 3 (Summer 1964): 881–909; Waltz, *Theory of International Politics*.

28. Waltz, "The Stability of a Bipolar World," 881–909; Glenn H. Snyder and Paul Diesing, *Conflict Among Nations: Bargaining, Decision Making, and System Structure in International Crises* (Princeton, N.J.: Princeton University Press, 1977), 28–29.

29. Wohlforth, "The Stability of a Unipolar World."

30. It has been argued that the international system has been bipolar prior to this period. See Hopf, "Polarity." However, there are important distinctions between a bipolar European system from 1529 to 1559 and the post–World War II global bipolar system.

31. Fox, *The Super-Powers*, 12.
32. Morgenthau, *Politics Among Nations*, 1st ed., 271.
33. Morgenthau, *Politics Among Nations*, 2nd ed., 324.
34. Morgenthau, *Politics Among Nations*, 1st ed., 273–274.
35. Stephen G. Brooks and William Wohlforth, *America Abroad: The United States' Global Role in the Twenty-First Century* (Oxford: Oxford University Press, 2016); Thomas J. Christensen, *The China Challenge: Shaping the Choices of a Rising Power* (New York: Norton, 2015); and Joseph S. Nye, *Is The American Century Over?* (Cambridge: Policy, 2015). Christensen argues that China has not become a superpower and states that "China's overall economic, military, and political clout . . . is nowhere near the United States" (see xviii–xix). China is "hardly a Soviet-style superpower" and "falls short of being a global superpower." However, Christensen's study does not consider whether China needs to obtain parity with the United States to become a superpower, does not assess the power gap between the second- and the third-ranking power, and does not compare the current distribution of capabilities with the distribution at the origins of the previous bipolar system, in order to establish whether China has reached superpower status.
36. Christensen, *The China Challenge*, 89.
37. Morgenthau, *Politics Among Nations*, 2nd ed., 328; Waltz, *Theory of International Politics*.
38. Wohlforth, "The Stability of a Unipolar World," 9n15.
39. The European Union cannot be regarded as a nation-state, superpower, or great power. Waltz, *Theory of International Politics*; Wohlforth, "The Stability of a Unipolar World," 31.
40. "National morals and the quality of government, especially in the conduct of foreign affairs, are the most important, but also most elusive, components of national power." Morgenthau, *Politics Among Nations*, 2nd ed., 186.
41. Waltz, *Theory of International Politics*, 131.
42. Monteiro, *Theory of Unipolar Politics*, 48–49. This argument, however, is puzzling given Monteiro's discussion of Waltz's proposition ("only when a state possesses ample capabilities in all these areas can it be considered a great power") and his acknowledgment that a unipolar world requires "that the unipole also possess first-rate latent economic resources." See 37, 48.
43. Mearsheimer, *The Tragedy*, 60–82, 67.
44. Monteiro, *Theory of Unipolar Politics*, 47.
45. Paul Kennedy, *The Rise and the Fall of the Great Powers* (New York: Vintage, 1989), 358.
46. The Soviet Union built its first helicopter carrier in the late 1960s and first aircraft carrier in the 1970s. Britain operated aircraft carriers during the Second World War and participated in the Pacific War against Japan. The Soviet Union's navy remained smaller than that of the United Kingdom for most of the Cold War.
47. Pillsbury notes that in the aftermath of the collapse of the Soviet Union, Chinese military analysts adjusted their measures of global strength and national progress toward a stronger emphasis on economics, foreign investment, technological innovation, and the ownership of natural resources instead of military strength. Michael Pillsbury, *The Hundred-Year Marathon: China's Secret Strategy to Replace America*

as the Global Superpower (New York: Henry Holt, 2015), 47. See also Yan, "The Rise of China."

48. Waltz, *Theory of International Politics*, 180.
49. Waltz, *Theory of International Politics*, 180. My emphasis.
50. Joshua R. Itzkowitz Shifrinson and Michael Beckley, "Correspondence: Debating China's Rise and U.S. Decline," *International Security* 37, no. 3 (Winter 2012/2013): 172–181; Morgenthau, *Politics Among Nations*, 2nd ed., 139–140.
51. Beckley, "China's Century"; Brooks, *Producing Security*.
52. Beckley, "China's Century," 59.
53. Wohlforth, "Unipolar Stability," 46–47.
54. The Soviet Union's GDP throughout the Cold War was less than 50 percent of U.S. GDP.
55. With a population roughly four times that of the United States, it is unrealistic to expect China in the foreseeable future to reach U.S. per capita GDP.
56. Leading economists are also struggling to assess China's real GDP. For a higher estimate, see Daniel H. Rosen and Beibei Bao, "A Better Abacus for China," Rhodium Group Note, December 12, 2014, http://rhg.com/notes/a-better-abacus-for-china; Gabriel Wildau, "China Data Revision Lift GDP by $308bn," *Financial Times*, December 19, 2014, http://www.ft.com/intl/cms/s/0/b569efb6-8736-11e4-8a51-00144feabdco.html#axzz3VJQmEzOJ; and Daniel H. Rosen and Beibei Bao, "An Independent Look at China's Economic Size," *Center for Strategic and International Studies* 1 (September 11, 2015), http://csis.org/files/publication/150911_Rosen_Bao_China's_Economic_Size.pdf. For a more skeptical assessment, see Michael Pettis, "Bad Debt Cannot Simply Be 'Socialized,'" *China Financial Markets*, July 14, 2014, http://carnegieendowment.org/2014/07/14/bad-debt-cannot-simply-be-socialized/hftd; Michael Pettis, *Avoiding the Fall: China's Economic Restructuring* (Washington, D.C.: Carnegie Endowment for International Peace, September 2013); Daniel Drezner, "Bad Debts: Assessing China's Financial Influence in Great Power Politics," *International Security* 34, no. 1 (2009): 7–45.
57. Arvind Subramanian, "The Inevitable Superpower: Why China's Dominance Is a Sure Thing," *Foreign Affairs* 90, no. 5 (September/October 2011); Aaron L. Freidberg, *A Contest for Supremacy: China, America, and the Struggle for Mastery in Asia* (New York: Norton, 2011).
58. Albert O. Hirschman, *National Power and the Structure of Foreign Trade* (1945; Berkeley: University of California Press, 1980).
59. Robert S. Ross, "Balance of Power Politics and the Rise of China: Accommodation and Balancing in East Asia," *Security Studies* 15, no. 3 (July–September 2006): 355–395, 368.
60. Edward S. Steinfeld, *Playing Our Game: Why China's Rise Doesn't Threaten the West* (Oxford: Oxford University Press, 2010), esp. chap. 4; Organization for Economic Cooperation and Development (OECD), "OECD/WTO Trade in Value Added (TIVA) Indicators," May 2013, http://www.oecd.org/sti/ind/TiVA_CHINA_MAY_2013.pdf; Daniel Drezner, "Perception, Misperception, and Sensitivity: Chinese Economic Power and Preferences After the 2008 Financial Crisis," in *Strategic Adjustment and the Rise of China: Power and Politics in East Asia*, ed. Robert S. Ross and Øystein Tunsjø (Ithaca, N.Y.: Cornell University Press, 2017), 69–99.

61. It should be noted that China's foreign reserves have now been drawn down from $4 trillion in 2014 to $3 trillion in 2017 in an effort to defend its currency, the yuan. See "China's Foreign-Exchange Reserves Swell to $3.03 Trillion, Beating Forecasts," *Wall Street Journal*, May 7, 2017, https://www.wsj.com/articles/chinas-foreign -exchange-reserves-continue-to-expand-1494129841.

62. The China Development Bank and the Export-Import Bank of China are so far much more important for Chinese overseas investments and in providing loans to foreign countries and development, infrastructure, and business projects.

63. Evan MacAskill, "Wikileaks: Hillary Clinton's Question: How Can We Stand Up to Beijing?" *Guardian*, December 4, 2010, http://www.theguardian.com/world/2010 /dec/04/wikileaks-cables-hillary-clinton-beijing.

64. Daniel Kruger, "China's Selling Tons of U.S. Debt. Americans Couldn't Care Less," *Bloomberg*, October 18, 2015, http://www.bloomberg.com/news/articles/2015-10-18 /china-s-selling-tons-of-u-s-debt-americans-couldn-t-care-less-/; Christensen, *The China Challenge*, 70.

65. Grace Zhu, "China Forex Reserves Fall to Lowest Level in More Than Two Years," *Wall Street Journal*, December 7, 2015, http://www.wsj.com/articles/china-forex-reserves -fall-to-lowest-level-in-more-than-two-years-1449476991.

66. Daniel Drezner, *The System Worked: How the World Stopped Another Great Depression* (New York: Oxford University Press, 2014).

67. "Moody's Downgrades China's Rating to A1 from Aa3 and Changes Outlook to Stable from Negative," *Moody's*, May 24, 2017, https://www.moodys.com/research/Moodys -downgrades-Chinas-rating-to-A1-from-Aa3-and-changes-PR_366139; Martin Wolff, "China Faces a Tough Fight to Escape Its Debt Trap," *Financial Times*, April, 11, 2017 https://www.ft.com/content/1c096f7e-1ddc-11e7-b7d3-163f5a7f229c; Li Zengxin and Fran Wang, "IMF Raises China Growth Forecast, but Warns of Debt-Related Risks," *Caixin*, April 19, 2017, http://www.caixinglobal.com/2017-04-19/101080395 .html; Pettis, *Avoiding the Fall*; Beckley, "China's Century," 60.

68. Andy Rothman, Teresa Kong, and Satya Patel, "The Puzzle of Moody's China Downgrade," *Matthews Asia Perspective*, May 2017, https://matthewsasia.com/resources /docs/pdf/Perspectives/US-Moody-May-17.pdf; Andrew Sheng and Ng Chow Soon, "Bringing Shadow Banking Into the Light: Opportunity for Financial Reform in China," *Fung Global Institute*, March 16, 2015, http://www.fungglobalinstitute.org /en/bringing-shadow-banking-light-opportunity-financial-reform-china/; Nicholas R. Lardy, *Markets Over Mao: The Rise of Private Business in China* (Washington, D.C.: Peterson Institute for International Economics, 2014).

69. Development Research Center of the State Council, and the World Bank, *China 2030: Building a Modern, Harmonious, and Creative Society* (Washington D.C.: World Bank Publications, 2013).

70. Daniel Rosen, *Avoiding the Blind Alley: China's Economic Overhaul and Its Global Implications*, Asia Society Policy Institute, October 2014, http://asiasociety.org /policy-institute/avoiding-blind-alley-chinas-economic-overhaul-and-its-global -implications; Barry Naughton, "Is There a 'Xi Model' of Economic Reform?—Acceleration of Economic Reforms Since Fall 2014," *China Leadership Monitor* 46 (Winter 2015), http://www.hoover.org/sites/default/files/research/docs/clm46bn.pdf.

71. Wagner, "What Was bipolarity?" 85.

72. Waltz, *Theory of International Politics*, 161–162; Morgenthau, *Politics Among Nations*, 2nd ed., 322–326.

73. This refers to the modern state system since 1648.

74. Waltz ("Reflections," 342) writes that "the victors in World War II thought of themselves as fighting a defensive war. In doing so, they nevertheless fought a war that changed the system from one of multipolarity to one of bipolarity."

75. Posen, "From Unipolarity to Multipolarity," 320.

76. Morgenthau, *Politics Among Nations*, 1st ed., 274.

77. Monteiro, *Theory of Unipolar Politics*, 56–57.

78. However, as chapter 6 argues, geopolitics heightens the risk of a limited war largely confined to East Asian waters.

79. Waltz, *Theory of International Politics*, 177.

80. Spykman, *The Geography of Peace*, 61.

81. John H. Herz, *International Politics in the Atomic Age* (New York: Columbia University Press, 1959), 29.

82. Herz, *International Politics*, 34. See Waltz's critique of such views in *Theory of International Politics*.

83. Wagner, "What Was Bipolarity?" 89.

84. Waltz, *Theory of International Politics*, 168–169; Robert Jervis, "Unipolarity: A Structural Perspective," in *International Relations Theory and the Consequences of Unipolarity*, ed. John G. Ikenberry, Michael Mastanduno, and William C. Wohlforth (Cambridge: Cambridge University Press, 2011), 252–281, 254.

85. Waltz, *Theory of International Politics*, 98.

86. Waltz, *Man, the State, and War*.

87. Waltz, "The Stability of a Bipolar World"; Waltz, *Theory of International Politics*, chap. 5, pp. 180–183.

88. Wagner, "What Was Bipolarity?" 86.

89. Waltz, *Theory of International Politics*, 158–159.

90. Waltz, "The Stability of a Bipolar World"; Morgenthau, *Politics Among Nations*, 2nd ed., 327.

91. Wagner, "What Was Bipolarity?" 101–103.

92. Mearsheimer, *The Tragedy*, 44.

93. Wohlforth argues that since the British and the Russian empires retained preponderant power in separate domains, "neither empire was unambiguously the top dog" until the Crimean War tested their strengths. William Wohlforth, "Hegemonic Decline and Hegemonic War Revisited," in *Power, Order, and Change in World Politics*, ed. John G. Ikenberry (Cambridge: Cambridge University Press, 2014), 109–130, 123–124.

94. Wohlforth, "Hegemonic Decline," 124.

95. Fox, *The Super-Powers*, 12.

96. Fox, *The Super-Powers*, 21–23.

97. Robert Jervis, *System Effects: Complexity in Political and Social Life* (Princeton, N.J.: Princeton University Press, 1997), 94–98. The bipolar system in the second half of the twentieth century had accommodated revolutionary political, military, and economic challenges. See Waltz, "The Stability of a Bipolar World."

98. Waltz, *Theory of International Politics*, 161–163.

99. Wohlforth, "The Stability of a Unipolar World," 8n11.
100. Richard Little, *The Balance of Power in International Relations: Metaphors, Myths, and Models* (Cambridge: Cambridge University Press, 2007), 209; Morgenthau, *Politics Among Nations*, 2nd ed., 327.
101. Waltz, *Theory of International Politics*, 168, 193.
102. Waltz, *Theory of International Politics*, 134–136, 163.
103. Mearsheimer (*The Tragedy*, 338–347) distinguishes between (1) unbalanced bipolarity, (2) balanced bipolarity, (3) unbalanced multipolarity, and (4) balanced multipolarity, but he still agrees with Waltz that "bipolar systems are more stable than multipolar systems."
104. Jack S. Levy, *War in the Modern Great Power System, 1495–1975* (Lexington: University Press of Kentucky, 1983); Bruce Bueno de Mesquita, "Neorealism's Logic and Evidence: When Is a Theory Falsified?" in *Realism and the Balance of Power: A New Debate*, ed. Colin Elman and John A. Vasquez (Upper Saddle River, N.J.: Prentice Hall, 2003), 166–199. Hopf ("Polarity") has argued that the "international situation in sixteenth century Europe became only marginally more stable after the shift from multipolarity to bipolarity." However, the origins of the "modern" international state system is conventionally considered the Peace of Westphalia in 1648.
105. Henry Kissinger, *World Order* (New York: Penguin, 2014).
106. Karl W. Deutsch and David J. Singer, "Multipolar Power Systems and International Stability," *World Politics* 16, no. 3 (April 1964): 390; Morton A. Kaplan, *System and Process in International Politics* (New York: John Wiley & Sons, 1957).
107. Raymond Aron, *Peace and War: A Theory of International Relations* (London: Weidenfeld and Nicolson, 1962), 149.
108. Wohlforth adds to this argument: "And, as an offshore power separated by two oceans from all other major states, the United States can retain its advantages without risking a counterbalance." See Wohlforth, "The Stability of a Unipolar World," 8.
109. Monteiro argues in *Theory* that the unipolar system has been war prone. But this is not the case if we consider the relations between the superpower, great powers, and major powers. Moreover, several studies conclude that wars and deaths in battle have declined and been at its lowest in the unipolar period. See among others, Nils Petter Gleditsch, Steven Pinker, Bradley A. Thayer, et al., "The Forum: The Decline of War," *International Studies Review* 15, no. 3 (2013): 396–419; Bethany Ann Lacina and Nils Petter Gleditsch, "The Waning of War Is Real: A Response to Gohdes and Price," *Journal of Conflict Resolution* 57, no. 6 (2013): 1109–1127; Lotta Themnér and Peter Wallensteen, "Armed Conflicts, 1946–2012," *Journal of Peace Research* 50, no. 4 (July 2013): 509–521.
110. Waltz, *Theory of International Politics*, 179–180.
111. Little, *Balance of Power*, 210–211; Wagner, "What Was Bipolarity?" 87.
112. William C. Wohlforth, "Measuring Power—and the Power of Theories," in *Realism and the Balance of Power: A New Debate*, ed. Colin Elman and John A. Vasquez (Upper Saddle River, N.J.: Prentice Hall, 2003), 257. Mearsheimer has taken a similar position, writing in the preface to the second edition of *The Tragedy* (xiii–xiv) that the book "is virtually unchanged from the first edition" and that he has not modified or altered his theory in order to engage with criticism of his book.
113. Waltz, "Evaluating Theories."

114. Morgenthau, *Politics Among Nations*, 2nd ed., 398.

115. See Mearsheimer, *The Tragedy*, 356–359.

116. Morgenthau, *Politics Among Nations*, 2nd ed., 356.

117. Wohlforth, "The Stability of a Unipolar World"; Robert S. Ross, "The Geography of Peace: East Asia in the Twenty-First Century," *International Security* 23, no. 4 (Spring 1999).

118. Robert S. Ross, "The Rise of Russia, Sino-Russian Relations, and U.S. Security Policy," Brief, Royal Danish Defence College, 2012, http://forsvaret.dk/FAK/Publikationer /Briefs/Documents/TheRiseofRussiaSino-RussianRelationsandUSSecurityPolicy.pdf. Lim characterizes Russia as "little more than an interested bystander in East Asia." Robyn Lim, *The Geopolitics of East Asia: The Search for Equilibrium* (London: Routledge, 2003), 11.

119. Robert S. Ross, "The Rise of the Chinese Navy: From Regional Naval Power to Global Naval Power?" in *China's Global Engagement: Cooperation, Competition, and Influence in the Twenty-First Century*, ed. Jacques deLisle and Avery Goldstein (Washington, D.C., Brookings Institution, 2017), 207–234.

120. Mearsheimer, *The Tragedy*.

121. Craig Campbell, *Glimmer of a New Leviathan: Total War in the Realism of Niebuhr, Morgenthau, and Waltz* (New York: Columbia University Press, 2003); Hopf, "Polarity"; Wagner, "What Was Bipolarity?"; and Arthur Lee Burns, "From Balance to Deterrence: A Theoretical Analysis," *World Politics* 9 (July 1964): 494–529.

122. Richard Little, *The Balance of Power in International Relations: Metaphors, Myths, and Models* (Cambridge: Cambridge University Press, 2007), 211; Edward Rhodes, "A World Not in Balance: War, Politics, and Weapons of Mass Destruction," in *Balance of Power: Theory and Practice in the Twenty-First Century*, ed. T. V. Paul, James J. Wirtz, and Michel Fortmann (Stanford, Calif.: Stanford University Press, 2004), 150–176; Daniel Deudney, "Unipolarity and Nuclear Weapons," in *International Relations Theory and the Consequences of Unipolarity*, ed. John G. Ikenberry, Michael Mastanduno, and William C. Wohlforth (Cambridge: Cambridge University Press, 2011), 282–316, 286; Wohlforth, "Hegemonic Decline"; Thomas Schelling, *The Strategy of Conflict* (Oxford: Oxford University Press, 1960), 230–254; Jervis, *System Effects*, 122–124.

123. Ross, "The Geography of Peace," 82; Mearsheimer, *The Tragedy*, 128.

124. Bernard Brodie, ed., *The Absolute Weapon: Atomic Power and World Order* (New York: Harcourt, Brace and Company, 1946). T. V. Paul, Richard J. Harknett, and James J. Wirtz, eds., *The Absolute Weapon Revisited: Nuclear Arms and the Emerging International Order* (Ann Arbor: University of Michigan Press, 1998).

125. Robert Jervis, *The Illogic of Nuclear Strategy* (Ithaca, N.Y.: Cornell University Press, 1985); Robert Jervis, *The Meaning of the Nuclear Revolution* (Ithaca, N.Y.: Cornell University Press, 1989); Kenneth N. Waltz, "The Spread of Nuclear Weapons: More May Be Better," *Adelphi Papers* 171 (London: International Institute for Strategic Studies, 1981); John Lewis Gaddis, "The Long Peace: Elements of Stability in the Postwar International System," *International Security* 10, no. 4 (Spring 1986): 99–142; and John H. Herz, *International Politics in the Atomic Age* (New York: Columbia University Press, 1959).

126. Waltz, "Reflections"; Waltz, *Realism*, 99–122; and Waltz, "The Spread of Nuclear Weapons." Waltz ("Reflections," 327) states, "in my view, the two biggest changes

in international politics since World War II are the structural shift from multi- to bipolarity and the unit-level change in the extent and rapidity with which some state can hurt others." Waltz's argument was controversial and led to a strong debate. See Scott D. Sagan and Kenneth N. Waltz, *The Spread of Nuclear Weapons: A Debate Renewed* (New York: Norton, 2003).

127. Waltz, *Theory of International Politics*, 136; Waltz, *Man, the State, and War*, 186.

128. Waltz, "The Stability of a Bipolar World"; Waltz, *Theory of International Politics*, 180. Some even maintain that nuclear weapons "do not seem to have been necessary to contain World War III, to determine alliance patterns, or to cause the United States and the Soviet Union to behave cautiously." John Mueller, "The Essential Irrelevance of Nuclear Weapons: Stability in the Postwar World," *International Security* 13, no. 2 (Fall 1988), 56.

129. Waltz, *Theory of International Politics*, 160.

130. Øystein Tunsjø, "The Cold War as a Guide to the Risk of War in East Asia," *Global Asia* 9, no. 3 (Fall 2014): 15–19; Mearsheimer, *The Tragedy*, 395–398.

131. Kenneth N. Waltz, "Reflections on *Theory of International Politics*: A Response to My Critics," in *Neorealism and Its Critics*, ed. Robert O. Keohane (New York: Columbia University Press, 1986), 333.

132. Kissinger, *World Order*, 78–79.

133. Peter L. Hahn, *The United States, Great Britain, and Egypt, 1945–1956* (Chapel Hill: University of North Carolina Press, 1991), 233.

134. *Foreign Relations of the United States*, 1955–1957, Vol. 16, Suez Crisis, July 26–December 31, 1956, Document 411, "Memorandum of a Conference with the President, White House, Washington, October 29, 1956, 7:15pm," 836.

135. Scott W. Lucas, *Divided We Stand* (London: Hodder and Stoughton, 1991), 293; Keith Kyle, *Suez* (London: Weidenfeld and Nicholson, 1991), 464–465.

136. Selwyn Lloyd, *Suez 1956: A Personal Account* (London: Cape, 1978), 209; Alistair Horne, *Macmillan* (London: Macmillan, 1989), 440.

137. Waltz, *Theory of International Politics*, 169.

138. Morgenthau, *Politics Among Nations*, 2nd ed., 326–327; Jervis, "Unipolarity," 254.

139. Christensen, *The China Challenge*, 51.

140. Morgenthau, *Politics Among Nations*, 2nd ed., 326.

3. CONTEMPORARY U.S.-CHINA BIPOLARITY

1. Graham Allison, "The Thucydides Trap: Are the U.S. and China Headed for War?" *The Atlantic*, September 24, 2015; Graham Allison, *Destined for War: Can America and China Escape Thucydides's Trap?* (New York: Houghton Mifflin Harcourt, 2017), chap. 1. Not only has no other state increased its relative power so much and so fast, but China's rise has been peaceful. This is unprecedented in the modern state system.

2. Allison, "The Thucydides Trap." The Netherlands in 2014 ranked as the seventeenth largest economy in the world.

3. This is based on a US$11 trillion estimate for the Chinese economy and a US$18 trillion estimate for the U.S. economy.

206 3. CONTEMPORARY U.S.-CHINA BIPOLARITY

4. The World Bank, "GDP (current US$)," http://data.worldbank.org/indicator/NY.GDP .MKTP.CD?page=1.

5. Arvind Subramanian, *Eclipse: Living in the Shadow of China's Economic Dominance* (Washington, D.C.: Peterson Institute of International Economics, 2011).

6. Michael Beckley, "China's Century? Why America's Edge Will Endure," *International Security* 36, no. 3 (Winter 2011/2012): 41–78; Michael Beckley and Joshua R. Itzkowitz, "Correspondence: Debating China's Rise and U.S. Decline," *International Security* 37, no. 3: 172–181.

7. According to the data presented by Mearsheimer, the Soviet Union's relative share of superpower wealth in the period 1945–1990 was never above 40 percent. John J. Mearsheimer, *The Tragedy of Great Power Politics*, 2nd ed. (New York: Norton, 2014), 74–75. Other studies place the Soviet Union's GDP in some years during the Cold War above 40 percent but never more than 50 percent. See, among others, Charles Wolf Jr., Gregory Hildenbrandt, Michael Kennedy, et al., "Long-Term Economic and Military Trends, 1950–2010" (Santa Monica: RAND, April 1989).

8. National Intelligence Council (NIC), *Global Trends 2030: Alternative Worlds* (Washington, D.C.: December 2012), 15na.

9. World Bank, "GDP ranking, PPP based," July 1, 2015, http://data.worldbank.org /data-catalog/GDP-PPP-based-table; Joseph E. Stiglitz, "The Chinese Century," *Vanity Fair*, January 2015, http://www.vanityfair.com/news/2015/01/china-worlds-largest -economy.

10. Similarly, market exchange spending is also the main source for comparing military spending. This will also apply to the analysis of comparative power distribution between China, Russia, India, Japan, Germany, and the United Kingdom in chapter 4.

11. Beckley and Itzkowitz, "Correspondence," 178.

12. The next year the professor would be earning $320,000 and the banker $1,420,000. The year after, the professor would be earning $1,280,000 and the banker $1,704,000. After three years, the professor would be earning $5,120,000 and the banker $2,044,000. It is doubtful that the banker would be satisfied with such an outcome.

13. Josef Joffe, *The Myth of America's Decline: Politics, Economics, and a Half-Century of False Prophecies* (New York: Norton, 2014), 85–87.

14. U.S. exports and imports in 2012 totaled US$3.82 trillion, compared to China's US$3.87 trillion. "China Eclipses U.S. as Biggest Trading Nation," *Bloomberg News*, February 10, 2013, http://www.bloomberg.com/news/2013-02-09/china-passes-u-s -to-become-the-world-s-biggest-trading-nation.html.

15. Peter Marsh, "U.S. Manufacturing Crown Slips," *Financial Times*, June 20, 2010, http://www.ft.com/intl/cms/s/0/af2219cc-7c86-11df-8b74-00144feabdc0.html#axzz 2IcWJjtvC.

16. World Trade Organization, "Trade Patterns and Global Value Chain in East Asia: From Trade in Goods to Trade in Tasks," IDE-JETRO and World Trade Organization, 2011, https://www.wto.org/english/res_e/booksp_e/stat_tradepat_globval chains_e.pdf; Yuqing Xing, "Measuring Value Added in the People's Republic of China's Exports: A Direct Approach," Asian Development Bank Institute Working Paper 493, August 2014, https://www.adb.org/sites/default/files/publication/156348 /adbi-wp493.pdf; David Shambaugh, "China at the Crossroads: Ten Major Reform

Challenges," Brookings Institution (Washington, D.C., October 1, 2014), http://www.brookings.edu/~/media/research/files/papers/2014/10/01-china-crossroads-reform-challenges-shambaugh-b.pdf; Edward S. Steinfeld, *Playing Our Game: Why China's Rise Doesn't Threaten the West* (Oxford: Oxford University Press, 2010), esp. chap. 4.

17. China has the largest number of Internet users and the fastest supercomputer, and it has surpassed the United States to become the world's largest automobile market, smartphone market, e-commerce market, and luxury-goods market.

18. Allison, "The Thucydides Trap."

19. Michael Pettis, *Avoiding the Fall: China's Economic Restructuring* (Washington, D.C.: Carnegie Endowment for International Peace, 2013), 8.

20. Daniel Rosen, "Avoiding the Blind Alley: China's Economic Overhaul and Its Global Implications," *Asia Society Policy Institute*, October 2014, http://asiasociety.org/files/pdf/AvoidingtheBlindAlley_FullReport.pdf.

21. "Spotlight: China's Thirteenth Five-Year Plan Creates New Economic Opportunities: Overseas Experts," *Xinhua*, November 3, 2015, http://news.xinhuanet.com/english/2015-11/04/c_134783590.htm.

22. Daniel H. Rosen and Anna Snyder, "China's Outlook—Now and in 2020," Note, Rhodium Group, August 8, 2014, http://rhg.com/notes/chinas-outlook-now-and-in-2020.

23. Lawrence H. Summers and Lant Pritchett, "Asiaphoria Meets Regression to the Mean," National Bureau of Economic Research Working Paper 20573, October 2014, http://www.nber.org/papers/w20573.

24. The Conference Board, a business-research group based in New York, forecasts that China's annual economic growth will slow to an average of 5.5 percent between 2015 and 2019 and downshift further to an average of 3.9 percent between 2020 and 2025. Bob Davis, "China Growth Seen Slowing Sharply Over Decade," *Wall Street Journal*, October 20, 2014, http://online.wsj.com/articles/china-growth-seen-slowing-sharply-over-decade-1413778141.

25. "The Great Fall of China," *The Economist*, August 29, 2015.

26. Thomas J. Christensen, *The China Challenge: Shaping the Choices of a Rising Power* (New York: Norton, 2015), chap. 3.

27. IMF, *Regional Economic Outlook: Asia and Pacific, Stabilizing and Outperforming other Regions* (Washington, D.C., April 2015), http://www.imf.org/external/pubs/ft/reo/2015/apd/eng/pdf/areo0415.pdf; Richard Dobbs, Susan Lund, Jonathan Woetzel, and Mina Mutafchieva, "Debt and (Not Much) Deleveraging," McKinsey Global Institute, February 2015, http://www.mckinsey.com/insights/economic_studies/debt_and_not_much_deleveraging.

28. Jonathan Woetzel, "Is China Really Collapsing?" *Forbes*, October 5, 2015, http://www.forbes.com/sites/forbesasia/2015/10/05/is-china-really-collapsing/.

29. Pettis, *Avoiding the Fall*, 96.

30. The 2013 annual U.S. Department of Defense report to Congress on military and security developments involving the PRC "estimates that China's total actual military-related expenditure for 2012 falls between US$135 and US$215 billion." U.S. Department of Defense, *Annual Report to Congress: Military and Security Developments Involving the People's Republic of China 2013*, http://archive.defense.gov/pubs/2013_China_Report_FINAL.pdf, 45.

31. Zachary Cohen, "Trump Proposes $54 Billion Defense Spending Hike," *CNN*, March 16, 2017, http://edition.cnn.com/2017/03/16/politics/donald-trump-defense-budget -blueprint/index.html.

32. Bernard D. Cole, *China's Quest for Great Power: Ships, Oil, and Foreign Policy* (Annapolis, Md.: Naval Institute Press, 2016), 55–56.

33. Richard A. Bitzinger, "China Double-Digit Defense Growth: What It Means for a Peaceful Rise," *Foreign Affairs*, March 19, 2015.

34. Joseph S. Nye, *Is The American Century Over?* (Cambridge: Policy, 2015), 57.

35. Stephen G. Brooks and William Wohlforth, *America Abroad: The United States' Global Role in the Twenty-First Century* (Oxford: Oxford University Press, 2016), 15–22.

36. Christensen, *The China Challenge*, 82.

37. Michael S. Chase, Jeffrey Engstrom, Tai Ming Cheung, et al., *China's Incomplete Military Transformation: Assessing the Weaknesses of the People's Liberation Army (PLA)* (Santa Monica, Calif.: RAND Corporation, February 2015), http://www.uscc .gov/sites/default/files/Research/China%27s%20Incomplete%20Military%20Trans formation_2.11.15.pdf; Dennis J. Blasko, "Ten Reasons Why China Will Have Trouble Fighting a Modern War," *War on the Rocks*, February 18, 2015, http://warontherocks .com/2015/02/ten-reasons-why-china-will-have-trouble-fighting-a-modern-war/; Bernard D. Cole, *The Great Wall at Sea: China's Navy in the Twenty-First Century*, 2nd ed. (Annapolis, Md.: Naval Institute Press, 2010).

38. Andrew S. Erickson and Adam P. Liff, "Demystifying China's Defense Spending: Less Mysterious in the Aggregate," *China Quarterly* 216 (December 2013): 825.

39. See also Andrew S. Erickson, ed., *Chinese Naval Shipbuilding: An Ambitious and Uncertain Course* (Newport, RI: Naval Institute Press, 2015).

40. Cole, *China's Quest for Great Power*, 74. For an in-depth analysis, see esp. chaps. 2 and 3. In addition, see Andrew S. Erickson, "Evaluating China's Conventional Military Power: The Naval and Air Dimension," in *Assessing China's Power*, ed. Jae Ho Chung (New York: Palgrave Macmillan, 2015), 65–90.

41. Patrick M. Cronin, Mira Rapp-Hooper, Harry Krejsa, et al., *Beyond the San Hai: The Challenge of China's Blue-Water Navy*, Center for a New American Security, May 2017, https://s3.amazonaws.com/files.cnas.org/documents/CNASReport-Blue WaterNavy-Finalb.pdf.

42. Eric Heginbotham et al., *The U.S.-China Military Scorecard: Forces, Geography, and the Evolving Balance of Power 1996–2017* (Santa Monica: Rand Corporation, 2015), xxx, http://www.rand.org/pubs/research_reports/RR392.html; Roger Cliff, *China's Military Power: Assessing Current and Future Capabilities* (Cambridge: Cambridge University Press, 2015). See also David C. Gompert, Astrid Stuth Cevallos, and Cristina L. Garafola, *War with China: Thinking Through the Unthinkable* (Santa Monica, Calif.: RAND Corporation, 2016), http://www.rand.org/pubs/research_reports /RR1140.html.

43. Robert S. Ross, "The Rise of the Chinese Navy: From Regional Naval Power to Global Naval Power?" in *China's Global Engagement: Cooperation, Competition, and Influence in the Twenty-First Century*, ed. Jacques deLisle and Avery Goldstein (Washington, D.C.: Brookings Institution, 2017), 207–234.

44. U.S. Office of Naval Intelligence, *The PLA Navy: New Capabilities and Missions for the Twenty-First Century* (Washington D.C., April 2015), http://news.usni.org/2015/04/09

/document-office-of-naval-intelligence-2015-assessment-of-chinese-peoples
-liberation-army-navy.

45. U.S Department of Defense, *Asia-Pacific Maritime Security Strategy* (Washington, D.C., July 27, 2015), http://www.defense.gov/Portals/1/Documents/pubs/NDAA%20 A-P_Maritime_SecuritY_Strategy-08142015–1300-FINALFORMAT.PDF.

46. Cole, *The Great Wall at Sea*, xvi; Cole, *China's Quest for Great Power*.

47. Ronald O'Rourke, "China's Naval Modernization: Implications for U.S. Navy Capabilities—Background and Issues for Congress," *Congressional Research Service*, September 21, 2015, https://www.fas.org/sgp/crs/row/RL33153.pdf. My emphasis.

48. David Tweed and Adrian Leung, "How China's Growing Naval Fleet Is Shaping Global Politics," *Bloomberg*, June 1, 2017, https://www.bloomberg.com/politics /articles/2017-05-31/china-s-growing-naval-might-challenges-u-s-supremacy-in-asia.

49. Hans J. Morgenthau, *Politics Among Nations: The Struggle for Power and Peace*, 2nd ed. (New York: Knopf, 1954), 325–326.

50. Nuno P. Monteiro, *Theory of Unipolar Politics* (Cambridge: Cambridge University Press, 2014), 43.

51. Morgenthau, *Politics Among Nations*, 2nd ed., 113.

52. Mearsheimer, *The Tragedy*, 2nd ed., 60–61.

53. In 2011, the share of the Chinese workforce was 74.4 percent (out of 1,347,350,000). See "One Billion Workers," *The Economist*, January 23, 2012, http://www.economist .com/blogs/freeexchange/2012/01/chinas-labour-force. However, the workforce has now declined as a percentage of the population, and the National Bureau of Statistics of China announced in January 2016 that the "population at the working age of 16–59 was 910.96 million, a decrease of 4.87 million as compared with that at the end of 2014, and it accounted for 66.3 percent of the total population." See http:// www.stats.gov.cn/english/PressRelease/201601/t20160119_1306072.html.

54. Brooks and Wohlforth, *America Abroad*, 35–38; Timothy Beardson, *Stumbling Giant: The Threats to China's Future* (New Haven, Conn.: Yale University Press, 2013), 6; Robert Stowe England, *Aging China: The Demographic Challenge to China's Economic Prospect* (Westport, Conn.: Praeger, 2005); Martin Jacques, *When China Rules the World: The End of the Western World and the Birth of a New World Order*, 2nd ed. (London: Penguin, 2012), 202–206; NIC, *Global Trends 2030*, 15.

55. Brooks and Wohlforth, *America Abroad*, 35–38.

56. Xizhe Peng, "China's Demographic History and Future Challenges," *Science* 333 (July 29, 2011): 583–584.

57. Kevin Sneader and Jonathan Woetzel, "China's Impending Robot Revolution," *Wall Street Journal*, August 3, 2016, http://www.wsj.com/articles/chinas-impending -robot-revolution-1470241843.

58. The National Bureau of Statistics of China reported in January 2016 that "in terms of gender, the male population was 704.14 million, and female population was 670.48 million; the sex ratio of the total population was 105.02 (the female is 100); the sex ratio at birth was 113.51" (http://www.stats.gov.cn/english/PressRelease/201601 /t20160119_1306072.html). The sex ratio at birth is lower than in previous years and it will decline further in coming years. But there is a twenty-year cohort of the population for which the sex ratio was higher, and this cohort is beginning to reach marriageable age.

59. UN University—International Human Dimensions Programme and the UN Environment Programme, *Inclusive Wealth Report 2014: Measuring Progress Toward Sustainability* (Cambridge: Cambridge University Press, 2014), 121–122.

60. The World Bank, "Fertility rate, total (births per woman)," http://data.worldbank .org/indicator/SP.DYN.TFRT.IN.

61. "China Unveils Proposals for Formulating Thirteenth Five-Year Plan," *Xinhua*, November 3, 2015, http://news.xinhuanet.com/english/2015-11/03/c_134780050.htm.

62. Martin King Whyte, Wang Feng, and Yong Cai, "Challenging Myths About China's One-Child Policy," *China Journal* 74 (2015): 144–159.

63. UN University, *Inclusive Wealth Report 2014*, 121–122; Stratford, "In China, an Unprecedented Demographic Problem Takes Shape," August 21, 2013, http://www.stratfor .com/analysis/china-unprecedented-demographic-problem-takes-shape.

64. Xizhe Peng, "China's Demographic History," 586.

65. Yanzhong Huang, "Population Aging in China: A Mixed Blessing," *The Diplomat*, November 10, 2013, http://thediplomat.com/2013/11/population-aging-in-china -a-mixed-blessing/.

66. Francois Godement, "China's Economic Power: Catching Up with the United States by 2025?" in *Assessing China's Power*, ed. Jae Ho Chung (New York: Palgrave Macmillan, 2015), 35.

67. China's total area of 9,388,211 km² is similar to the United States' 9,147,420 km² and much larger than the European Union's 7,708,000 km².

68. Morgenthau, *Politics Among Nations*, 2nd ed., 104.

69. Peter Dutton, Robert S. Ross, and Øystein Tunsjø, eds., *Twenty-First Century Seapower: Cooperation and Conflict at Sea* (London: Routledge, 2012); Robert D. Kaplan, *The Revenge of Geography: What the Map Tells Us About Coming Conflicts and the Battle Against Fate* (New York: Random House, 2012), 188–227.

70. Robert S. Ross, "China's Naval Nationalism: Sources, Prospects, and the U.S. Response," *International Security* 34, no. 2 (Fall 2009): 56–57.

71. Ross, "The Rise of the Chinese Navy."

72. Kaplan, *The Revenge*, 189, 200, 211.

73. Launched in 2013, the Belt and Road initiative has become China's most prestigious project abroad. See, for instance, the website of the State Council of the PRC (http:// english.gov.cn/beltAndRoad/) and National Development and Reform Commission, *Vision and Actions on Jointly Building Silk Road Economic Belt and Twenty-First-Century Maritime Silk Road*, issued jointly by the National Development and Reform Commission, Ministry of Foreign Affairs, and Ministry of Commerce of the People's Republic of China, March 28, 2015, http://en.ndrc.gov.cn/newsrelease/201503 /t20150330_669367.html.

74. Tian Shaohui, "Chronology of China Road and Belt Initiative," *Xinhuanet*, March 28, 2015, http://news.xinhuanet.com/english/2015-03/28/c_134105435.htm.

75. Jo Inge Bekkevold and Øystein Tunsjø, "Sustaining Growth: Energy and Natural Resources," in *SAGE Handbook of Contemporary China*, ed. Wu Weiping and Mark Frazier (forthcoming).

76. Daniel Yergin, *The Quest: Energy, Security, and the Remaking of the Modern World* (London: Allen Lane, 2011), 221; Philip Andrews-Speed and Roland Dannreuther, *China, Oil, and Global Politics* (London: Routledge, 2011).

77. Spencer Swartz and Shai Oster, "China Tops U.S. in Energy Use," *Wall Street Journal,* July 18, 2010, http://online.wsj.com/article/SB100014240527487037205045753767123 53150310.html. China's position as the largest net oil importer is not simply attributable to its growing demand but also to the development of fracking, oil sand, and unconventional reserves in the United States. See Edward L. Morse, "Energy 2020: North America, the New Middle East?" *Citi GPS,* March 20, 2012, http://csis.org/files /attachments/120411_gsf_MORSE_ENERGY_2020_North_America_the_New _Middle_East.pdf.

78. China's energy mix is currently about 62 percent coal, 20 percent oil, 7 percent hydro, 7 percent gas, 2 percent nuclear, 1 percent bio, and 1 percent other renewables.

79. Yergin, *The Quest,* 196.

80. China is the world's largest producer of hydroelectric power, which accounts for roughly 7 percent of its energy mix. It also has indigenous gas reserves, is strongly building up its nuclear-power production, and is a leading investor in alternative and renewable energy.

81. "International Energy Statistics," Energy Information Administration, https://www .eia.gov/beta/international/rankings/#?prodact=53-1&cy=2016.

82. Shi Hongtao, "China's 'Malacca Straits,'" *Qingnian Bao,* June 15, 2004, in Foreign Broadcast Information Service (hereafter cited as FBIS), CPP20040615000042; Wu Lei and Shen Qinyu, "Will China Go to War Over Oil?" *Far Eastern Economic Review* 160, no. 3 (April 2006): 38–40; Robert D. Kaplan, "Center Stage for the Twenty-first Century: Power Plays in the Indian Ocean," *Foreign Affairs* 88, no. 2 (March/April 2009): 16–32; Ian Storey, "China's 'Malacca Dilemma,'" *China Brief* (Jamestown Foundation) 6, no. 8 (April 12, 2006); You Yi, "Dealing with the Malacca Strait Dilemma: China's Efforts to Enhance Energy Transportation Security," *EAI Background Brief* 329 (April 12, 2007).

83. Øystein Tunsjø, *Security and Profit in China's Energy Policy: Hedging Against Risk* (New York: Columbia University Press, 2013).

84. See Gabriel B. Collins and William S. Murray, "No Oil for the Lamps of China?" *Naval War College Review* 61, no. 2 (2008): 81.

85. "China's Oil Refinery Capacity From 1970 to 2014," *Statista,* 2015, http://www.statista .com/statistics/273578/oil-refinery-capacity-of-china/.

86. Tunsjø, *Security and Profit.* China is also sitting on large reserves of shale gas and oil, which potentially can be added to China's energy mix.

87. World Bank, http://data.worldbank.org/indicator/AG.LND.ARBL.ZS; "Water in China: Desperate Measures," *The Economist,* October 12, 2013, http://www.economist .com/news/leaders/21587789-desperate-measures.

88. OECD-FAO Agricultural Outlook 2013, "Feeding China: Prospects and Challenges in the Next Decade," June 27, 2013, http://www.oecd-ilibrary.org/agriculture-and-food /oecd-fao-agricultural-outlook-2013_agr_outlook-2013-en.

89. The growth of Chinese agricultural production is mainly driven by technical progress. China's per capita grain production increased from about 200 kg per capita in 1949 to about 400 kg in the early 1990s. During this period, a 2.5-fold population increase was accompanied by a 4.5-fold increase in total grain production. See Jianhua Zhang, "China's Success in Increasing Per Capita Food Production," *Journal of Experimental Botany* 62, no. 11 (2011): 3707–3711; "China Issues Guidelines

for Agricultural Development," *Xinhua*, May 27, 2015, http://news.xinhuanet.com /english/2015–05/27/c_134275861.htm.

90. Morgenthau, *Politics Among Nations*, 2nd ed., 104.

91. Morgenthau, *Politics Among Nations*, 2nd ed., 105.

92. David Pimentel and Marcia Pimentel, "Sustainability of Meat-Based and Plant-Based Diets and the Environment," *American Journal of Clinical Nutrition* 78, no. 3 (2003): 660S–663S.

93. Damien Ma and William Adams, *In Line Behind a Billion People: How Scarcity Will Define China's Ascent in the Next Decade* (New Jersey: FT, 2014), 6.

94. Elizabeth Economy, "China's Water Challenge: Implications for the U.S. Rebalance to Asia," prepared statement before the Senate Foreign Relations Subcommittee on East Asian and Pacific Affairs, July 24, 2013.

95. Ma and Adams, *In Line*, 44–45, 64.

96. Elizabeth Economy, *The River Runs Black: The Environmental Challenge to China's Future* (Ithaca, N.Y.: Cornell University Press, 2004); Barry Naughton, *The Chinese Economy: Transition and Growth* (Cambridge, Mass.: MIT Press, 2007), 30.

97. Economy, *The River*; Economy, "China's Water Challenge."

98. Jian Xie et al., *Addressing China's Water Scarcity: A Synthesis of Recommendations for Selected Water Resource Management Issues* (Washington, D.C.: World Bank, 2009).

99. "Water in China: Desperate Measures," *The Economist*, October 12, 2013, http://www .economist.com/news/leaders/21587789-desperate-measures.

100. Agence France-Presse and Stephen Chen, "Beijing's Massive Water Project Opens to Doubts from Critics," *South China Morning Post*, December 28, 2014, http:// www.scmp.com/news/china/article/1669498/beijings-massive-water-project-opens -reservations-critics.

101. Scott Moore, "Water Resource Issues, Policy and Politics in China," Issue Brief (Washington, D.C.: Brookings, February 12, 2013), http://www.brookings.edu/research /papers/2013/02/water-politics-china-moore.

102. See the website of China's Ministry of Land and Resources: http://www.mlr.gov.cn /mlrenglish/about/facts/.

103. David Shambaugh, "The Coming Chinese Crackup," *Wall Street Journal*, March 6, 2015, http://www.wsj.com/articles/the-coming-chinese-crack-up-1425659198; Minxin Pei, "The Twilight of Communist Party Rule in China," *American Interest*, November 12, 2015, http://www.the-american-interest.com/2015/11/12/the-twilight-of-communist -party-rule-in-china/.

104. Gordon Chang, *The Coming Collapse of China* (New York: Random House, 2001); He Qinglian, *The Pitfalls of Modernization* (Tokyo: Soshisha, 2002); Arthur Waldron, "The China Sickness," *Commentary*, July/August 2003; Gordon Chang, "The Coming Collapse of China: 2012 Edition," *Foreign Policy*, December 29, 2011.

105. Arthur R. Kroeber, "Here Is Xi's China: Get Used to It," *ChinaFile*, December 11, 2014, http://www.chinafile.com/reporting-opinion/viewpoint/here-xis-china-get-used-it.

106. Michael Forsyth, "Q. and A.: Roderick MacFarquhar on Xi Jinping's High-Risk Campaign to Save the Communist Party," *Sinosphere*, January 30, 2015, http://sinosphere .blogs.nytimes.com/2015/01/30/q-and-a-roderick-macfarquhar-on-xi-jinpings-high -risk-campaign-to-save-the-communist-party/. MacFarquhar argues that Xi is the strongest leader in China since Mao, since he has no peers of equal status who are

able to challenge him because of their past record. Others contend that Xi is the strongest leader since Deng. See Zhuang Chen, "Xi Jinping: The Heir to Deng Xiaoping?" *BBC News*, August 22, 2014, http://www.bbc.com/news/world-asia-28892043.

107. David M. Lampton, "How China Is Ruled: Why It's Getting Harder for Beijing to Govern," *Foreign Affairs*, January/February 2014; David M. Lampton, *Following the Leader: Ruling China, from Deng Xiaoping to Xi Jinping* (Berkeley: University of California Press, 2014).

108. David Shambaugh, *China's Future* (Cambridge: Polity, 2016), 11.

109. Bruce J. Dickson, *The Dictator's Dilemma: The Chinese Communist Party's Strategy for Survival* (Oxford: Oxford University Press, 2016).

110. Jo Inge Bekkevold and Robert S. Ross, eds., *China in the Era of Xi Jinping: Domestic and Foreign Policy Challenges* (Washington, D.C.: Georgetown University Press, 2016).

111. Andrew J. Nathan, "Authoritarian Resilience," *Journal of Democracy* 14, no. 1 (January 2003), 6–17; David Shambaugh, *China's Communist Party: Atrophy and Adaptation* (Berkeley: University of California Press, 2008). It should be noted that both these scholars are now questioning the resilience of the CCP. Andrew J. Nathan, "Foreseeing the Unforeseeable," *Journal of Democracy* 24, no. 1 (2013): 20–25; Shambaugh, "The Coming Chinese Crackup."

112. Bo Xilai was the Chongqing party boss whose fall from power during the first months of 2012 posed a potential threat to the CCP and political stability. Bo is a "princeling," as his father Bo Yibo was a revolutionary veteran and one of the eight immortals of the CCP. Bo's family has ties to Chengdu Military Region and some quarters of the PLA. Zhou was China's former domestic security chief and CCP Politburo Standing Committee member and allegedly a supporter of Bo Xilai. Both Bo and Zhou were sentenced to life in prison after an internal power struggle in the CCP. Jeremy Page and Lingling Wei, "Bo's Ties to Army Alarmed Beijing," *Wall Street Journal*, May 17, 2012, http://online.wsj.com/article/SB10001424052702304203604577398034072800836.html. On the importance of consensus in the Politburo and stability during leadership transition, see Alice Miller, "The Bo Xilai Affair in Central Leadership Politics," *China Leadership Monitor* 38 (2012), http://media.hoover.org/sites/default/files/documents/CLM38AM.pdf.

113. Kenneth Allen, Dennis J. Blasko, and John F. Corbett, "The PLA's New Organizational Structure: What Is Known, Unknown, and Speculation (Part 1)," *China Brief* 16, no. 3 (February 4, 2016), http://www.jamestown.org/single/?tx_ttnews%5Btt_news%5D=45069&no_cache=1#.VrspbNvhC1t.

114. Ross Terrill, *The New Chinese Empire and What It Means for the United States* (New York: Basic Books, 2003), 1.

115. Dan Breznitz and Michael Murphree, "The Rise of China in Technology Standards: New Norms in Old Institutions," U.S.-China Economic and Security Review Commission, January 16, 2013, http://origin.www.uscc.gov/sites/default/files/Research/RiseofChinainTechnologyStandards.pdf; Battelle, "2013 Global R&D Funding Forecast," *R&D Magazine*, December 2012. See UNESCO Science Report 2015; OECD, "China Headed to EU, US in Science & Technology Spending," November 12, 2014, http://www.oecd.org/newsroom/china-headed-to-overtake-eu-us-in-science-technology-spending.htm; Yutao Sun and Cong Cao, "Demystifying Central Government R&D spending in China: Should Funding Focus on Scientific Research?"

Science 345, no. 6200 (August 29, 2014): 1006; Richard Van Noorden, "China Tops Europe in R&D intensity," *Nature*, January 8, 2014, http://www.nature.com/news /china-tops-europe-in-rd-intensity-1.14476.

116. UN Educational, Scientific, and Cultural Organization, *UNESCO Science Report: Towards 2030* (Paris, 2015), 26; UN World Intellectual Property Organization (UN-WIPO), "World Intellectual Property Report: The Changing Face of Innovation and Intellectual Property," http://www.wipo.int/econ_stat/en/economics/wipr/pdf /wipr_2011_chapter1.pdf, 34–35.

117. Sun and Cao, "Demystifying Central Government R&D Spending in China," 1006; Van Noorden, "China Tops Europe in R&D Intensity."

118. UNESCO Science Report 2015.

119. UNESCO Science Report 2015, 36.

120. UNWIPO, "World Intellectual Property Report," 37-38; *Knowledge, Networks, and Nations: Global Scientific Collaboration in the Twenty-First Century*, The Royal Society (2011), http://royalsociety.org/uploadedFiles/Royal_Society_Content/Influencing _Policy/Reports/2011-03-28-Knowledge-networks-nations.pdf.

121. UNESCO Science Report 2015, 32.

122. Allison, *Destined for War*, 16.

123. Felicia Sonmez, "Chinese University Tops MIT in Engineering Rankings," *Wall Street Journal*, October 8, 2015, http://blogs.wsj.com/chinarealtime/2015/10/08/chinese -university-tops-mit-in-engineering-rankings/.

124. Cong Cao, "China," UNESCO Science Report 2015, 623–627.

125. "Shenzhen Is a Hothouse of Innovation," *The Economist*, April 8, 2017, http:// www.economist.com/news/special-report/21720076-copycats-are-out-innovators -are-shenzhen-hothouse-innovation.

126. Paul Davidson, "Why China Is Beating the U.S. at Innovation," *USA Today*, April 17, 2017, https://www.usatoday.com/story/money/2017/04/17/why-china-beating-us -innovation/100016138/.

127. Beckley, "China's Century?"; Guy de Jonquiéres, "Who's Afraid of the China's High-Tech Challenge?" Policy Briefs, European Centre for International Political Economy, no. 07/2013, http://www.ecipe.org/media/publication_pdfs/PB7.pdf; Christensen, *The China Challenge*, 73.

128. Conversely, after receiving about three times more and granting twice as many patent applicants than the United States, China can allow itself some junk patterns to serve as tools for Chinese companies to retaliate against foreign competitors. See Giacopello, "Rise in Quantity, Fall in Quality."

129. Comparatively, Japan and Germany's share in 2013 were 19 percent and 6.3 percent respectively. UNESCO Science Report 2015, 38, 39.

130. Beckley, "China's Century," 64–65.

131. UNWIPO, "World Intellectual Property Report," 37–38.

132. Steinfeld, *Playing Our Game*, 146–147, 173.

133. Gideon Rose and Jonathan Tepperman, "Dysfunction Junction: Trouble on the Home Front," *Foreign Affairs* 93, no. 5 (2014): 2; Francis Fukuyama, "America in Decay: The Sources of Political Dysfunction," *Foreign Affairs* 93, no. 5 (2014): 5–26.

134. Daniel Lynch, "The End of China's Rise," *Foreign Affairs*, January 11, 2016.

135. Jacques, *When China Rules*.

4. DISTINGUISHING TOP-RANKING STATES AND COMPARING BIPOLARITY

1. Kenneth N. Waltz, *Theory of International Politics* (1979; Long Grove, Ill.: Waveland, 2010), 131.
2. IMF, "World Economic Database, Outlook," April 2016.
3. For an early optimistic assessment of India's great-power potential, see the special issue "The Rise of India," *Foreign Affairs* 84, no. 4 (June 2006).
4. Robert S. Ross, "The Geography of Peace: East Asia in the Twenty-First Century," *International Security* 23, no. 4 (Spring 1999): 81–118, 87–90; Robert S. Ross, "The Rise of the Chinese Navy: From Regional Naval Power to Global Naval Power?" in *China's Global Engagement: Cooperation, Competition, and Influence in the Twenty-First Century*, ed. Jacques deLisle and Avery Goldstein (Washington, D.C.: Brookings Institution, 2017), 207–234.
5. Denny Roy, *The Return of the Dragon: Rising China and Regional Security* (New York: Columbia University Press, 2013), 106.
6. See the UN Department of Economic and Social Affairs, Population Division, "Population Estimates and Projections," http://esa.un.org/wpp/.
7. Editorial, "India's Youth Challenge," *New York Times*, April 17, 2014, http://www.nytimes.com/2014/04/18/opinion/indias-youth-challenge.html.
8. World Bank, "Mortality rate, infant (per 1,000 live births)," http://data.worldbank.org/indicator/SP.DYN.IMRT.IN; World Bank, "Life expectancy at birth, total (years)," http://data.worldbank.org/indicator/SP.DYN.LE00.IN.
9. Sebastian James, "Why Is China Ahead of India?" blog, *World Bank*, July 17, 2013, http://blogs.worldbank.org/psd/why-china-ahead-india-fascinating-analysis-amartya-sen.
10. Yogesh Vajpeyi, "Tackling the Challenges to India's Demographic Dividend," UNICEF, http://www.unicef.org/india/health_3081.htm; Danielle Rajendram, "The Promise and Perils of India's Youth Bulge," *The Diplomat*, March 10, 2013, http://thediplomat.com/2013/03/the-promise-and-peril-of-indias-youth-bulge/.
11. Marshall I. Goldman, *Petrostate: Putin, Power, and the New Russia* (Oxford: Oxford University Press, 2010).
12. Simi Metha and Mohsin Amin, "Reliance on Oil and Gas Imports and Economic Growth—India's New Challenge," *SAIS Review of International Affairs*, April 27, 2017, http://www.saisreview.org/2017/04/27/indias-new-challenge/; U.S. Energy Information Administration, "India Is Increasingly Dependent on Imported Fossil Fuels as Demands Continue to Increase," August 14, 2015, http://www.eia.gov/todayinenergy/detail.cfm?id=17551.
13. Food Security Portal, "Global Huger Index 2015," International Food Policy Research Institute (IFPRI), http://www.foodsecurityportal.org/countries.
14. World Bank, *World Governance Indicators*, http://info.worldbank.org/governance/wgi/index.aspx#home.
15. India, however, is apparently doing better on some less conventional indicators of creativity and innovation emanating from its robust private sector and civil society, but the lack of organization, infrastructure, and state leadership might prevent India from becoming a leader in terms of competency. Davesh Kapur, "Unleashing Potential in Innovation and Creativity," *East Asia Forum Quarterly* 4, no. 1

(January–March 2012): 10–11, http://press.anu.edu.au//wp-content/uploads/2012/02/whole2.pdf.

16. Robert Farley, "America, Take Notice: China's Five Military Game Changes," *National Interest*, August 23, 2014, http://nationalinterest.org/feature/america-take-notice-chinas -five-military-game-changers-11138; Tai Ming Chung, ed., *Forging China's Military Might: A New Framework for Assessing Innovation* (Washington, D.C.: Johns Hopkins University Press, 2014); Tai Ming Chung, ed., *China's Emergence as a Defense Technological Power* (London: Routledge, 2013); Evan S. Medeiros, Roger Cliff, Keith Crane, and James C. Mulvenon, *A New Direction for China's Defense Industry* (Santa Monica, Calif.: RAND Corporation, 2005).

17. Alexander Cooley, *Great Games, Local Rules: The New Great Power Contest in Central Asia* (Oxford: Oxford University Press, 2012); Gilbert Rozman, *The Sino-Russian Challenge to the World Order: National Identities, Bilateral Relations, and East Versus West in the 2010s* (Washington, D.C.: Woodrow Wilson Center Press, 2014); Martha Brill Olcott, "China's Unmatched Influence in Central Asia," Carnegie Endowment for International Peace, Washington, D.C., September 18, 2013, http://carnegieendowment .org/2013/09/18/china-s-unmatched-influence-in-central-asia; "Rising China, Sinking Russia," *Economist*, September 14, 2013, http://www.economist.com/news/asia/21586304 -vast-region-chinas-economic-clout-more-match-russias-rising-china-sinking.

18. IMF, "World Economic Database, Outlook," https://www.imf.org/external/pubs/ft /weo/2015/02/weodata/index.aspx.

19. World Bank, "Energy imports, net (% of energy use)," http://data.worldbank.org /indicator/EG.IMP.CONS.ZS.

20. Charles Wolf Jr., Gregory Hildenbrandt, Michael Kennedy, et al., "Long-Term Economic and Military Trends, 1950–2010" (Santa Monica, Calif.: RAND, April 1989), 4; John G. Ikenberry, Michael Mastanduno, and William C. Wohlforth, "Introduction: Unipolarity, State Behavior, and Systemic Consequences," *World Politics* 61, no. 1 (January 2009): 1–27. The export and import rates in the United States were much higher than those in the Soviet Union, and the United States was the world's leading manufacturer. See tables in Waltz, *Theory of International Politics*, 178, 215, 219. Gareth Porter, *Perils of Dominance: Imbalance of Power and the Road to War in Vietnam* (Berkeley: University of California Press, 2005), 3; Barry Posen, "From Unipolarity to Multipolarity: Transition in Sight?" in *International Relations Theory and the Consequences of Unipolarity*, ed. John G. Ikenberry, Michael Mastanduno, and William C. Wohlforth (Cambridge: Cambridge University Press, 2011), 317–341, 321, 324. For the period 1970–1990, see Carmel Davis, *Power, Threat, or Military Capabilities: U.S. Balancing in the Later Cold War, 1970–1982* (Lanham, Md.: University Press of America, 2011). The United States' percentage of world trade and manufacturing was ahead of the Soviet Union. See Waltz, *Theory of International Politics*, appendix, 215–220.

21. Wolf et al., "Long-Term Economic and Military Trends."

22. Waltz, *Theory of International Politics*, 179–180.

23. The population in the Soviet Union and the United States in 1950 was respectively roughly 180 and 150 million.

24. Close to half of the population in the Soviet Union in 1950 was composed of non-Russian ethnic groups, and the Soviet Union was made up of fifteen union republics.

25. The Soviet Union developed a comprehensive railway system, but its road network, civil-aviation transport, and automobile industry remained underdeveloped. See David Wilson, *The Demand for Energy in the Soviet Union* (London: Rowman & Littlefield, 1983); John Ambler, Denis J. B. Shaw, and Leslie Symons, *Soviet and East European Transport Problems* (New York: St. Martin's Press, 1985).

26. Loren R. Graham, *Science in Russia and the Soviet Union: A Short History* (Cambridge: Cambridge University Press, 1994); Audra J. Wolfe, *Competing with the Soviets: Technology and the State in Cold War America* (Baltimore, Md.: Johns Hopkins University Press, 2012); and Waltz, *Theory of International Politics*, 217.

27. Graham, *Science in Russia*, 5.

28. Peter H. Beckman, *World Politics in the Twentieth Century* (Englewood Cliffs, N.J.: Prentice Hall, 1984); Porter, *Perils of Dominance*.

29. Porter, *Perils of Dominance*, 4.

30. Waltz, *Theory of International Politics*, 163; Paul Kennedy, *The Rise and the Fall of the Great Powers* (New York: Vintage, 1989); John H. Hertz, *International Politics in the Atomic Age* (New York: Columbia University Press, 1959); John Lewis Gaddis, *Strategies of Containment: A Critical Appraisal of American National Security Policy During the Cold War*, rev. and exp. ed. (Oxford: Oxford University Press, 2005), 386. Snyder and Diesing wrote in 1977 that "since 1945 it [the international system] has been bipolar" but then added that the "international system at present seems to be in a transition period leading to a new form of multipolarity." Glenn H. Snyder and Paul Diesing, *Conflict Among Nations: Bargaining, Decision Making, and System Structure in International Crisis* (Princeton, N.J.: Princeton University Press, 1977), 419.

31. Kennedy, *The Rise and the Fall*, chap. 7.

32. Gaddis, "The Long Peace," 102.

33. As pointed out in chapter 3, according to the OECD, China spent 1.98 percent of GDP on R&D in 2012, which is more than the Soviet Union did in 1950 (about 1.4 percent). William Easterly and Stanley Fischer, "The Soviet Economic Decline: Historical and Republican Data," Working Paper 4735 (Cambridge, Mass.: National Bureau of Economic Research, May 1994), fig. 3.

34. China has the second-largest rail transportation network in the world behind the United States, but it has the world's most extensive network of high-speed rail. China and India's share the second place in term of road-network size behind the United States, but China has many more expressways than any country in the world. China is ranked second in the world in terms of number of international airports, and seven out of the ten largest ports in the world are located in China.

35. World Bank, "Military expenditure (% of GDP)," http://data.worldbank.org/indicator /MS.MIL.XPND.GD.ZS.

36. According to Easterly and Fischer, the Soviet Union defense burden as a share of GDP was 9 percent in 1950, 12 percent in 1960, 13 percent in 1970, and 16 percent in 1980. See Easterly and Fischer, "The Soviet Economic Decline," table 3. This suggests that China has learned from the Soviet Union and adopted a policy subordinating defense modernization and military buildup to, but in coordination with, the national objective of economic development (that is, China's defense budget has increased in step with its economic growth).

37. Jae Ho Chung, "Assessing China's Power," in *Assessing China's Power*, ed. Jae Ho Chung (New York: Palgrave Macmillan, 2015), 4.

38. Wolf et al., "Long-Term Economic and Military Trends," 4.

39. According to Maddison, U.S. GDP in 1950 was 1,455 billion; the Soviet Union's was 510 billion; the United Kingdom, 347 billion; Germany, 265 billion; France, 220 billion; India, 222 billion; Japan, 160 billion, and the world total GDP, 5,329 billion. Maddison uses 1990 International Geary Kharmis dollars. See "Statistics on World Population, GDP, and Per Capita GDP, 1–2008 AD," http://www.ggdc.net/maddison /Maddison.htm.

40. GDP numbers in 1990 using International Geary Kharmis dollars were: United States, 9,485 billion; China, 8,908 billion; India, 3,415 billion; Japan, 2,904 billion; Germany, 1,713 billion; United Kingdom, 1,446 billion; France, 1,423 billion; Russia, 1,281 billion; Brazil, 1,262; and the world total, 50,973 billion.

41. Conference Board, "Global Economic Outlook 2013, May 2013 Update," http://www .conference-board.org/data/globaloutlook.cfm.

42. IMF World Economic Outlook, "IMF Data Mapper," October 2015, http://www.imf .org/external/datamapper/index.php.

43. Wolf et al., "Long-Term Economic and Military Trends," 17.

44. The gap between China and Russia is closer if we use the IISS figure; others, however, such as the U.S. Department of Defense, estimate that China's defense spending is much higher than the IISS estimates and more in accordance with the SIPRI figures.

45. Waltz, *Theory of International Politics*, 131.

46. The PLA had no air force or navy during the Korean War. Although the Soviet Union eventually decided to offer air support, it was delayed and not provided at the front lines. Zhihua Shen, *Mao, Stalin, and the Korean War: Trilateral Communist Relations in the 1950s* (London: Routledge, 2012).

47. Ross, "The Rise of the Chinese Navy"; Peter Dutton, Andrew S. Erikson, and Ryan Martinson, eds., *China's Near Seas Combat Capabilities*, China Maritime Studies 11, (Newport, R.I.: U.S. Naval War College, 2014), https://www.usnwc.edu /Research-Gaming/China-Maritime-Studies-Institute/Publications/documents/Web -CMS11-(1)-(1).aspx; Seth Cropsey, *Mayday: The Decline of American Naval Supremacy* (New York: Overlook, 2013); James R. Holmes, "China's Navy Is Already Challenging the U.S. in the Asia Pacific," *The Diplomat*, October 16, 2014, http://thediplomat .com/2014/10/chinas-navy-is-already-challenging-the-us-in-asia/.

48. David Shambaugh, *China Goes Global: The Partial Power* (New York: Oxford University Press, 2013).

49. Hans J. Morgenthau, *Politics Among Nations: The Struggle for Power and Peace*, 2nd ed. (New York: Knopf, 1954), 324; Kennedy, *The Rise and the Fall*, 358.

50. Donald P. Steury, ed., *Intentions and Capabilities: Estimates on Soviet Strategic Forces, 1950–1983* (Washington, D.C.: CIA, 1996).

51. Andrew S. Erickson and Austin Strange, "China's Global Maritime Presence: Hard and Soft Dimensions of PLAN Antipiracy Operations," *China Brief* 15, no. 9 (May 1, 2015), http://www.jamestown.org/single/?tx_ttnews%5Btt_news%5D=43868&no _cache=1#.VktZhlUve1s.

52. Yan Meng and Yao Chun, "Chinese Navy Completes Escort Mission of Transporting Syria's Chemical Weapons," *People's Daily Online*, February 13, 2014, http://en.people .cn/90786/8534903.html.

53. Ross, "The Rise of the Chinese Navy"; Bernard D. Cole, *The Great Wall at Sea: China's Navy in the Twenty-First Century*, 2nd ed. (Annapolis, Md.: Naval Institute Press, 2010); Nan Li, "The Evolution of China's Naval Strategy and Capabilities: From 'Near Coast' and 'Near Seas' to 'Far Seas,'" *Asian Security* 5, no. 2 (June 2009): 144–169; Michael McDevitt and Fredric Vellucci Jr., "The Evolution of the People's Liberation Army and Navy: The Twin Missions of Area-Denial and Peacetime Operations," in *Sea Power and the Asia-Pacific: The Triumph of Neptune?* ed. Geoffrey Till and Patrick C. Bratton (London: Routledge, 2012), 75–92; Roy Kamphausen and Andrew Scobell, eds., *Right Sizing the People's Liberation Army: Exploring the Contours of China's Military* (Carlisle, Penn.: Strategic Studies Institute, U.S. Army War College, 2007).

54. "Full Text: China's Military Strategy," *Xinhua*, May 26, 2015, http://www.chinadaily.com.cn/china/2015-05/26/content_20820628.htm; "Xi Advocates Efforts to Boost China Maritime Power," *Xinhua*, July 31, 2013, http://news.xinhuanet.com/english/china/2013-07/31/c_132591246.htm; and Sukjoon Yoon, "Implications of Xi Jinping's 'True Maritime Power,'" *Naval War College Review* 68, no. 3 (Summer 2015): 40–63.

55. Jeremy Page and Gordon Lubold, "Five Chinese Navy Ships Are Operating in Bering Sea off Alaska," *Wall Street Journal*, September 2, 2015.

56. Ross, "The Rise of the Chinese Navy."

5. STRONG BALANCING POSTPONED

1. Kenneth N. Waltz, "Reflections on Theory of International Politics: A Response to My Critics," in *Neorealism and Its Critics*, ed. Robert O. Keohane (New York: Columbia University Press, 1986), 322–345, 344.

2. Kenneth N. Waltz, *Theory of International Politics* (1979; Long Grove, Ill.: Waveland, 2010), 127–128.

3. Robert Jervis, *System Effects: Complexity in Political and Social Life* (Princeton, N.J.: Princeton University Press, 1997), 104.

4. The present situation in East Asia does not yet resemble an arms race in the sense provided by Ian Storey as "two or more antagonistic parties that match each other's military capabilities by rapidly increasing defence spending as a percentage of GDP." There is no mad rush in the Asia-Pacific today, Storey maintains, comparable to the Anglo-German naval arms race in the lead up to the First World War. See Ian Storey, "Naval Modernization in China, Japan and South Korea: Contrasts and Comparisons," in *Naval Modernisation in South East Asia: Nature, Causes, and Consequences*, ed. Geoffrey Till and Jane Chan (London: Routledge, 2014), 105.

5. Stephen M. Walt, "Alliances in a Unipolar World," in *International Relations Theory and the Consequences of Unipolarity*, ed. John G. Ikenberry, Michael Mastanduno, and William C. Wohlforth (Cambridge: Cambridge University Press, 2011), 99–139, 117; Robert S. Ross, "Balance of Power Politics and the Rise of China: Accommodation and Balancing in East Asia," *Security Studies* 15 (2006): 355–395; Robert S. Ross, "Bipolarity and Balancing in East Asia," in *Balance of Power: Theory and Practice in the Twenty-First Century*, ed. T. V. Paul, James J. Wirtz, and Michel Fortmann (Stanford, Calif.: Stanford University Press, 2004), 267–304.

6. Mearsheimer argues for the "the primacy of land power." See John J. Mearsheimer, *The Tragedy of Great Power Politics*, 2nd ed. (New York: Norton, 2014), chap. 4.

7. One could foresee a situation, based on trends in military technology such as missile technology and other platforms, in which sea power becomes less important to obtaining and retaining regional hegemony in East Asia.

8. This is similar to the shifting distribution of capabilities that allowed the Soviet Union to challenge the regional balance of power in Europe in the post–World War II period.

9. John L. Gaddis, *Strategies of Containment: A Critical Appraisal of American National Security Policy During the Cold War*, rev. and exp. ed. (Oxford: Oxford University Press, 2005), 80.

10. William T. R. Fox, *The Super-Powers: The United States, Britain, and the Soviet Union—Their Responsibility for Peace* (New York: Harcourt, Brace and Company, 1944), 22.

11. Jack S. Levy and William R. Thompson, "Balancing on Land and at Sea: Do States Ally Against the Leading Global Power?" *International Security* 35, no. 1 (Summer 2010): 7–43.

12. Robert S. Ross, "The Geography of Peace: East Asia in the Twenty-First Century," *International Security* 23, no. 4 (Spring 1999): 81–118.

13. Jennifer M. Lind, "Correspondence: Spirals, Security, and Stability in East Asia," *International Security* 24, no. 4 (Spring 2000): 191.

14. Thomas Risse-Kappen, *Cooperation Among Democracies: The European Influence on U.S. Foreign Policy* (Princeton, N.J.: Princeton University Press, 1997), 16–17.

15. Navies can cross the ocean and land troops in enemy territory relatively easily, but they are not able to put large forces ashore and support them for long periods when confronted by strong land powers. Mearsheimer, *The Tragedy*, 44, 114–125.

16. Antonio Varsori, "Reflections on the Origins of the Cold War," in *Reviewing the Cold War: Approaches, Interpretations, Theory*, ed. Odd Arne Westad (London: Frank Cass, 2000), 281–302, 281.

17. Thomas G. Paterson and Robert J. McMahon, eds., *The Origins of the Cold War*, 3rd ed. (Lexington, Mass.: D. C. Heat and Company, 1991), xxi.

18. Odd Arne Westad, "Introduction: Reviewing the Cold War," in *Reviewing the Cold War: Approaches, Interpretations, Theory*, ed. Odd Arne Westad (London: Frank Cass, 2000), 1–26, 4.

19. Stephen M. Walt, *The Origins of Alliances* (Ithaca, N.Y.: Cornell University Press, 1987).

20. Walter Lippman, *The Cold War: A Study in U.S. Foreign Policy* (New York: Harper & Brothers, 1947), 33–34.

21. George F. Kennan, *Realities of American Foreign Policy* (Princeton, N.J.: Princeton University Press, 1954), 63.

22. Kennan, *Realities*, 66–67; Eric Hobsbawm, *Age of Extremes: The Short Twentieth Century, 1914–1991* (London: Penguin, 1994), 226–227.

23. Levy and Thompson, "Balancing on Land and at Sea," 15.

24. Levy emphasizes this in Jack S. Levy, "Power Transition Theory and the Rise of China," in *China's Ascent: Power, Security, and the Future of International Politics*, ed. Robert S. Ross and Zhu Feng (Ithaca, N.Y.: Cornell University Press, 2008), 11–33.

25. I thank Robert S. Ross for drawing my attention to this geographical distinction.

26. Hans J. Morgenthau, *Politics Among Nations: The Struggle for Power and Peace*, 2nd ed. (New York: Knopf, 1954), 104.

27. Kenneth N. Waltz, "Evaluating Theories," *American Political Science Review* 91, no. 4 (December 1997): 915; Kenneth N. Waltz, "The Emerging Structure of International Politics," *International Security* 18, no. 2 (Fall 1993): 44-79; Christopher Layne, "The Unipolar Illusion: Why New Great Powers Will Rise," *International Security* 17, no. 4 (Spring 1993): 5-51; Mearsheimer, *The Tragedy*.

28. John J. Mearsheimer, "Back to the Future: Instability in Europe After the Cold War," *International Security* 15, no. 1 (Summer 1990): 5-56.

29. Ross, "The Geography of Peace," 82.

30. Thomas J. Christensen, *The China Challenge: Shaping the Choices of a Rising Power* (New York: Norton, 2015); James Steinberg and Michael E. O'Hanlon, *Strategic Reassurance and Resolve: U.S.-China Relations in the Twenty-First Century* (Princeton, N.J.: Princeton University Press, 2014), 6.

31. Noah Feldman, *Cool War: The Future of Global Competition* (New York: Random House, 2013). For emphasis on economic interdependence in Sino-U.S. relations, see, among others, Christensen, *The China Challenge*, 41-49; Joseph S. Nye Jr., *The Future of Power* (New York: PublicAffairs, 2011), 56-57; Rosemary Foot and Andrew Walter, *China, the United States, and Global Order* (Cambridge: Cambridge University Press, 2011), 18; David M. Lampton, *The Three Faces of Chinese Power: Might, Money, and Minds* (Berkeley: University of California Press, 2008); David Lampton, *Same Bed, Different Dreams: Managing U.S.-China Relations 1989-2000* (Berkeley: University of California Press, 2001).

32. Helge Hveem and T. J. Pempel, "China's Rise and Economic Interdependence," in *China in the Era of Xi Jinping: Domestic and Foreign Policy Challenges*, ed. Jo Inge Bekkevold and Robert S. Ross (Washington, D.C.: Georgetown University Press, 2016), 196-232.

33. Peter Dicken, *Global Shift: Mapping the Changing Contours of the World Economy* (London: Sage, 2015), 37; Coker, *The Improbable War*.

34. Paul Bairoch and Richard Kozul-Wright, "Globalization Myths: Some Historical Reflections on Integration, Industrialization, and Growth in the World Economy," United Nations Conference on Trade and Development Discussion Paper 113, March 1996; Paul Hirst, Grahame Thompson, and Simon Bromley, *Globalization in Question*, 3rd ed. (Malden, Mass.: Polity, 2009); Waltz, *Theory of International Politics*, 138-160.

35. "Taking a Tumble—Briefing: China and the World Economy," *Economist*, August 29, 2015; World Bank, "World Integrated Trade Solution," September 3, 2014, http://wits.worldbank.org/Default.aspx.

36. Hveem and Pempel, "China's Rise."

37. Christensen, *The China Challenge*, 42.

38. Edward Steinfeld, *Playing Our Game: Why China's Rise Doesn't Threaten the West* (Oxford: Oxford University Press, 2010); Ho-fung Hung, *The China Boom: Why China Will Not Rule the World* (New York: Columbia University Press, 2016).

39. Steinfeld, *Playing Our Game*, 22.

40. Aaron L. Freidberg, *A Contest for Supremacy: China, America, and the Struggle for Mastery in Asia* (New York: Norton, 2011), 4; James D. Morrow, *Game Theory for*

Social Scientists (Princeton, N.J.: Princeton University Press, 1994); Bruce Bueno de Mesquita, James D. Morrow, and Ethan R. Zorick, "Capabilities, Perception, and Escalation," *American Political Science Review* 91 (1997): 15–27.

41. Ross, "Balance of Power Politics."
42. Japan and the Philippines have also strengthened their security ties with the United States but are not as dependent on the Chinese market as Singapore, Malaysia, and Australia. For a discussion of whether China's economic power is a sufficient force to compel states' strategic realignment in East Asia, see the contributions to Robert S. Ross and Øystein Tunsjø, eds., *Strategic Adjustment and the Rise of China: Power and Politics in East Asia* (Ithaca, N.Y.: Cornell University Press, 2017).
43. Mark O. Yeisley, "Bipolarity, Proxy Wars, and the Rise of China," *Strategic Studies Quarterly* 5, no. 4 (Winter 2011): 82–83.
44. Robert Kaplan, "The Geography of Chinese Power," *Foreign Affairs* 89, no. 3 (May/June 2010): 22–41; Kaplan, *The Revenge of Geography*, 199.
45. The fundamental national interest is maintaining the power of the CCP. In this respect, there is sometimes a tension between China's national interests and the interests of the CCP.
46. Øystein Tunsjø, *Security and Profit in China's Energy Policy: Hedging Against Risk* (New York: Columbia University Press, 2013).
47. Philip Andrews-Speed and Roland Dannreuther, *China, Oil, and Global Politics* (London: Routledge, 2011), 74, 138.
48. John Lewis Gaddis, "The Long Peace: Elements of Stability in the Postwar International System," *International Security* 10, no. 4 (Spring 1986): 99–142. See also Waltz, *Theory of International Politics*, 138.
49. Robert Gilpin, *War and Change in World Politics* (Cambridge: Cambridge University Press, 1981); Henry Kissinger, *World Order* (New York: Penguin, 2014).
50. John G. Ikenberry, "The Liberal Sources of American Unipolarity," in *International Relations Theory and the Consequences of Unipolarity*, ed. John G. Ikenberry, Michael Mastanduno, and William C. Wohlforth (Cambridge: Cambridge University Press, 2011), 216–251.
51. Ikenberry, "The Liberal Sources," 245.
52. Ikenberry, "The Liberal Sources," 244n46, 246–247.
53. Nicholas R. Lardy, *Markets Over Mao: The Rise of Private Business in China* (Washington, D.C.: Peterson Institute for International Economics, 2014).
54. Richard C. Longworth, "U.S.-China: A Shared Vision of Global Economic Partnership," Chicago Council on Global Affairs, December 17, 2014, http://www.thechicago council.org/event/us-china-shared-vision-global-economic-partnership.
55. Hung, *The China Boom*; Supachai Panitchpakdi and Mark L. Clifford, *China and the WTO: Changing China, Changing World Trade* (Wiley, 2002); Elizabeth Economy, *China Joins the World: Progress and Prospects* (New York: Council of Foreign Relations, 1999).
56. Andrew J. Nathan, "China's Rise and International Regimes: Does China Seek to Overthrow International Norms?" in *China in the Era of Xi Jinping: Domestic and Foreign Policy Challenges*, ed. Jo Inge Bekkevold and Robert S. Ross (Washington, D.C.: Georgetown University Press, 2016), 165–195. On China's socialization into existing institutions, norms, and regimes, see Alastair Iain Johnston, *Social States: China in International Institutions, 1980–2000* (Princeton, N.J.: Princeton University Press, 2007).

57. Daniel W. Drezner, *The System Worked: How the World Stopped Another Great Depression* (Oxford: Oxford University Press, 2014), 158; Hung, *The China Boom*.

58. Gilpin, *War and Change*, 210.

59. Ikenberry, "The Liberal Sources," 245.

60. Geoff Dyer, *The Contest of the Century: The New Era of Competition with China* (London: Penguin, 2014).

61. Gregory Shaffer and Henry Gao, "China's Rise: How It Took on the U.S. at the WTO," *University of Illinois Law Review* 1 (2018).

62. Gilpin, *War and Change*, 187.

63. Denny Roy, *The Return of the Dragon: Rising China and Regional Security* (New York: Columbia University Press, 2013).

64. China surpassed the United States in 2009 as Africa's largest trading partner.

65. China is Saudi Arabia's largest petroleum customer; China has developed close ties with Iran and has managed to play a central role in Iraq's petroleum industry after the U.S. military drawdown.

66. National Development and Reform Commission, *Vision and Actions on Jointly Building Silk Road Economic Belt and Twenty-First-Century Maritime Silk Road*, issued jointly by the National Development and Reform Commission, Ministry of Foreign Affairs, and Ministry of Commerce of the People's Republic of China, March 28, 2015, http://en.ndrc.gov.cn/newsrelease/201503/t20150330_669367.html.

67. See the contributions to the special issue "China's New Silk Roads: What's Driving Beijing's 'Pivot to the West,'" *Global Asia* 10, no. 3 (Fall 2015); Jo Inge Bekkevold and Sunniva Engh, "Silk Road Diplomacy: China's Strategic Interest in South Asia," in *South Asia and the Great Powers: International Relations and Regional Security*, ed. Sten Rynning (London: I. B. Tauris, 2017), 147–173.

68. Halford J. Mackinder, "The Geographical Pivot of History," *Geographical Journal* 23, no. 4 (April 1904): 421–437.

69. Wang Jisi, "China's Search for a Grand Strategy: A Rising Great Power Finds Its Way," *Foreign Affairs*, March/April 2011, https://www.foreignaffairs.com/articles/china/2011-02-20/chinas-search-grand-strategy.

70. Øystein Tunsjø, "Global Power Shifts, Geography, and Maritime East Asia," in *International Order at Sea: How It Is Challenged, How It Is Maintained*, ed. Jo Inge Bekkevold and Geoffrey Till (London: Palgrave Macmillan, 2016), 41–62.

71. China's maritime economy now accounts for about 10 percent of China's GDP. See State Council, "China's Maritime Economy Outpaces GDP Growth," Beijing, June 23, 2015, http://english.gov.cn/state_council/ministries/2015/06/23/content_281475132986863.htm. Shanghai became the world's busiest port in 2010, and seven out of ten of the world's busiest container ports are in China (including Hong Kong).

72. Ministry of Foreign Affairs of the PRC, "Keynote Speech by Vice Foreign Minister Zhang Ming at the China Country Session of the Third Arctic Circle Assembly," October 17, 2015, http://www.fmprc.gov.cn/mfa_eng/wjdt_665385/zyjh_665391/t1306858.shtml; Ingrid Lundestad and Øystein Tunsjø, "The United States and China in the Arctic," *Polar Record* (May 2015): 1–12.

73. Jakub J. Grygiel, *Great Powers and Geopolitical Change* (Baltimore, Md.: Johns Hopkins University Press, 2006).

74. I thank Professor Wu Zhengyu at Renmin University for emphasizing this aspect in a meeting in Beijing, December 2015.

75. Ikenberry, "The Liberal Sources," 222–223.

76. Paul Kennedy, *The Rise and the Fall of the Great Powers* (New York: Vintage, 1989), 372.

77. Hobsbawm, *Age of Extremes*, 232. One leading Cold War historian believes he "understated the role of ideology" but nonetheless concludes that the Cold War in Europe was a result of "a unique set of geopolitical configurations in the international system interacting with equally unique sets of indigenous variables within their own countries." See Melvin P. Leffler, "Bringing It Together: The Parts and the Whole," in *Reviewing the Cold War: Approaches, Interpretations, Theory*, ed. Odd Arne Westad (London: Frank Cass, 2000), 44–45, 53.

78. Kennan, *Realities*, 70.

79. Anders Stephanson, "Liberty or Death: The Cold War as U.S. Ideology," in *Reviewing the Cold War: Approaches, Interpretations, Theory*, ed. Odd Arne Westad (London: Frank Cass, 2000), 81–100; Joyce and Gabriel Kolko, "American Capitalist Expansion," in *The Origins of the Cold War*, 3rd ed., ed. Thomas G. Paterson and Robert J. McMahon (Lexington, Mass.: D. C. Heat and Company, 1991), 14–21; Daniel Yergin, "American Ideology: The Riga and Yalta Axioms," in *The Origins of the Cold War*, 3rd ed., ed. Thomas G. Paterson and Robert J. McMahon (Lexington, Mass.: D. C. Heat and Company, 1991), 35–48.

80. Hobsbawm, *Age of Extremes*, 235; Øystein Tunsjø, "U.S.-China Relations: From Unipolar Hedging Toward Bipolar Balancing," in *Strategic Adjustment and the Rise of China: Power and Politics in East Asia*, ed. Robert S. Ross and Øystein Tunsjø (Ithaca, N.Y.: Cornell University Press, 2017), 41–68.

81. Hobsbawm, *Age of Extremes*, 230–242.

82. Douglas J. Macdonalds, "Formal Ideologies in the Cold War: Toward a Framework for Empirical Analysis," in *Reviewing the Cold War: Approaches, Interpretations, Theory*, ed. Odd Arne Westad (London: Frank Cass, 2000), 180–206, 183.

83. Leffler, "Bringing It Together," 46.

84. For example, the outbreak of the Korean War undoubtedly changed strong balancing in Europe. See, among others, Gaddis, *Strategies of Containment*, chap. 4. For an emphasis on how ideologies shaped U.S. and Soviet foreign policy and patterns of behavior globally during the previous bipolar period, see Odd Arne Westad, *The Global Cold War: Third World Interventions and the Making of Our Time* (Cambridge: Cambridge University Press, 2007).

85. Deborah Welch Larson, *Origins of Containment: A Psychological Explanation* (Princeton, N.J.: Princeton University Press, 1985), 351–352.

86. Kennan, *Realities*, 86–87. Kennan was no longer at the policy-planning department in the U.S. administration in 1954, and the containment strategy laid out in NSC 68 focused on U.S. balancing of the Soviet Union. All the same, winning the ideological contest in the noncommunist world was still a core objective of the strategies of containment.

87. Edward Rhodes, "A World Not in Balance: War, Politics, and Weapons of Mass Destruction," in *Balance of Power: Theory and Practice in the Twenty-First Century*, ed. T. V. Paul, James J. Wirtz, and Michel Fortmann (Stanford, Calif.: Stanford University Press, 2004), 173; Craig Campbell, *Glimmer of a New Leviathan: Total War in the*

Realism of Niebuhr, Morgenthau, and Waltz (New York: Columbia University Press, 2003); Thomas Schelling, *Strategy of Conflict* (Cambridge, Mass.: Harvard University Press, 1960), 230–254; Jervis, *System Effects*, 122–124; Craig Campbell, "American Power Preponderance and the Nuclear Revolution," *Review of International Studies* 35, no. 1 (2009): 27–44.

88. Keir A. Lieber and Daryl G. Press, "The End of MAD? The Nuclear Dimension of U.S. Primacy," *International Security* 30, no. 4 (Spring 2006): 7–44; Keir A. Lieber and Daryl G. Press, "The Rise of American Nuclear Primacy," *Foreign Affairs* 85, no. 2 (March/April 2006): 42–54. For a debate about Lieber and Press' analysis, see Jeffrey S. Lantis, Tom Sauer, James J. Wirtz, et al., "The Short Shadow of U.S. Nuclear Primacy?" *International Security* 31, no. 3 (Winter 2006/2007): 174–193; Peter C. Flory, Keith Payne, Pavel Podvig, et al., "Nuclear Exchange: Does Washington Really Have (or Want) Nuclear Primacy?" *Foreign Affairs* 85, no. 5 (September/October 2006): 149–157.

89. Fiona S. Cunningham and Taylor M. Fravel, "Assuring Assured Retaliation: China's Nuclear Posture and U.S.-China Strategic Stability," *International Security* 40, no. 2 (Fall 2015): 7–50. Taylor M. Fravel and Evan S. Medeiros, "China's Search for Assured Retaliation: The Evolution of Chinese Nuclear Strategy and Force Structure," *International Security* 35, no. 2 (Fall 2010): 51, 57; Michael S. Chase, "China's Transition to a More Credible Nuclear Deterrent: Implications and Challenges for the United States," *Asia Policy* 16 (July 2013): 69–101.

90. Stephen Biddle and Ivan Oelrich, "Future Warfare in the Pacific: Chinese Anti-access/Area Denial, U.S. AirSea Battle, and Command of the Commons in East Asia," *International Security* 41, no. 1 (Summer 2016): 40–41.

91. Hans N. Kristensen and Robert S. Norris, "Chinese Nuclear Forces 2016," *Bulletin of Atomic Scientists* 72, no. 4: 205–211.

92. U.S. Department of Defense, "Military and Security Developments Involving the People's Republic of China 2017 Annual Report to Congress," May 15, 2017, https://www.defense.gov/Portals/1/Documents/pubs/2017_China_Military_Power_Report.PDF?ver=2017-06-06-141328-770.

93. Bernard D. Cole, *China's Quest for Great Power: Ships, Oil, and Foreign Policy* (Annapolis, Md.: Naval Institute Press, 2016).

94. Intelligence estimates in the early 1960s recalculated Soviet missile and manpower capabilities and concluded that the United States had achieved a sense of overall parity with the Soviet Union (Gaddis, *Strategies of Containment*, 206).

95. Christensen, *The China Challenge*, 52–53.

96. Waltz, *Theory of International Politics*, 182.

97. Nuno P. Monteiro, *Theory of Unipolar Politics* (Cambridge: Cambridge University Press, 2014).

98. Waltz, *Theory of International Politics*, 118, 128, 163; Kenneth Waltz, *Realism and International Politics* (New York: Routledge, 2008), 213; Waltz, "Reflections"; Mearsheimer, *The Tragedy*.

99. Waltz, *Realism and International Politics*, 213.

100. Waltz, "Reflections," 343.

101. Avery Goldstein, *Rising to the Challenge: China's Grand Strategy and International Security* (Stanford, Calif.: Stanford University Press, 2005), 205, 212.

102. Jervis, *System Effects*, 104. For a neoclassical realist approach, see Gideon Rose, "Neoclassical Realism and Theories of Foreign Policy," *World Politics* 51, no. 1 (October 1998): 144–172; Randall L. Schweller, "Domestic Politics and Nationalism in East Asian Security," in *Strategic Adjustment and the Rise of China: Power and Politics in East Asia*, ed. Robert S. Ross and Øystein Tunsjø (Ithaca, N.Y.: Cornell University Press, 2017), 15–40.

103. Thomas J. Christensen and Jack Snyder, "Chain Gangs and Passed Bucks: Predicting Alliance Patterns in Multipolarity," *International Organization* 44, no. 2 (Spring 1990): 137–168.

104. Walt, *The Origins of Alliances*.

6. U.S.-CHINA RELATIONS AND THE RISK OF WAR

1. For instance, Jervis writes: "irrational as it may be, the chance of devastation has made our world unusually safe." See Robert Jervis, *The Illogic of American Nuclear Strategy* (Ithaca, N.Y.: Cornell University Press, 1984), 13. For a quantitative study on the nuclear peace hypothesis, see Robert Rauchhaus, "Evaluating the Nuclear Peace Hypothesis: A Quantitative Approach," *Journal of Conflict Resolution* 53, no. 2 (2009): 258–277.

2. For an argument that nuclear weapons are a force for stability in U.S.-China relations, see, among others, Avery Goldstein, "First Things First: The Pressing Danger of Crisis Instability in U.S.-China Relations," *International Security* 37, no. 4 (Spring 2013): 49–89; Fiona S. Cunningham and Taylor M. Fravel, "Assuring Assured Retaliation: China's Nuclear Posture and U.S.-China Strategic Stability," *International Security* 40, no. 2 (Fall 2015): 7–50; Thomas J. Christensen, *The China Challenge: Shaping the Choices of a Rising Power* (New York: Norton, 2015). However, as Coker emphasizes, despite the role of nuclear weapons, economic interdependence, and the improbability of a U.S.-China war, it is important to discuss the possibility of a conflict and beware of complacency regarding the obsolescence of superpower and great-power wars. See Christopher Coker, *The Improbable War: China, the United States, and the Continuing Logic of Great Power Conflict* (London: Hurst, 2015).

3. There are other nonmaritime regional flashpoints that might pull China and the United States into a conflict. The Korean Peninsula is the most dangerous one. However, both the United States and China share the goals of a nuclear-free Korean Peninsula and the avoidance of war. China has a security buffer in North Korea and is eager to avoid its collapse. The United States has few interests in being pulled into a land war with China on the mainland in Northeast Asia. If war broke out or North Korea collapsed, it is likely that South Korean, Chinese, and U.S. troops would confront one another on the peninsula, but it is uncertain whether this would lead to a shooting war. Washington and Beijing might agree to withdraw their troops from the peninsula and allow the government in South Korea to head a unified Korea.

4. Robert Osgood, *Limited War: The Challenge to American Strategy* (Chicago: University of Chicago Press, 1957), 1–4. It should be noted that the Korean War, the

Vietnam War, and the Soviet-Afghan War were major wars for the North and South Koreans, the North and South Vietnamese, and the Democratic Republic of Afghanistan and the Afghan mujahedeen. See Harold Stein's review of Osgood's "Limited War," *American Political Science Review* 52, no. 2 (June 1958): 533–535.

5. See John J. Mearsheimer, *The Tragedy of Great Power Politics*, 2nd ed. (New York: Norton, 2014).

6. Thomas C. Schelling, *The Strategy of Conflict* (Cambridge, Mass.: Harvard University Press, 1980), 74–77. According to Schelling, the Korean War was an example of a limited war. It had the potential to become a major war, but geography prevented it from escalating. Schelling also points out that the "Formosa Strait made it possible to stabilize a line between the Communist and the Nationalist forces of China." Water was crucial in limiting the war. When referring to a limited war or a battle at sea, the analysis in this chapter draws on Schelling's interpretation of a limited war and the geopolitical factors that make it possible.

7. A limited war at sea or a battle at sea is likely to include cyberwar and potentially war in outer space. This will increase the risk of escalation, but it will still remain a limited war, since the risk of a land invasion, which might pose an existential threat, remains remote.

8. Thomas C. Schelling, *Arms and Influence* (New Haven, Conn.: Yale University Press, 1966), 48–49, 105, 123.

9. This refers to the early years of the Cold War. In 1961, the Kennedy administration shifted to a flexible-response strategy.

10. Schelling, *Arms and Influence*, 46.

11. Hans J. Morgenthau, *Politics Among Nations: The Struggle for Power and Peace*, 2nd ed. (New York: Knopf, 1954), 190; Robert Gilpin, *War and Change in World Politics* (Cambridge: Cambridge University Press, 1981); A. F. K Organski and Jacek Kugler, *The War Ledger* (Chicago: University of Chicago Press, 1980).

12. Robert S. Ross, "The Rise of the Chinese Navy: From Regional Naval Power to Global Naval Power?" in *China's Global Engagement: Cooperation, Competition, and Influence in the Twenty-First Century*, ed. Jacques deLisle and Avery Goldstein (Washington, D.C.: Brookings Institution, 2017), 207–234.

13. Øystein Tunsjø, "The Cold War as a Guide to the Risk of War in East Asia," *Global Asia* 9, no. 3 (Fall 2014): 15–19; Mearsheimer, *The Tragedy*, 394.

14. Robert D. Kaplan, *Asia's Cauldron: The South China Sea and the End of a Stable Pacific* (New York: Random House, 2014), 6–7, 175.

15. The United States, after it had obtained territorial security in the late nineteenth century, is an interesting comparison. See Øystein Tunsjø, "Global Power Shifts, Geography, and Maritime East Asia," in *International Order at Sea: How It Is Challenged, How It Is Maintained*, ed. Jo Inge Bekkevold and Geoffrey Till (London: Palgrave Macmillan, 2016), 41–62; Ross, "The Rise of the Chinese Navy."

16. Alastair Iain Johnston, "China's New 'Old Thinking': The Concept of Limited Deterrence," *International Security* 20, no. 3 (Winter 1995–1996): 9n12.

17. David M. Finkelstein, "National Missile Defense and China's Current Security Perceptions," Report 42, presented to the Stimson/CAN NMD-China Project, December 14, 2001, http://www.stimson.org/images/uploads/research-pdfs/42.pdf.

18. Bernard D. Cole, *The Great Wall at Sea: China's Navy in the Twenty-First Century*, 2nd ed. (Annapolis, Md.: Naval Institute Press, 2010), 16.

19. "China to Cut Troops by 300,000: Xi," *Xinhua*, September 3, 2015, http://news .xinhuanet.com/english/2015-09/03/c_134583730.htm.

20. Ross, "The Rise"; Geoff Dyer, *The Contest of the Century: The New Era of Competition with China* (London: Penguin, 2014).

21. "Full Text: China's Military Strategy," *China Daily*, May 25, 2015, http://www.china daily.com.cn/china/2015-05/26/content_20820628_4.htm.

22. Spykman, *America's Strategy*, 468.

23. Andrew S. Erickson, Lyle J. Goldstein, and Carnes Lord, eds., *China Goes to Sea: Maritime Transformation in Comparative Historical Perspective* (Annapolis, Md.: U.S. Naval Institute Press, 2009).

24. See Jakub J. Grygiel, *Great Powers and Geopolitical Change* (Baltimore, Md.: Johns Hopkins University Press, 2006); Peter Padfield, *Maritime Power and the Struggle for Freedom: Naval Campaigns That Shaped the Modern World, 1788–1851* (New York: Overlook, 2005); Robert S. Ross, "China's Naval Nationalism: Sources, Prospects, and the U.S. Response," *International Security* 34, no. 2 (Fall 2009): 46–81; Peter Dutton, Robert S. Ross, and Øystein Tunsjø, eds., *Twenty-First-Century Seapower: Cooperation and Conflict at Sea* (London: Routledge, 2012).

25. French naval aspirations were also demolished when the British Copenhagenized the Royal Danish-Norwegian Fleet in 1807 to prevent France from taking advantage of its allies' naval power.

26. Grygiel distinguishes between "naval power," which "refers to the technical capabilities of the navy," and "seapower," which "denotes the ability to bring naval capabilities to bear on the interests and security of another state, thereby altering its behavior." See Jakub Grygiel, "Geography and Seapower," in *Twenty-First-Century Seapower: Cooperation and Conflict at Sea*, ed. Peter Dutton, Robert S. Ross, and Øystein Tunsjø (London: Routledge, 2012), 18–41, 19.

27. Spykman, *America's Strategy*, 468–469.

28. Andrew S. Erickson and Connor M. Kennedy, "China's Maritime Militia: What It Is and How to Deal with It," *Foreign Affairs*, June 23, 2016.

29. Taylor Fravel, "Threading the Needle: The South China Sea Dispute and U.S.-China Relations," in *Strategic Adjustment and the Rise of China: Power and Politics in East Asia*, ed. Robert S. Ross and Øystein Tunsjø (Ithaca, N.Y.: Cornell University Press, 2017), 233–260.

30. Thomas J. Christensen, "The Meaning of the Nuclear Evolution: China's Strategic Modernization and U.S.-China Security Relations," *Journal of Strategic Studies* 35, no. 4 (2012): 452.

31. Goldstein, "First Things First," 59; Christensen, "The Meaning," 452, 472–474, 484.

32. John Lewis Gaddis, "The Long Peace: Elements of Stability in the Postwar International System," *International Security* 10, no. 4 (Spring 1986): 133.

33. Eric Hobsbawm, *Age of Extremes: The Short Twentieth Century, 1914–1991* (London: Penguin, 1994), 226–228.

34. Robert S. Ross, "The Geography of Peace: East Asia in the Twenty-First Century," *International Security* 23, no. 4 (Spring 1999): 81–118.

35. Dennis J. Blasko, *The Chinese Army Today: Tradition and Transformation for the Twenty-First Century*, 2nd ed. (London: Routledge, 2012), 19.

36. Thomas J. Christensen, "Posing Problems Without Catching Up: China's Rise and Challenges for U.S. Security Policy," *International Security* 25, no. 4 (Spring 2001): 5–40. Other studies that discuss China's asymmetric strategies, the modernization of the PLA, and how it poses increasing challenges to the United States include, among others: Roger Cliff, *China's Military Power: Assessing Current and Future Capabilities* (Cambridge: Cambridge University Press, 2015); Seth Cropsey, *Mayday: The Decline of American Naval Supremacy* (New York: Overlook, 2013); Larry M. Wortzel, *The Dragon Extends Its Reach: Chinese Military Power Goes Global* (Washington, D.C.: Potomac, 2013); Robert Haddick, *Fire on the Water: China, America, and the Future of the Pacific* (Annapolis, Md.: Naval Institute Press, 2014); Avery Goldstein, "Parsing China's Rise: International Circumstances and National Attributes," in *China's Ascent: Power, Security, and the Future of International Politics*, ed. Robert S. Ross and Zhu Feng (Ithaca, N.Y.: Cornell University Press, 2008), 59–67; Aaron L. Friedberg, "Here Be Dragons: Is China a Military Threat?" *National Interest* 103 (September/October 2009): 19–25.

37. Christensen ("Posing Problems," 13–14) has emphasized four situations in which China might challenge the United States: (1) Chinese leaders believe they are backed into a corner and care more about the issue in dispute than Washington, (2) Chinese leaders believe they can deter effective U.S. intervention or compel the United States to withdraw, (3) Chinese leaders perceive the U.S military as distracted or tied down in other parts of the world, or (4) Chinese leaders believe the United States can be separated from its regional allies by targeting those allies with political persuasion or military coercion. Goldstein ("First Things First," 52, 75–78) focuses on five dangers in a plausible U.S.-China crisis: stark asymmetry, crisis communications, strategic beliefs, technology, and geography.

38. On the challenges inherent with the distance a military must travel, see Kenneth E. Boulding, *Conflict and Defense: A General Theory* (New York: Harper and Row, 1962), 230–231, 245–245.

39. Ross, "The Rise of the Chinese Navy."

40. Christensen, "Posing Problems," 10–11.

41. Evan Braden Montgomery, "Time to Worry About China's Military Rise," policy brief, Belfer Center for Science and International Affairs, Cambridge, Mass., Harvard Kennedy School, June 2014; Evan Braden Montgomery, "Contested Primacy in the Western Pacific: China's Rise and the Future of U.S. Power Projection," *International Security* 38, no. 4 (Spring 2014): 125–126.

42. Robert S. Ross, "Navigating the Taiwan Strait: Deterrence, Escalation Dominance, and U.S.-China Relations," *International Security* 27, no. 2 (Fall 2002): 53; Christensen, "Posing Problems," 11–12.

43. Montgomery, "Contested Primacy"; Christensen, "The Meaning of the Nuclear Evolution," 451.

44. Nicholas J. Spykman, *America's Strategy in World Politics: The United States and the Balance of Power* (New York: Harcourt, Brace & World, 1942; New York: Archon, 1970), esp. 75–82.

45. This is informed by Xi Jinping's China Dream policy, which is described as the "two 100s": becoming a moderately well-off society by 2021, the hundredth anniversary of the founding of the CCP, and a fully developed nation by 2049, the hundredth anniversary of the founding of the PRC. Robert Lawrence Kuhn, "Xi Jinping's China

Dream," *New York Times*, June 4, 2013, http://www.nytimes.com/2013/06/05/opinion/global/xi-jinpings-chinese-dream.html; Michael Pillsbury, *The Hundred-Year Marathon: China's Secret Strategy to Replace America as the Global Superpower* (New York: Henry Holt, 2015).

46. Graham Allison, "The Thucydides Trap: Are the U.S. and China Headed for War?" *The Atlantic*, September 24, 2015.

47. Coker, *The Improbable War*, 91–98, 92; Ross, "The Rise of the Chinese Navy."

48. Russia might regain some territory in the Baltic or Eastern Europe in the first half of the twenty-first century, but this does not challenge the balance of power in Europe in ways similar to Germany during the First and Second World War or the Soviet Union after World War II. Russian aggression can in large part be balanced by Western European powers, and the United States can concentrate on balancing the rise of China.

49. Taylor M. Fravel and Evan S. Medeiros, "China's Search for Assured Retaliation: The Evolution of Chinese Nuclear Strategy and Force Structure," *International Security* 35, no. 2 (Fall 2010): 51, 57; Michael S. Chase, "China's Transition to a More Credible Nuclear Deterrent: Implications and Challenges for the United States," *Asia Policy* 16, (July 2013): 82.

50. Fravel and Medeiros, "China's Search," 64; Johnston, "China's New 'Old Thinking,'" 9; Jeffrey Lewis, "China's Nuclear Modernization: Surprise, Restraint, and Uncertainty," in *Asia in the Second Nuclear Age*, ed. Ashley J. Tellis, Abraham M. Denmark, and Travis Tanner (Washington, D.C.: National Bureau of Asian Research, 2013), 67–96.

51. Jervis, *The Illogic of American Nuclear Strategy*, 31.

52. Glenn H. Snyder, *Deterrence and Defense: Towards a Theory of National Security* (Princeton, N.J.: Princeton University Press, 1961); Glenn H. Snyder, "The Balance of Power and the Balance of Terror," in *The Balance of Power*, ed. Paul Seabury (San Francisco: Chandler, 1965), 191–201.

53. Goldstein, "First Things First," 65–66; See also Christensen, "The Meaning"; Ross, "Navigating."

54. Christensen, "The Meaning," 451.

55. Since stability at the nuclear level could not guarantee caution at the conventional level, U.S. nuclear strategy evolved during the Cold War from massive retaliation to a countervailing strategy and a flexible response "to meet potential Soviet threats on their own terms" once the Soviet Union gained second-strike capability in the early 1960s. See Jervis, *The Illogic of American Nuclear Strategy*, 20.

56. Goldstein, "First Things First," 78.

57. Schelling, *Arms and Influence*, 71.

58. Schelling, *Arms and Influence*, 47.

59. Schelling, *Arms and Influence*, 48.

60. Schelling, *Arms and Influence*, 47.

61. Goldstein, "First Things First."

62. Schelling, *Arms and Influence*, 48.

63. Goldstein, "First Things First," 77–78.

64. Schelling, *Arms and Influence*, 48.

65. See the various *Annual Report to Congress on the Military Power of the People's Republic of China*, by the Pentagon; hearings on the Taiwan question in the U.S. House of Representatives and the U.S. Senate; and several reports by the U.S.-China

Economic and Security Review Commission. See also Mearsheimer, *The Tragedy*; Joseph A. Bosco, "Taiwan and Strategic Security," *The Diplomat*, May 15, 2015, http://thediplomat.com/2015/05/taiwan-and-strategic-security/.

66. Charles L. Glaser, "A U.S.-China Grand Bargain? The Hard Choice Between Military Competition and Accommodation," *International Security* 39, no. 4 (Spring 2015): 49–90.

67. U.S. support for Taiwan's democracy interrelates with strategic calculations. Taiwan's democracy is often differentiated from the authoritarian regime on the mainland. If Taiwan is coerced or threatened by China, then contemporary U.S. support for Taiwan's "flourishing democracy" is likely to grow stronger. Øystein Tunsjø, *U.S. Taiwan Policy: Constructing the Triangle* (London: Routledge, 2008).

68. Thomas J. Christensen, "Correspondence: Spirals, Security, and Stability in East Asia," *International Security* 24, no. 4 (Spring 2000): 196; Goldstein, "First Things First," 53–58. Christensen also emphasizes the role of nationalism and divergent interpretations of history as issues that could spark tension and conflict. On the role of nationalism, see Ross, "China's Naval Nationalism."

69. Jennifer Lind, "Correspondence: Spirals, Security, and Stability in East Asia," *International Security* 24, no. 4 (Spring 2000): 191.

70. Christensen, "Correspondence."

71. Schelling, *Arms and Influences*, 49, 105, 123; Christensen, "The Meaning of the Nuclear Evolution"; Goldstein, "First Things First"; Avery Goldstein, "China's Real and Present Danger: Now Is the Time for Washington to Worry," *Foreign Affairs*, September/October 2013.

72. Sam LaGrone, "Pentagon Drops Air Sea Battle Name, Concept Lives On," *USNI News*, January 20, 2015, http://news.usni.org/2015/01/20/pentagon-drops-air-sea-battle-name-concept-lives.

73. Strikes against the Chinese mainland carry with them the danger that a conventional attack might be misconstrued as an attempt at preemptively destroying nuclear facilities and capabilities, thereby unwittingly escalating the conflict to the nuclear level. On the conventional/nuclear overlap, see John Lewis and Xue Litai, "Making China's Nuclear War Plan," *Bulletin of the Atomic Scientists* 68, no. 5 (2012): 45–65. Cunningham and Fravel ("Assuring Assured Retaliation") have demonstrated that very few of China's launch brigades contain both nuclear and conventional missiles. Other experts on the PLA, such as Mark A. Stokes, argue that the PLA maintains a firewall between nuclear and conventional brigades and the broader command-and-control infrastructure.

74. Admiral Jonathan Greenert and General Mark Welsh, "Breaking the Kill Chain: How to Keep America in the Game When Our Enemies Are Trying to Shut Us Out," *Foreign Policy*, May 17, 2013, http://foreignpolicy.com/2013/05/17/breaking-the-kill-chain/.

75. Stephen Biddle and Ivan Oelrich, "Future Warfare in the Pacific: Chinese Antiaccess/Area Denial, U.S. AirSea Battle, and Command of the Commons in East Asia," *International Security* 41, no. 1 (Summer 2016): 7–48; Cheryl Pellerin, "Deputy Secretary: Third Offset Strategy Bolsters America's Military Deterrence," *DoD News*, October 31, 2016, https://www.defense.gov/News/Article/Article/991434/deputy-secretary-third-offset-strategy-bolsters-americas-military-deterrence/.

76. Aaron Friedberg, *Beyond Air-Sea Battle: The Debate Over U.S. Military Strategy in Asia* (London: International Institute for Strategic Studies, 2014); T. X. Hammes, "Sorry, AirSea Battle Is No Strategy," *National Interest*, August 7, 2013, http://nationalinterest.org/commentary/sorry-airsea-battle-no-strategy-8846; T. X. Hammes, "Offshore Control vs. AirSea Battle: Who Wins?" *National Interest*, August 21, 2013, http://nationalinterest.org/commentary/offshore-control-vs-airsea-battle -who-wins-8920.

77. Ronald O'Rourke, *China Naval Modernization: Implications for U.S. Navy Capabilities—Background and Issues for Congress*, September 8, 2014, https://www.fas.org /sgp/crs/row/RL33153.pdf, 54–58.

78. Goldstein, "First Things First," 59.

7. THE RETURN OF BIPOLARITY: GLOBAL AND REGIONAL EFFECTS

1. Kenneth N. Waltz, "The Stability of the Bipolar World," *Daedalus* 93, no. 3 (Summer 1964): 881–909.

2. Jon D. Glassman, *Arms for the Arabs: The Soviet Union and War in the Middle East* (Baltimore, Md.: Johns Hopkins University, 1975); Ray Takeyh, *The Origins of the Eisenhower Doctrine: The U.S., Britain, and Nasser's Egypt, 1953–57* (New York: Palgrave Macmillan, 2000).

3. David Reynolds, *One World Divisible: A Global History Since 1945* (London: Penguin, 2001), 36.

4. Paul Kennedy, *The Rise and the Fall of the Great Powers* (New York: Vintage, 1989), 359.

5. Hans J. Morgenthau, *Politics Among Nations: The Struggle for Power and Peace*, 2nd ed. (New York: Knopf, 1954), 327–336.

6. Jack S. Levy, "Power Transition Theory and the Rise of China," in *China's Ascent: Power, Security, and the Future of International Politics*, ed. Robert S. Ross and Zhu Feng (Ithaca, N.Y.: Cornell University Press, 2008), 11–33, 32.

7. Mark O. Yeisley, "Bipolarity, Proxy Wars, and the Rise of China," *Strategic Studies Quarterly* (Winter 2011): 75–91.

8. Waltz, "The Stability."

9. Nicholas J. Spykman, *America's Strategy in World Politics: The United States and the Balance of Power* (New York: Harcourt, Brace & World, 1942; New York: Archon, 1970).

10. Kenneth N. Waltz, *Man, the State, and War: A Theoretical Analysis* (New York: Columbia University Press, 1959), 200; Robert S. Ross, "U.S. Grand Strategy, the Rise of China, and U.S. National Security Strategy for East Asia," *Strategic Studies Quarterly* 7, no. 2 (Summer 2013): 20–40; John J. Mearsheimer, *The Tragedy of Great Power Politics*, 2nd ed. (New York: Norton, 2014), 40–42.

11. Spykman, *America's Strategy*, 465–470; Nicholas J. Spykman, *The Geography of Peace* (New York: Harcourt, Brace and Co., 1944), 45; Melvyn P. Leffler, *A Preponderance of Power: National Security, the Truman Administration, and the Cold War* (Stanford, Calif.: Stanford University Press, 1992), 11.

12. Spykman, *America's Strategy*, 467.

13. Thomas G. Paterson and Robert J. McMahon, *The Origins of the Cold War*, 3rd ed. (Lexington, Mass.: D. C. Heat and Company, 1991), xxii; John L. Gaddis, *The United States and the Origins of the Cold War* (New York: Columbia University Press, 1972), 354.
14. George F. Kennan, *Realities of American Foreign Policy* (Princeton, N.J.: Princeton University Press, 1954), 65–67; Walter Lippmann, *The Cold War: A Study in U.S. Foreign Policy* (New York: Harper & Brothers, 1947), 61–62; John L. Gaddis, *Strategies of Containment: A Critical Appraisal of American National Security Policy During the Cold War*, 2nd ed. (Oxford: Oxford University Press, 2005), 24–31, 83.
15. On Washington's downsizing of its European flank, see Øystein Tunsjø, "Europe's Favourable Isolation," *Survival* 55, no. 6: 94–95. On the redeployment from Europe to East Asia, see Ross, "U.S. Grand Strategy," 26–28; Robert S. Ross, "Bipolarity and Balancing in East Asia," in *Balance of Power: Theory and Practice in the Twenty-First Century*, ed. T. V. Paul, James J. Wirtz, and Michel Fortmann (Stanford, Calif.: Stanford University Press, 2004), 267–304.
16. Nicholas J. Wheeler, *Saving Strangers: Humanitarian Intervention in International Society* (Oxford: Oxford University Press, 2002).
17. Thomas J. Christensen, *The China Challenge: Shaping the Choices of a Rising Power* (New York: Norton, 2015), 248; Shirley A. Kan, *Guam: U.S. Defense Deployments* (Washington, D.C.: Congressional Research Service 2014); Nina Silove, "The Pivot Before the Pivot: U.S. Strategy to Preserve the Power Balance in Asia," *International Security* 40, no. 4 (Spring 2016): 45–88; Austin Long, "The U.S.: A New Wary Titan: U.S. Defense Policy in an Era of Military Change, Asian Growth, and European Austerity," in *Security, Strategy, and Military Change in the Twenty-First Century*, ed. Jo Inge Bekkevold, Ian Bowers, and Michael Raska (London: Routledge, 2015), 241–265, 252.
18. Christensen, *The China Challenge*.
19. Jeffrey A. Bader, *Obama and China's Rise: An Insider's Account of America's Asia Strategy* (Washington, D.C.: Brookings Institution, 2012).
20. Hillary Clinton, "America's Pacific Century," *Foreign Policy*, October 11, 2011, http://foreignpolicy.com/2011/10/11/americas-pacific-century/.
21. Barack Obama, "Remarks by President Obama to the Australian Parliament," White House, Office of the Press Secretary, November 17, 2011, https://www.whitehouse.gov/the-press-office/2011/11/17/remarks-president-obama-australian-parliament.
22. Obama, "Remarks by President."
23. Bruce D. Klingner, "Rebalancing to the Pacific: Asia Pivot or Divot?" in *2015 Index of U.S. Military Strength: Assessing America's Ability to Provide for the Common Defense*, ed. Dakota L. Wood (Washington, D.C.: Heritage Foundation, 2015), 37–46, http://ims-2015.s3.amazonaws.com/2015_Index_of_US_Military_Strength_FINAL.pdf.
24. Mercy A. Kuo and Angelica O. Tang, "The Next U.S. President: Asia's Impact on America's Future: Insight from Admiral Dennis Blair," *The Diplomat*, June 15, 2015, http://thediplomat.com/2015/06/the-next-us-president-asias-impact-on-americas-future/.
25. U.S. Department of Defense, "Deputy Secretary of Defense Bob Work Delivers Remarks at the Council on Foreign Relations," September 30, 2014, http://www.defense.gov/transcripts/transcript.aspx?transcriptid=5509.

26. Andrew F. Krepinevich, *Preserving the Balance: A U.S. Eurasia Defense Strategy*, Center for Strategic and Budgetary Assessments (Washington, D.C., January 2017); U.S. Department of Defense, *Sustaining U.S. Global Leadership: Priorities for Twenty-First-Century Defense*, January 2012, http://www.defense.gov/news /Defense_Strategic_Guidance.pdf. See also U.S. Department of Defense, *Defense Budget Priorities and Choices*, January 2012, http://www.defense.gov/news /Defense_Budget_Priorities.pdf.

27. U.S. Department of Defense, *The Asia-Pacific Maritime Security Strategy*, July 27, 2015, 20–25, http://www.defense.gov/Portals/1/Documents/pubs/NDAA%20A-P_Maritime _SecuritY_Strategy-08142015–1300-FINALFORMAT.PDF.

28. Tyler Hlavac, "USS *Ronald Reagan* Heads to Yokosuka to Replace USS *George Washington*," *Stars and Stripes*, August 31, 2015, http://www.stripes.com/news/uss-ronald -reagan-heads-to-yokosuka-to-replace-george-washington-1.365419; Erik Slavin, "Upgraded Destroyer USS *Benfold* Arrives at New Home in Japan," *Stars and Stripes*, October 19, 2015, http://www.stripes.com/news/pacific/upgraded-destroyer-uss -benfold-arrives-at-new-home-in-japan-1.373937.

29. Department of Defense, *The Asia-Pacific*, 20.

30. David Tweed and Mira Rojanasakul, "The Great Asian Arms Buildup," *Bloomberg*, May 31, 2016, http://www.bloomberg.com/graphics/2016-shangrila/.

31. Department of Defense, *The Asia-Pacific*, 22. These numbers may be misleading, since growth to 60 percent might reflect a reduction in the size of the entire navy. The U.S. Navy might even station more than 60 percent of naval and overseas air assets in the Pacific. However, giving priority to sustain the U.S. military presence in East Asia is in itself significant for the U.S. counterbalancing of China.

32. Bader, *Obama and China's Rise*.

33. The White House, "Joint Statement on the U.S.-ASEAN Strategic Partnership," Office of the Press Secretary, Washington D.C., November 21, 2015, https://www .whitehouse.gov/the-press-office/2015/11/21/joint-statement-asean-us-strategic -partnership. As Christensen (*The China Challenge*, 247–251) emphasizes, the TPP and other economic policies were initiated during the Bush administration. Still, the Obama administration managed to secure a deal on the TPP, which would not been possible without strong diplomatic efforts. Christensen also recognizes that the Obama administration engaged more robustly in regional diplomacy.

34. Although the SIPRI world military expenditure database shows that military spending in East Asia in percentage of GDP has declined since the end of the Cold War, the same data show that the share of military spending in the economies of most of China's neighbors has remained the same since 2000 or grown at a faster rate than China's. Moreover, especially since 2010, the growth rate of year-on-year military spending in countries such as Vietnam, Indonesia, and the Philippines has been catching up with or passing China's.

35. Øystein Tunsjø, "U.S.-China Relations: From Unipolar Hedging Toward Bipolar Balancing," in *Strategic Adjustment and the Rise of China: Power and Politics in East Asia*, ed. Robert S. Ross and Øystein Tunsjø (Ithaca, N.Y.: Cornell University Press, 2017), 41–68.

36. Bjørn Elias Mikalsen Grønning, "Japan's Shifting Military Priorities: Counterbalancing China's Rise," *Asian Security* (2014): 1–21.

37. Ayako Mie, "Defense Ministry Request ¥5.1 Trillion for Fiscal 2017 to Address New Threats," *Japan Times*, August 31, 2016, http://www.japantimes.co.jp/news/2016/08/31/national/japan-seeks-%C2%A55-1-trillion-defense-next-year-2-3-rise-reflects-new-threats/#.V-unlSGLS1s.

38. Andrew S. Erickson and Carnes Lord, *Rebalancing U.S. Forces: Basing and Forward Presence in the Asia Pacific* (Annapolis, Md.: Naval Institute Press, 2014); Andrew S. Erickson and Carnes Lord, "Bases for America's Asia Pacific Rebalance," *The Diplomat*, May 2, 2014.

39. Ian Bowers and Bjørn Grønning, "Protecting the Status Quo: Japan's Response to the Rise of China," in *Strategic Adjustment and the Rise of China: Power and Politics in East Asia*, ed. Robert S. Ross and Øystein Tunsjø (Ithaca, N.Y.: Cornell University Press,2017), 137–168.

40. See Shinzō Abe, "Japan Is Back," speech at the CSIS, February 22, 2013, http://www.mofa.go.jp/announce/pm/abe/us_20130222en.html.

41. Peter A. Dutton, "The Sino-Philippine Maritime Row: International Arbitration and the South China Sea," *Center for New American Security*, March 15, 2013, http://www.cnas.org/files/documents/publications/CNAS_Bulletin_Dutton_TheSinoPhilippine MaritimeRow_0.pdf. A summary of the tribunal's decision can be found at http://www.pcacases.com/web/sendAttach/1503.

42. Franz-Stefan Gady, "Philippines Push for Military Modernization in New Budget Proposal," *The Diplomat*, August 21, 2015, http://thediplomat.com/2015/08/philippines-push-for-military-modernization-in-new-budget-proposal/.

43. Juliet Eilperin, "U.S., Philippines Reach 10-Year Defense Agreement Amidst Rising Tension," *Washington Post*, April 27, 2014, https://www.washingtonpost.com/world/us-philippines-to-sign-10-year-defense-agreement-amid-rising-tensions/2014/04/27/a04436c0-cddf-11e3-a75e-463587891b57_story.html.

44. Philippine Department of Foreign Affairs, "Q&A on the Enhanced Defense Cooperation Agreement," April 28, 2014, http://www.gov.ph/2014/04/28/qna-on-the-enhanced-defense-cooperation-agreement/.

45. Andrew Brown, "For China, 'Clouds Are Fading Away' in the Philippines," *Wall Street Journal*, October 4, 2016, http://www.wsj.com/articles/for-china-clouds-are-fading-away-in-the-philippines-1475554864.

46. Prashanth Parameswaran, "Philippines to Hold Military Exercise with U.S., Japan," *The Diplomat*, June 19, 2015, http://thediplomat.com/2015/06/philippines-to-hold-military-exercises-with-us-japan/.

47. Prashanth Parameswaran, "What's Next for Japan-Philippines Defense Ties?" *The Diplomat*, June 30, 2015, http://thediplomat.com/2015/06/whats-next-for-japan-philippines-defense-ties/.

48. See the announcements, press statements, and updates on the Republic of Philippines, Department of National Defense webpage: http://www.dnd.gov.ph/.

49. New Zealand's part in the ANZUS defense pact ended in 1986 when New Zealand in the late 1980s barred nuclear-powered or nuclear-armed ships from using New Zealand ports or entering New Zealand waters. The United States consequently suspended its treaty obligations. However, New Zealand and the United States have resumed military cooperation in recent years.

50. Chung-in Moon, "China's Rise and Security Dynamics on the Korean Peninsula," in *Strategic Adjustment and the Rise of China: Power and Politics in East Asia*, ed.

Robert S. Ross and Øystein Tunsjø (Ithaca, N.Y.: Cornell University Press, 2017), 196–232.

51. Domestic politics, not just geostructural conditions, also matter in shaping such realignment and explaining why South Korea and Japan, two U.S. treaty allies, are responding to the rise of China differently. Nationalist sentiment is strong in South Korea, but South Korea and China have both experienced Japanese occupation and brutality.

52. Jim Garamone, "U.S., India Sign 10-Year Defense Framework Agreement," *U.S. Department of Defense News*, June 4, 2015, http://www.defense.gov/News-Article-View /Article/604775; Anil Sasi, "'Look East' Has Become 'Act East Policy,' Says PM Modi at ASEAN Summit," *Indian Express*, November 13, 2014, http://indianexpress.com /article/india/india-others/look-east-has-become-act-east-policy-pm-modi-at-asean/.

53. "India, U.S., Japan Kick Off Naval Drills Likely to Annoy China," *CNBC*, October 12, 2015, http://www.cnbc.com/2015/10/12/.

54. Gardiner Harris, "Vietnam Arms Embargo to Be Fully Lifted, Obama Says in Hanoi," *New York Times*, May 23, 2016, http://www.nytimes.com/2016/05/24/world/asia /vietnam-us-arms-embargo-obama.html.

55. Morgenthau, *Politics Among Nations*, 2nd ed., chap. 12.

56. Yan, "China-U.S. Competition for Strategic Partnerships."

57. U.S. House Armed Services Committee, "Testimony of Admiral James Stavridis, United States Navy Commander, United States European Command," 2013, http:// www.eucom.mil/mission/background/posture-statement; Tunsjø, "Europe's Favourable Isolation."

58. Andrew Tilghman, "EUCOM Chief: Time to Stop the Drawdown in Europe," *DefenseNews*, July 7, 2014, http://archive.defensenews.com/article/20140707 /DEFREG01/307070016/EUCOM-Chief-Time-Stop-Drawdown-Europe.

59. See the fact sheets on Operation Atlantic Resolve published on the U.S. European Command webpage: http://www.eucom.mil/operation-atlantic-resolve; U.S. Department of Defense, "America's Continued Commitment to European Security: Operation Atlantic Resolve," http://www.defense.gov/News/Special-Reports/0514 _Atlantic-Resolve; Tilghman, "EUCOM Chief."

60. U.S. Department of Defense, "Press Briefing by General Breedlove in the Pentagon Briefing Room," October 30, 2015, http://www.defense.gov/News/News-Transcripts /Transcript-View/Article/626787/department-of-defense-press-briefing-by-general -breedlove-in-the-pentagon-brief. When General Breedlove is stating "we accept" in the press briefing, he refers to General Mark A. Milley, the U.S. Army chief, and General Raymond T. Odierno, the former chief of staff of the U.S. Army.

61. North Atlantic Treaty Organization, "Warsaw Summit Communiqué," July 9, 2016, http://www.nato.int/cps/en/natohq/official_texts_133169.htm.

62. Tunsjø, "Europe's Favourable Isolation."

63. Italy's defense spending combined with France's or the United Kingdom's would be larger than Russia's but not in combination with Germany's. See "The 15 Countries with the Highest Military Expenditure in 2014," Stockholm International Peace Research Institute, April 13, 2015, http://books.sipri.org/product_info?c_product_id=496.

64. John J. Mearsheimer and Stephen M. Walt, "The Case for Offshore Balancing: A Superior U.S. Grand Strategy," *Foreign Affairs*, June 13, 2016.

65. Michael Birnbaum and Rick Noack, "Following Trump's Trip, Merkel Says Europe Can't Rely on 'Others.' She Means the U.S.," *Washington Post*, May 28, 2017, https://www.washingtonpost.com/world/following-trumps-trip-merkel-says-europe-cant-rely-on-us-anymore/2017/05/28/4c6b92cc-43c1-11e7-8de1-cec59a9bf4b1_story.html.

66. Gaddis, *Strategies of Containment*, 55.

67. Similarly, Kennan's insistence "that if competition was to take place, it do so on terrain and with instruments best calculated to apply American strengths against Soviet weaknesses, thereby preserving the initiative while minimizing costs," is most likely to shape U.S. decision making. For instance, the Baltics are probably one of the least favorable places to fight Russia's armed forces, and maritime East Asia is probably one of the more favorable places to fight the PLA. See Gaddis, *Strategies of Containment*, 55.

68. Lippmann, *The Cold War*, 24.

69. Mearsheimer, *The Tragedy*, xii, 360–361; Nuno P. Monteiro, *Theory of Unipolar Politics* (Cambridge: Cambridge University Press, 2014).

70. Such as terrorism, refugee crises, piracy, organized crime, and instability in Africa and the Middle East. It can be argued that the wars with minor powers during the unipolar era have created more risks and challenges for Europe. Nonetheless, one cannot bring back a stable Iraq under Saddam Hussein, a stable Libya under Gaddafi, or a stable Syria under Assad. Whatever caused instability in Europe's neighborhood is not the point. It poses a security risk to Europe, and, in a new bipolar system, Europeans are compelled to play a stronger role in managing security in their neighborhood.

71. Øystein Tunsjø, "China's Rise: Towards a Division of Labor in Transatlantic Relations," in *Responding to China's Rise*, ed. Vinod K. Aggarwal and Sara A. Newland (Berkeley APEC Study Center, 2014), 151–174.

72. Tunsjø, "Europe's Favourable Isolation."

73. Rene Wagner and Michael Nienaber, "China Steams Past U.S., France to be Germany's Biggest Trading Partner," *Reuters*, February 24, 2017, https://www.reuters.com/article/us-germany-economy-trade-idUSKBN1622SO. For an early analysis of such trends, see Robert S. Ross, Øystein Tunsjø, and Zhang Tuosheng, eds., *U.S.-China-EU Relations: Managing the New World Order* (London: Routledge, 2010); Øystein Tunsjø, "Testimony for the U.S.-China Economic and Security Review Commission Hearing on 'China-Europe Relationship and Transatlantic Implications,'" April 19, 2012, http://www.uscc.gov/hearings/2012hearings/written_testimonies/hr12_04_19.php; Tunsjø, "China's Rise."

74. Øystein Tunsjø, "Geopolitical Shifts, Great Power Relations, and Norway's Foreign Policy," *Cooperation and Conflict* 46, no. 1 (2011): 60–77.

75. Bobo Lo, *Axis of Convenience: Moscow, Beijing, and the New Geopolitics* (Washington, D.C.: Brookings and Chatham House, 2008); Bobo Lo, *Russia and the New World Disorder* (Washington, D.C.: Brookings and Chatham House, 2015).

76. Robert S. Ross, "Balance-of-Power Politics and the Rise of China: Accommodation and Balancing in East Asia," *Security Studies* 15, no. 3 (2006): 355–395; Ross, "Bipolarity and Balancing"; Robert S. Ross, "The Rise of Russia, Sino-Russian Relations, and U.S. Security Policy," brief, Royal Danish Defence College, June 2009. Today, however, Ross remains doubtful about significant security cooperation because Russia cannot be of much help to China in dealing with the United States.

77. Edward Lucas, *The New Cold War* (London: Palgrave, 2008); Robert Kagan, *The Return of History and the End of Dreams* (New York: Knopf, 2008).

78. Stephen M. Walt, "The Ties That Fray: Why Europe and America Are Drifting Apart," *National Interest* 54 (Winter 1999). See also Richard Betts, "The Three Faces of NATO," *National Interest* (March/April 2009); Ross, "The Rise of Russia."

79. Mehreen Khan, "Russia Crisis Deepens as Economy Suffers Worst Recession in Six Years," *Telegraph*, August 10, 2015, http://www.telegraph.co.uk/finance/economics /11794653/Russia-crisis-deepens-as-economy-suffers-worst-recession-in-six-years .html.

80. Randall L. Schweller, *Maxwell's Demon and the Golden Apple: Global Disorder in the New Millennium* (Baltimore, Md.: Johns Hopkins University Press, 2014); Geoff Dyer, *The Contest of the Century: The New Era of Competition with China* (London: Penguin, 2014).

81. For example, the Korean War, the Vietnam War, and the Iran-Iraq War were far more deadly and posed a greater threat to order than the wars in the post–Cold War era. The recent wars in Afghanistan, Iraq, Libya, and Syria have not produced anywhere near the death rates of wars of preceding decades and the previous bipolar period. See Steven Pinker, "Guess What? More People Are Living in Peace Now. Just Look at the Numbers," *Guardian*, March 20, 2015, http://www.theguardian.com /commentisfree/2015/mar/20/wars-john-gray-conflict-peace.

82. Barry R. Posen, *Restraint: A New Foundation for U.S. Grand Strategy* (Ithaca, N.Y.: Cornell University Press, 2014); Schweller, *Maxwell's Demon*, 8–9.

83. Robert S. Ross, "The Rise of the Chinese Navy: From Regional Naval Power to Global Naval Power?" in *China's Global Engagement: Cooperation, Competition, and Influence in the Twenty-First Century*, ed. Jacques deLisle and Avery Goldstein (Washington, D.C.: Brookings Institution, 2017), 207–234.

84. Christensen, *The China Challenge*, 176–177.

85. Bader, *Obama and China's Rise*, 102–103, 143.

86. John J. Mearsheimer, "Imperial by Design," *National Interest* 111 (January/February 2011): 33.

87. G. John Ikenberry, Michael Mastanduno, and William C. Wohlforth, "Introduction: Unipolarity, State Behavior, and Systemic Consequences," *World Politics* 61, no. 1 (January 2009): 1–27, 4.

88. Robert Gates (former U.S. secretary of defense), "Reflections on the Status and the Future of the Transatlantic Alliance," *Security & Defence Agenda*, Brussels, June, 10, 2011, http://www.securitydefenceagenda.org/Contentnavigation/Activities /Activitiesoverview/tabid/1292/EventType/EventView/EventId/1070/EventDateID/1087 /PageID/5141/Reflectionsonthestatusandfutureofthetransatlanticalliance.aspx.

89. Kenneth N. Waltz, *Theory of International Politics* (1979; Long Grove, Ill.: Waveland, 2010), 71; Robert D. Putnam, "Diplomacy and Domestic Politics: The Logic of Two-Level Games," *International Organization* 42, no. 3 (1988): 427–460.

90. See, among others, Thomas J. Christensen and Jack Snyder, "Progressive Research on Degenerate Alliances," in *Realism and the Balance of Power: A New Debate*, ed. Colin Elman and John A. Vasquez (Upper Saddle River, N.J.: Prentice Hall, 2003), 66–73.

8. CONCLUSION: GEOSTRUCTURAL REALISM

1. Kenneth N. Waltz, "Evaluating Theories," in *Realism and the Balancing of Power: A New Debate*, ed. John A. Vasquez and Colin Elman (New Jersey: Prentice Hall, 2003), 49–65.

2. Kenneth N. Waltz, "Reflections on *Theory of International Politics*: A Response to My Critics," in *Neorealism and Its Critics*, ed. Robert O. Keohane (New York: Columbia University Press, 1986), 322–345, 344.

3. Hans J. Morgenthau, *Politics Among Nations: The Struggle for Power and Peace*, 2nd ed. (New York: Knopf, 1954), 16.

4. Morgenthau, *Politics Among Nations*, 2nd ed., 16.

5. See the references to this debate in chapter 1.

6. Barry R. Posen, "From Unipolarity to Multipolarity: Transition in Sight?" in *International Relations Theory and the Consequences of Unipolarity*, ed. John G. Ikenberry, Michael Mastanduno, and William C. Wohlforth (Cambridge: Cambridge University Press, 2011), 317–341, 321.

7. Even if one argues, as Ikenberry does, that the international system is not yet bipolar, the trend toward bipolarity is much stronger than the trend toward multipolarity. See John G. Ikenberry, "The Liberal Sources of American Unipolarity," in *International Relations Theory and the Consequences of Unipolarity*, ed. John G. Ikenberry, Michael Mastanduno, and William C. Wohlforth (Cambridge: Cambridge University Press, 2011), 216–251, 223.

8. John J. Mearsheimer, *The Tragedy of Great Power Politics*, 2nd ed. (New York: Norton, 2014); Graham Allison, *Destined for War: Can America and China Escape Thucydides's Trap?* (New York: Houghton Mifflin Harcourt, 2017).

9. China's peaceful "rise" has officially been labeled China's peaceful "development" by Beijing. Never in the history of international politics has one state become so powerful, in such a short time, relative to all other states in the international system, without waging war or other states waging war against it. China's unprecedented peaceful rise, however, was not achieved by China acting alone. The United States has been a very important factor in accommodating China's peaceful rise.

10. A. F. K Organski and Jacek Kugler, *The War Ledger* (Chicago: University of Chicago Press, 1980).

11. Øystein Tunsjø, "East Asia at the Center: Power Shifts and Theory," in *Strategic Adjustment and the Rise of China: Power and Politics in East Asia*, ed. Robert S. Ross and Øystein Tunsjø (Ithaca, N.Y.: Cornell University Press, 2017), 41–68. Current developments correspond more with Gilpin's emphasis on how "the law of uneven growth" undermines "the status quo established by the last hegemonic struggle." See Robert Gilpin, *War and Change in World Politics* (Cambridge: Cambridge University Press, 1981), 210.

12. Stephen G. Brooks and William C. Wohlforth, *World Out of Balance* (Princeton, N.J.: Princeton University Press, 2008); Steve Chan, *Looking for Balance: China, the United States, and Power Balancing in East Asia* (Stanford, Calif.: Stanford University Press, 2012); John G. Ikenberry, Michael Mastanduno, and William C. Wohlforth, eds., *International Relations Theory and the Consequences of Unipolarity* (Cambridge: Cambridge University Press, 2011); Jack S. Levy and William R. Thompson,

"Balancing on Land and at Sea: Do States Ally Against the Leading Global Power?" *International Security* 35, no. 1: 7–43.

13. Kenneth N. Waltz, *Theory of International Politics* (1979; Long Grove, Ill.: Waveland, 2010), 128.

14. Waltz, "Evaluating Theories," 52.

15. Waltz, *Theory of International Politics*, 128.

16. Waltz, *Realism and International Politics* (London: Routledge, 2008), 213, 221, could only partly answer the "what will happen" question he claimed his theory is "better at saying." Moreover, his theory could not answer when it would happen.

17. Waltz, "Evaluating Theories," 55

18. Øystein Tunsjø, "U.S.-China Relations: From Unipolar Hedging Toward Bipolar Balancing," in *Strategic Adjustment and the Rise of China: Power and Politics in East Asia*, ed. Robert S. Ross and Øystein Tunsjø (Ithaca, N.Y.: Cornell University Press, 2017), 41–68.

19. Waltz, "Evaluating Theories," 55.

20. Levy and Thompson, "Balancing on Land and at Sea."

21. Robert A. Pape, "Soft Balancing Against the United States," *International Security* 30, no. 1 (2005): 7–45. For counterarguments to soft balancing, see Keir A. Lieber and Gerard Alexander, "Waiting for Balancing: Why the World Is Not Pushing Back," *International Security* 30, no. 1 (2005): 109–139; Stephen G. Brooks and William C. Wohlforth, "Hard Times for Soft Balancing," *International Security* 30, no. 1 (2005): 72–108; Robert J. Art, "Correspondence: Striking a Balance," *International Security* 30, no. 3 (2006): 177–185.

22. William T. R. Fox, *The Super-Powers: The United States, Britain, and the Soviet Union—Their Responsibility for Peace* (New York: Harcourt, Brace & World, 1944), 21–23.

BIBLIOGRAPHY

Allen, Kenneth, Dennis J. Blasko, and John F. Corbett. "The PLA's New Organizational Structure: What Is Known, Unknown, and Speculation." Part 1. *China Brief* 16, no. 3 (February 4, 2016).

Allison, Graham. *Destined for War: Can America and China Escape Thucydides's Trap?* New York: Houghton Mifflin Harcourt, 2017.

——. "The Thucydides Trap: Are the U.S. and China Headed for War?" *The Atlantic*, September 24, 2015.

Ambler, John, Denis J. B. Shaw, and Leslie Symons. *Soviet and East European Transport Problems.* New York: St. Martin's Press, 1985.

Andrews-Speed, Philip, and Roland Dannreuther. *China, Oil, and Global Politics.* London: Routledge, 2011.

Aron, Raymond. *Peace and War: A Theory of International Politics.* London: Weidenfeld and Nicolson, 1966.

Art, Robert J. "Correspondence: Striking a Balance." *International Security* 30, no. 3 (2006): 177–185.

Bachrach, Peter, and Morton S. Baratz. "Two Faces of Power." *American Political Science Review* 56, no. 4 (December 1962): 947–952.

Bader, Jeffrey A. *Obama and China's Rise: An Insider's Account of America's Asia Strategy.* Washington, D.C.: The Brookings Institution, 2012.

Bairoch, Paul, and Richard Kozul-Wright. "Globalization Myths: Some Historical Reflections on Integration, Industrialization, and Growth in the World Economy." United Nations Conference on Trade and Development Discussion Paper 113. March 1996.

Beardson, Timothy. *Stumbling Giant: The Threats to China's Future.* New Haven, Conn.: Yale University Press, 2013.

Beckley, Michael. "China's Century? Why America's Edge Will Endure." *International Security* 36, no. 3 (Winter 2011/2012), 41–78.

Beckley, Michael, and Joshua R. Itzkowitz. "Correspondence: Debating China's Rise and U.S. Decline." *International Security* 37, no. 3: 172–181.

Beckman, Peter H. *World Politics in the Twentieth Century*. Englewood Cliffs, N.J.: Prentice Hall, 1984.

Bekkevold, Jo Inge, and Øystein Tunsjø. "Sustaining Growth: Energy and Natural Resources." In *SAGE Handbook of Contemporary China*, ed. Wu Weiping and Mark Frazier. Thousand Oaks, Calif.: Sage, forthcoming.

Bekkevold, Jo Inge, and Robert S. Ross, eds. *China in the Era of Xi Jinping: Domestic and Foreign Policy Challenges*. Washington, D.C.: Georgetown University Press, 2016.

Bekkevold, Jo Inge, and Sunniva Engh. "Silk Road Diplomacy: China's Strategic Interest in South Asia." In *South Asia and the Great Powers: International Relations and Regional Security*, ed. Sten Rynning, 147–173. London: I. B. Tauris, 2017.

Betts, Richard. "The Three Faces of NATO." *National Interest*, March/April 2009.

Biddle, Stephen, and Ivan Oelrich. "Future Warfare in the Pacific: Chinese Antiaccess/Area Denial, U.S. AirSea Battle, and Command of the Commons in East Asia." *International Security* 41, no. 1 (Summer 2016): 7–48.

Bitzinger, Richard A. "China Double Digit Defense Growth: What It Means for a Peaceful Rise." *Foreign Affairs*, March 19, 2015.

Blasko, Dennis J. *The Chinese Army Today: Tradition and Transformation for the Twenty-First Century*. 2nd ed. London: Routledge, 2012.

——. "Ten Reasons Why China Will Have Trouble Fighting a Modern War." *War on the Rocks*, February 18, 2015.

Bosco, Joseph A. "Taiwan and Strategic Security." *The Diplomat*, May 15, 2015.

Boulding, Kenneth E. *Conflict and Defense: A General Theory*. New York: Harper and Row, 1962.

Bowers, Ian, and Bjørn Grønning. "Protecting the Status Quo: Japan's Response to the Rise of China." In *Strategic Adjustment and the Rise of China: Power and Politics in East Asia*, ed. Robert S. Ross and Øystein Tunsjø, 137–168. Ithaca, N.Y.: Cornell University Press, 2017.

Breznitz, Dan, and Michael Murphree. "The Rise of China in Technology Standards: New Norms in Old Institutions." *U.S.-China Economic and Security Review Commission*, January 16, 2013.

Brill Olcott, Martha. "China's Unmatched Influence in Central Asia." Carnegie Endowment for International Peace. Washington D.C., September 18, 2013.

Brodie, Bernard, ed. *The Absolute Weapon: Atomic Power and World Order*. New York: Harcourt, Brace, 1946.

Brooks, Stephen G. "Dueling Realisms." *International Organization* 51, no. 3 (Summer 1997): 445–477.

——. *Producing Security: Multinational Corporations, Globalization, and the Changing Calculus of Conflict*. Princeton, N.J.: Princeton University Press, 2005.

Brooks, Stephen G., and William Wohlforth. *America Abroad: The United States' Global Role in the Twenty-First Century*. Oxford: Oxford University Press, 2016.

——. "Hard Times for Soft Balancing." *International Security* 30, no. 1 (2005): 72–108.

——. "The Rise and the Fall of the Great Powers in the Twenty-first Century: China's Rise and the Fate of America's Global Position." *International Security* 40, no. 3 (Winter 2015/2016): 7–53.

——. *World Out of Balance: International Relations and the Challenge of American Primacy.* Princeton, N.J.: Princeton University Press, 2008.

Brzezinski, Zbigniew. *Strategic Vision: America and the Crisis of Global Power.* New York: Basic Books, 2012.

Bueno de Mesquita, Bruce. "Neorealism's Logic and Evidence: When Is a Theory Falsified." In *Realism and the Balance of Power: A New Debate*, ed. Colin Elman and John A. Vasquez, 166–199. Upper Saddle River, N.J.: Prentice Hall, 2003.

Bueno de Mesquita, Bruce, James D. Morrow, and Ethan R. Zorick. "Capabilities, Perception, and Escalation." *American Political Science Review* 91 (1997): 15–27.

Burns, Arthur Lee. "From Balance to Deterrence: A Theoretical Analysis." *World Politics* 9 (July 1964): 494–529.

Campbell, Craig. "American Power Preponderance and the Nuclear Revolution." *Review of International Studies* 35, no. 1 (2009): 27–44.

——. *Glimmer of a New Leviathan: Total War in the Realism of Niebuhr, Morgenthau, and Waltz.* New York: Columbia University Press, 2003.

Chan, Steve. *Looking for Balance: China, the United States, and Power Balancing in East Asia.* Stanford, Calif.: Stanford University Press, 2012.

Chang, Gordon. *The Coming Collapse of China.* New York: Random House, 2001.

——. "The Coming Collapse of China: 2012 Edition." *Foreign Policy*, December 29, 2012.

Chase, Michael S. "China's Transition to a More Credible Nuclear Deterrent: Implications and Challenges for the United States." *Asia Policy* 16 (July 2013).

Chase, Michael S., Jeffrey Engstrom, Tai Ming Cheung, et al. *China's Incomplete Military Transformation: Assessing the Weaknesses of the People's Liberation Army (PLA).* Santa Monica: RAND Corporation, February 2015.

Chong, Ja Ian, and Todd H. Hall. "The Lessons of 1914 for East Asia Today: Missing the Trees for the Forest." *International Security* 39, no. 1 (Summer 2014): 7–43.

Christensen, Thomas J. *The China Challenge: Shaping the Choices of a Rising Power.* New York: Norton, 2015.

——. "The Meaning of the Nuclear Evolution: China's Strategic Modernization and U.S.-China Security Relations." *Journal of Strategic Studies* 35, no. 4 (2012): 447–487.

——. "Posing Problems Without Catching Up: China's Rise and Challenges for U.S. Security Policy." *International Security* 25, no. 4 (Spring 2001): 5–40.

Christensen, Thomas J., and Jack Snyder. "Chain Gangs and Passed Bucks: Predicting Alliance Patterns in Multipolarity." *International Organization* 44, no. 2 (Spring 1990): 137–168.

——. "Progressive Research on Degenerate Alliances." In *Realism and the Balance of Power: A New Debate*, ed. Colin Elman and John A. Vasquez, 66–73. Upper Saddle River, N.J.: Prentice Hall, 2003.

Christensen, Thomas J., and Jennifer M. Lind. "Correspondence: Spirals, Security, and Stability in East Asia." *International Security* 24, no. 4 (Spring 2000): 190-200.

Chung, Jae Ho. "Assessing China's Power." In *Assessing China's Power*, ed. Jae Ho Chung, 1–20. New York: Palgrave Macmillan, 2015.

Cliff, Roger. *China's Military Power: Assessing Current and Future Capabilities.* Cambridge: Cambridge University Press, 2015.

Clinton, Hillary. "America's Pacific Century." *Foreign Policy*, October 11, 2011.

Coker, Christopher. *The Improbable War: China, the United States, and the Continuing Logic of Great Power Conflict.* London: Hurst & Company, 2015.

Cole, Bernard D. *China's Quest for Great Power: Ships, Oil, and Foreign Policy.* Annapolis, Md.: Naval Institute Press, 2016.

——. *The Great Wall at Sea: China's Navy in the Twenty-First Century.* 2nd ed. Annapolis, Md.: Naval Institute Press, 2010.

Collins, Gabriel B., and William S. Murray. "No Oil for the Lamps of China?" *Naval War College Review* 61, no. 2 (2008): 79–95.

Cooley, Alexander. *Great Games, Local Rules: The New Great Power Contest in Central Asia.* Oxford: Oxford University Press, 2012.

Cronin, Patrick M., Mira Rapp-Hooper, Harry Krejsa, et al. *Beyond the San Hai: The Challenge of China's Blue-Water Navy.* Center for a New American Security, May 2017.

Cropsey, Seth. *Mayday: The Decline of American Naval Supremacy.* New York: Overlook, 2013.

Cunningham, Fiona S., and Taylor M. Fravel. "Assuring Assured Retaliation: China's Nuclear Posture and U.S.-China Strategic Stability." *International Security* 40, no. 2 (Fall 2015): 7–50.

Dahl, Robert A. *Who Governs: Democracy and Power in an American City.* New Haven, Conn.: Yale University Press, 1961.

Davis, Carmel. *Power, Threat, or Military Capabilities: U.S. Balancing in the Later Cold War, 1970–1982.* Lanham, Md.: University Press of America, 2011.

Dempsey, Judy. "The United States and China: The Return of a Bipolar World." *Carnegie Europe*, November 12, 2012. http://carnegieeurope.eu/strategiceurope/?fa=49969.

Deudney, Daniel. "Unipolarity and Nuclear Weapons." In *International Relations Theory and the Consequences of Unipolarity*, ed. John G. Ikenberry, Michael Mastanduno, and William C. Wohlforth, 282–316. Cambridge: Cambridge University Press, 2011.

Deutsch, Karl W., and David J. Singer. "Multipolar Power Systems and International Stability." *World Politics* 16, no. 3 (April 1964): 390–406.

Development Research Center of the State Council, and the World Bank. *China 2030: Building a Modern, Harmonious, and Creative Society.* Washington D.C.: World Bank Publications, 2013.

Dicken, Peter. *Global Shift: Mapping the Changing Contours of the World Economy.* London: Sage, 2015.

Dickson, Bruce. *The Dictator's Dilemma.* Oxford: Oxford University Press, 2016.

Drezner, Daniel W. "Bad Debts: Assessing China's Financial Influence in Great Power Politics." *International Security* 34, no. 1 (2009): 7–45.

——. "Perception, Misperception and Sensitivity: Chinese Economic Power and Preferences after the 2008 Financial Crisis." In *Strategic Adjustment and the Rise of China: Power and Politics in East Asia*, ed. Robert S. Ross and Øystein Tunsjø, 69–99. Ithaca, N.Y.: Cornell University Press, 2017.

——. *The System Worked: How the World Stopped Another Great Depression.* New York: Oxford University Press, 2014.

Dutton, Peter A. "The Sino-Philippine Maritime Row: International Arbitration and the South China Sea." Center for New American Security, March 15, 2013.

Dutton, Peter, Andrew S. Erikson, and Ryan Martinson, eds. *China's Near Seas Combat Capabilities.* China Maritime Studies 11. Newport, R.I.: U.S. Naval War College, 2014.

Dutton, Peter A., Robert S. Ross, and Øystein Tunsjø, eds. *Twenty-First Century Seapower: Cooperation and Conflict at Sea.* London: Routledge, 2012.

Dyer, Geoff. *The Contest of the Century: The New Era of Competition with China*. London: Penguin, 2014.

Easterly, William, and Stanley Fischer. "The Soviet Economic Decline: Historical and Republican Data." Working Paper 4735. Cambridge, Mass.: National Bureau of Economic Research, May 1994.

Economy, Elizabeth. *China Joins the World: Progress and Prospects*. New York: Council of Foreign Relations, 1999.

——. *The River Runs Black: The Environmental Challenge to China's Future*. Ithaca, N.Y.: Cornell University Press, 2004.

Erickson, Andrew S., ed. *Chinese Naval Shipbuilding: An Ambitious and Uncertain Course*. Newport, R.I.: Naval Institute Press, 2015.

——. "Deterrence by Denial: How to Prevent China From Using Force." *National Interest*, December 16, 2013.

——. "Evaluating China's Conventional Military Power: The Naval and Air Dimension." In *Assessing China's Power*, ed. Jae Ho Chung, 65–90. New York: Palgrave Macmillan, 2015.

Erickson, Andrew S., and Adam P. Liff. "Demystifying China's Defense Spending: Less Mysterious in the Aggregate." *China Quarterly* 216 (December 2013): 805–830.

Erickson, Andrew S., and Austin Strange. "China's Global Maritime Presence: Hard and Soft Dimensions of PLAN Antipiracy Operations." *China Brief* 15, no. 9 (May 1, 2015).

Erickson, Andrew S., and Carnes Lord. "Bases for America's Asia Pacific Rebalance," *The Diplomat*, May 2, 2014.

——. *Rebalancing U.S. Forces: Basing and Forward Presence in the Asia Pacific*. Annapolis, Md.: Naval Institute Press, 2014.

Erickson, Andrew S., Lyle J. Goldstein, and Carnes Lord, eds. *China Goes to Sea: Maritime Transformation in Comparative Historical Perspective*. Annapolis, Md.: U.S. Naval Institute Press, 2009.

Farley, Robert. "America, Take Notice: China's Five Military Game Changes." *National Interest*, August 23, 2014.

Feldman, Noah. *Cool War: The Future of Global Competition*. New York: Random House, 2013.

Finkelstein, David M. "National Missile Defense and China's Current Security Perceptions." Report 42. Presented to the Stimson/CAN NMD-China Project, December 14, 2001.

Flory, Peter C., Keith Payne, Pavel Podvig, et al. "Nuclear Exchange: Does Washington Really Have (or Want) Nuclear Primacy?" *Foreign Affairs* 85, no. 5 (September/October 2006): 149–157.

Foot, Rosemary, and Andrew Walter. *China, the United States, and Global Order*. Cambridge: Cambridge University Press, 2011.

Forsyth, Michael. "Q. and A.: Roderick MacFarquhar on Xi Jinping's High-Risk Campaign to Save the Communist Party." *Sinosphere*, January 30, 2015.

Fox, William T. R. *The Super-Powers: The United States, Britain, and the Soviet Union—Their Responsibility for Peace*. New York: Harcourt, Brace & World, 1944.

Fravel, Taylor. "Threading the Needle: The South China Sea Dispute and U.S.-China Relations." In *Strategic Adjustment and the Rise of China: Power and Politics in East Asia*, ed. Robert S. Ross and Øystein Tunsjø, 233–260. Ithaca, N.Y.: Cornell University Press, 2017.

Fravel, Taylor M., and Evan S. Medeiros. "China's Search for Assured Retaliation: The Evolution of Chinese Nuclear Strategy and Force Structure." *International Security* 35, no. 2 (Fall 2010): 48–87.

Friedberg, Aaron L. *Beyond Air-Sea Battle: The Debate Over U.S. Military Strategy in Asia.* London: International Institute for Strategic Studies, 2014.

——. *A Contest for Supremacy: China, America, and the Struggle for Mastery in Asia.* New York: Norton, 2011.

——. "Here Be Dragons: Is China a Military Threat?" *National Interest* 103 (September/October 2009): 19–25.

——. "Ripe for Rivalry: Prospect for Peace in a Multipolar Asia." *International Security* 18, no. 3 (Winter 1993/1994): 5–33.

Fukuyama, Francis. "America in Decay: The Sources of Political Dysfunction." *Foreign Affairs* 93, no. 5 (2014): 5–26.

Gaddis, John L. "The Long Peace: Elements of Stability in the Postwar International System." *International Security* 10, no. 4 (Spring 1986): 99–142.

——. *Strategies of Containment: A Critical Appraisal of American National Security Policy During the Cold War.* Rev. and exp. ed. Oxford: Oxford University Press, 2005.

——. *The United States and the Origins of the Cold War.* New York: Columbia University Press, 1972.

Gady, Franz-Stefan. "Philippines Push for Military Modernization in New Budget Proposal," *The Diplomat,* August 21, 2015.

Gilpin, Robert. *War and Change in World Politics.* Cambridge: Cambridge University Press, 1981.

Glaser, Charles L. "A U.S.-China Grand Bargain? The Hard Choice Between Military Competition and Accommodation." *International Security* 39, no. 4 (Spring 2015): 49–90.

——. "Why Unipolarity Doesn't Matter (Much)." *Cambridge Review of International Affairs* 24, no. 2 (June 2011): 135–147.

Glassman, Jon D. *Arms for the Arabs: The Soviet Union and War in the Middle East.* Baltimore, Md.: Johns Hopkins University Press, 1975.

Gleditsch, Nils Petter, Steven Pinker, Bradley A. Thayer, et al. "The Forum: The Decline of War." *International Studies Review* 15, no. 3 (2013): 396–419.

Goldman, Marshall I. *Petrostate: Putin, Power, and the New Russia.* Oxford: Oxford University Press, 2010.

Goldstein, Avery. "China's Real and Present Danger: Now Is the Time for Washington to Worry." *Foreign Affairs,* September/October 2013.

——. "First Things First: The Pressing Danger of Crisis Instability in U.S.-China Relations." *International Security* 37, no. 4 (Spring 2013): 49–89.

——. "Parsing China's Rise: International Circumstances and National Attributes." In *China's Ascent: Power, Security, and the Future of International Politics,* ed. Robert S. Ross and Zhu Feng, 59–67. Ithaca, N.Y.: Cornell University Press, 2008.

——. *Rising to the Challenge: China's Grand Strategy and International Security.* Stanford, Calif.: Stanford University Press, 2005.

Goldstein, Lyle. *Meeting China Half Way: How to Defuse the Emerging U.S.-China Rivalry.* Washington, D.C.: Georgetown University Press, 2015.

Gompert, David C., Astrid Stuth Cevallos, and Christina L. Garafola. *War with China: Thinking Through the Unthinkable.* Santa Monica, Calif.: RAND Corporation, 2016.

Graham, Loren R. *Science in Russia and the Soviet Union: A Short History.* Cambridge: Cambridge University Press, 1994.

Greenert, Jonathan, and Mark Welsh. "Breaking the Kill Chain: How to Keep America in the Game When Our Enemies Are Trying to Shut Us Out." *Foreign Policy*, May 17, 2013.

Grønning, Bjørn Elias Mikalsen. "Japan's Shifting Military Priorities: Counterbalancing China's Rise." *Asian Security* (2014): 1–21.

Grygiel, Jakub J. "Geography and Seapower." In *Twenty-First Century Seapower: Cooperation and Conflict at Sea*, ed. Peter Dutton, Robert S. Ross, and Øystein Tunsjø, 18–41. London: Routledge, 2012.

——. *Great Powers and Geopolitical Change*. Baltimore, Md.: Johns Hopkins University Press, 2006.

Haass, Richard N. "The Age of Nonpolarity: What Will Follow U.S. Dominance?" *Foreign Affairs* 77, no. 2 (May/June 2008): 44–56.

Haddick, Robert. *Fire on the Water: China, America, and the Future of the Pacific*. Annapolis, Md.: Naval Institute Press, 2014.

Hahn, Peter L. *The United States, Great Britain, and Egypt, 1945–1956*. Chapel Hill: University of North Carolina Press, 1991.

Hammes, T. X. "Offshore Control vs. AirSea Battle: Who Wins?" *National Interest*, August 21, 2013.

——. "Sorry, AirSea Battle Is No Strategy." *National Interest*, August 7, 2013.

Handel, Michael I. *Weak States in the International System*. London: Frank Cass, 1981.

Hansen, Birthe. *Unipolarity and World Politics: A Theory and Its Implications*. London: Routledge, 2011.

Hart, Jeffrey. "Three Approaches to the Measurement of Power in International Relations." *International Organization* 30, no. 2 (Spring 1976): 289–305.

Heginbotham, Eric, Michael Nixon, Forrest E. Morgan, et al. *The U.S.-China Military Scorecard: Forces, Geography, and the Evolving Balance of Power 1996–2017*. Santa Monica, Calif.: RAND Corporation, 2015.

Hertz, John H. *International Politics in the Atomic Age*. New York: Columbia University Press, 1959.

Hirschman, Albert O. *National Power and the Structure of Foreign Trade*. 1945; Berkeley: University of California Press, 1980.

Hirst, Paul, Grahame Thompson, and Simon Bromley. *Globalization in Question*. 3rd ed. Malden, Mass.: Polity, 2009.

Hobsbawm, Eric. *Age of Extremes: The Short Twentieth Century, 1914–1991*. London: Penguin, 1994.

Holmes, James R. "China's Navy Is Already Challenging the U.S. in the Asia Pacific." *The Diplomat*, October 16, 2014.

Holslag, Jonathan. *China's Coming War with Asia*. Cambridge: Polity, 2015.

Hopf, Ted. "Polarity, the Offense-Defense Balance, and War." *American Political Science Review* 85, no. 2 (June 1991): 475–493.

Horne, Alistair. *Macmillan*. London: Macmillan, 1989.

Hu Angang. *China in 2020: A New Type of Superpower*. Washington D.C.: Brookings, 2011.

Hung, Ho-fung. *The China Boom: Why China Will Not Rule the World*. New York: Columbia University Press, 2016.

Huntington, Samuel P. "The Lonely Superpower." *Foreign Affairs* 78, no. 2 (March/April 1999).

Hurt, Martin. "Preempting Further Russian Aggression Against Europe." *2016 Index of U.S. Military Strength: Assessing America's Ability to Provide for the Common Defense.* Washington, D.C.: Heritage Foundation, 2015.

Hveem, Helge, and T. J. Pempel. "China's Rise and Economic Interdependence." In *China in the Era of Xi Jinping: Domestic and Foreign Policy Challenges*, ed. Jo Inge Bekkevold and Robert S. Ross, 196–232. Washington, D.C.: Georgetown University Press, 2016.

Ikenberry, John G., ed. *America Unrivaled: The Future of the Balance of Power.* Ithaca, N.Y.: Cornell University Press, 2002.

——. "The Liberal Sources of American Unipolarity." In *International Relations Theory and the Consequences of Unipolarity*, ed. John G. Ikenberry, Michael Mastanduno, and William C. Wohlforth, 216–251. Cambridge: Cambridge University Press, 2011.

Ikenberry, John G., Michael Mastanduno, and William C. Wohlforth. "Introduction: Unipolarity, State Behavior, and Systemic Consequences." In *International Relations Theory and the Consequences of Unipolarity*, ed. John G. Ikenberry, Michael Mastanduno, and William C. Wohlforth, 1–32. Cambridge: Cambridge University Press, 2011.

——. "Introduction: Unipolarity, State Behavior, and Systemic Consequences." *World Politics* 61, no. 1 (January 2009): 1–27.

International Monetary Fund. *Regional Economic Outlook: Asia and Pacific, Stabilizing and Outperforming Other Regions.* Washington D.C., April 2015.

——. *World Economic Outlook: Slowing Growth, Rising Risks.* September 2011.

Jacques, Martin. *When China Rules the World: The End of the Western World and the Birth of a New World Order.* 2nd ed. London: Penguin, 2012.

Jervis, Robert. *The Illogic of American Nuclear Strategy.* Ithaca, N.Y.: Cornell University Press, 1984.

——. *The Meaning of the Nuclear Revolution.* Ithaca, N.Y.: Cornell University Press, 1989.

——. *System Effects: Complexity in Political and Social Life.* Princeton, N.J.: Princeton University Press, 1997.

——. "Unipolarity: A Structural Perspective." In *International Relations Theory and the Consequences of Unipolarity*, ed. John G. Ikenberry, Michael Mastanduno, and William C. Wohlforth, 252–281. Cambridge: Cambridge University Press, 2011.

Jian Xie et al. *Addressing China's Water Scarcity: A Synthesis of Recommendations for Selected Water Resource Management Issues.* Washington, D.C.: World Bank, 2009.

Jianhua Zhang. "China's Success in Increasing Per Capita Food Production." *Journal of Experimental Botany* 62, no. 11 (2011): 3707–3711.

Joffe, Josef. *The Myth of America's Decline: Politics, Economics, and a Half-Century of False Prophecies.* New York: Norton, 2014.

Johansson, Åsa, et al. *Looking to 2060: Long-Term Global Growth Prospects for the World.* OECD, November 2012.

Johnston, Alastair Iain. "China's New 'Old Thinking': The Concept of Limited Deterrence." *International Security* 20, no. 3 (Winter 1995/1996): 5–42.

——. *Social States: China in International Institutions, 1980–2000.* Princeton, N.J.: Princeton University Press, 2007.

Jonquiéres, Guy de. "Who's Afraid of the China's High-Tech Challenge?" Policy Brief, European Centre for International Political Economy, no. 07/2013.

Kagan, Robert. *The Return of History and the End of Dreams.* New York: Knopf, 2008.

Kamphausen, Roy, and Andrew Scobell, eds. *Right Sizing the People's Liberation Army: Exploring the Contours of China's Military*. Carlisle, Penn.: Strategic Studies Institute, U.S. Army War College, 2007.

Kaplan, Morton A. *System and Process in International Politics*. New York: John Wiley & Sons, 1957.

Kaplan, Robert D. *Asia's Cauldron: The South China Sea and the End of a Stable Pacific*. New York: Random House, 2014.

——. "Center Stage for the Twenty-First Century: Power Plays in the Indian Ocean." *Foreign Affairs* 88, no. 2 (March/April 2009): 16–32.

——. "The Geography of Chinese Power." *Foreign Affairs* 89, no. 3 (May/June 2010): 22–41.

——. *The Revenge of Geography: What the Map Tells Us About Coming Conflicts and the Battle Against Fate*. New York: Random House, 2012.

Kapstein, Ethan B., and Michael Mastanduno, eds. *Unipolar Politics: Realism and State Strategies After the Cold War*. New York: Columbia University Press, 1999.

Kapur, Davesh. "Unleashing Potential in Innovation and Creativity." *East Asia Forum Quarterly* 4, no. 1 (January–March 2012): 10–11.

Kelly, Phil. *Classical Geopolitics: A New Analytical Model*. Stanford, Calif.: Stanford University Press, 2016.

Kennan, George F. *Realities of American Foreign Policy*. Princeton, N.J.: Princeton University Press, 1954.

Kennedy, Paul. *The Rise and the Fall of the Great Powers*. New York: Vintage, 1989.

Kissinger, Henry. *World Order*. New York: Penguin, 2014.

Klingner, Bruce D. "Rebalancing to the Pacific: Asia Pivot or Divot?" In *2015 Index of U.S. Military Strength: Assessing America's Ability to Provide for the Common Defense*, ed. Dakota L. Wood, 37–46. Washington D.C.: Heritage Foundation, 2015.

Knorr, Klaus. *The Power of Nations*. New York: Basic Books, 1975.

Kolko, Joyce, and Gabriel Kolko. "American Capitalist Expansion." In *The Origins of the Cold War*, 3rd ed., ed. Thomas G. Paterson and Robert J. McMahon, 14–21. Lexington, Mass.: D. C. Heat and Co., 1991.

Krauthammer, Charles. "The Unipolar Moment." *Foreign Affairs* 70, no. 1 (1990/1991): 23–33.

——. "The Unipolar Moment Revisited." *National Interest* 70, no. 5 (2002/2003): 5–17.

Krepinevich, Andrew F. *Preserving the Balance: A U.S. Eurasia Defense Strategy*. Center for Strategic and Budgetary Assessments. Washington, D.C., January 2017.

Kuo, Mercy A., and Angelica O. Tang. "The Next U.S. President: Asia's Impact on America's Future: Insight from Admiral Dennis Blair." *The Diplomat*, June 15, 2015.

Kupchan, Charles A. "After Pax Americana: Benign Power, Regional Integration, and the Sources of Stable Multipolarity." *International Security* 23, no. 3 (Fall 1998): 40–79.

Kyle, Keith. *Suez*. London: Weidenfeld and Nicholson, 1991.

Lacina, Bethany Ann, and Nils Petter Gleditsch. "The Waning of War Is Real: A Response to Gohdes and Price." *Journal of Conflict Resolution* 57, no. 6 (2013): 1109–1127.

Lantis, Jeffrey S., Tom Sauer, James J. Wirtz, et al. "The Short Shadow of U.S. Nuclear Primacy?" *International Security* 31, no. 3 (Winter 2006/2007): 174–193.

Lampton, David M. *Following the Leader: Ruling China, from Deng Xiaoping to Xi Jinping*. Berkeley: University of California Press, 2014.

——. "How China Is Ruled: Why It's Getting Harder for Beijing to Govern." *Foreign Affairs*, January/February 2014.

——. *Same Bed, Different Dreams: Managing U.S.-China Relations, 1989–2000*. Berkeley: University of California Press, 2001.

——. *The Three Faces of Chinese Power: Might, Money, and Minds*. Berkeley: University of California Press, 2008.

Lardy, Nicholas R. *Markets Over Mao: The Rise of Private Business in China*. Washington, D.C.: Peterson Institute for International Economics, 2014.

Layne, Christopher. "China's Challenge to U.S. Hegemony." *Current History* 107, no. 705 (January 2008): 13–18.

——. "China's Role in American Grand Strategy: Partner, Regional Power, or Great Power Rival?" In *The Asia Pacific: A Region in Transition*, ed. Jim Rolfe, 54–80. Honolulu: Asia-Pacific Center for Security Studies, 2004.

——. *The Peace of Illusions: American Grand Strategy from 1940 to the Present*. Ithaca, N.Y.: Cornell University Press, 2006.

——. "This Time It's Real: The End of Unipolarity and the *Pax Americana*." *International Studies Quarterly* 56, no. 1 (March 2012): 203–213.

——. "The Unipolar Illusion Revisited: The Coming End of the United States' Unipolar Moment." *International Security* 31, no. 2 (Fall 2006): 7–41.

——. "The Unipolar Illusion: Why New Great Powers Will Rise." *International Security* 17, no. 4 (Spring 1993): 5–51.

——. "U.S. Hegemony in a Unipolar World: Here to Stay or *Sic Transit Gloria*?" *International Studies Review* 11, no. 4 (2009): 784–787.

Leffler, Melvin P. "Bringing It Together: The Parts and the Whole." In *Reviewing the Cold War: Approaches, Interpretations, Theory*, ed. Odd Arne Westad, 43–63. London: Frank Cass, 2000.

——. *A Preponderance of Power: National Security, the Truman Administration, and the Cold War*. Stanford, Calif.: Stanford University Press, 1992.

Levy, Jack S. "Power Transition Theory and the Rise of China." In *China's Ascent: Power, Security, and the Future of International Politics*, ed. Robert S. Ross and Zhu Feng, 11–33. Ithaca, N.Y.: Cornell University Press, 2008.

——. *War in the Modern Great Power System, 1495–1975*. Lexington: University Press of Kentucky, 1983.

Levy, Jack S., and William R. Thompson. "Balancing on Land and at Sea: Do States Ally Against the Leading Global Power?" *International Security* 35, no. 1 (Summer 2010): 7–43.

Lewis, Jeffrey. "China's Nuclear Modernization: Surprise, Restraint, and Uncertainty." In *Asia in the Second Nuclear Age*, ed. Ashley J. Tellis, Abraham M. Denmark, and Travis Tanner, 67–96. Washington, D.C.: National Bureau of Asian Research, 2013.

Lewis, John, and Xue Litai. "Making China's Nuclear War Plan." *Bulletin of the Atomic Scientists* 68, no. 5 (2012): 45–65.

Lieber, Keir A., and Daryl G. Press. "The End of MAD? The Nuclear Dimension of U.S. Primacy." *International Security* 30, no. 4 (Spring 2006): 7–44.

——. "The Rise of American Nuclear Primacy." *Foreign Affairs* 85, no. 2 (March/April 2006): pp. 42–54.

Lieber, Keir A., and Gerard Alexander. "Waiting for Balancing: Why the World Is Not Pushing Back." *International Security* 30, no. 1 (2005): 109–139.

Lim, Robyn. *The Geopolitics of East Asia: The Search for Equilibrium.* London: Routledge, 2003.

Lippman, Walter. *The Cold War: A Study in U.S. Foreign Policy.* New York: Harper & Brothers, 1947.

Little, Richard. *The Balance of Power in International Relations: Metaphors, Myths, and Models.* Cambridge: Cambridge University Press, 2007.

Lloyd, Selwyn. *Suez 1956: A Personal Account.* London: Cape, 1978.

Lo, Bobo. *Axis of Convenience: Moscow, Beijing, and the New Geopolitics.* Washington, D.C.: Brookings and Chatham House, 2008.

——. *Russia and the New World Disorder.* Washington, D.C.: Brookings and Chatham House, 2015.

Long, Austin. "The U.S.: A New Wary Titan: U.S. Defense Policy in an Era of Military Change, Asian Growth, and European Austerity." In *Security, Strategy, and Military Change in the Twenty-First Century,* ed. Jo Inge Bekkevold, Ian Bowers, and Michael Raska, 241–265. London: Routledge, 2015.

Lucas, Edward. *The New Cold War.* London: Palgrave, 2008.

Lucas, Scott W. *Divided We Stand.* London: Hodder and Stoughton, 1991.

Lukes, Steven. *Power: A Radical View.* 2nd ed. London: MacMillan, 2005.

Lundestad, Ingrid, and Øystein Tunsjø. "The United States and China in the Arctic." *Polar Record* (May 2015): 1–12.

Lynch, Daniel. "The End of China's Rise." *Foreign Affairs,* January 11, 2016.

Ma, Damien, and William Adams. *In Line Behind a Billion People: How Scarcity Will Define China's Ascent in the Next Decade.* New Jersey: FT, 2014.

Macdonalds, Douglas J. "Formal Ideologies in the Cold War: Toward a Framework for Empirical Analysis." In *Reviewing the Cold War: Approaches, Interpretations, Theory,* ed. Odd Arne Westad, 180–204. London: Frank Cass, 2000.

Mackinder, Halford J. "The Geographical Pivot of History." *Geographical Journal* 23, no. 4 (April 1904): 421–437.

MacMillian, Margret. "The Rhyme of History: Lessons of the Great War." *Brookings Essay,* December 2013.

Maddison, Angus. *Statistics on World Population, GDP, and Per Capita GDP 1–2008 AD.*

Mahan, Alfred T. *The Influence of Seapower on History, 1660–1783.* Boston, 1890.

Mastanduno, Michael. "Preserving the Unipolar Moment: Realist Theories and U.S. Grand Strategy After the Cold War." *International Security* 21, no. 4 (Spring 1997): 44–98.

McDevitt, Michael, and Fredric Vellucci Jr. "The Evolution of the People's Liberation Army Navy: The Twin Missions of Area-Denial and Peacetime Operations." In *Sea Power and the Asia-Pacific: The Triumph of Neptune?* ed. Geoffrey Till and Patrick Bratton, 75–92. London: Routledge, 2012.

Mearsheimer, John J. "Back to the Future: Instability in Europe After the Cold War." *International Security* 15, no. 1 (Summer 1990): 5–56.

——. "China's Unpeaceful Rise." *Current History* 105, no. 690 (April 2006): 160–162.

——. *The Tragedy of Great Power Politics.* 2nd ed. New York: Norton, 2014.

Medeiros, Evan S., Roger Cliff, Keith Crane, and James C. Mulvenon. *A New Direction for China's Defense Industry.* Santa Monica, Calif.: RAND Corporation, 2005.

Miller, Alice. "The Bo Xilai Affair in Central Leadership Politics." *China Leadership Monitor* 38 (2012).

Minxin Pei. "The Twilight of Communist Party Rule in China." *American Interest*, November 12, 2015.

Monteiro, Nuno P. *Theory of Unipolar Politics*. Cambridge: Cambridge University Press, 2014.

Montgomery, Evan Braden. "Contested Primacy in the Western Pacific: China's Rise and the Future of U.S. Power Projection." *International Security* 38, no. 4 (Spring 2014): 115–149.

——. "Time to Worry About China's Military Rise." Policy Brief, Belfer Center for Science and International Affairs, Cambridge, Mass., Harvard Kennedy School, June 2014.

Moon, Chung-in. "China's Rise and Security Dynamics on the Korean Peninsula." In *Strategic Adjustment and the Rise of China: Power and Politics in East Asia*, ed. Robert S. Ross and Øystein Tunsjø, 196–232. Ithaca, N.Y.: Cornell University Press, 2017.

Morgenthau, Hans J. *Politics Among Nations: The Struggle for Power and Peace*. New York: Knopf, 1948.

——. *Politics Among Nations: The Struggle for Power and Peace*. 2nd ed. New York: Knopf, 1954.

Morrow, James D. *Game Theory for Social Scientists*. Princeton, N.J.: Princeton University Press, 1994.

Mueller, John. "The Essential Irrelevance of Nuclear Weapons: Stability in the Postwar World." *International Security* 13, no. 2 (Fall 1988): 55–79.

Mulvenon, James. "The New Central Military Commission." *China Leadership Monitor* 40 (2013).

Murray, Donette, and David Brown, eds. *Multipolarity in the Twenty-First Century: A New World Order*. London: Routledge, 2012.

Nan Li. "The Evolution of China's Naval Strategy and Capabilities: From 'Near Coast' and 'Near Seas' to 'Far Seas.'" *Asian Security* 5, no. 2 (June 2009): 144–169.

Nathan, Andrew J. "Authoritarian Resilience." *Journal of Democracy* 14, no. 1 (January 2003): 6–17.

——. "China's Rise and International Regimes: Does China Seek to Overthrow International Norms?" In *China in the Era of Xi Jinping: Domestic and Foreign Policy Challenges*, ed. Jo Inge Bekkevold and Robert S. Ross, 165–195. Washington, D.C.: Georgetown University Press, 2016.

——. "Foreseeing the Unforeseeable." *Journal of Democracy* 24, no. 1 (2013): 20–25.

National Development and Reform Commission. *Vision and Actions on Jointly Building Silk Road Economic Belt and Twenty-First-Century Maritime Silk Road*. Issued jointly by the National Development and Reform Commission, Ministry of Foreign Affairs, and Ministry of Commerce of the People's Republic of China, March 28, 2015.

National Intelligence Council (NIC). *Global Trends 2030: Alternative Worlds*. Washington D.C.: December 2012.

Naughton, Barry. *The Chinese Economy: Transition and Growth*. Cambridge, Mass.: MIT Press, 2007.

——. "Is There a 'Xi Model' of Economic Reform?—Acceleration of Economic Reforms Since Fall 2014." *China Leadership Monitor* 46 (Winter 2015).

Noorden, Richard Van. "China Tops Europe in R&D Intensity." *Nature*, January 8, 2014.

Nye, Joseph S. *The Future of Power*. New York: PublicAffairs, 2011.

——. *Is The American Century Over?* Cambridge: Policy, 2015.

——. *Soft Power: The Means to Success in World Politics*. New York: PublicAffairs, 2004.

O'Rourke, Ronald. *China's Naval Modernization: Implications for U.S. Navy Capabilities—Background and Issues for Congress.* September 8, 2014.

——. "China's Naval Modernization: Implications for U.S. Navy Capabilities—Background and Issues for Congress." *Congressional Research Service,* September 21, 2015.

Organski, A. F. K., and Jacek Kugler. *The War Ledger.* Chicago: University of Chicago Press, 1980.

Padfield, Peter. *Maritime Power and the Struggle for Freedom: Naval Campaigns That Shaped the Modern World, 1788–1851.* New York: Overlook, 2005.

Panitchpakdi, Supachai, and Mark L. Clifford. *China and the WTO: Changing China, Changing World Trade.* New York: Wiley, 2002.

Pape, Robert A. "Soft Balancing Against the United States." *International Security* 30, no. 1 (2005): 7–45.

Parameswaran, Prashanth. "Philippines to Hold Military Exercise with U.S., Japan." *The Diplomat,* June 19, 2015.

——. "What's Next for Japan-Philippines Defense Ties?" *The Diplomat,* June 30, 2015.

Parent, Joseph M., and Sebastian Rosato. "Balancing in Neorealism." *International Security* 40, no. 2 (Fall 2015): 51–86.

Paul, T. V., Richard J. Harknett, and James J. Wirtz, eds. *The Absolute Weapon Revisited: Nuclear Arms and the Emerging International Order.* Ann Arbor: University of Michigan Press, 1998.

Pettis, Michael. *Avoiding the Fall: China's Economic Restructuring.* Washington, D.C.: Carnegie Endowment for International Peace, September 2013.

Pillsbury, Michael. *The Hundred-Year Marathon: China's Secret Strategy to Replace America as the Global Superpower.* New York: Henry Holt, 2015.

Pimentel, David, and Marcia Pimentel. "Sustainability of Meat-Based and Plant-Based Diets and the Environment." *American Journal of Clinical Nutrition* 78, no. 3 (2003): 660S–663S.

Porter, Gareth. *Perils of Dominance: Imbalance of Power and the Road to War in Vietnam.* Berkeley: University of California Press, 2005.

Posen, Barry. "Command of the Commons: The Military Foundations for U.S. Hegemony." *International Security* 20, no. 1 (2003): 5–46.

——. "Emerging Multipolarity: Why Should We Care?" *Current History* 108, no. 721 (November 2009): 347–352.

——. "From Unipolarity to Multipolarity: Transition in Sight?" In *International Relations Theory and the Consequences of Unipolarity,* ed. John G. Ikenberry, Michael Mastanduno, and William C. Wohlforth, 317–341. Cambridge: Cambridge University Press, 2011.

——. *Restraint: A New Foundation for U.S. Grand Strategy.* Ithaca, N.Y.: Cornell University Press, 2014.

Putnam, Robert D. "Diplomacy and Domestic Politics: The Logic of Two-Level Games." *International Organization* 42, no. 3 (1988): 427–460.

Qinglian, He. *The Pitfalls of Modernization.* Tokyo: Soshisha, 2002.

Rajendram, Danielle. "The Promise and Perils of India's Youth Bulge." *The Diplomat,* March 10, 2013.

Rangang, Apoorva. "The Myth of the Thucydides Trap: Examining U.S.-China Relations." *Harvard Political Review,* October 16, 2015.

Rauchhaus, Robert. "Evaluating the Nuclear Peace Hypothesis: A Quantitative Approach." *Journal of Conflict Resolution* 53, no. 2 (2009): 258–277.

Reynolds, David. *One World Divisible: A Global History Since 1945*. London: Penguin, 2001.

Rhodes, Edward. "A World Not in Balance: War, Politics, and Weapons of Mass Destruction." In *Balance of Power: Theory and Practice in the Twenty-First Century*, ed. T. V. Paul, James J. Wirtz, and Michel Fortmann, 150–176. Stanford, Calif.: Stanford University Press, 2004.

Risse-Kappen, Thomas. *Cooperation Among Democracies: The European Influence on U.S. Foreign Policy*. Princeton, N.J.: Princeton University Press, 1997.

Rose, Gideon, and Jonathan Tepperman. "Dysfunction Junction: Trouble on the Home Front." *Foreign Affairs* 93, no. 5 (2014): 2.

Rosen, Daniel. "Avoiding the Blind Alley: China's Economic Overhaul and Its Global Implications." *Asia Society Policy Institute*, October 2014.

Rosen, Daniel H., and Anna Snyder. "China's Outlook—Now and in 2020." Note, Rhodium Group, August 8, 2004.

Rosen, Daniel H. and Beibei Bao. "A Better Abacus for China." Rhodium Group, December 12, 2014.

——. "An Independent Look at China's Economic Size." *Center for Strategic and International Studies* 1 (September 11, 2015).

Ross, Robert S. "Balance of Power Politics and the Rise of China: Accommodation and Balancing in East Asia." *Security Studies* 15, no. 3 (July–September 2006): 355–395.

——. "Bipolarity and Balancing in East Asia." In *Balance of Power: Theory and Practice in the Twenty-First Century*, ed. T. V. Paul, James J. Wirtz, and Michel Fortmann, 267–304. Stanford, Calif.: Stanford University Press, 2004.

——. "China's Naval Nationalism: Sources, Prospects, and the U.S. Response." *International Security* 34, no. 2 (Fall 2009): 46–81.

——. "The Geography of Peace: East Asia in the Twenty First Century." *International Security* 23, no. 4 (Spring 1999): 81–118.

——. "Navigating the Taiwan Strait: Deterrence, Escalation Dominance, and U.S.-China Relations." *International Security* 27, no. 2 (Fall 2002): 48–85.

——. "The Problem with the Pivot." *Foreign Affairs* 91, no. 6 (November/December 2012): 70–82.

——. "The Rise of the Chinese Navy: From Regional Naval Power to Global Naval Power?" In *China's Global Engagement: Cooperation, Competition, and Influence in the Twenty-First Century*, ed. Jacques deLisle and Avery Goldstein, 207–234. Washington, D.C.: Brookings Institution, 2017.

——. "The Rise of Russia, Sino-Russian Relations, and U.S. Security Policy." Brief, Royal Danish Defence College, June 2009.

——. "The United States and China in Northeast Asia: Third-Party Coercion and Alliance Relations." In *Strategic Adjustment and the Rise of China: Power and Politics in East Asia*, ed. Robert S. Ross and Øystein Tunsjø, 261–284. Ithaca, N.Y.: Cornell University Press, 2017.

——. "U.S. Grand Strategy, the Rise of China, and U.S. National Security Strategy for East Asia." *Strategic Studies Quarterly* 7, no. 2 (Summer 2013): 20–40.

Ross, Robert S., Øystein Tunsjø, and Zhang Tuosheng, eds. *US-China-EU Relations: Managing the New World Order*. London: Routledge, 2010.

Roy, Denny. *The Return of the Dragon: Rising China and Regional Security*. New York: Columbia University Press, 2013.

Rozman, Gilbert. *The Sino-Russian Challenge to the World Order: National Identities, Bilateral Relations, and East Versus West in the 2010s*. Washington, D.C.: Woodrow Wilson Center Press, 2014.

Sagan, Scott D., and Kenneth N. Waltz. *The Spread of Nuclear Weapons: A Debate Renewed*. New York: Norton, 2003.

Schelling, Thomas C. *Arms and Influence*. New Haven, Conn.: Yale University Press, 1966.

——. *The Strategy of Conflict*. Cambridge, Mass.: Harvard University Press, 1980.

Schweller, Randall L. "Domestic Politics and Nationalism in East Asian Security." In *Strategic Adjustment and the Rise of China: Power and Politics in East Asia*, ed. Robert S. Ross and Øystein Tunsjø, 15–40. Ithaca, N.Y.: Cornell University Press, 2017.

——. *Maxwell's Demon and the Golden Apple: Global Disorder in the New Millennium*. Baltimore, Md.: Johns Hopkins University Press, 2014.

Shaffer, Gregory, and Henry Gao. "China's Rise: How It Took on the U.S. at the WTO." *University of Illinois Law Review* 1 (2018).

Shambaugh, David L. *China at the Crossroads: Ten Major Reform Challenges*. Washington, D.C.: The Brookings Institution, October 1, 2014.

——. *China Goes Global: The Partial Power*. New York: Oxford University Press, 2013.

——. *China's Communist Party: Atrophy and Adaptation*. Berkeley: University of California Press, 2008.

——. *China's Future*. Cambridge: Polity, 2016.

Sharma, Shefalia. *The Need for Feed: China's Demands for Industrialized Meat and Its Impacts*. Washington, D.C.: Institute for Agriculture and Trade Policy, February 17, 2014.

Sheng, Andrew, and Ng Chow Soon. "Bringing Shadow Banking Into the Light: Opportunity for Financial Reform in China." *Fung Global Institute*, March 16, 2015.

Shi Hongtao. "China's 'Malacca Straits.'" *Qingnian bao*, June 15, 2004. Foreign Broadcast Information Service, CPP20040615000042.

Snyder, Glenn H. "The Balance of Power and the Balance of Terror." In *The Balance of Power*, ed. Paul Seabury, 191–201. San Francisco: Chandler, 1965.

——. *Deterrence and Defense: Towards a Theory of National Security*. Princeton, N.J.: Princeton University Press, 1961.

——. "Mearsheimer's World—Offensive Realism and the Struggle for Security: A Review Essay." *International Security* 27, no. 1 (Summer 2002): 149–173.

Snyder, Glenn H., and Paul Diesing. *Conflict Among Nations: Bargaining, Decision Making, and System Structure in International Crises*. Princeton, N.J.: Princeton University Press, 1977.

Sprout, Harold, and Margaret Sprout. *Foundations of International Politics*. Princeton, N.J.: Van Nostrand, 1962.

Spykman, Nicholas J. *America's Strategy in World Politics: The United States and the Balance of Power*. New York: Harcourt, Brace & World, 1942; Hamden, Conn.: Archon, 1970.

——. *The Geography of the Peace*. New York: Harcourt, Brace, 1944; Hamden, Conn.: Archon, 1970.

Steinberg, James, and Michael E. O'Hanlon. *Strategic Reassurance and Resolve: U.S.-China Relations in the Twenty-First Century*. Princeton, N.J.: Princeton University Press, 2014.

Steinfeld, Edward S. *Playing Our Game: Why China's Rise Doesn't Threaten the West*. Oxford: Oxford University Press, 2010.

Stephanson, Anders. "Liberty or Death: The Cold War as U.S. Ideology." In *Reviewing the Cold War: Approaches, Interpretations, Theory*, ed. Odd Arne Westad, 81–100. London: Frank Cass, 2000.

Steury, Donald P., ed. *Intentions and Capabilities: Estimates on Soviet Strategic Forces, 1950–1983*. Washington D.C.: CIA, 1996.

Storey, Ian. "China's 'Malacca Dilemma.'" *China Brief* 6, no. 8 (April 12, 2006).

——. "Naval Modernization in China, Japan, and South Korea: Contrasts and Comparisons." In *Naval Modernisation in South East Asia: Nature, Causes, and Consequences*, ed. Geoffrey Till and Jane Chan, 104–118. London: Routledge, 2014.

Stowe England, Robert. *Aging China: The Demographic Challenge to China's Economic Prospect*. Westport, Conn.: Praeger, 2005.

Subramanian, Arvind. *Eclipse: Living in the Shadow of China's Economic Dominance*. Washington, D.C.: Peterson Institute of International Economics, 2011.

——. "The Inevitable Superpower: Why China's Dominance Is a Sure Thing." *Foreign Affairs* 90, no. 5 (September/October 2011).

Summers, Lawrence H., and Lant Pritchett. "Asiaphoria Meets Regression to the Mean." National Bureau of Economic Research Working Paper 20573, October 2014.

Tai Ming Chung, ed. *China's Emergence as a Defense Technological Power*. London: Routledge, 2013.

——, ed. *Forging China's Military Might: A New Framework for Assessing Innovation*. Baltimore, Md.: Johns Hopkins University Press, 2014.

Takeyh, Ray. *The Origins of the Eisenhower Doctrine: The U.S., Britain, and Nasser's Egypt, 1953–57*. New York: Oxford University Press, 2000.

Tellis, Ashley J., Janice Bially, Christopher Layne, and Melissa McPherson. *Measuring National Power in the Postindustrial Age*. Santa Monica, Calif.: RAND, 2000.

Terrill, Ross. *The New Chinese Empire and What It Means for the United States*. New York: Basic Books, 2003.

Themnér, Lotta, and Peter Wallensteen. "Armed Conflicts, 1946–2012." *Journal of Peace Research* 50, no. 4 (July 2013): 509–521.

Tunsjø, Øystein. "China's Rise: Towards a Division of Labor in Transatlantic Relations." In *Responding to China's Rise*, ed. Vinod K. Aggraval and Sara A. Newland, 151–174. Springer and Berkeley APEC Study Center, 2014.

——. "The Cold War as a Guide to the Risk of War in East Asia." *Global Asia* 9, no. 3 (Fall 2014): 15–19.

——. "East Asia at the Center: Power Shifts and Theory." In *Strategic Adjustment and the Rise of China: Power and Politics in East Asia*, ed. Robert S. Ross and Øystein Tunsjø, 285–298. Ithaca, N.Y.: Cornell University Press, 2017.

——. "Europe's Favourable Isolation." *Survival* 55, no. 6 (2013): 91–106.

——. "Geopolitical Shifts, Great Power Relations, and Norway's Foreign Policy." *Cooperation and Conflict* 46, no. 1 (2011): 60–77.

——. "Global Power Shifts, Geography, and Maritime East Asia." In *International Order at Sea: How It Is Challenged, How It Is Maintained*, ed. Jo Inge Bekkevold and Geoffrey Till, 41–62. London: Palgrave Macmillan, 2016.

——. *Security and Profit in China's Energy Policy: Hedging Against Risk*. New York: Columbia University Press, 2013.

——. Testimony for the U.S.-China Economic and Security Review Commission hearing on "China-Europe Relationship and Transatlantic Implications." April 19, 2012.

——. "U.S.-China Relations: From Unipolar Hedging Toward Bipolar Balancing." In *Strategic Adjustment and the Rise of China: Power and Politics in East Asia*, ed. Robert S. Ross and Øystein Tunsjø, 41–68. Ithaca, N.Y.: Cornell University Press, 2017.

——. *U.S. Taiwan Policy: Constructing the Triangle*. London: Routledge, 2008.

UN Environment Programme. *Inclusive Wealth Report 2014: Measuring Progress Toward Sustainability*. Cambridge: Cambridge University Press, 2014.

UN Educational, Scientific, and Cultural Organization (UNESCO). *UNESCO Science Report: Towards 2030*. Paris, 2015.

UN World Intellectual Property Organization (UNWIPO). "World Intellectual Property Report: The Changing Face of Innovation and Intellectual Property." http://www.wipo.int/edocs/pubdocs/en/intproperty/944/wipo_pub_944_2011.pdf.

U.S. Department of Defense. *Asia-Pacific Maritime Security Strategy*. Washington D.C., July 27, 2015.

——. *Sustaining U.S. Global Leadership: Priorities for Twenty-First-Century Defense*. January 2012.

U.S. Navy. *A Cooperative Strategy for Twenty-First-Century Seapower*. March 2015.

U.S. Office of Naval Intelligence. *The PLA Navy: New Capabilities and Missions for the Twenty-First Century*. Washington D.C., April 2015.

Varsori, Antonio. "Reflections on the Origins of the Cold War." In *Reviewing the Cold War: Approaches, Interpretations, Theory*, ed. Odd Arne Westad, 281–302. London: Frank Cass, 2000.

Wagner, Harrison R. "What Was Bipolarity?" *International Organization* 47, no. 1 (Winter 1993): 77–106.

Waldron, Arthur. "The China Sickness." *Commentary*, July–August 2003.

Walt, Stephen M. "Alliances in a Unipolar World." In *International Relations Theory and the Consequences of Unipolarity*, ed. John G. Ikenberry, Michael Mastanduno, and William C. Wohlforth, 99–139. Cambridge: Cambridge University Press, 2011.

——. *The Origins of Alliances*. Ithaca, N.Y.: Cornell University Press, 1990.

——. "The Ties That Fray: Why Europe and America Are Drifting Apart." *National Interest* 54 (Winter 1999).

Waltz, Kenneth N. "The Emerging Structure of International Politics." *International Security* 18, no. 2 (Fall 1993): 44–79.

——. "Evaluating Theories." *American Political Science Review* 91, no. 4 (December 1997): 913–917.

——. "International Politics Is Not Foreign Policy." *Security Studies* 6, no. 1 (1996): 54–57.

——. *Man, the State, and War: A Theoretical Analysis*. New York: Columbia University Press, 1959.

——. "The Origins of War in Neorealist Theory." *Journal of Interdisciplinary History* 18, no. 4 (Spring 1988): 39–52.

——. *Realism and International Politics*. London: Routledge, 2008.

——. "Reflections on *Theory of International Politics*: A Response to My Critics." In *Neorealism and Its Critics*, ed. Robert O. Keohane, 322–345. New York: Columbia University Press, 1986.

——. "The Spread of Nuclear Weapons: More May Be Better." Adelphi Papers 171. London: International Institute for Strategic Studies, 1981.

——. "The Stability of a Bipolar World." *Daedalus* 93, no. 3 (Summer 1964): 881–909.

——. *Theory of International Politics.* 1979; Long Grove: Ill.: Waveland, 2010.

Wang Jisi. "China's Search for a Grand Strategy: A Rising Great Power Finds Its Way." *Foreign Affairs*, March/April 2011.

Welch Larson, Deborah. *Origins of Containment: A Psychological Explanation.* Princeton, N.J.: Princeton University Press, 1985.

Westad, Odd Arne. *The Global Cold War: Third World Interventions and the Making of Our Time.* Cambridge: Cambridge University Press, 2007.

——. "Introduction: Reviewing the Cold War." In *Reviewing the Cold War: Approaches, Interpretations, Theory,* ed. Odd Arne Westad, 1–26. London: Frank Cass, 2000.

Wheeler, Nicholas J. *Saving Strangers: Humanitarian Intervention in International Society.* Oxford: Oxford University Press, 2002.

Whyte, Martin K., Wang Feng, and Yong Cai. "Challenging Myths About China's One-Child Policy." *China Journal* 74 (2015): 144–159.

Wilson, David. *The Demand for Energy in the Soviet Union.* London: Rowman & Littlefield, 1983.

Wohlforth, William C. "Hegemonic Decline and Hegemonic War Revisited." In *Power, Order, and Change in World Politics,* ed. John G. Ikenberry, 109–130. Cambridge: Cambridge University Press, 2014.

——. "How Not to Evaluate Theories." *International Studies Quarterly* 56, no. 1 (March 2012): 219–222.

——. "Measuring Power—and the Power of Theories." In *Realism and the Balance of Power: A New Debate,* ed. Colin Elman and John A. Vasquez, 250–265. Upper Saddle River, N.J.: Prentice Hall, 2003.

——. "The Perception of Power: Russia in the Pre-1914 Balance." *World Politics* 39, no. 3 (April 1987): 353–381.

——. "The Stability of a Unipolar World." *International Security* 24, no. 1 (Summer 1999): 5–41.

——. "Unipolar Stability: The Rules of Power Analysis." *Harvard International Review* (Spring 2007): 44–48.

Wolf Jr., Charles, Gregory Hildenbrandt, Michael Kennedy, et al. *Long-Term Economic and Military Trends, 1950–2010.* Santa Monica, Calif.: RAND, April 1989.

Wolfe, Audra J. *Competing with the Soviets: Technology and the State in Cold War America.* Baltimore, Md.: Johns Hopkins University Press, 2012.

Wortzel, Larry M. *The Dragon Extends Its Reach: Chinese Military Power Goes Global.* Washington, D.C.: Potomac, 2013.

Wu Lei and Shen Qinyu. "Will China Go to War Over Oil?" *Far Eastern Economic Review* 160, no. 3 (April 2006): 38–40.

Wu Zurong. "No Thucydides Trap." *China & U.S. Focus,* October 7, 2015.

Xizhe Peng. "China's Demographic History and Future Challenges." *Science* 333 (July 29, 2011): 581–587.

Yan Xuetong. "A Bipolar World Is More Likely Than a Unipolar or Multipolar One." *China-U.S. Focus Digest,* April 20, 2015. http://www.chinausfocus.com/foreign-policy /a-bipolar-world-is-more-likely-than-a-unipolar-or-multipolar-one/.

——. "China-U.S. Competition for Strategic Partners." *China & U.S. Focus,* October 29, 2015.

——. "The Rise of China and Its Power Status." *Chinese Journal of International Politics* 1 (2006): 5–33.

Yanzhong Huang. "Population Aging in China: A Mixed Blessing." *The Diplomat*, November 10, 2013.

Yeisley, Mark O. "Bipolarity, Proxy Wars, and the Rise of China." *Strategic Studies Quarterly* 5, no. 4 (Winter 2011): 75–91.

Yergin, Daniel. "American Ideology: The Riga and Yalta Axioms." In *The Origins of the Cold War*, 3rd ed., ed. Thomas G. Paterson and Robert J. McMahon, 35–48. Lexington, Mass.: D. C. Heat and Company, 1991.

——. *The Quest: Energy, Security, and the Remaking of the Modern World*. London: Allen Lane, 2011.

Yoon, Sukjoon. "Implications of Xi Jinping's 'True Maritime Power.'" *Naval War College Review* 68, no. 3 (Summer 2015): 40–63.

Yoshihara, Toshi, and James Holmes. "Asymmetric Warfare, American Style." *Proceedings Magazine*, April 2012.

You Yi. "Dealing with the Malacca Strait Dilemma: China's Efforts to Enhance Energy Transportation Security." EAI Background Brief 329 (April 12, 2007).

Yutao Sun and Cong Cao. "Demystifying Central Government R&D Spending in China: Should Funding Focus on Scientific Research?" *Science* 345, no. 6200 (August 29, 2014).

Zakaria, Fareed. *The Post-American World*. New York: Norton, 2008.

Zhihua Shen. *Mao, Stalin, and the Korean War: Trilateral Communist Relations in the 1950s*. London: Routledge, 2012.

INDEX

Abe, Shinzō, 161–62
Afghan-Soviet war, 30
Africa, 116, 223n64
AIIB. *See* Asian Infrastructure Investment Bank
AirSea Battle (ASB), 148
Allison, Graham, 9–10, 54, 193n37
American-led liberal institutional order, 116
American Mediterranean, 132
anarchy, 15
antiship ballistic missile (ASBM), 148
arms race, with U.S.-China, 3
Aron, Raymond, 9, 43
ASB. *See* AirSea Battle
ASBM. *See* antiship ballistic missile
ASEAN Regional Forum, 175
ASEAN Treaty of Amity and Cooperation, 161
Asia, 161–64; Central, 78, 81, 113, 116, 117, 151; multipolarity with, 185. *See also* East Asia
Asian Infrastructure Investment Bank (AIIB), 116
Asia-Pacific Maritime Security Strategy, 160, 234n31

Asia-Pacific pivot, of U.S., 150–51, 152, 156–61, 174
Asiatic Mediterranean, 132
Austria-Hungary, 48, 49
authoritarian regimes, 176

balance of power: in Europe, 14, 157, 165; external, internal and, 43; preventive war relating to, 129–30; theory of, 6, 46, 102–3
balancing, 183–84; under bipolarity, 43, 94, 203n103; contemporary, 3, 101, 102, 121, 125; degree and intensity of, 185; East Asia relating to, 100–102, 103, 107, 150, 173; imbalance, 44, 54; importance of, 2, 20; limited, 100; moderate, 100; rebalancing, 56, 152, 156–61; strong, 3, 18, 99–102, 190n5
balancing behaviors: conclusion to, 123–25; geographical terrain and, 108–9; geopolitics and, 102–5, 112, 138–39; nuclear weapons role, 109, 121–23; power vacuums role, 105–7, 154–56, 174; unit-level factors, 109–21; of U.S.-China, 12–13, 17, 111–14, 123, 182
Baltic States, 165

behaviors: bipolarity and, 90–93; patterns of, 47, 94, 107, 113. *See also* balancing behaviors

Belt and Road initiative, 16, 35, 65, 116–19, 175, 210n73

Big Three, 27

bilateral relationship, of U.S.-China, 99–100, 219n4

bipolar distribution of capabilities, 29–30, 36; with China, 87–88, 217nn33–34; with Soviet Union, 87–88; with U.S., 87–88

bipolar distribution of power, 26–27, 40, 47, 87, 164

bipolar era, 143

bipolarity, 194n50; balancing under, 43, 94, 203n103; of China, 1, 29, 87–88, 90–93, 217nn33–34; during Cold War, 3, 20, 155; distribution relating to, 2, 4, 6; geographic impact on, 2; geopolitics and, 14; of international system, 8, 11, 18, 29, 39–40, 41, 76, 93; meaning of, 17, 23, 39–40; from multipolarity, 37; perfect, 84; sameness of, 11, 99, 101–2, 123, 151; stability with, 44, 126; Suez case relating to, 47–48; thesis of, 4–6, 190nn8–9; top-ranking powers and, 88–90, 218n40, 218n44; from unipolarity, 37–38, 103, 184; to unipolarity, 37; with U.S., 1–2, 87–88, 90–93, 174; of U.S.-China, 13, 18, 119

bipolarity, behaviors with: with China, 90–93; with other powers, 92–93; with Soviet Union, 90–93; with U.S., 90–93

bipolarity, return of, 1, 6, 16, 184; conclusion to, 176–77; impact of, 9, 19–20, 39, 126, 150–51; instability, stability and, 151–56; questions about, 99; shifting distribution of capabilities, 156–76

bipolar-stability thesis, 9, 11, 46–47

bipolar systems: comparison of, 181–82; contemporary, 14, 186–87; differences in, 3; in Europe, 14–15, 18, 151; new, 3, 176–77; stability of, 46–47; of twenty-first century, 38; of U.S.-China, 13, 18, 119; Waltz on, 1, 5, 15, 151

border security, of China, 64

Bo Xilai, 70, 213n112

Bretton Woods system, 35

BRICS New Development Bank, 116

buffer zones, for security, 133–38

Bush, George W., 158, 160

Buzan, Barry, 7

capabilities: bipolar distribution of, 29–30, 36, 87–88, 217nn33–34; of China, 25–26, 28; global distribution of, 44–46; global power-projection, 4–5, 6, 26–30, 33, 61, 199n46; naval, 29–31, 59–61, 60, 103, 138, 228nn25–26; nuclear, 103–5; of PLA, 59–62, 90–91, 135, 138, 218n46; power-projection, 153; second-strike, 121–23, 142, 143. *See also* distribution of capabilities; economic capabilities

capitalist-oriented system, 111

CCP. *See* China's Communist Party

Center for a New American Security (CNAS), 59–60

Central Asia, 78, 81, 113, 116, 117, 151

China, 32; ambitions of, 153–54, 155, 160; assertiveness of, 158; contemporary, 29, 87, 91, 103, 123, 131–36; critics of, 4; diverging views of rise of, 169–70; domestic stability of, 154; domination of, 153, 164; dream policy of, 140, 229n45; East Asia relating to, 100, 101–2, 103–5, 111, 116, 139–41, 154, 174; emergence of, 9, 12, 15–16, 17–18, 41; Eurasia and, 175; geographical size of, 16, 35, 63–65, 107, 116–17, 210n67, 210n73; geographical terrain of, 108; geostructural conditions and, 64–65, 141; as global hub, 118; globalization, market forces, and, 112–14; global scientific publications in, 71; India and, 44; innovation in, 71–73; international order established by, 174; Iran and, 113; land power of, 131; leadership role of, 175; major powers and, 81–83, 83; Morgenthau on, 67; next step for, 93–94; oil in, 113; Philippines and, 145, 162–63, 222n42; political stability of, 24, 69–73, 80, 81, 84, 87, 214nn128–29;

population of, 61–63, 77, 209n53,
209n58, 210n59; power lacked by, 4,
5, 28; PRC, 31, 34, 64–65, 70–71, 112;
rank of, 2, 7–8, 16, 18, 34, 37, 45, 73–75,
76–77; R&D progress of, 71–73, 81;
regional hegemony of, 4, 14, 28, 29, 63,
107, 122, 129–30, 137, 140–41, 146, 166;
rise of, 50, 76, 93–95, 103, 179–80; status
quo relating to, 134; strength of, 16,
133; superpower status of, 179–80, 186;
Taiwan and, 146; U.S. allies relating
to, 161, 234n34; White Paper of, 131–32;
world order changed by, 116–19. *See
also* U.S.-China
China, bipolarity of, 1, 29; behaviors with,
90–93
China, capabilities of, 25–26, 28; bipolar
distribution of capabilities, 87–88,
217nn33–34; naval, 30, 59–61, 60, 130,
131–32, 137–38, 227n15
China, economy of, 109, 163; challenges
of, 54–57; consumption relating to,
54–55; economic-stimulus programs,
36; economic strength, 16, 30, 33, 34–36,
38, 51–57, 73–75, 200nn61–62, 206n12;
GDP, 16, 34–35, 50–54, 56, 59, 71, 74–75,
77–78, 87–89, 100–102, 110, 200nn55–
56, 205n2, 217nn34–35; global economic
program, 30, 33; high growth rates
impact on, 55–57, 207n24; imbalance of,
54; influence of, 156; investments relating to, 54–55; as major creditor, 35–36,
200nn61–62; management of, 56; maritime, 117, 223n71; productive capacity,
35; public debt of, 36; rebalancing of,
56; reforms for, 36, 55; with regional
states, 111–12; with stock market, 56;
survival of, 112; trading power of, 35,
116–17, 223nn64–65
China, great powers and: with economy,
77–78; with geography, 79; with India,
77–81, 215n15; with natural resources,
65–69, 80, 211n78, 211n89; with Soviet
Union, 45–46, 77–81
China, military power of: ICBMs of,
121–22; modernization of, 139; nuclear

strategy of, 141–42, 143; in proxy wars,
30, 150; SSBNs of, 122
China, security of, 45, 112–13, 132–33, 134;
with border, 64; energy, 65–67; with
food and water, 67–68, 211n89; fundamental, 131; military, 59–60, 66, 211n80
China-India bipolar system, 186–87
Chinese Communist Party (CCP), 69–71,
81, 84, 87, 112, 135, 145, 222n45
China's Military Strategy, 59
Christensen, Thomas J., 10, 12, 49
CNAS. *See* Center for a New American
Security
Cold War, 99, 102–4, 143; anticommunist/
procapitalism polarity of, 119; bipolarity during, 3, 20, 155; contemporary
bipolarity and, 181–82; Europe during,
18–19; geography and, 40–42; literature
of, 120; nuclear weapons during, 31;
origins of, 105–6; procommunist/anti-
capitalist polarity of, 119; Soviet Union
during, 5, 34, 44; superpowers during,
32; U.S.-Soviet relations during, 155
Cold War, post: global distribution of
capabilities, 44–46; multipolarity, 45;
polarity, 6; superpowers, 32; unipolarity, 1, 7, 33
collapse, of Soviet Union, 32, 37, 45, 157
Communist Party, 69, 121
consumption, with Chinese economy,
54–55
contemporary balancing, 3, 101, 102, 121,
125
contemporary bipolarity: bipolar systems
comparison, 181–82; Cold War and,
181–82; geostructural realism, 179–83;
power change, power transition vs.,
182–83; second- and third-ranking
power, 180–81, 239nn7–8
contemporary bipolar systems, 14, 186–87
contemporary polarity, 180
Crimea, 165, 173

defense, national, collective, and out-of-
area, 168
defense dominant, East Asia as, 148

destabilizing forces, in China, 69
distribution, bipolarity and, 2, 4, 6
distribution, of power: bipolar, 26–27, 40, 47, 87, 164; power attributes of states vs., 28–32; unipolar, 24
distribution of capabilities, 15, 17, 32, 93, 181, 220n8; as bipolar, 29–30, 36; global, 44–46; in international system, 29, 31, 50; measurement of, 26–28; post-Cold War, 44–46; superpower concept relating to, 5, 28–29; systemic, 99, 103; in 2050, 30; U.S.-Soviet, 84–87, 85, 216nn23–24, 217n25; Waltz on, 30, 36, 99; after World War Two, 29, 37, 41, 186–87, 202n74; before World War Two, 29
distribution of capabilities, shifting: China, diverging views of rise of, 169–70; European security, transatlantic ties and, 165–66; global implications of, 156–76; national, collective, out-of-area defense, 168; NATO deterrence credibility, 166–68, 172; nontraditional security challenges, institutions, world order, 173–76; rebalance, Asia-Pacific pivot and, 156–61; Soviet Union, power shifts and, 171–73; U.S. allies, Asian nonaligned and, 161–64
domination, of China, 153, 164

East Asia, 31, 61, 93; balancing relating to, 100–102, 103, 107, 150, 173; China relating to, 100, 101–2, 103–5, 111, 116, 139–41, 154, 174; contemporary, 18, 45, 49, 102, 105–7, 120, 122, 128, 152, 155, 164, 183; contested waters in, 19, 103, 138, 141; as defense dominant, 148; geographical terrain of, 108–9, 134, 139; geopolitics relating to, 128–33; hegemony in, 47, 141; influences of, 41; instability in, 3, 18, 155; land-sea region of, 107, 127, 130, 132, 139–41; limited war in, 126–29, 134; maritime, 3, 14, 16, 18–19, 104, 112, 126, 130, 134, 151, 159, 161, 190n6; military operations in, 138; risk of war with, 126–27, 226n3; U.S. and, 14, 16, 101, 112, 130, 136–37, 150

Eastern Europe, 152, 153
East Germany, 137, 138
East-West European divide, 134, 137, 145, 147, 164
economic capabilities: of China, 16, 30, 33, 34–36, 38, 51–57, 73–75, 200nn61–62, 206n12; of Soviet Union, 77–78; of U.S., 33, 51–54, 109–11, 206n12
economic interdependence, globalization and, 109–14
economic-stimulus programs, in China, 36
economy: evaluation of, 34–37; factors in, 34; with great powers, 77–78; qualitative data, quantitative data and, 34; state power impacted by, 34
EDCA. See Enhanced Defense Cooperation Agreement
Egypt, 31, 48, 131
Eisenhower, Dwight D., 47–48
energy security, of China, 65–67
Enhanced Defense Cooperation Agreement (EDCA), 163
Eurasian landmass, 40, 117–18, 130, 153, 175, 181–82
Europe: balance of power preservation in, 14, 157; bipolar system in, 14–15, 18, 151; borders within, 182; during Cold War, 18–19; Eastern, 152, 153; East-West divide in, 134, 137, 145, 147, 164; GDP in, 165–66, 236n63; geographical terrain of, 108; geopolitical security order in, 155; geostructural conditions in, 155; stability in, 155, 159; U.S. forces in, 165; Western, 14–15, 143–44, 187, 199n47
"European continental system," 104, 152
European security, transatlantic ties and, 165–66
European theater, Soviet Union in, 18, 137
European Union, 80, 152, 173, 199n39
expenditure, military, 57–59, 58, 78, 101

failed states, 154–55
FDI. See foreign direct investors
First Indochina War, 31
first island chain, 134, 135
First World War. See World War One

flanking regions, of U.S., 16, 156, 157, 160, 161, 171
flashpoints, 141–47
food and water security, of China, 67–68, 211n89
foreign direct investments (FDI), 54, 207n17
Fox, William T. R., 5, 26, 38, 41
France, 29, 31, 32, 47–49, 180

GDP, 206n10; of China, 16, 34–35, 50–54, 56, 59, 71, 74–75, 77–78, 87–89, 100–101, 110, 200nn55–56, 205n2, 217nn33–34; in European countries, 165–66, 236n63; of Soviet Union, 16, 34, 52, 77–78, 84, 85, 87–89, 165–66, 206n7, 217n36; of U.S., 34–35, 51–54, 71, 84, 85, 87–89, 110, 166, 205n3
geographical size, of China, 63, 107, 210n67; Belt and Road initiative relating to, 16, 35, 65, 116–17, 175, 210n73; disadvantage of, 64; geostructural conditions relating to, 64–65
geographical terrain: of China, 108; of East Asia, 108–9, 134, 139; of Europe, 108
geography: bipolarity and, 2; of China and great powers, 79; Cold War and, 40–42; of U.S., 140–41; U.S.-China relating to, 15
geography, risk of war with, 128–29; geopolitics, asymmetry, risk of limited war, 138–39, 229n37; land powers at sea, 130–33; regional hegemonic ambitions, 139–41; status quo, buffer zones, spheres of influence, 133–38
"geography trumps structure," 3, 94, 108, 190n7
geopolitical security order, in Europe, 155
geopolitics, 41, 47, 101–2, 155, 160; asymmetry, risk of limited war, and, 138–39, 229n37; bipolarity and, 14; classical, 13–14; critical, 13; East Asia relating to, 128–33; neorealist theory and, 11, 13–17, 194n58; structural realism complemented by, 178
geopolitics, balancing and: formal military alliances with, 104; nuclear capabilities impact on, 103–5; power-projection

problems with, 104, 112, 130; U.S.-China with, 102–5, 138–39
geostructural conditions, 161; in China, 64–65, 141; in Europe, 155
geostructural realism, 2, 126, 178; components of, 12, 20, 124–25, 127; contemporary bipolarity, 179–83; polarity shifts and, 185–87; structural realism, building on, 183–87
geostructural-realist theory, 2, 3, 11–12, 13, 20
GERD. See gross domestic expenditure of research and development
GERD/GDP, 71
Germany, 9, 10, 29, 48–49, 166; division of, 128; East, 137, 138; Nazi, 41, 107, 128, 137; West, 19, 106, 136; West Berlin in, 128, 136, 138, 144, 145
global confrontation, proxy wars and, 151–54
global distribution of capabilities, 44–46
global economic program, of China, 30, 33
global finance actor, U.S. as, 36
global hub, China as, 118
global implications, of shifting distribution of capabilities, 156–76
global international system, 27, 198n30
globalization, 109–14
global maritime system, 107
global power-projection capabilities, 61; of Great Britain, 29; of Japan, 29; Soviet Union lack of, 4–5, 6, 29–30, 33, 199n46
global power shift, 150, 165
global rivalry, 150
global scientific publications, in China, 71
global-security actor, Soviet Union as, 131
Great Britain, 31, 41, 140; global power-projection capability of, 29; Suez case relating to, 47–49; as third-ranking power, 8, 10, 26–28, 33; U.S. and, 27–28, 157
great-power politics, 15–16
gross domestic expenditure of research and development (GERD), 71

hegemony. See regional hegemony
high growth rates, impact of, 55–57, 207n24

Himalayas, 186, 187
humanitarian interventions, of U.S., 157, 175–76

ICBMs, of China, 121–22
ideology, credibility and, 119–21
India, 32, 44, 77–81, 150, 186–87, 189n3, 215n15
Industrial Revolution, 41, 202n93
instability: in East Asia, 3, 18, 155; stability-instability paradox, 142–44, 230n55; of U.S.-China, 19
instability, stability and: power vacuums role, 105–7, 154–56, 174; proxy wars, global confrontation and, 151–54
interdependence, economic, 109–14
international institutional order, 182; changing of, 15, 116, 175; existence of, 3, 94, 102, 109, 114–15, 119, 125, 156, 174; U.S.-led, 36, 118, 174
international politics, structural realism and, 182, 184
international system, 42; bipolarity of, 8, 11, 18, 29, 39–40, 41, 76, 93; distribution of capabilities in, 29, 31, 50; global, 27, 198n30; multipolarity of, 7, 9–10, 29, 76; polarity of, 7–8, 29, 111; unipolarity of, 1, 6, 7, 29, 118; Waltz on, 12
investments, of China, 54–55
Iran, China and, 113
Israel, 31, 48

JAM-GC. See Joint Concept for Access and Maneuver in the Global Commons
Japan, 32, 130, 161; ambitions of, 162; aspirations of, 164; economy of, 74; global power-projection capability of, 29; military enhancing of, 162; strategic diplomacy of, 162
Joint Concept for Access and Maneuver in the Global Commons (JAM-GC), 121, 148

Kennan, George F., 106, 120, 166–67, 224n86, 237n67
Kissinger, Henry, 8–9, 43, 48

Korean Peninsula, 62, 90–91, 151
Korean War, 31, 90, 153, 224n84

land powers: of China, 131; at sea, 130–33; of Soviet Union, 40–41, 130–31
land-sea region, of East Asia, 107, 127, 130, 132, 139–41
limited war: in East Asia, 126–29, 134; geopolitics, asymmetry and risk of, 138–39, 229n37; U.S.-China risk of, 126–28, 138–39, 147–49, 227nn6–7, 231n73

market exchange rate (MER), 51–52, 53, 88
market forces, China, globalization and, 112–14
"Markets over Mao," 115
massive retaliation, by U.S., 128–29
material resources, power and, 23–24
Mearsheimer, John J., 10, 195n67, 196n75; on multipolarity, 45; on power, 23–24, 196n5
MER. See market exchange rate
military alliances, 104
military conflict, conventional, 143
military enhancement, of Japan, 162
military expenditure, 57–59, 58, 78, 101
military operations, in East Asia, 138
military power, 28–29, 42, 57–61; of China, 30, 121–22, 130–32, 137–38, 139, 141–43, 150, 227n15; of Soviet Union, 33, 106–7; of U.S., 33, 129, 159–61
military security, of China, 59–60, 66, 211n80
military strength. See U.S.-China military strength
military threat, from Soviet Union, 165
minerals, in China, 69
modernization, of military strength, 59–61
Monteiro, Nuno P., 33, 199n42, 203n109
Morgenthau, Hans J., 38, 49, 61; on China, 67; on power, 25–28, 33, 198n25, 199n40; on superpowers, 5, 154
multilateralism, 174
multipolarity, 1, 4, 12, 34, 39; arrival of, 180, 184; with Asia, 185; to bipolarity, 37; of international system, 7, 9–10, 29,

76; Mearsheimer on, 45; perspective, of U.S.-China, 9, 29; of post-Cold War, 45
multipolar systems: peace preserved by, 43; polarity and, 43–44; stability with, 43–44, 47

national security, military strength for, 59–60, 66, 211n80
NATO. *See* North Atlantic Treaty Organization
NATO deterrence credibility, 166–68, 172
natural resources, of China, 65–69, 80, 211n78, 211n89
naval capabilities, 31, 228nn25–26; of China, 30, 59–61, *60*, 130, 131–32, 137–38, 227n15; of Soviet Union, 29–30, 138; of U.S., 59–61, *60*, 103
Nazi Germany, 41, 107, 128, 137
neorealism, 37, 94, 123, 126
neorealist theory, 3, 151, 186; geopolitics and, 11, 13–17, 194n58
New Zealand, 163
nonpolarity, 1
nonrealist theory, of Waltz, 13, 17, 94
North Atlantic Treaty Organization (NATO), 127–28, 138, 147, 152, 165
nuclear peace, stability and, 46–47
nuclear strategy, of China, 141–42, 143
nuclear weapons, 64; balancing behaviors with, 109, 121–23; during Cold War, 31; geopolitics and balancing impact on, 103–5; role of, 141; of Soviet Union, 103–4; with superpowers, 47, 126–28; tripwires, maritime flashpoints and, 128, 141–48; of U.S., 103–4, 129; Waltz on, 39, 46, 204n126, 205n128

Obama, Barack, 158–59, 161
oil, 66, 113, 211n80
"1+1+X" system, 7
"1+X" system, 7
"1+Y+X" system, 7
Operation Atlantic Resolve, 165

parity, 37; power, 50, 53, 155, 179–80, 182–83; PPP, 34–35, 52, 54, 58, 89
Peace of Westphalia, 43

Pearl Harbor, 130
People's Liberation Army (PLA), 100, 104, 129, 131–32, 146; capabilities of, 59–62, 90–91, 135, 138, 218n46; on Korean Peninsula, 31; reorganization of, 70, 73
People's Liberation Army Navy (PLAN), 30, 59–60, 122, 131, 132
People's Republic of China (PRC), 31, 34, 64–65, 70–71, 112, 145, 166
Philippines: China and, 145, 162–63, 222n42; South China Sea relating to, 162–63; U.S. and, 162–63, 164
PLA. *See* People's Liberation Army
PLAN. *See* People's Liberation Army Navy
Poland, 165
polarity, 119; behavior patterns and, 47; debate on, 6–8, 20; defining power and measurement of, 23–26, 196n12; distribution of power, power attributes of states vs., 28–32; economic strength evaluation, 34–37; explaining and understanding of, 23; importance of, 42–49; of international system, 7–8, 29, 111; measuring distribution of capabilities and, 26–28; multipolar systems, 43–44; 1956 Suez case, 47–49; nuclear peace, stability and, 46–47; peacefulness of unipolarity, 44–46; post-Cold War, 6; stability and, 42–43; of superpowers, 32; Waltz on, 44–45, 47; weighing components of power, 33–34
polarity shifts, 95, 158, 160; establishment of, 37–39; geostructural realism and, 185–87
political stability, of China, 80; CCP impact on, 69–71, 81, 84, 87; competence and, 24, 71–73, 214nn128–29; destabilizing forces relating to, 69; leadership and, 69–71; Xi and, 69–70
politics: geopolitics, 11, 13–17, 41, 47, 101–5, 112, 194n58; great-power, 15–16
Politics Among Nations (Morgenthau), 27, 28
population, of China, 61–63, 77, 209n53, 209n58, 210n59

Posen, Barry R., 5, 25, 37, 194n61
power: assessment of, 25, 198n19; balance
    of, 6, 14, 43, 46, 102–3, 129–30, 157;
    defining of, 23–26, 196n12; distribu-
    tion of, 24, 26–32, 40, 47; elements of
    national, 25; gap between U.S.-China,
    2, 29, 50, 73, 76, 93; global power-pro-
    jection capabilities, 4–5, 6, 29–30, 33,
    61, 199n46; great-power politics, 15–16;
    imbalance of, 44; material resources
    and, 23–24; Mearsheimer on, 23–24,
    196n5; Morgenthau on, 25–28, 33,
    198n25, 199n40; PPP, 34–35, 52, 54, 58,
    89; shifts of, 171–73; of Soviet Union,
    27, 152, 167; "stopping power of water,"
    3, 189n4; structural-realist theory
    and, 23–24; superpowers, 5, 18–19, 20,
    196n76; unipolar distribution of, 24; of
    U.S., 27, 40; Waltz on measurement
    of, 24, 25, 26, 30, 33, 34, 36, 38, 193n7,
    196n7; weighing components of, 33–34;
    Wohlforth on, 24, 25, 41, 42, 196n9,
    197n17. See also military power; super-
    powers; third-ranking power
power, of China: lack of, 4, 5, 28; military,
    30, 121–22, 130–32, 137–38, 139, 141–43,
    150, 227n15; naval, 30, 130, 131–32,
    137–38, 227n15; scholars on, 25–26
power-as-influence, 24
power-as-resources, 24
power attributes of states, distribution of
    power vs., 28–32
power change, power transition vs., 182–83
power parity, 50, 53, 155, 179–80, 182–83
power-projection: capabilities of, 153; prob-
    lems of, 104, 112, 130
powers, 92–93; great, 77–81, 215n15; land to
    sea, 77–78; major, 81–83, 83
power-transition theory, 182–83
power vacuums role, 105–7, 154–56, 174
PPP. See purchasing power parity
PRC. See People's Republic of China
preventive war, balance of power and,
    129–30
productive capacity, of China, 35
proxy wars, 30, 150, 151–54, 173, 238n81

public debt, of China, 36
purchasing power parity (PPP), 34–35, 52,
    54, 58, 89

RAND reports, 59–60, 88–89
rank: of China, 2, 7–8, 16, 18, 34, 37, 45,
    73–75, 76–77; of Great Britain, 8, 10,
    26–38; top-ranking powers, bipolarity
    and, 88–90, 218n40, 218n44; of U.S., 2,
    7–8, 16, 18, 37
R&D. See research and development
realism: geostructural, 2, 12, 20, 124–25,
    126, 127; structural, 107, 108
rebalancing: Asia-Pacific pivot and, 156–61;
    of Chinese economy, 56; of U.S., 152,
    156–61
reform agenda, of Xi, 36, 55
regional hegemony, 103, 157; ambitions for,
    139–41; of China, 4, 14, 28, 29, 63, 107,
    122, 129–30, 137, 140–41, 146, 166; in
    East Asia, 47, 141; of Soviet Union, 105,
    129, 141, 155; of U.S., 6, 16, 29, 140
regional states, 111–12
research and development (R&D), 71–73,
    81
rivalry: global, 150; of superpowers, 18–19,
    116, 151–52, 175–76; of U.S.-China, 3, 14,
    103, 132–33, 150, 151, 154, 164, 174, 220n7
"rules of power analysis," 34
Russia. See Soviet Union

sameness, of bipolarity, 11, 99, 101–2, 123,
    151
scholarship, challenge to, 8–11
SCO. See Shanghai Cooperation Organi-
    zation
second-strike capabilities, 121–23, 142, 143
Second World War. See World War Two
security: buffer zones for, 133–38; of China,
    45, 59–60, 64–68, 112–13, 131–33, 134,
    211n80, 211n89; national security,
    military strength for, 59–60, 66, 211n80;
    nontraditional institutions, world
    order, and challenges of, 173–76; risk,
    168, 237n70; of Soviet Union, 106–7
Shanghai Cooperation Organization
    (SCO), 116

Sino-Russian strategic partnership, 171–72
Sino-Soviet split, 172
Sino-Soviet Treaty of Friendship, Alliance, and Mutual Assistance, 123
SLOCs, 66, 107, 117, 132, 134, 147
Snyder, Jack, 12, 124, 142
South China Sea, 136, 138, 152, 162–63, 175
South Korea, 163, 236n51
Soviet Red Army, 41, 103, 104, 106, 111, 129, 136
Soviet Union, 140, 230n48; bipolar distribution of capabilities with, 87–88; bipolarity behaviors with, 90–93; China and, 45–46, 77–81; during Cold War, 5, 34, 44; collapse of, 32, 37, 45, 157; in Crimea, 165, 173; decline of, 16–17; economic capabilities of, 77–78; empire of, 40–41; in European theater, 18, 137; GDP of, 16, 34, 52, 77–78, 84, 85, 87–89, 165–66, 206n7, 217n36; global power-projection capability lacked by, 4–5, 6, 29–30, 33, 199n46; as global-security actor, 131; India and, 189n3; land power of, 40–41, 130–31; massive retaliation against, 128–29; military power of, 33, 106–7; military threat from, 165; naval capabilities of, 29–30, 138; nuclear weapons of, 103–4; power of, 27, 152, 167; power shifts and, 171–73; regional hegemony of, 105, 129, 141, 155; security, 106–7; as superpower, 29, 32, 45; transition of, 153; in Ukraine, 31, 165, 172; U.S. and, 5, 7–8, 26, 27, 136; westward expansion of, 181–82; during World War Two, 134
spheres, of influence, 133–38
SSBNs, of China, 122
stability: with bipolarity, 44, 126; bipolar-stability thesis, 9, 11, 46–47; of bipolar system, 46–47; domestic, 154; in Europe, 155, 159; importance of, 2, 18–19, 195n73; instability, 3, 18, 19; with multipolarity, 43–44, 47; nuclear peace and, 46–47; with polarity, 42–43; political, 24, 69–73, 80–81, 84, 87, 214nn128–29; Waltz on, 42

stability-instability paradox, 142–44, 230n55
states: definition of, 25, 197n15; economic power of, 34; failed, 154–55; interaction between, 156; power attributes of, 28–32; regional, 111–12. See also United States
status quo, buffer zones, and spheres of influence, 133–38
STEM subjects, 71
stock market, 56
"stopping power of water," 3, 38, 40, 103–4, 143, 189n4, 202n78
strategic diplomacy, of Japan, 162
structural realism, 107, 108, 177; geopolitics and, 178; international politics and, 182, 184
structural realism, building on: balancing, degree and intensity of, 185; with more balanced system, 183–84; polarity shifts, geostructural realism and, 185–87
structural-realist theory, 32, 46, 195n67; power and, 23–24; U.S.-China relating to, 8–9, 193n30; Waltz on, 2–3, 6, 8–9, 11–13, 17, 29, 39, 178, 187, 193n30
Suez case, 1956: bipolarity relating to, 47–48; blockade, 48; Eisenhower relating to, 47–48; France relating to, 47–49; Great Britain relating to, 47–49; multiparity relating to, 47–48; polarity relating to, 49; U.S. relating to, 47–49
superpowers, 25, 26, 27; China as, 179–80, 186; during Cold War, 32; concept of, 5, 28–29; definition of, 28, 32; "long peace" between, 181; Morgenthau on, 5, 154; nuclear weapons with, 47, 126–28; number of, 41–42; polarity of, 32; rivalry of, 18–19, 116, 151–52, 175–76; on same landmass, 19, 196n76; shaping of, 49; Soviet Union as, 29, 32, 45; understanding of, 20
surplus wealth, 34
systemic distribution of capabilities, 99, 103

Taiwan, 146–48, 152, 157, 231n67
technical sophistication, of military strength, 58–59

third-ranking power: of Great Britain, 8, 10, 26–28, 33; with U.S., 2, 7–8, 16, 18, 37

"third world," 19

Thucydides trap, 9

top-ranking powers, bipolarity and, 88–90, 218n40, 218n44

trading power: of China, 35, 116–17, 223nn64–65; of U.S., 53, 206n14

Tragedy of Great Power Politics, The (Mearsheimer), 45

transatlantic alliance, 169–70

Trans-Pacific Partnership, 118

tripwires, 128, 141–48

Twenty-First Century Maritime Silk Road Initiative, 116

"2+X" system, 7

Ukraine, 31, 165, 172

UN. *See* United Nations

UN Educational, Scientific, and Cultural Organization (UNESCO), 71, 72

unipolar distribution, of power, 24

unipolarity, 4, 11, 34, 35, 168; from bipolarity, 37; to bipolarity, 37–38, 103, 184; emergence of, 44–45; end of, 7; of international system, 1, 6, 7, 29, 118; peacefulness of, 44–46; of post-Cold War, 1, 7, 33; U.S., 6–7, 174; Wohlforth on, 44, 203n108

"unipolar moment," in 1990s, 158

United Nations (UN), 174

United States (U.S.): Asia-Pacific pivot of, 150–51, 152, 156–61, 174; credibility of, 143; decline of, 1, 76, 103; East Asia and, 14, 16, 101, 112, 130, 136–37, 150; economy of, 33, 51–54, 109–11, 206n12; European balance of power maintained by, 14, 157, 165; flanking regions of, 16, 156, 157, 160, 161, 171; GDP of, 34–35, 51–54, 71, 84, 85, 87–89, 110, 166, 205n3; geography of, 140–41; as global finance actor, 36; Great Britain and, 27–28, 157; humanitarian interventions of, 157, 175–76; massive retaliation by, 128–29; power of, 27, 140; rebalancing of, 152, 156–61; regional

hegemony of, 6, 16, 29, 140; Soviet Union and, 5, 7–8, 26, 27, 136; Suez case and, 47–49; tit-for-tat strategy relating to, 153; as trading nation, 53, 206n14; unipolarity of, 6–7, 174

United States, bipolarity of, 1–2, 174; behaviors with, 90–93; distribution of capabilities with, 87–88

United States, military of: naval capabilities, 59–61, 60, 103; nuclear weapons, 103–4, 129; power of, 33, 129, 159–61; presence of, 101, 136–37

unit-level factors: China, globalization, market forces, 112–14; Chinese economic ties, with regional states, 111–12; economic interdependence, globalization and, 109–14; ideology, credibility and, 119–21; world order, changing, 116–19; world order, establishment of, 114–15

UN Security Council, 174

UN World Intellectual Property Organization (UNWIPO), 71

U.S. *See* United States

U.S. allies, Asian nonaligned and: Australia, 163, 235n49; China, 161, 234n34; India, 164; Japan, 161–62; Philippines, 162–63, 164; power shifts relating to, 161; South Korea, 163, 236n51

U.S.-ASEAN relationship, 161

U.S.-China: arms race with, 3; balancing behaviors of, 12–13, 17, 111–14, 123, 182; bilateral relationship of, 99–100, 219n4; bipolar system of, 13, 18, 119; characteristics of, 8–9; consequences of, 8; geography relating to, 15; geopolitics and balancing with, 102–5, 138–39; instability of, 19; multipolar perspective of, 9, 29; parity with, 37; on path to tragedy, 10–11; power gap between, 2, 29, 50, 73, 76, 93; rivalry of, 3, 14, 103, 132–33, 150, 151, 154, 164, 174, 220n7; structural-realist theory relating to, 8–9, 193n30; studies relating to, 10; third-ranking power with, 2, 7–8, 16, 18, 37

U.S.-China, risk of war with, 226n1; Chinese nuclear strategy, 141–42;

conclusion to, 147–49; with East
Asia, 126–27, 226n3; geography and,
128–41; limited, 126–28, 138–39, 147–49,
227nn6–7, 231n73; nukes, tripwires, and
maritime flashpoints with, 128, 141–48;
stability-instability paradox relating to,
142–44, 230n55
U.S.-China bipolarity, contemporary,
107, 168, 184; conclusion to, 73–75;
economic power, 51–54, 206n12; natural
resources, 65–69; political stability,
69–71; power parity, 50, 53, 155
U.S.-China military strength: expenditure
for, 57–59, 58, 78, 101; foreign weapons
and equipment, 57, 207n30; modernization of, 59–61; for national security,
59–60, 66, 211n80; with navies, 59–61,
60; with PLA, 31, 59–62, 70, 73; with
PLAN, 33, 59–60, 122, 131, 132; technical
sophistication of, 58–59
U.S.-Japan Security Treaty, 145
U.S.-led international institutional order,
36, 118, 174
U.S. Patent and Trademark Office
(USPTO), 72
U.S.-Soviet distribution of capabilities,
84–87, 85, 216nn23–24, 217n25
U.S.-Soviet relations, during Cold War, 155
U.S.-Taiwan policy, 145

Very High Readiness Joint Task Force, 165

Wagner, Harrison R., 37, 39–40
Waltz, Kenneth, 48; on bipolarity, 1, 5,
15, 151; on distribution of capabilities,
30, 36, 99; on international system,
12; neorealist theory of, 13, 17, 94; on
nuclear weapons, 39, 46, 204n126,
205n128; on polarity, 44–45, 47; on
power measurement, 24, 25, 26,
30, 33, 34, 36, 38, 193n7, 196n7; on
stability, 42; structural-realist theory
of, 2–3, 6, 8–9, 11–13, 17, 29, 39, 178,
187, 193n30
war. See specific wars
Warsaw Pact, 128
weapons: equipment and, 57, 207n30. See
also nuclear weapons
West Berlin, Germany, 128, 136, 138, 144,
145
Western Europe, 14–15, 143–44, 187,
199n47
West Germany, 19, 106, 136
White Paper, of China, 131–32
Wohlforth, William, 24, 25, 41, 42, 196n9,
197n17; on unipolarity, 44, 203n108
World Bank, 51, 55, 88
world order: changing of, 116–19; establishment of, 114–15
World War One, 43, 48
World War Two, 33, 39; bipolar power
distribution after, 26–27, 40, 47, 87;
distribution of capabilities after, 29,
37, 41, 186–87, 202n74; Soviet Union
during, 134

Xi Jinping (president): China dream policy
of, 140, 229n45; China political stability
and, 69–70; PLA speech of, 131–32;
reform agenda of, 36, 55